Tikkunei Zohar Revealed

תיקיני הזחר גלה

Mark Siet

Books by the Author available on Amazon.com and Kindle Books

Thought Into Form

360 Degrees of Good

The Bahir Revealed

Reach For the Sky (novel)

Cover art by Jane Siet

May all who venture within receive the blessings of above and the insights of Shekinah who lies in wait to share her light about which these pages are proof of in every category of influence.

Master of all thy will flows through all and we thank you for this moment and the ones yet to come…

Open Thou mine eyes, that I may behold wondrous things out of Thy law. (Tehilim 119:18)

Foreword	vii
Introduction:	1
First Tiqun	93
Tiqun 2	95
Tiqun 2 (Tiqun 3)	96
Tiqun 3	96
Tiqun 4	97
Tiqun 5	99
Tiqun 6	111
Tiqun 7	119
Tiqun 8	120
Tiqun 9	120
Tiqun 10	121
Tiqun 11	127
Tiqun 12	130
Tiqun 13	132
Tiqun 14	146
Tiqun 15	148
Tiqun 16	150
Tiqun 17	151
Tiqun 18	153
Tiqun 19	183
Tiqun 20	203
Tiqun 21	203
Tiqun 22	277
Tiqun 23	293
Tiqun 24	294
Tiqun 25	298

Tiqun 26   304

Tiqun 27 (part of the introduction Tiqun 6-7)   310

Tiqun 28   310

Tiqun 29   311

Tiqun 30   313

Tiqun 31   324

Tiqun 32   326

Tiqun 33   329

Tiqun 34   330

Tiqun 35   331

Tiqun 36   331

Tiqun 37   334

Tiqun 38   336

Tiqun 39   338

Tiqun 40   341

Tiqun 41   343

Tiqun 42   344

Tiqun 43   347

Tiqun 44   349

Tiqun 45   350

Tiqun 46   353

Tiqun 47   354

Tiqun 48   362

Tiqun 49   364

Tiqun 50   367

Tiqun 51   371

Tiqun 52   372

Tiqun 53   374

Tiqun 54	377
Tiqun 55	377
Tiqun 56	384
Tiqun 57	392
Tiqun 58	395
Tiqun 59	398
Tiqun 60	398
Tiqun 61	401
Tiqun 62	403
Tiqun 63	406
Tiqun 64	408
Tiqun 65	412
Tiqun 66	414
Tiqun 67	419
Tiqun 68	423
Tiqun 69	424
Tiqun 70	510
Second Tiqun 22	595
Second Tiqun 23	595
Second Tiqun 24	599
Second Tiqun 25	606
Second Tiqun 26	607
Tiqun 27 also additional Tiqun 6	618
Seventh Tiqun or Tiqun 27	632
Eighth Tiqun Tiqun 28	635
Ninth Tiqun Tiqun 29	635
Tenth Tiqun –Tiqun 30	637
Tiqun 11 - Second Tiqun 30	639

Foreword

The Tikkunei HaZohar is part of a group of mystical writings grouped together under the general topic Zohar. It is an exposition via Kabbalah that studies the deep connection of Shekinah throughout the verses of Torah and the underlying themes of mystical thought. There seventy Tiqun or sections each dealing with a variation of the word Bereishis and how it relates to just about everything in the Jewish thought of the times and also relating to that which is called the Oral Torah.

Up until this moment there has never been an English commentary on Tikkunei HaZohar that has covered the entire range of topics. This is now a complete English commentary that with Hashem's help will reach those true seekers of wisdom gathering those insights from Torah in the harvest of the mind that awakens to its fruit.

The topics included in here concern the ritual, specific prayers, the elements, the Tree of Life, the Tree of the Knowledge of Good and Evil, cantillation trope, the specific vowels and their mystical meanings and a whole host of allegories that explain the mystical side of Jewish thought. Central to this thought is Shekinah, the Divine Presence, the bride of Ha Kodesh Barachu, Father, Mother, daughter and son all relationships on the Tree of Life are examined in great detail.

My methodology for producing my commentary was to examine each paragraph and extract the meanings from there and then tie it into the whole picture as it went along.

I have included the hebrew as well as the translation of certain sections to set the tone for the text as well as clarify in a broad sense the letter combinations that are referenced here.

This information is made available during certain periods of time in order to raise the level of consciousness in order to bring about unity and peace. It is important that this English commentary be understood in the context of practical thought and the relationships that we have with the Creator and the created. It is in that spirit that my study commenced and continued for over two and a half years.

While I was working on this commentary I realized that the essence of Kabbalah is to study Torah and bring forth the hidden mysteries that are available for those with eyes to see and ears to hear. The unifications that take place during the text guided me as true as a sextant and the North Star.

As our sages used to say…'if it were only first this moment it would have been enough.'

For Hashem who got it right the first time

Introduction:

Rabbi Shimon departed and fled into the wilderness of Lod and concealed himself in a cave he and Rabbi Elazar his son were exiled. There came to be a miracle of nature that happened that reproduced a special carob tree and a special spring where water issued forth and fed them from the same carob and they drank from same water and there was Eliyahu of blessed memory who came two times every day and they learned the knowledge that man did not have in them. In the Zohar there are new things to be written about the name…

The opening to this adventure in consciousness begins with Rabbi Shimon and his son El'azar. They are in a cave and Elijah comes to speak with them. Everything that comes afterwards is a result of those conversations on the seventy revelations of the word Bereishis. At no time does it say that they ever leave the cave.

1a) Rabbi Shimon represents the seeker in Consciousness that is ultimately seeking its own self-awareness. He seeks refuge in the wilderness of Lod or the wilderness of forty (Lamed-Vav-Daleth), which is the same forty years of wandering, and the same forty days and nights spent on Sinai. The soul surrounded by the world needs respite in order to enter into the holy connection above. Rabbi Shimon is taught by Elijah and miraculously fed from the carob tree and the running stream. Both the teaching and the feeding are one in the same thing. Where does the soul feed? It is from the Tree of Life where both sustenance and higher wisdom are both generated and received.

What is the water? It is the flowing emanation of Shekinah. Think of Shekinah as the link that connects as in one verse of Torah to another or even one concept to another. Until there is this linking there is an absence of understanding.

So Eliyahu says, "Let learn some new insights about Torah. We'll call these insights Tikkunei Zohar."

This is to be called the Tikkunei Zohar about the seventy faces of Torah that R. Shimon bar Yochai made up about the word Bereishis in the secrets of Torah.

The seventy faces of Torah references the refuge taken at Elim (Shemos 15:27) where the children of Israel sojourned amongst the seventy palms and twelve springs. This was a time of learning and inspiration and introspection alluding to the same type of sojourning that Rabbi Shimon is speaking of here.

A light bulb may only shine when the circuit between itself and its source is opened. The enlightened ones, the maskilim, connect to this source via the Tree of Life. Now the circuit that runs between the enlightened and the Tree of Life is Shekinah.

Here we find the various radiances compared to the chayot, the firmament -heavens, and the various illuminations that are received from the Tree of Life and its Sephiros. All of these references are points of connection that the soul reaches for and attaches itself to.

And the knowledgeable will be radiant like the bright expanse of the sky (Daniel 12;3),

And the knowledgeable of Rabbi Shimon are warned that they have been given the attached permission given to them by Eliyahu who is with them and with all those souls in the houses of study to bring down between them that which the angels (learn) are guided by in secret.

Why does the soul or indeed Elijah need permission to connect to the Tree of Life? This permission has more to do with a harmony of relationship rather than the direct granting of permission. It is analogous to the answer that lies in waiting and is only evoked when the right question is asked. In this way the maskilim align themselves by their questions in order to receive the answers that are continuously being radiated by an ongoing Creation. Elijah who is acting as intermediary becomes an amplifier that is placed in between the signal and the output allowing for the question not only to be heard but to also be responded to as well.

The question and the answer are a primary component that together define the inner workings of Creation as we discover thought by thought that all of our thoughts are intertwined and are signals within the super awesome unity that we are becoming aware of coming online to produce the experience of unification.

What is this main principle (Iquar) or the foundation of the chariot? It is the conceptual reality of the Tree of Life. This is where our thoughts attach themselves to and become as a result of this attachment imbued with the radiant brilliance that is the status quo of the continuous creation that always becomes more than it was by compression and expansion.

And he who is in the firmament above the living creatures about which is written Yecheziel `1:26 ' *above the firmament that was over their heads'*.

And opposite heaven and obtaining the same main point and foundation of the chariot whereon stand the living creatures and throne of the chariot and it was said to me of them and righteous foundation of world on the righteous ones that were above knowing the world cover, And on the righteous one that to the many exists the worlds that get discovered.

1b) The righteous one refers to the thought that is aligned perfectly with the Tree of Life. It is the 'revolving intention' that is both emanated from and directed towards this center of radiance described previously. There out of this radiance arise those states of being called 'your people' which is composed of your thoughts those that you pay attention to.

It is in fact this attention that brings out Shekinah which is the divine connection between those higher thoughts arranged in their hierarchies anchored below by Malchus the realm of the 'righteous one.'

There are different degrees of thought one above the other arranged as the ten Sephiros also known in the Torah as the Patriarchs with their ideas seeding Israel along with the resultant thoughts which are categorized as sages, Masters of Torah, pious ones, etc.

Each thought, every category, each of the Sephiros either as a single unit of ten or individualized in their various representations is recognized as a unit of measure whereby we may track our journey above and back again.

The permission is given to those souls of the righteous that is always with The Holy One blessed be He and the Shekinah to dwell in your (Rabbi Shimones) writing of the Zohar.

It said (Proverbs 27:8) *Like a bird wanders from her nest so is the man that wanders from his place,*

And the bird refers to the Shekinah that is sent away from her place and for that it is said (Deuteronomy 22:7) thou shalt in any wise let the dam go, but the young thou mayest take unto thyself. That includes the Shekinah of the lower level. The mother is the upper level Shekinah.

In Isaiah 50:1 we read "*because of your sins, your mother was sent away.* And for that "you shall send away" twice, one for the first Holy Temple and one for the Second Holy temple, in order to make true to the verse "I am YKVK and my name and honor won't be given to another. "I won't give" that is Shekinah below and "my glory" that is the upper Shekinah.

So Ha Kodesh Barachu He wanders from his place, which is the Holy Temple. When it said YKVH is a man of war, it is for the need to wander because of the sins of the Israelites.

The 'He who wanders from his place' refers to one who having become attached to Torah then is led away from it by the outer things of the world. Shekinah or the bird that is driven away is the aspect of holiness that may only be present when we connect with Torah.

In Consciousness when we are meditating upon a thing this is what our thoughts are wrapped around as the center of our focus. When that focus wanders we lose the center so to speak and with that center the sense of connection which is referred to as Shekinah

The idea of attachment to Torah is reiterated by the 'bird returning home' which is Shekinah returning to the person whose focus once again resumes with Torah. The process of Creation is a continuous building operation that always requires our focus. That focus is inherently promoted via the aegis of Torah study. What is implied here is that there is no building of that inner house without words of Torah that are spoken meaning where the connection with Shekinah has been established.

Now there are levels of learning that are categorized here since all knowledge is built upon the foundation that is established via the special openings that Kabbalah makes possible. Kabbalah may also be described in terms of an 'acute listening' that is for the express purpose of making connections between verses of Torah and by extension the surrounding Consciousness linking the parts to the whole.

(Deuteronomy 22:) *If a bird's nest chance to be before thee in the way, in any tree or on the ground, with young ones or eggs, and the mother sitting upon the young, or upon the eggs, thou shalt not take the mother with the young;"*

When you send away the mother which is the inherent understanding symbolized by Binah a vessel is created, "the eggs" wherein the insights of Kabbalah are drawn within the mold. In essence without the "mother" a need is created that brings about the flowing of Shekinah just as the question is the need that brings out the answer.

The Saba reinforces this concept of a filling of wisdom meaning the flowing connections between the higher wisdom Chokmah flowing into Binah so that even though the "mother" leaves it is only for the purpose of encouraging the children to fly on their own or in the imagery just spoken of to connect via Shekinah above and below.

Shekinah is the temple and when it is damaged it must be repaired.

The masters of Torah et al. make this nest for the Holy One Blessed Be He by their overflowing trust in Hashem thereby becoming in effect a vehicle for the Divine immanence that is Shekinah an abode that continuously fills becoming in the moment the place of the Divine or the dwelling of the most high in effect repairing the temple.

The Righteous ones followers of Abraham
live on the level of Chesed
so that there you do not embody Chesed
unless you have a suitable place for it to call home.

2a) This idea of Chesed comes into play because there is an overflowing that takes place due to the consistent focus that is maintained by the 'righteous' giving rise to the unity that comes from Shekinah and the connection that is established. Out of this connection the further flowing of thought takes place increasing in holiness as it goes along. What is this like?

"A King has a vast treasury and each day it is filled to overflowing so that soon he can no longer build more room to house his treasures. What does he do? He devises a plan to open his treasury via two doors where each day ministers from his kingdom load up their wagons with the excess treasure and distribute it back to the people in the form of all that their needs require. In this way his kingdom not only becomes the richest in the world but his people are known for their vast generosity towards others."

Intention that lacks direction or whose direction is scattered subverts the plan of Chesed. When there is a proper passing through of the overflowing of thought into the realm here of Gevurah there is the conviction or strength of thought that is like the knot that is tied in Tephilin.

The SHMA functions as the unifier of Consciousness always coalescing into the One. However, this unification requires the discipline of Tephilin, which represent the knot of Intention that regroups itself for the purpose of unification. Tephilin is the knot that regulates the flow of thought. Without the spigot of Tephilin thought does not compress and becomes miserly, thin and unfocused.

(Proverbs 30:22) *For a servant when he reigns…*
(Proverbs 30:22) *…and a handmaid that is heir to her mistress.*

Specifically when we have a thought that rises above it is up to us to continue that upward motion. The same dynamic takes place in terms of Torah study. Once an insight is gained it must not become a static occurrence but must be used as a stepping-stone for further progress, increased learning and a greater sense of unity with Hashem. The mistress or master that thought serves is the directive to go on going continuously mirroring the actions of Creation along the way.

What happens at midnight? Those thoughts of the day rise and become one with Shekinah called 'night' meaning they are ripe for the bearing of insights into Torah. This process is another instance of the overflowing of thought into its appropriate vessels for the fulfillment of the intention that has promoted the thought in the first place.

Visionaries and Prophets symbolize what happens when we look deeply into the secrets of Torah. We not only see the underlying essence we are also given intimations of what will come next leading to an understanding of the whole.

If we juxtapose the ten Sephiros with the 613 commandments then we may see that unity is its purpose. 613 or 6+1+3 adds together becoming ten and then reducing to one.

So too does the dual divine name (ADNY YKVK = Y-A-H-D-V-N-H-Y) represents the unity of purpose in that YKVK when placed together in Torah is pronounced YKVK Elohim showing how Creation brings forth that which already is in a sequence of becoming revelation upon revelation.

Therefore Ezekiel's ten visions in like manner all stem from a single insight that is expanded due to their holy nature. The cluster of commandments described is as if to say that when we partake of or fulfill each commandment we are entering more fully into the unity that makes up the inherent basis for all of Torah.

Those who do not strive in Torah lose that holy connection sending away the mother or Binah the understanding that comes with Torah study.

Then by observing the Sabbath the unification of mother and father is observed which is the joining together of the intention and its subsequent mode of discovery that takes place through a continuing focus. In Consciousness there ensues a raised level of awareness.

(Deuteronomy 30:20) ...for it is your life, and the way of your days upon the land which the Lord your God gives you ....

For there are three worlds , this world, the garden below, and the world to come. When Eliyahu finished speaking they pondered this meaning.

There are three worlds in this verse that refers to how Creation builds upon itself. The first two are the father and mother that is inherited by honoring both the Intention and its antecedent Understanding. This is called "your life, and the 'way of your days' is the lower garden. This alludes to living your life in such as way in order to understand each day in its context. Torah is the integration of the two becoming one.

This lower garden leads to the world to come and as a result the low world or the world of manifestation is what appears 'upon the land that the KVYK Elohim gives you.' All three unified via the verses that describe them in their various appearances throughout Torah.

If you do not pursue Torah and its deeper meanings it is as though you were abandoning the divine intention. The only way we reach the Divine is to ponder its mysteries. When you bind the Tephilin it is as though you are attaching yourself to *Ha Kodesh Barachu.*

When it says 'do not take the mother upon the children' it implies the connection that occurs when we are studying Torah. This connection is in response to our questions and our sincere intention to receive the fruits of Torah.

There is a unity of relationship that cannot be broken by 'taking the mother' or the understanding away from the children, who are described earlier as masters of Kabbalah.

You must become immersed in Torah and then the understanding you receive makes you master of Kabbalah.

The second part of this is also its converse, "you shall surely send away the mother," which shows us that without the understanding the "children" are vulnerable meaning that without understanding the masters of Kabbalah are bereft of that holy connection.

Keep the sign eight days in the field. Keep the Sabbath.
Those that do this reiterate the dual divine name.

2b) The direct purpose of Creation is to become that which is envisioned. When you start with a perfect image you end up with a perfect form. The idea of perfection is included in both Yud's one from ADNY and one from YKVK.

Therefore what you have respectively is the image and its reflection. The image is feminine and its reflection is masculine. Tephilin is feminine. The scrolls are the vessel for the holiness contained within. It is what we absorb in its wearing and daily observance. The sign of the covenant is discussed in detail next.

The circumcision is symbolic of the attachment to heaven and the letting go of the earthly nature that seeks only for itself as in the ego and its limited view.

Here the acronym milah (who will go up for us to heaven) expresses that aspiration for connection that is only accomplished by a conscious act of awareness. Tephilin is the reminder that we are becoming one with heaven.

The central idea here is the covering with the bird that covers her children, Shekinah that covers the sign of the covenant and the lulav and myrtle branches, the Sukkah itself all of these are covers. Without these covers, which also include Tefillin, there is no separation of Keter and Chokmah from the remaining eight Sephiros symbolized by the dual divine name.

There is a distinction then between what is covered and what is separated continuing the theme of 'you shall not take the mother upon the children," and "You will surely send away."

When you are attached to, absorbed in or peering deeply into the mysteries of Torah you are covered by Torah. This means that not only are you open to everything that pertains to the particular area you are studying but you are also open to the whole of Torah which in its totality is the unity of Hashem.

Bava Batra Rabbah bar Bar hana was going on a boat and saw the same bird in the sea that comes up to her ankles. And this bird here cr one of those chicks are from those eggs..

The bird with the sea that reaches to its ankles is Netzach and Hod called eggs or chicks that are the resultant of the higher Imma, which could be called Tipheres.

The sons are the six Sephiros from Keter through Tipheres whereas the eggs are the result of the gestation of above now emanating from the lower Imma in Yesod and by extension Malchus. At the level of Tzaddik chicks emerge from Malchus through Yesod or from below to above.

The sea that spreads to the fifty gates is called the Higher Mother-Binah and then flows below to the ankles of the fowl called Netzach and Hod. These pillars of Netzach and Hod represent a filling from above and then the immersion from below. This is Consciousness that is being developed.

Yesod the foundation integrates the fifty gates from the ten expanded Sephiros from Chesed to Hod. Yesod is the lower throne called judgment, which takes place just prior to the manifestation field called Malchus.

The sound that is carried is the echo of intention that is kept intact via the middle pillar, which gathers together this sound and transmits it below and above.

It is Metatron symbolized in the SHMA that maintains this essence of unity as a part of the process of the continuous Creation that takes place and is recognized via the voice of God upon the waters.

The voice of God upon the waters is Consciousness becoming aware of its own making. The six sounds or perhaps echoes are Zeir Anpin with the seventh echo being Yesod. Every instance of Imma refers to a gathering then of thought that is then released through the abundance of overflowing or the Infinite Mercy of the Holy One Blessed Be He.

Prayer ascends has wings and refers to our thoughts in line with holiness that are reaching above. The eighteen blessings are the ladder through which our thoughts ascend providing a consistent anchoring above and below in effect becoming the current or life force that gives prayer its upward direction.

Shekinah rides upon the current of prayer, which is her chariot. There are two aspects to prayer. One is ADNY which is the kavannah of the heart's desire and the second is YKVK which is the actualization of prayer; its rising up becomes the image of the reflection of that intention. The angel or malakh is the synthesis or the connection that links between the two producing the current of thought or Shekinah.

During Shabbat the connection between the two names ADNY and YKVK is not established side to side but rather through the middle pillar which is called the righteous one meaning that a simple understanding of the unity of the SHMA is enough to carry the blessings filled with prayer during its recital.

– the sound of the recital of the Shm'a.
(Ecclesiastes 10:20) ...*and the one with wings will tell a thing*
– this is the speech of direct prayer;
and not through an agent.

3a) Creation works in a prescribed manner meaning that these two Names together are the dynamic that is ever present. The "foundation of the world" is the unity of intention with its actualization. The simple recognition of this process is the meaning behind "the trees of the forest rejoice." In this way prayer is unified with blessings or fulfillment.

That ten Sephiros of Atzilus has the king in them
He is one with the life in each of those
What is not so with the ten Sephiros of Briah is that
They do not have a life of their own.

And on high above all he decreed the ten Sephiros of Atzilus.
And the ten Sephiros of Briah.
And in the ten sephiros (circles) of the heavens.
They are changeless in all places

Ezekiel the prophet established those (sephiros) are as mirrors to the gardens of the Shekinah.

And in them (Daniel 12:3) *and the enlightened will be radiant like the bright expanse in the sky* and the enlightened are these letters.

Be radiant from these points taken from the Zohar which indicates in them that the Shekinah is included in all of them

And she it was said (Yechezkiel 1:13) *kept moving about amongst the creatures* That they are creatures of superiority (higher thought) of the indications of the vowel points

And the lower creatures of the vowel points of the characters like this (Heh with three dots above) – and they the segol are superior and the top three creatures are superior are hinted by the Y'Y"Y in creation of the boxes containing YKV'K, YKV'K, YKV"K (contained in Tefillir)

And they YKV'K was king and YKV'K is the king, YKV'K will be king
The face of the three higher creatures is Chesed, Gevurah and Tipheres

Herein are the secrets of the Merkavah as related to Consciousness. Imagine for a moment the holiness within that is the perceptual reality of all your thoughts about Hashem including your questions and the answers you have received. Now forming the latticework of this inner framework are the Sephiros, the unification of Shekinah and Ha Kodesh Barachu, and the recitation of the SHMA. All of these have built up within Consciousness that at some point spontaneously glows with the brilliance of the combination of YKVK and ADNY. The result of this combining is self-awareness.

There is a cascade of this self-awareness that is shown via the expansion of the above mentioned framework so that it produces a spinning motion making this framework accessible and visible from all aspects of life revealing its true inner nature.

We attach ourselves in thought speaking and listening to prayers that join in unity combining predestination with fulfillment.

The SHMA and its holy sound gives wings to prayers moving the chariot via the ten praises called Sephiros.

These are vibrations interpenetrating one another and subsequently all of Israel via the middle pillar. These vibrations establish the thought into speech into sound into the manifestation fulfillment.

Thought must be tied to its fulfillment through the unique vibration of unity produced by he SHMA. Any interruption lowers the vibration thus reducing it efficacy to the point of not getting off the ground.

Tefillin and tzitzit symbolize the knotting together of thought and its outcome, which is echad, the unity of aleph chet to dalet.

In order that mind should have the physical imagery of the internal process, meditation on tefillin brings out the Yud or the essence of Hashem via the two Heh's with the head tefillin or the initial idea and the arm tefillin or the action that is taken.

The four texts and the four housings of tephilin symbolize the four worlds of Kabbalah, Atzilus, Briah, Yetzirah, and

Assaiah, one inside the other demonstrating the dynamic of unity of thought and outcome.

E-H-Y-H ASHER E-H-Y-H; this is the way things work.

Thoughts one inside the other each with their connections symbolized by the straps of Tephilin. The Supernal Imma out of which all utterances come especially those contained with the head and hand Tephilin shows its entire nature which is to remind us of the current or Shekinah that is produced by the awakening self awareness or the Consciousness that knows itself.

The great wisdom is the Supernal Chokmah that produces Yisrael or the middle pillar, and is surrounded by the Levites and Kohanim who are the support of the righteous.

Thoughts are supported and surrounded by other thoughts some higher some lower, some to the left and some to the right. This is the organization of Consciousness that is the continuous creation of Hashem.

The mother descends with the Kedushas of the Levites from the left, and through it 'one who wants to become wealthy should head north.' Both stand in the Middle Pillar that unites them,

Even so is yesod the life-force of worlds
And is the connection of the Middle Pillar and the lower Shekinah.
In which place in prayer in which is included the eighteen blessings
and in it the two names YAKDVNK'Y stand together as one .

And both names should be secretly attached.

3b) It is within prayer that thoughts rise up and are surrounded by other thoughts. What is created within is a virtual holy of holies so that thoughts are imbued with the connection of Yesod and Shekinah. This establishes the current that produces the two names unified in silence that produce the lift that is crucial to the upward journey of prayer.

The 'still thin sound' is the voice of nothing that is the void out of which all things come to be.

Thoughts assume their rightful shape within made up of varying levels of awareness. The north represents the eternal connection that is the link above. Yud is the motive force or the turning force out of which the experience of Hashem is found within both holy names. It is this realization that unites within in the same way as a star is compressed into dark matter.

The feminine aspect of the one calls to the masculine aspect of the other. Imagine thought establishing itself and then being open to expansion via compression. The awareness of one induces the recognition of the other.

The garments for Ha Kodesh Barachu and Shekinah are the four aspects previously discussed (the tempest wind, the fire, the cloud, the thin still voice). When you make the combination between between ADNY and YKVK the awareness of being called Hashem fills your entire being.

Just him yes his throne is his clothing and in those who are dressed
For it is written: (Isaiah 50:3) *I will dress the sky with darkness...*

And the Shekinah it was said about her...(Song of Songs 1:6) 'Look not upon me that I am dark,' because she was in exile her seat damaged because of Israel's sins.

Shekinah is in exile because unification does not take place because of sin. There is no recognition of the process of 'the way things work.' Therefore the "sky is dressed in blackness," meaning that the inner world of Consciousness is without that holy connection. Israel represents the unified holiness of thought.

There can be no approach to holiness in the blemished soul because first the blemish must be taken away.

The soul is perfected via the contemplation of the unity of male and female the action and the result along with the working out of the intention that is fulfilled via YAHDVNHY. This is the garment of thought.

Within Briah resides the creative aspect of spontaneity that produces the horse that drives the chariot. That horse signifies our intention and is surrounded by the garments of the ten Sephiros that subsequently arrange our thoughts.

Within Atzilus resides the totality of being and the ten Sephiros that are here cannot be separated. The King is One including the life force that emanates from the King. In Briah the separation may be experienced as cause and effect whereas in Atzilus all is one.

Mirrors-visions gardens of Shekinah.
(Yechezkiel 1:13) *As for the likeness of the living creatures, their appearance was like coals of fire, burning like the appearance of torches; it flashed up and down among the living creatures; and there was brightness to the fire, and out of the fire went forth lightning.*
These are the points and taste of Torah.

4a) The image of the chayot is revealed and its various connections. The Segol, the inverted Segol the appearance of "is King, was King KVYK will be King" show the connections between cause and effect. Prayers are pillars and channels for thoughts culminating in the central point chayah (life) called Adam or the awareness of the process going on. This awareness is like that of the architect whose plans start out as a sketch and then little by little details are filled in until a working plan emerges.

Three rise and three chayot fall and yet the connecting link gives the appearance of four for every three and then in the next cycle seven to every six. Viewpoint is paramount in this vision. It is man who asks the question generating the answer. (The power of what) Contemplation of the Heh above and below expresses this same dynamic of connection, of one coming from the other and of the connecting link itself.

The meaning of the Heh is expanded by the words it is associated with. Heh also represents the spiritual framework of thought that sits on high and is reflected below.

The Sephiros are expanded via the chayot, which connect via the higher level of one Keter to the Malchus that ascends until Tipheres and the lower emanations from Keter through Gevurah, or the fifth to four higher and lower chayot.

The mystery of Ezekiel's vision is that these chayot are the expanded versions of the Sephiros that appear throughout the worlds described in levels of appearance as compared to the levels of the King's image.

The suspension of the world is our image of the world and that image appears fixed like the vowel point kamatz.

The diaspora is our exile from the connection of "the way things work." What Ezekiel witnesses are the flowing thoughts and he has the insight that these attach themselves in specific ways above or they are rejected.

During the New Year the three books, or Torahs that are read from mirrored by the three Torah's that are read on Simchat Torah. These books are the right side, the left side and the middle pillar.

Eighteen thousand descend with Metatron
Eighteen blessings of prayer raising the world,

before them HKBK eighteen worlds the righteous foundation of the worlds

(Proverbs 10:25) ...*the righteous one is a foundation of the world·*

4b) Metatro"n is a vehicle of the reflection of Hashem. It is the operation of the consciousness of holiness. This consciousness includes the angels of holiness and the chariots of holiness. In order to exist in the unity of Ha Kodesh Barachu our thoughts must have the direction to rise above.

The prayers of the Amidah with its eighteen blessings provide this direction. They act as the chariots which ascend with our prayers with each prayer carrying the advocate of an angel and the entire procession lifted up by Metatro"n rises above with the unity of the image of Hashem and the image from below, our prayers.

The heavens open in response to the connection of Shekinah which by extension is the light of the heavens calling to one another. When we are in diaspora the outer visions consume us. It is only when we attend to the inner heavens that Shekinah then begins to rise up making the connections from spiritual heaven to heaven always keeping as its source YKVK KVYK or Hashem of the heavens.

And visions of Elokim... the five lights of the first day.
the five occurrences of light-*aur* (in Torah)
of the first day - corresponding to the first Hei 5
Each by the different vowels under each Aleph.

א א א א א (qametz, tzeirei, cholem, chireq and shureq)

The five occurrences of aur (light) are compared to the five vowel points. What does light do? It literally defines the darkness just as these vowel points define that first Heh in the five Alephs with their respective vowel sounds.

When thoughts come together they proceed accordingly level-by-level achieving stasis. The Aleph gives rise to EHYH and the vowel points equate to Elohim. Thoughts arrange themselves accordingly to holiness in terms how close in value and substance they are like their Creator.

The discernment of thought allows for its unification. The reason for this is that in order to receive you must first conceive. This is being shown here since the vowel points are the delineations of the letters that describe the concepts that are coming into being.

These points are of Elokim in which there are seven points three up and three down. Relating to the seven planets,There are three here and three there, Center is the sun, fourth to three and seventh to six.
And it is the in the form of the cholem.
In the those five and the (Vayikra 2:2) (Cohen)shall scoop out
of it a handful of its Chamatz his Yud " when he opened it in the five points his Heh'

The planets represent the fixed spheres that are concentrations of holiness presenting as the seven sparks or the seven levels of awareness. These are generated by the concentration of the sun-Tipheres with Hod Netzach and Yesod below and Chesed, Gevurah, and Binah above. The five fingers that indicate Yud and the fifty gates are the principalities that evolve into those fifty gates of understanding issuing from Binah.

The arm, the shoulder and the finger joints derive from Yud hei. Cholem is in the middle all are part of the architecture of thought. What is this like?

"A King desires to build a road to where the Queen has her summer palace. He sends workman to choose the perfect bricks, aligns them along the path and then cements the bricks into place creating a road where nothing more than a meandering path was before."

The road leading back to Hashem is within the power of our consciousness but only if we continue to make the connections throughout Torah that are then cemented with the insights of our discoveries keeping always open the line of communication that allows for revelation at every level.

It is only through the recognition of the great name that the way of return may be entered into. This way of return is truth. This truth is the continuous revelation that is Torah revealing itself to those who are willing to toil in its mysteries. It is in this way that decrees are annulled and redemption is brought near.

When we call upon Hashem we are seeking the unity that is His namesake. In order to "know our way upon the earth," we must be "close to the Lord," or become conversant with the 'way things work.' Now when we deny the truth there is diaspora and conversely when we embrace and integrate that "truth" the time of Moshiach is upon us.

That in the letters were created four animals of the throne that was said on them in idea of Yechezkiel…(1:13) *'Such then was the appearance of the creatures that looked like the burning coals of fire'*, those are the points of Torah that they are nine.
In which they were created nine circular wheels of the throne
The throne is tenth for nine wheels
And in them they were created,
Four letters that are KVYK that shine in the four animals in which they were created.
And there standing true in the middle is KVYK and his Shekinah.
This is the truth of Torah.

(Proverbs 3:35) *the wise shall obtain shine…*

The wise shine because they are surrounded by Torah and out of that brilliance the definition of holiness is made clear. Torah creates through its nine points the architecture of holiness which then creates the throne of holiness. What this is alluding to is the continuous creation that takes place within Consciousness as a whole and each individual whose Torah study shines alike in spinning the wheels of heaven above. The Chayot or Sephiros transform that energy of intention into the connections that establish the holy abode above.

KVYK the central pillar called truth also the vehicle through which Shekinah ascends. Shekinah is the current which when traveled upon leads to the throne called Elohim. Through Torah study all insights evoke Shekinah that produces the current giving snapshots of holiness that in each turn fix the throne in place.

The Torah of Atzilus has existed forever it is the essence of Hashem indeed its perfection. All that has come into and is entering into being are the direct result of this Torah of Atzilus. The higher order of being is already in place.

This Torah of is also directly related to the mitvzos in that their performance provides a vehicle for their verification.

Imagine then a device which has built into it every function necessary to fulfill its own operation including being able to transcend time and account for every circumstance. Therefore is the Beit the precursor not only of Bereishis but also of the first two commandments given to Moshe.

And above everything, And not below everything is the Cause Above,
Not beneath him or it, not to any of the four sides of the world,
and He fills all the worlds and surrounds them.

5a) When you study Torah you are studying man's relationship to Hashem. Out of this study comes our inheritance of the insight or awareness that is the signpost or the badge that confers this awareness leading to our interpretation of Torah.

Now what is conferred is by grace, as a King would endow his servants. This is the emanated glory coming at the level of the world of Atzilus. The created glory occurs when we are aware of and live inside of this "cause of everything." In this way we are surrounded by holiness.

When we study Torah it is as though we are entering a causeway that is already moving merging with the flow of holiness. We are attracted by its brightness and the discovery of its hidden levels which occur at the same time.

There are those who study Torah who may be lacking perhaps in education into its ways, however, they will soon be taught by Torah itself and will become knowledgeable in its ways.

The highest of the levels of "fear of God" is the fear of sin. This is because when we sin it is directly opposed to the path of holiness that we aspire to. Even though we may acquire wisdom, the highest wisdom is "fear of sin." When you are aligned with the "way things work," everything else tracks on course.

The "fear of Hashem" awakens you to the awareness of holiness. This awakening may be compared to the outer keys or the letters of ADN"Y. KVYK represents the inner keys that are the insights that a continuing awareness allows you to enter into. In the Amidah this fear of Hashem is evoked for the purpose of reaching that inner place of revelation. What is this like?

"A King wishes to take a journey but it is too far to walk so he rides a horse. Along the way the horse grows tired and hungry so the King stops to feed and rest the horse."
In the Amidah we too take a journey but within that journey what must be fed with meditation is revelation. Otherwise the journey is for naught.

The one who ascends in holiness does so because he is mindful of the journey. The vowel shv"a from the side of

Gevurah symbolizes the restraint that is necessary in meditation in order to produce the focus that becomes one with the holiness above.

The three hundred and sixty five negative precepts precede the two hundred and forty eight positive precepts because we have to turn away from that which doesn't lead to holiness and run towards that which promotes and defines holiness. Both are necessary in that the negative precepts make possible the performance of the positive precepts.

The "faith of your times" refers to what you have by way of background in Consciousness. This refers to the various orders of Mishnah which extend the field of contemplation providing the basis for the attachments above. The "Fear of God" points directly to the presence of the infinite with the finite. The only way to recognize this wonder is through Torah study and its corollary the Mishnah.

The primary focus of awareness is Shekinah the current that links us up with Ha Kodesh Barachu. Without Shekinah even though a person has learned all six orders of Mishnah the holy connection does not exist without Shekinah.

Keep in mind that as we go along in the introduction here each section although dealing with separate descriptions is nevertheless tied to the whole work. The primary focus of this work continues to show Shekinah and its connection to Ha Kodesh Barachu. In this focus the Sephiros add colors to the overall picture as we see how verses of Torah are linked together to bring us further inside of this mystery.

Faith may be looked at as the downward flow that emanates from Chesed through Tipheres or the upward flow from Lower Shekinah rising from Yesod to Tipheres. What is this Faith? It is the attachment both above and below of the holiness that is ever present within. This is to say that no matter where we enter into or become aware of its presence we are destined to reach the heart of the matter or the essence of Tipheres, which is the harmonization of both above and below.

Just as there is no Torah without fear, so is there no fear without Torah
and there will be no lack in his household alt. his learning;
there will be no lack in his soul,
and there will be no lack in his good deeds.

5b) The six orders of Mishnah are aligned with the Sephiros from Da'at through the central pillar with Chesed-Gevurah connected above in conjunction with Hod and Netzach connected below upward to Tipheres. These are aligned in this way due to the nature of Consciousness, which is like the "blade of a revolving sword."

Thoughts do go every which way and are pulled according to their various attractions. The internal conception of the Mishnah is to direct thoughts according to their energies or orders so that we are all the while training Consciousness in its supreme aspiration which is the unification which takes place above and below.

Fear of God in the seventh level is the awareness of the way things work. There is at first "fear" because of potential missteps due to unconscious actions-reactions, however, when this "fear" becomes in fact the raised awareness of God then the entire psyche is placed upon a higher footing.

The sixth level in the fear of Hashem
And the faith of thy times (Isaiah 33:6)
This faith is in the order Zeraim (Seeds) (1st order)
inheritance of the order of Moed (Festivals) (2nd order)
Have control of the order of Nashim (Women) (3rd Order)
Salvation of the order of damages Nezikin (4th order)
Intelligence of the order of Kodashim holiness –(5th order of Mishnah)
And the knowledge of the order of Tohorot- (purity) (6th order of Mishnah)

A person who has no knowledge of Torah cannot have "fear of God" because they would not understand the impact of these actions. With Torah we gain the understanding and the fulfillment of "fear of God" since in every sense of the word we learn to flow with the "way things work."

Mishnah prepares the mind for the sword that revolves which is the playback of thoughts that are either subjugated and then dissipated by our recognition of their lower nature or are placed into higher orbits of internal unification provided by the pathways that are the details the Mishnah offers as guide points for our awareness.

Torah study and good deeds are for the purpose of building the temple within. Through this kind of intention (to study Torah and do good deeds) our imagination is raised to the level of holiness. If however our thoughts are debased this causes not only an apparent detachment from above it also decays the body, which cannot be sustained without the holiness of above.

Therein the secret of destruction of the Holy Temple is explained both in the actual occurrences of long ago and within each soul as it seeks it own avenue of awareness to the temple within.

Imagine the awesome experience of Sinai. It is the unification of Hashem experienced by Israel. A spark of this experience lives in every Jew and some say that this is an ongoing experience that never ended and that our own stubborn way of looking at things prevents us from the full immersion once again in that Sinai experience.

Since we still retain that spark within us whenever we do something that takes away our vision into the greater unified reality should be cause for the deepest regret or what is called shame of face. Perhaps even it could be called shadow of face since what is being covered up is the spark of Sinai.

The word Bereishis suggests both "shame of face" and the "fear of Shabbat." Both of these are related to this idea of covering or making less that awesome experience of Hashem that resides within the secret compartments to their innermost levels.

Humility is the eight level of "fear of God." It is the higher Shekinah because before rising above you must kneel down below in order to be lifted up. You have to be open to your higher awareness letting it guide you in the same way Moshe was guided in his journeys.

A person becomes praiseworthy before God as in the ninth level in the fear of God by attending to the divine precepts. These precepts all six hundred and thirteen of them are mystically intertwined with learning about and working with the knowledge of 'the way things work.' We become aligned subsequently with the thoughts of Hashem. Praise is defined now as the image above that is reflected below.

The tenth degree of fear of the Lord...
Here is fear that will show and there is fear that will not show
Not every face is equal, there will show that a person HKBK in order that will not afflict the same in the land that was said in her...(Bereishis 1:2) 'the earth being unformed and void,' from the side of the tree of good and evil, which is the empty land the evil maidservant.

6a) The tenth level in the fear of God is the sudden realization that you have been neglecting your higher calling. What happens is that you see that you have nothing and nowhere to turn and it is like being in a pit with no escape. This seems to come directly as a pronouncement from above. This sudden realization can only come with the fear of God otherwise like the boor a person would be oblivious to this fear of God.

Now understand that his fear of God is the awareness or the awe of God. This awareness it is stately clearly travels via the middle pillar where centrally located Tipheres becomes its nexus. From this nexus Torah study proceeds above and below giving both inspiration to higher thinking and righteous action below in Malchus.

The simple doctrine of Torah is expressed meaning that we are to know the precedent and the antecedent and where we stand in relation to both.

Those who do not understand the inner workings of Torah will not experience fear of God even though they will still be bound by all manner of circumstance that is described and discussed in Torah.

Torah is given from the level of Chesed and the level of Gevurah. These two levels combined with the numerical value of Torah, which is six hundred eleven, make up the six hundred and thirteen mitvzos. The ignorant cannot therefore be kind or have fear of God since they do not recognize these distinctions.

There is always a reflection from above to below as through Chesed-Gevurah becoming the fulfillment in Malchus or Torah study leading to righteous action. It is one thing to become aware of (fear of) God and another to become wise in the ways of God, wisdom. These ways lead to acting as one with God.

This idea of reflection from above to below is continued with Tipheret called man the lower hei reflecting the upper hei in the higher Chokmah. Man first in thought then the extension of man becoming Israel through Tipheret via another extension culminating in the last of thought, the Yud of

ADNY here called the lower Chokmah, fear of God or Malchus.

It is stated here (of woman)
(Vayikra 12:2) *...a woman who shall conceive....*
And last that it is from Yud from ADNY the lower wisdom, fear of Hashem His kingdom.
This is the reason is said of woman in Tazria that
she has to anticipate all the mitzvos as it is said (Mishlei 31:30) *'it is for her fear of Hashem.'* that is her praise.
And before this found a woman in the first found good, that we will say in him it good ' for all His works (Tehilim 145:8)
(Proverbs 18:22) *He who has found a woman...*
And it is said
(Psalms 145:9) *God is good to all...*

The woman that conceives is the first priority in all commandments because it is through conception that all ideas are thereby developed. The man "who has found a woman... has found good," meaning the inspiration that is developed is derived from holiness and proceeds accordingly to holiness.

The priority in prayer is the inspiration that develops from prayer the female who conceives and then provides the mold for all thought to come through.

And because of this intention in thought brings forth the mitzvah.
And because of this name of wisdom there is the prayer that is expressed first.
That is which is placed in first blessing (intention)
And because of this awe-fear needs to come from the side of the Shekinah between the Torah there inside of the Mitzvos.
But from the side of of HKBK awe-fear is placed first of all the commandments in Torah.

Intention in thought comes first, which opens the gates of awareness. Shekinah makes possible the divine connection with Ha Kodesh Barachu, which attaches us to Torah during prayer.

The oral Torah or fear of Torah comes to us when we have opened the doors to receive. We are filled with insights.

Every time that we pray with the proper intention we are entering the operation that is called "repairing the throne of his master." What is this like?

A King desired to live in a palace that would be accessible to all. His workmen toiled for years and finally it was ready. The King upon inspection said yes this is good but something is not quite right. So the workmen persisted and twice more they presented the palace for his inspection and twice more he told them no it wasn't ready yet. Finally one of the workmen noticed that the throne was on high and that the King had to peer down at his subjects. He lowered the throne and made it possible for the King to see eye to eye with his people. "Yes," declared the King, "this is perfect."

Our prayers form the basis for the throne above for the purpose of making a suitable place within for Ha Kodesh Barachu to reside. The perfect place is where the divine influence merges with the yearnings of our soul.

This connection is made possible only by the truth of our prayers that pass above and formulate the throne that allows us to meet Ha Kodesh Barachu eye to eye.

That he includes the three blessings of prayer and the last three
And this is the ten Sephiros without what. *(blimah)*
They derive from each other two names YKVK ADNY
And eight characters
They are ten, ten scales of the holy shekel
(Numbers 7:86) *...ten, ten, each spoon (kaph) in weight of the holy shekel....*

The ten Sephiros are the eight that become ten meaning the expansion of ADNY and KVYK that are the Sephiros aligning themselves within the internal architecture of thought. These Sephiros are considered from below to above or from "what is, what was and what will be," to "nothingness," and then back again.

And at the end of the redemption *'Skipping over the mountains'* (Shir Hashirim 2:8),
The mountains only refers to the patriarchs who are the chariot
Even one who so skips on the mountains are in service to YKVK ADNY

6b) The patriarch's symbolize the levels of awareness of the divine experience that is flowing out while the matriarch's similarly relate to the divine experience that is flowing in mirroring the upward and downward flow of Sephiros.

It is through Yesod that the thought of intention becomes transformed into the act of fulfillment. Each of the eighteen blessings then becomes the support for the throne (blessings of the head of the righteous) that is internalized.

Every thought that you have has its own destination and resting place that are determined by the intention placed behind each thought.

The eighteen blessings might be called the first fence of awareness that acts both to keep in holiness and repel the evil inclination. They are like children in that they must be watched-prayed over and like servants because they serve the holy connection that is established above. They are called glory because they are ever increasing.

ADN"Y is the chariot of YKV"K,
and it is wrapped in Her.
Even so YKVK is contained within AKVK to create a world.
But there YKVK is a supreme Keter to the chariot of ADNY most high..
And because of this *there is no holy one like the Lord* (Samuel 1 2:2)

ADN"Y is the chariot of YKV"K, (Hashem – Yud Heh Vav Heh) since in the dual divine name the latter is contained within the former which is in turn the chariot for Ha Kodesh Barachu or that which has no name the essence of divinity continuously awakening to its own presence infinitely.

The same kind of paradox resides within the seal, which is a depiction of the image of the image. What does this mean and why consider the paradox in the first place?

The meaning has to do with the symbolism that Consciousness employs in its increasing levels of awareness. Yes we cannot encompass the divine although we most certainly can suggest by inference using the letters of Torah to give us an idea of what we are thinking about.

Where we see the symbols we can infer or envision the actual, which is exactly what Ezekiel's vision is all about.

On a deeper level we can consider the paradox and yet even though it may come as a surprise to we do not have to figure it out completely. The answer is a moving target that is always coming into being expanding and requiring greater and greater levels of comprehension. Therefore it is enough to simply be aware of the movement and then infer by means of symbolic representation where we stand in relation to it, to the paradox.

The thing is that we are not meant to make any graven image because in doing so we have limited the same thing that we are trying to understand which is our own expansion of comprehension.

(Ezekiel 1:26) *And above the firmament that was over their heads,*
There was א *like the appearance of sapphire stone, was the likeness of a throne.*
This covered sapphire and white sapphire is actually more like this
Above, like this
(Shemos 24:10) *...and beneath His feet, like a work of sapphire stone....*
And under his feet like white sapphire like this (Aleph)
And it is all one א

7a) The point of the Aleph that is like a Yud is the sapphire stone alluding to the higher Keter where Y"K Chokmah and

Binah come together. This is the beginning of Ezekiel's vision and the basis for what follows. This vision then is rooted in Malchus meaning it represents the entire tree since it is the representation of YKV"K.

There within YKV"K is rakia the Central Pillar Zeir Anpin extending like a curtain with the diagonal line of the Aleph. This is the natural or predominate mode of Consciousness that extends itself by the specific nature of its being. What are the heavens? They are the myriad worlds-pathways of creation.

These pathways suggest the journeys we are making in Consciousness that bring forth the idea of the 'way things work.'

This idea of returning to the one is central to thought. There must a center to every purpose that is brought forth. This center is the divine name YKVK that is the image of the one that cannot be described. This is the beginning of man, the Aleph that unfolds into all that can be.

Shekinah acts as a current for the soul. The synagogue on high is the location of a transformer to that current that merges with the soul showing both the Garden of Eden and Gehinom.

A return to the first day acts to reignite the soul from the center above and below. While this is happening the permutations of Yud Hei Vav Hei flow along this current transforming it via the Sephiros.

It is the building of the world that promoted by the current of Shekinah. It takes the intention through the Sephiros up until Hod revealing fifty gates and their aspects above and below. The awareness transforms the fire in six visions or tSephiros from Binah to Hod forming Zeir Anpin that is the building of the world.

The seventh of the points of Yud Hei Vav Hei alludes to Yesod or the foundation of the world whose counterpart below is Metatron or the vision that is seen by Ezekiel.

These visions appear within one another like a mirror that reflects itself over and over again. The image flows below into the lower Shekinah.

The brightness or nogah of the lower Shekinah is because it has become imbued with the image above. In this way it has taken on this image and then seeks to surround the male or the incoming appearance of the image to take on all of its transmitted qualities. Thought carries the impression until it transmits its expression and then that expression encompasses the impression drawing it continuously into manifestation.

Just prior to the realization of the totality of the image that is YKVK here in the ninth level the reflection or likeness of the glory of God is seen from below presenting itself as the Higher Chokmah. This is the awareness of the initial awakening that is now culminated in form. What is this like?

A King instructs a minister to carry out his instructions for improving his impoverished lands to the south. The minister makes many changes and finally just prior to the King's arrival on the next day he looks around and realizes the depth of his accomplishments. The entire area is thriving due to the King's instruction which has been perfectly carried out.

Therefore when the King does come wearing his crown (Keter) at the tenth level of YKVK there can only be the awareness of the King throughout everything. The higher conceptions of Bria'h and Atzilus become increasingly higher in their conceptions so that even their expressions are unable to be contained within an adequate description regardless of the magnificence of the visions.

Think of your mind as a landscape of thought. Due to the unconscious nature of mind and not of thought this landscape needs to be explored. The vowel points in fact give depth to each letter and because of this the letters can be enunciated. Without the vowels those letters retain their structure but are lacking in meaning.

The same thing is true in mind in that without awareness mind retains the structure of thought but not its deeper meanings. It could be said that mind without self discovery is one dimension instead of being six dimensional as when the wheels turn this way and that. Each turning reveals another aspect all integral to the whole.

In the shorthand of Kabbalah and the TKZ the Vav represents these six dimensions also called Zeir Anpin referencing the six Sephiros from Binah through Hod. Holiness is incomplete without its connecting links. The Vav is that connecting link.

Ezekiel's construction is none other than the architecture of thought as we see that there is one inside another as the Vav is contained within the form of the Aleph. Learning how to delineate this construction is contained in the deepening awareness that is the result of its contemplation.

And all this is the mystery of Ezekiel's construction within the mystery of the points. And furthermore, (regarding) the mystery of the points, they are to be revised.

(Concerning)Patach – the numerical value of the letters are equal to YU"D. And it is written:
(Psalms 145:16) You *open Your Hand and satisfy every living thing with favor*, and they have determined: do not read Your hand, but rather, Your Yuds.

7b) First the Patach delineates the flowing forth of divine abundance showing the unity of the dual divine name in that one is inside the other. It is kind of like cutting a diamond in that every cut still reveals the diamond albeit in different aspect though still retaining its diamond essence. Patach alludes to the firmament in that it is the context against which all meanings are derived.

Qametz in the heavens a spark of Yud Vav
Sixteen points, sixteen faces of chayot
A totality of points one facing the other.

Qametz extends the firmament adding more depth becoming the reflecting mirror that the chayot all turn in relationship to. It is the continuous spark of thought that recognizes itself and the maker that has revealed it's sending forth as in the hand that opens to share its blessings.

Tzeirei equals Vav-Vav or twelve. And beneath tzaddi are two sparks which are Yud-Yud: (Shemos 1:16) ...*the two great luminaries*.... And these are Vav-Vav and Yud-Yud adding to thirty two. And these are 'the thirty two wonderful paths of chokmah.' And (added) the point under the Reish of tzeirei there is Yud — (meaning) ten sephiros, - see there forty two.

Tzeirei indicate one inside the other side by side as with two Yuds and two Vav's and the two great luminaries resolving then to the numerical equivalent of man forty-five. Special attention may be focused on the way we have arrived at this meaning. We always start with something we know and build upon this extending it to reveal first one then another dimension. In this way we establish a chain of association or a histashelut.

Shva, which comes to be: (Shemos 1:16) ... *the greater light to dominate the day, and the lesser light,'* And there is the mystery of forty two; and the mystery of man.

Shva equals is six, (321 or 3+2+1) with three sparks and a heaven, it is: YYYV, adding to thirty six; then see forty two; plus the three letters of the word *Shva* — here is forty five. And the mystery of this word is:

36

(Shemos 3:13) ... *when they ask me what is his name what shall I say to them?* (*mah- what -45*) And the vowel point *Shva* is a point of the Name YKV"K in the Torah.

Shva also delineates the name of God in both the forty-two letter and the forty five letter name. This gives us another way in which Torah even in its smallest detail is speaking about the recognition of Hashem via the awareness of man. The luminaries represent both conscious awareness or the big luminary and subconscious awareness the smaller luminary. Their resolution, their unity takes place within the name YKV"K.

Segol eighteen counted Vav, Vav, Vav
Shemos 14:19-21, (ויסע ויבא ויס)
Yud Yud Yud plus three Vav's is forty-eight
Add the four letters of Segol to make חמישים ושתיים or fifty two.

Segol represents what happens as the recognition of the name unfolds within as in Moses whose face shines like the face of the sun.

Cholem without Vav – its number is YA"H 15. And three sparks Yud Yud Yud 30 are forty five; like the Tetragrammaton Yu"d H"ai Va"v H"ai spelt with Alephs and which equals 45. And, together with the three letters of the word *cholem*, and the word itself, they are forty nine, like the value of the forty nine letters of: (Deuteronomy 6:4) *Hear O Israel (Shema Yisrael)* Blessed be the Name of the glory...

And in the Mishnah the Rabbis say Fifty gates of wisdom in the way
Given to Moses all but one
(Psalms 8:6) *Yet You have made him slightly less than Elohim*

Now below the angels forty nine pure faces
Of Metatron they show their traces
As angels over cholem in all their places.

Cholem represents the ascendency of the seeker whose thought approaches the sublime holiness. Each instance of unification where the Tetragrammaton is discovered anew opens up another of these fifty gates of wisdom less one, which is the final step to Moshiach. The cholem is that last step with Metatron representing the unique crossover that makes this last step possible.

When you place the vowels in conjunction with the letters of the Tetragrammaton it produces the various aspects of the unfolding of the divine. This is to show the interconnections that may be found within each instance of the holy name and amongst each of its holy letters.

Shureq – the numerical value of its letters is six, and with five sparks are fifty, this is fifty six. Three letters and the word are sixty. (Psalms 25:14) *The secret* (*sod*) *of* YKV"K *is with those who fear him....* And through it: (Jeremiah 31:6) *Sing to Jacob of joy...* is an acronym of Shureq.

Shureq its letters numbering to six (600 - 6)
Five sparks (the Vav's) are fifty
Making fifty six together.
Then the three letters of Shureq making sixty.

(Psalms 25:14) *The secret of* YKV"K *is with those who fear him....*
(Jeremiah 31:6) *Sing to Jacob of joy...* is an acronym of Shureq.

The secret of YKV"K is that all things combine to point to and emanate from there including all the variations of the adding together of the vowels. Shureq is included in this compilation of examples that point to the holiness of YKV"K

Every meaning comes by definition from Chokmah since it is there where the initial sparks are derived from. There is the extension of meaning that culminates in Malchus. At every step in the hishtalshelus there is a leap of faith as seen where Yesod contains the mystery of sod. We are being pointed to the realization of one thing that resides inside another.

Here we are shown the relationships of the vowels with their points-sparks and their firmaments-straight lines forming underneath the letters giving meanings to the archetypes that are written within Torah.

We can illustrate these relationships between the vowels and infer their counterparts within the structure of the Sephiros. There is a fluid nature presented here just as Consciousness is made up of a fluid design with interpenetrating thoughts that become concepts, The resultant field calls all into action producing the demonstration of being.

The chamatz combines the sparks and the firmament making up the divine relationship that is compared to YKV"K wherein the Keter of creation is highlighted. Within thought we are directed its highest conception

Patach illustrates the forty two-letter name of God as various combinations all result in the numeric of forty-two. Look closely as the references here. First desire and rescue, and then opening the gates of righteousness and subsequently entering through them; this describes the pathways of holiness.

And so mysteries of the points abound.
And like this;
(Psalms 118:19) *I shall come through them, I shall give thanks to God* (YA"H).

And how many mysteries there are of the points.
And this is seems to be: it is:
(Psalms 118:19) *I shall come through them, I shall give thanks to God* (YA"H). *Now patach it is said:*
Of this it was said (Tehilim 118:19)*Open to me the gates of righteousness; I will enter into them, I will give thanks unto the LORD.*

8a) Following this we give thanks and then reaffirm the intention as in "this is the gate for God." This is the formula revealed by patach using the holy name as a chariot of revelation.

Cantillation notes are now added to the vision of letters and vowel points. This is not merely now the relationships that are being explained but is rather a unification that is taking place. This unification allows us to see the not only what is taking place within these particular verses but also serves to lay the groundwork for everything that is to come forth in the overall body of work.

The order established is with letters directed (given their meaning) by the vowel points and the combined letters-vowel points are directed by the cantillation marks.

Here we find one thing inside of the other. Letters are fire, the wind that directs the letters and water and is not mentioned in context with the cantillation marks, plays its part in the overall mixture, which is why we see another description that includes all four elements together becoming the legs of the Divine throne separating the points which are symbolized by Adam upon the throne.

The combinations that are expressed via YKVK and their permutations relate to the aspect ratios that occur between the Sephiros. Notably the feminine and masculine aspects are considered from above to below and below to above.

With consciousness there is an initial sending forth (masculine) and then an acceptance (feminine). Father passing to daughter is masculine becoming feminine while father passing to son retains the masculine aspect. The arrangements that these divine letters make generate the pathways that flows both below and above.

The signature realization is that what we are learning is the construction of Ha Kodesh Barachu. This is the construction of the holiness within that is linked with all the unifications that we have ever experienced within Torah, Mishnah and throughout life itself.

These constructions form themselves out of the divine letters and become like super charged nodes within Consciousness. They have to power to topple if we sin or as well to build themselves whole with our prayers.

It is this construction in mind that is central to Torah study and the contemplation of the divine name. What is this like?

"A King constructs his palace using the finest materials placing his foundation stones in strategic locations to insure the stability of his palace. The palace is tied together with cement that binds the stones and the foundation in place."

In our prayers we must be mindful of YKVK for this is where we are attaching our thoughts. It is this attachment that ensures not only the foundation of our prayers but also their raising on high to become imbued with the flow of thought becoming from idea to fulfillment.

We are building the altar with Yud as its foundation and upon this foundation via Vav as beam and post we place bayit the house. The house is the eternal within framed by Beit the building, Malchus, Yesod the foundation and Tav as Tipheret the beauty of the thing itself.

What dwells inside of this house upon this altar? It is our prayers that reside there and partake in the eternal construction within. When we bless we are building the bayit -house continuous in our prayers.

Once our attention is focus upon the building of this eternal within more is revealed. We see that the entrance is Keter or the Cause of Causes. Because of this there is not anything perceivable through this entrance. since what we are building cannot be directly accessed. This is why man or Adam is above the tabernacle considering it as an image or like the seal of the King discussed earlier or also like the khaf is an extension of the image of yud.

Once we have the revelation of the divine flow (Shekinah) and can conceive it in terms of the 'eternal within' this illuminates or anchors our awareness so that this imagery may be processed there. The actual work that takes place is symbolized by Chesed, which represents the abundance of the flow. This abundance generates the seventy-two permutations that develop from this overflowing of unification.

The head of the sword is yud the (head of the)name YKV"K
No one surpasses the master of the sword, On all sides victorious,
No one stands before it.

8b) What is yud other than yichud or unification? The name of YKV"K begins with yud at the head or handle of the sword. Think about every thought you have being focused with the intention of unifying with this name.

The yud itself represents that intention for unification. It becomes the deciding factor throughout every decision you make. The question then always becomes, "will this bring me closer to unification or farther away? "No matter what thought comes in from whichever direction it comes, you designate for yourself the empowerment of yud. Once you are established in yud then your pathways become clear. These pathways are symbolized by the Vav or Zeir Anpin meaning that once unification is your insistent goal the directions that you take are along the pathways of the Sephiros. And this occurs on all four sides meaning in all four worlds from Keter through Malchus and back again to Keter. It is the chain of association that you gain mastery over.

The two hei's cut above and below but what is it they cut? It is circumstance. How does this work? It is the grounding of circumstance that either nullifies or sets it into motion. In either case it is the example of the vowelling of ELKY"M that allows the hei's to sweep into motion. Binah filled with intention also establishes the transformation of circumstance as in bringing it about or making it null.

There are thoughts in your mind that are errant or contrary to unification. These are the ones that are bound by the Shema so that no tendrils of confusion grow sowing seeds of doubt. The eternal momentum or the righteous momentum is found in prayers, which seek unification in the greater good. The Shema is our most powerful thought and therefore our most unique weapon against chaos.

When we recite the Shema it reaffirms our intention for unification and reestablishes our mastery over the domain of our thoughts.

It is the evil inclination that has to be slain without reservation. It is only a thought and must be summarily eliminated, erased, made to have never existed in the first place.

The evil inclination must be removed from the heaven of your thought atmosphere and every action you perform in deed. Now this evil inclination exists for a reason that is bound to our own definitions of holiness that has somehow become mixed up.

And upon their names is it stated in Scripture:
(Psalms 84:12) *) YKV"K ELKY"M is a sun and a shield...*
And so it comes true...
(Isaiah 60:20) *Thy sun shall no more go down,*
Neither shall thy moon withdraw itself;
for the LORD shall be thine everlasting light,
and the days of thy mourning shall be ended.

9a) There are two thrones; one is inside the other. Just as the moon is inside the orbit of the sun so too is Shekinah inside the orbit of Ha Kodesh Barachu. Thoughts reside likewise one inside the other. Sometimes we are seeking one thing and come up with another and realize that this unexpected thing was in fact the answer after all.

The evil inclination or the errant thought may be several layers deep but the alchemy of the wise is to learn how to catch that thread of evil and spin it away from the righteous thoughts so that you rid Israel or the body of thoughts that are surrounded by holiness from the taint of chaos.

The taint of the evil inclination (Sama"el) is insidious meaning our thoughts are permeated with chaos simply because the nature of thinking is vast. There are two kinds of thoughts; one may be characterized as children. These thoughts are the reactive thoughts that follow like children every shiny object of interest without discrimination.

The second kind are like servants in that they are directed by our intention, the inner will the good that seeks Hashem and wants to ferret out the evil inclination. This evil inclination has directly to do with right and wrong which lies in between judgment and mercy.

Then when She comes down in their presence
It is Vav that She is by a strap tied with
With the six words of the unification (Shema Yisroel…)
Now the meaning of
(Shemos 13:16) *And it shall be a sign upon your hand…* becomes clear

Using the imagery of Tephilin we bind the evil thought and then slaughter it with the SHMA. This prevents these thoughts from growing in power or becoming a part of your thought atmosphere in such a way that they become endemic to the entire space. In essence we stop or bind the evil inclination and then erase or slaughter it.

Understand then what must be bound. It is the head and the hand. It is thought and action. The weak hand is the subconscious or the reactive thought. This is what must be seasoned or seeded with praises, songs and thanksgivings simply because what it is given is what must be produced in kind. This in turn causes Shekinah to descend as the symbolism of the Vav suggests forming that connection between thought and action.

The SHMA forms the unity between above and below and is locked into place with the knot of yud. This knot of yud is the indisputable unity. Out of this unity proceeds the Vav and Hei. This is why any deviation of this process as in talking between putting on the head and hand tephilin causes a break in this flow. Sin is defined as a break in the circuit that is made active by tephilin and the SHMA.

The higher glory, higher hei, the higher Mother represent the connection that is directly established with the mystery.

The mystery or Ha Kodesh Barachu flows into and through this crown of Tipheret. Here is established the connection between head and hand or between thought and action as previously stated. The linking of head and hand is the intention the Vav in the middle connecting both head and hand tefillin.

"Israel saw the great hand meaning that our awareness rose to the level of Chesed and made its connection via Tipheret along this sacred pathway. In this way mercy revolves around Tipheret intersection the orbit of judgment or Gevurah, which is the binding of the evil inclination and then it, destruction via the sword of Vav.

The three times hand refers to the pathways above and below that pass through Tipheret. In this way the 42 names of God are revealed. These forty two names are seven times six or seven times the pathways of Zeir Anpin (six) from Chesed to through Yesod as spheres and then seven pathways leading to Malchus.

Within Consciousness the main emphasis of these pathways are in the holiness that they embrace in establishing the flowing of Shekinah.

It is important to realize that the great hand of the lower Shekinah refers to the pathway between Chesed and Chokmah. Shekinah is dependent upon this pathway.

In the same consideration the strong hand is the pathway between Gevurah and Binah. This symbolism is tied to the inner tephilin that is associated with the pathway of the Middle Pillar. The Master of the World is the source of all emanation. What we have here is the imaging of YKVK combined with the tephilin and then linked to the thought processes that are eternal within.

The SHMA and its blessings form the architecture of holiness within. The purpose of this architecture is to construct a dwelling place within to make that most sublime of all connections with the king seeing the entire chain of association from the initial thought that arises out of Keter to the fulfillment taking place in Malchus.

The sole impediment to holiness is the evil inclination. When it is bound and eradicated there is no exile and Shekinah flows. Unless this is taken care of the connection cannot be wholly made. Tipheret is trapped meaning Shekinah is blocked from its flow.

This blockage is concerned primarily with the recognition of that flow and then the awareness of being cut off becomes acute. The divine name exhibits itself only during a perfect connection. The emanation from Keter reaches Malchus and then reciprocates from below to above.

It is one thing to recognize that our thoughts produce our life experiences (the flow from above to below) and it is another thing to realize that our awareness of the fulfillment (from below to above) sets the stage for an eternity of fulfillment completing the circuit and in effect establishing Shekinah for all time.

The only way you can step outside of yourself is to identify with the holiness within while stepping outside of the box of those worldly thoughts that would limit your perception.

It is your awareness that rescues you. Out of this awareness is the realization of the forty-two mentions of the divine Name. What you understand is the unity of both your questions and answers and subsequently how both work together to draw you inside of the holiness within.

When you recite the SHMA you call or move into place the reality of "you will call and Hashem will answer. This is illustrated by ADNY who answers YKVK in the tephilin of the head that then directs the hand tephilin or the thought that directs the action that takes place.

The housing in the hand and the head are taken together so that there are in total five housings. It is called the weaker hand because actions are a diluted form of thought.

And the secret of thing is (Tehilim 91:14) *because he is devoted to me I will deliver him,*
Kaph Yud (30) and Bet Yud (12) in Gematria Mem-Bet (Forty Two) names of Tephilin (and of the head and of the arm.)

I will keep him safe for he knows my name (Ibid),
I will be with him in the Kriat SHMA and answer him.
This is that which is said... (Isaiah 58:9) *'Then when you call the Lord will answer.'*
YKV'K four houses for the front Tephillin (head) which are the four letters AHY'H.
And YY answers YKV'K that are the four houses of the hand Tefillin, ADN'Y.
And if you say they are not in hand but one house of five, they are the weak hand.

9b) Consider now the architecture of thought in that one thought ties to another and is subsequently linked on one side and then the other. In the same way the five housings are linked together via Hei from YKV"K which on one side links to YK"V and on another side to EKY"K.

The symbolism of tephilin is tied to Torah to the SHMA and syllogistically tied to the physicality of the head and hand. Imagine then that the head is the box wherein the four compartments of tephilin. These verses and their meditation form a permanent part of the holiness that is within. The arrangement of these verses is mirrored to the Sephiros beginning with Chokmah and Binah, flowing through Chesed and Gevurah, and reaching stasis with the SHMA in Tipheres. Then moving once again flowing through until Malchus. This is a map of the passing of thought into form.

The three straps indicate the pathways of Shekinah as it transforms the inner emanations via Hod Netzach and Yesod. It is the transformation of the higher hei into the lower hei of Malchus becoming the thing itself in stages discernible and yet maintaining its unification all along the way.

Transformation is the key here. The knot of the tephilin is the binding of thought in this case the higher thought symbolized by yud, which passes through and becomes the thing unto which it is sent. Binah flows through the five intervening Sephiros and is then turned into the essence via that becomes the image of itself in Malchus.

In Malchus is established the "mystery of the word," in that thought is guided by the middle horn alluding to the head tephilin specifically the knot that stays true to its nature. As it flows into manifestation - Malchus is resident in the strap of the hand tephilin. This is the binding strap that wraps physicality around the idea within.

Keter the crown is the home of the eternal conception. When we lay tephilin it is as though that plan of conception were impressed upon our body. The idea always remains above the fulfillment of its precepts. The mystery of the word is that through the ten Sephiros the word flows itself into being. This being in its fulfillment and its conception is none other than YKV"K.

The heavens are established with understanding meaning that through Binah the divine flow emanates from the left the side of tephilin. It is here that the transformation occurs via the interaction of Chokmah, the Yud upon the daughter that is the next phase to occur. The four watches refer to the staging of the flow. Stage one is from Chokmah to Binah. Stage two is from Binah to Zeir Anpin. Stage three is from Zeir Anpin to Yesod and then stage four is from Yesod to Malchus.

The arrangement of these four letters determines the particular pathway that comes into view and offers a corresponding connection. The pathways of HVY"ct in the middle refers to the phrases that reference the middle column of Sephiros. All of these verses point to the transcendence of Hashem to sanctify, give thanks, listen and hear the unity of that transcendence.

These acronyms that are presented here are shortcuts to these pathways that link the Sephiros together. The analogy here is to thoughts that reference each other in an endless chain of association. These thoughts are the pathways of mind and it is here that the divine flow is promoted throughout the world.

Through these shortcuts we see the connections in Torah to the divine name in its various permutations. All of this is to demonstrate that Hashem is written into the fabric of Torah.

Each example refers to the holiness that is about to be revealed. It is as if the divine name that appears couched in the end letters of a phrase are also its resting place where it can be perceived. What we find then within these Torah phrases are the persistent callings of the above that seem to be off the stage somewhere but all the while they are imminent and resident within.

The connection is then made via the name that is exalted that accomplishes (the hand) and brings forth the good (righteousness) that is revealed by their (the holy names) perception.

Each time a thought appears it is wrapped around a form. This is to give that thought a context against which it may be measured tracked and pass into greater reflections that illuminate this original thought that embodies the form.

And these points exist at the end of the tephilin like this,
The Lord is King, YKVK
The Lord was King, YKVK
The Lord will be King," YKVK
The names above. Their points are written underneath.

From every name four Names
As it is said: (Isaiah 6:3) *And this one* (*zeh* =12) *calls*
corresponding to the twelve faces of three *chayot*,
to the other (*zeh* =12... twelve wings of three chayot.
This is the secret of tefillin and tzitzit.

10a) The vowel points are the context against which we may view these divine emanations. These vowels are the shadows cast by the holiness giving it an explicit expression while still maintaining the all-encompassing quality of the thought embodied form.

The vowel points assume a special place within the divine names. Below they ascertain the meaning, substance of the emanation and above they act as points of connection above to below and so on. The same thing is true in terms of the letters that are found at the beginnings and endings of words or phrases configuring the divine name in its permutations.

What therefore is the aspect of choice that comes into being? It is the face of a man ruler over all these appellations. The face of man is his configuration the way he is linked above and the determination of his sovereignty below. The head tefillin acts in the manner of the face of man and the straps are wings he rides upon. The arm tefillin are the chayot and their faces as they call to one another the man gives the answer or the direction in terms of which way to ultimately go.

Now meditation into these mysteries gives rise to the establishment of the Name of 12 in that the various forces represented by these faces may be directed accordingly during prayers. This meditation is akin to holding mirrors in the mind that capture or simulate the higher forces interacting to arrange the flow of Shekinah below to activate the emanations that are flowing above in the sense of fixing them into the aspects of the realized prayers.

Tefillin and Tzitzit are the overt garments of prayer their inner significance is the meditative pathway that releases prayer from the potential to the actual.

The divine connections taken from YKV"K the divine name relate together according to the manner in which they are arranged together as brothers, sisters, mother, daughter including within these connections the operation of the sacrifices and their mode of rising above and below called the graded sacrifice.

Thoughts are connected together similarly with each idea ascending and descending to find its settled place via the connecting links that it shares accordingly with other thoughts. What we find in Torah are phrases that reveal these combinations and are the parallel operations of mind in its workings within the physical body to arrange the life experiences that result thereof.

First there has to be the recognition of being or the awareness of being. Then out of this assumption there is the reflection of being which is the endgame of divinity.

You might think that G-d would arise first and all else afterwards, however there must first be an awareness of being. Then that awareness aware of being contemplates the divine, its resident source.

The Egyptian who denigrated the name is the ignorance of that reflection that comes from the awareness of being. The name is that reflection and the confirmation of that awareness of being, the two becoming one simultaneously. What was killed with the name was that ignorance of the awareness of being.

Now these vowel points above are the awareness of being and those below the reflection of that awareness. This awareness of being is demonstrated then by the finding of the letters of the divine name at the beginning or the end of a phrase or word. This is true in general of all Torah study which exists

for the purpose of the recognition of the divine in its
awareness of being.

The word *Bereishis* is composed of the words:
bat roshi (daughter of my head):
(Shemos 6:14) *These are the heads*
of the house (*rashei beit* = *bat roshi*) *of their fathers…*

The daughter comes first because she is the precursor of sons
meaning that we first become aware the deepest (feminine)
mysteries within prior to our acting (the male influence) upon
these revelations. The illumination of these colors comes
from that constant lingering back and forth between
awareness of being and its reflection like a candle as the
example shows flickers inside of a chamber.

A ruby from the aspect of gevurah,
a diamond from the right side,
and a *bareqet* from the side of the central pillar.
It is ALe"Ph DaLe"T NU"N YU"D, comprising 12 colors,
and all of them tripled by the three patriarchs;
tripled by Priests, Levites and Israelites,
"Holiness to You they will triple…"

The tripling of the forty-two colors intimated by the three
patriarchs, Priests, Levites, and Israelites, and the threefold
priestly blessing and ADN"Y Melech, ADN"Y Malach,
ADN"Y Yimloch L'Olam Va"ed. The colors that come from
this represent the various gradients that appear throughout the
multiple dimensions of influence that makes up the worlds
without end.

Chesed makes up the composite of all color or everlasting
color referenced by "with everlasting love…(Jeremiah 31:2).
This is thought filled with all of its ramifications so that its
overflowing quality of love or unconditional acceptance is
brought forth.

Gevurah signifies the releasing of doubt in its animalistic core so that together this releasing from Gevurah and the overflowing of Chesed comprise the spiraling middle pillar.

Yellow צהוב like gold is from the side of higher mother which is repentance, a yellow line that surrounds the whole world. And there is a color that is simple, that is doubled, that is tripled, that is quadrupled until it adds up to ten colors in which shine ten letters, which are Yud, Yud Hei, Yud Hei Vav, Yud Hei Vav Hei. And these ten add up to seventy two ('A"B) lights that illuminate in seventy two colors.

The color yellow of the higher mother called repentance is another gradient of expression that contains within itself the number series that adds to seventy two from the ten letters, the four groupings of single, double triple and quadruple.

What this shows is that in order for the renewal of thought to take place much must be left behind. This is the purpose of repentance; that is the letting go of negativity in order to pursue the positive nature of things.

The illumination of Malchus shows thoughts passing through the gradients above gradually distilling its purpose below. There is a mirroring of one another finally coalescing in the unified awareness.

And furthermore,
Another Tiqun 6: (Daniel 12:3) *And the wise shall radiate....* they are wise who know, the mystery of the second commandment
there you find in it in the word Bereishis, -
which is ahavah (love) in the 'small counting' of Bereishis equals 13
Ascending in one weight thirteen here and thirteen there.
and this is the love of chesed being 72 in number,

This relates to the Shem Hamephorash from...
(Shemos 14:19-21) *vayis'a* vayavo vayeit
Here VA"V (complete spelling) is the same numeric value (as ahavah 13)
like *echad* אחד *which is one utterance,* Then see Bereishis,

where they have established, And could it not have been created with one utterance.

10b) Therefore is this unity (echad) found in the transformation of the divine name via the divine names found in Shemos 14:19-22 into the seventy two three letter combinations. There is a distillation and then a putting together as it should be since the end result of Torah study requires both for the enlightened to profit from their journeys within the mysteries.

Out of Bereishis comes the incomparable. There are two that become one. This is template of resolution. It is the awareness of being recognizing the creator of being simultaneously and yet also as in two that become one. When our purpose is constant unity then neither our money, nor our body nor our soul may interpose themselves to subvert this most basic of realities. There deep within is the eternal veracity of existence and the verification of its unity.

It is only through the unification of Consciousness that the void is bridged. This bridge can be as simple as the linking of phrases and their letters or as sublime as the addition of the letters of a phrase in Torah that brings a new insight. We may only grow by reflection of the unity within.

The order of Consciousness is in its connections. Without these connections thoughts are disparate leading to the chaos of separation. This is why he whose love for his Master transcends all is a lover of the unity that adheres to all and through these attractions the connections are established above and below.

Malchus represents the continuity of the union between above and below or the thought and its expression. It is only through this continuity that the world is built.

Conversely the bad maidservant does not attend to her duties meaning she is not connected to the ones she serves and this is the meaning of chaos in thought when we do not constantly seek connection that uplifts and unifies while promoting the expression of that thought which is characterized by Malchus.

It is the unity of purpose that is end result contained in the beginning. This is the primary love.

The perfection of Torah is contained within the name which gives rise to the 613 precepts. Therefore do we find the image and its reflection in the central purpose or pillar that culminates in Malchus.

The covenant is the connection between man and G-d and further this connection derives all manner of meaning including the fires that bring forth man and woman. The fire that makes man is the idea of action moving towards its source and the fire that makes woman is the acceptance that merges with its source and then shows forth its reflection.

Protecting the covenant means to protect the unifying principle. When the thought that misleads is transformed into the thought that protects; this is the covering that allows the illuminations (the ideas that promote connection) to remain undeterred by the sin of separation.

As previously stated unity is the overriding principle within and without. Those who seek to distance themselves from unity are pursued relentlessly by it throughout their lives and would suffer the most during chibut hakever. Those that give in to the unity via mitvzos and right action come to know its ways so that even in death it is unity that they are cooperating with in effect working in concert with the process of chibut hakever.

And he (Ha Kodesh Barachu) became separated from them; (havdalah)

(Shemos 3:7) ...*and they knew that they were naked...* - from them,

11a) The mystery of Havdalah is the recognition of the gradient of light that is added on Shabbat and taken away thereafter reminding us of the separation that occurs in the Garden of Eden following the unmasking of form from its spiritual sheath. By extension the covenant of circumcision is the removal of the veil that shields the light making the membrane once again permeable.

For Consciousness this is the thought that covers or obscures the true light of wisdom. It is the line of demarcation between the rising of Shekinah and its suppression. This is why the holidays including Shabbat shine with a special light.

The evil inclination represents the thought that takes you away from the contemplation of holiness. Conversely the prayers are what bind you to holiness. It is the YHV"H that is at the center of holiness and this is what destroys or slaughters the evil inclination.

It is during the recital of the SHEMA that the spear of unity slices through the chaos of the evil inclination and resolves the shattered pieces into the unity that is called "true."

The metaphors of sling, tephilin, Shema and ammunition have to do with the parsing of thought that takes place when we eliminate the negative attractions that the world accrues to us in our unconscious state. When we make a conscious effort to ameliorate these thoughts we do indeed break through that attraction in effect replacing the subconscious impulse with our conscious intention symbolized by the SHMA.

The spear or the Vav of the middle pillar mimics the actions of thought that centers itself on the deepest relationships that are established within prayer. Most notably it is our recognition of this relationship that is active in awakening our intention to remember the underlying mystery of thought.

It is one thing to understand the relationships within Tefillin and its adherence to the covenant; it is another thing to become aware of the practical aspects of these relationships in our daily affairs.

Now here is a deep mystery; the covenant the earth the foreskin the soil the blood and the altar and the saving from the angel of death are connected. Here we are making a connection (covenant), and then a dissolution (circumcision) the veils are parted and the earth or the result of intention is given life or spirit (the blood). This prevents the angel of death from ever coming near. The altar is the attention we give to our higher thoughts constantly weaving them ever higher and deeper into the fabric of our souls.

In the covenant (circumcision) what is taken away is the ability for the dominance of the evil inclination. Once taken away anytime it accrues it may be death with by shedding its skin as a snake sheds its own skin leaving the shell behind. Creation proceeds much in the same manner discarding its failed experiments for those that promote rather than destroy creation's purpose.

The evil inclination exists in this world because of the thoughts that have been left over from the chaos of its creation. These thoughts include those errant thoughts of the father that would unduly influence the child if not for the ritual of circumcision that acts to wipe clean the slate of birth to promote the natural state of innocence. The snake (that which is trod underfoot) is the remnant of those thoughts and must be in effect ritually slaughtered time and again.

Kelippos are those thoughts that failed to unite with their maker and exist in short cycles of embodiment only to lose their form due to the their lack of coherence to any unifying principle. This is the first husk or tohu.

The second husk or the void wherein there is the breaking apart of the tenuous attractions that causes the instability in the first place. The third husk or the darkness refers to that state of being where the nothing becomes compacted and suddenly becomes something i.e. "the light."

(Vayikra 19:23) ...*three years shall it be as forbidden unto you; it shall not be eaten.*
And, as to the fruit it is:
(Vayikra 19:24) *And in the fourth year all the fruit thereof shall be holy, for giving praise unto the LORD.*
And of them, from the aspect of the foreskin four entered Paradise.
Three who ate those husks and died. A fourth lived who ate the fruit and discarded the husk like Rabbi Meir who ate the inside of a pomegranate and discarded the shell.

11b) The fruit of the light is the brain that discerns its own innate connection within and without. It is like the passing of the idea through until Binah where its bursts into being overflowing with abundance of becoming symbolized by Chesed the fourth Sephirah. This is the fruit of holiness.

The three who ate the husks partook of the gleanings of wisdom and yet did not perceive its kernel could never be at peace since the unity was not coherent. In contrast the one, Rabbi Meir who ate of the kernel perceived the higher wisdom and learned the pathways of unification.

The rules of halakhah are in a similar way compared to the deeper meanings that occur in the various levels of interpretation of these laws.

The fourth commandment alluded to is seeing the end inside of the beginning. The lower Shekinah symbolizes the current that is realized via Malchus as a result of its flowing forth initially from Chokmah.

Although the focus seems changed the subject is still the unraveling of meaning. The Torah is taken from Keter representing a shell in itself and yet there is the reflection in Tipheret called the crown of glory that is brought about by the righteous one. To exploit the crown is to only see the surface of meaning and not all of its layers including its kernel.

There is then the oral (from Gevurah) and the written Torah (from Chesed) both of these layers of meaning that have been perceived.

All of these layers of Torah adhere to each other and interpenetrate one another. The central pillar is the connecting link out of which Shekinah flows. It is therefore called by its aspects and yet it retains its truth throughout.

This expression of the 'Torah of truth' is its opening signified by the female and represented as well in the drop down configurations of the divine name joining within each other.

Subsequently the Torah is given via its opening meaning that the level of meaning called Malchus is the direct reflection of above albeit the back of that reflection or "achora'I." The gate of YKV"K opens at first with the outer keys which are the Sephiros leading from Keter through Malchus. The inner key is the kernel that is sought.

The journey of wisdom then is to seek this kernel past all of its layers in effect becoming the receptacle for this kernel. This internal becoming of the receptacle for the kernel of meaning is the essence of Kabbalah. It is the answered question that rises above.

David understood that only by letting go could he go further within. He realized that the essence of thought is to become conscious of its kernel or source emanation. He recognized that all was taking place within.

Shekinah is the fire offering that takes place via the fire of consumption. This consumption is the unification of a series of revelations that literally brings about the fire that is within that is the holiness or connecting link with the source emanation.

Upon that which is received (Kabbalah)
Israel asks no other surety from Ha Kodesh Barachu
But for *Zot* to redeem them from exile.

Here is what is said:
(Vayikra 26:44) *And yet for all that (zot), when they are in the land of their enemies,.*

12a) Speaking of "this" refers to the kernel of which all inquiries are directed towards. This kernel is the destination and its starting point. It is through the operation of Shekinah that "this" is revealed.

In all inquiries including the Sephiros themselves and the vowels points, the cantillation notes all reveal what "this" is now specifically seen from the aspect of Cholem.

The numerical equivalent of words and phrases regardless of their method of reckoning exists purely for the relationships that may be shown in their comparisons. These relationships point to the various aspects of the divine in all things.

The ladder from Shemos 28:12 refers to the vowel points but also indicates the redemption of Israel since by rising above we negate the effects of the yetzer hara concentrating thereby on holiness and making that the object of our intended meditation.

The fifth commandment is to hold sacred that holiness which comes about through prayer. Its focus is therefore internal and does not embrace the outer world against which the thirty-nine prohibitions are to guard against. The sacred daughter is prayer and the result of prayer that is a cognizance of Shekinah that is the current upon which prayer travels.

Shekinah flows through all ten of the Sephiros which are called the 'many Sabbath's. Holiness transforms itself into the object of its awakening.

The mystery of the observance of the Sabbath is spoken of and compared to the limits and borders of the sea. Our thoughts reside within that sea called Consciousness numerous beyond counting and all of them like the children of Israel are sacred to Hashem. They (our thoughts) are the Torah of our lives. Now if we are not mindful of these thoughts (during the Sabbath or the time of reflection) then what is their purpose?

The Sabbath is the time of cohesion or the coming together of thought into a unified whole and is indeed the time and space for this covenant of unity wherein we reflect upon our thoughts in order to make sense of them and to unify them above. During the Sabbath we bind those thoughts that has been issued in error or the "warned ox."

What is the result of such unification and such binding? It is the awareness of Shekinah that is revealed in the divine name.

Therefore the delight of Shabbat is in fulfilling the recognition that we are tied intimately to our Consciousness and that we make repairs to that consciousness by binding and purifying the bad and opening ourselves up to the good that we have been thinking about. It lies within our domain to both rise above and to overcome within. When we rise above consciously we unify with that which is continuously rising above symbolized by Chesed.

Now the river that emerges is Shekinah the unifying current that waters the garden, which is in effect our Consciousness. The only thing we can compare this connecting influence is to the holiness above about which we have no comprehension of other than as an experience of faith. It is called muphia because we cannot conceive of a thought that would emanate from there even though we are the recipients of this higher flow. We say yes there is and then let go becoming the channel for this irrigation which is of the fields of mind that are nurtured by holiness.

A curious phenomena occurs during Torah study when we make the leap of faith from one part to another sensing and then knowing with an innate certainty the connections that we have just established. These moments of awakening are powered by this dew that is a drop of Shekinah making you aware of its essence and giving you a taste of holiness. It is this dew that opens the mind for its highest awakening literally bringing into being those pathways via which you travel in the realms of holiness.

And furthermore
(Daniel 12:3) *And the wise will shine....*
In the sixth commandment found in the word Bereishis
Bayit is there. This is what is said
(Psalms 84:4) *Yea, the sparrow hath found a house (bayit), and the swallow (dror) a nest for herself, where she may lay her young;*

12b) The concept of dror or bird and its nest or the bird its house refers to the idea that out of chaos the natural state of being is to produce order. This is to say that if a dror bird will have its nest how much more so will we build our house of prayer or house of study.

It is the agency then of the masters of Torah, Mishnah and Qabalah to continuously elicit the response of Shekinah building pathways within that open the soul to its own holy connection.

Creation proceeds via the letters that are woven inside of the Consciousness of the primordial person, the archetype that is coexistent with Gan Eden. These letters are made up of the colors (intention) of a person which then determines the events that come into being.

The vowel points accentuate the intention (colors) that makes up the background or firmament through which all that we see appears.

The cantillation notes are the vehicles. They carry the letters with their colors and vowel points to the destination the is envisioned.

All that we find is because of the active awareness of Shekinah that awakens through our Torah inquiry. We begin this process when we are open to Shekinah, which then illuminates the mysteries we are pondering.

Mar'ot or visions called by extension the bitter sign are transformations of consciousness that take place upon the realization of Ha Kodesh Barachu. It is as if at first an ordinary piece of quartz is transformed by shaping it into a prism that then reveals the colors already present.

The letters are the building blocks of Creation. First the bayit is built through visualization. In this visualization this house or temple contains the Sephiros within it that connects in active emanation flowing from the point within the Beit, the dagesh, which turns out to be Keter the sapphire that emanates the holiness from within. The 'wise that shine' do so in like manner from the inspiration of the 'Holy Lamp.'

The sapphires that shine in the letter Beit all emanate from one sapphire Keter that is the dagesh within the letter. All emanation therefore partakes of the brilliance of this initial emanation. It is the recognition of the "glory of God" that illuminates these emanations or Sephiros that follow. Therefore it is "wisdom that builds the house" meaning for the enlightened ones that their inspiration proceeds from the Holy Lamp.

The three patriarchs received the initial inspiration that verifies and completes Shekinah. It is their revelations upon which Israel is built. Yachin and Boaz, the light and dark pillars and their synthesis in the middle pillar refer also to the three patriarchs. Their influence is the connection with Shekinah whose connection is symbolized by the three hooks, the Vav's.

Hei, Hei, take from the Middle Pillar called the middle bar
called bars after its name. This is what is said:
(Shemos 26:27) *and five bars for the boards of the other side of the tabernacle ….*

13a) The Yud that extends from the higher to the lower hei is the pole that attaches from above to below in the Mishkan. The Middle Pillar refers to the supports that are the Hei's over, which the coverings drape. The five bars are an extension of this support on the side of the Mishkan. Our highest thoughts reside against the backdrop of our lower thoughts. When visualizing the temple we give special attention within to this inner construction.

The outer therefore reflects the inner construct of consciousness in terms of how thoughts are arranged in layers. We do not find out about these layers unless we discover them like taking the coverings off the temple reveal the framework within. It is this framework that is made up of holiness, thoughts of praise, certainty and ultimately the core which is 'the way things work.'

The Holy Lamp is the explanation for all. It is what gives these symbols their raison d'être. While these holy structures always exist it is up to the Holy Lamp to illuminate their purpose and mode of being. This Holy Lamp is none other than that light within that makes connection with Shekinah possible.

Rabbi Shimon speaks of making those that are wise of heart and wise in wisdom. It is those attributes that come from the truth of what is self evident i.e. the heart and those that infer from what has come to be...wisdom which remembers and makes its assumptions based upon subsequent reflections.

They comprise the six days of *Bereishis*,
Made up of ten sayings and thirty two paths,
these are the thirty two times ELKY"M appears in the work of creation.

The thirty-two paths are the associations with ELH"M within the first part of Bereishis and its six days and ten sayings. Specifically there cannot be Creation without ELKY"M which in this case refers absolutely to 'the way things work.' It is the operative power of Creation. Each pathway therefore refers to a realization of holiness or the innate creative principle, which reveals itself through its linked associations.

Creation brings forth the world into being through the power of the letters that create heaven and earth. Bezalel did not merely build the Mishkan but also as well brought a world into being or rather shifted that world from the dimension of the status quo into the dimension of holiness.

At first glance it would appear the world was brought into being at Bereishis, however, the power of Creation is everywhere present so that in the case of Bezalel his power was to rearrange the world into the world of holiness in essence going back to the beginning in terms of concept to awaken that holiness which is to be the temple.   It is important to note that this power is always present when we invoke with the right attention that initial phrase of creation.

The power that Israel had removed from them is the power to distinguish the holiness of 'the way things work.' It is this veil that the exile has imposed upon them via a simple lack of attention that Kabbalah in its highest purpose seeks to reinstate.   The prayers all have this intention whether or not those who pray are conscious of this underlying message. The hand that is upon the throne of YKV"K is attention.

The construct of the body is as the construct of the temple. What we make within via our thoughts and the attention we focus upon determines the holiness of the body and of the temple that is meant to be the body. The direction here is to recognize this temple within.

The cabinet of cedar wood is the Sabbath or the place of stasis within.   These six days are Zeir Anpin pointing to the inner organization of Consciousness.

You will find one inside the other meaning that the lower Shekinah-the body is built out of the construct of the temple-Metatron.   It is the intellectual purity, which transforms the purity of the body. This body is in effect the substance of the outcome of thought.   The essence of the heavens is after all the distilled thought made holy by its higher attachments

Shabbat is home to Shekinah on high.
There Torah of the enlightened the understanding heart

On Shabbat the extra soul has freedom from the dominion of
The lords of Hell who do not rule on Shabbat.

13b) So therefore we turn to the holiness of the heart out of which the thirty two paths emanate in this realm of holiness where the Sabbath or stasis is formed. Here is the higher Shekinah the higher connecting link above or that which is self evident to the wise.

This field of stasis elicits the extra soul called the realized reflection of above that is mirrored elsewhere and is readily apparent within the heart.

The copper alter removes the impurities just as the liver removes them from the body and by extension too there is the operation of the concept of transformation taking a lower thought and transforming it above.

The ark cover represents the extension of the field of stasis called the Sabbath acting as a sukkah when we contemplate the holiness within.

The Menorah is a symbol of the awakening of the light within and the oil is that inspiration that is fueled by the holiness above. What we take in (eyes, ears, nose and mouth) gives meaning to our thoughts raising them above.

This is wisdom. Now all of this information is processed in the brain in specific locations known or felt by the wise which in turn cause the Menorah to light bringing about the awareness of higher consciousness.

All the places in the body where we find a nexus of nerves could be said to be a places where information is being sent from one nerve end to another. This information travels via electrical and chemical impulses known as thoughts both conscious and unconscious.

What happens is that there are layers of thought that cascade throughout the body continuously. For example the breath from the lungs serves the purpose of providing transport of oxygen, aerating the blood supply and flooding the brain with oxygen as well. This is what is meant by 'the wings that spread upwards shielding the ark cover.' The ark cover is the processing center for the thoughts that emanate throughout the body.

The table-the heart-the lower Shekinah produce the intended focus that is to take form within the corporeal transformation that is the world of experience.

Now this place within the heart is a mystical location within and is the connecting link between the above and the below. This suggests that while we may reach up for higher thoughts we may also determine their efficacy by going South or investigating their effects to surmise the deeper meanings of their higher purpose.

When Shekinah (the connecting force within attaching itself to holiness above and below) takes from the left, meaning from the discernment of judgment then "She" is called a Table. The Table is where the transformation takes place removing the dross of thought and refining it into its higher essences.

When She goes northward to wealth this is referring to the abundance of good, of expectation, and a reuniting with the highest source that is both emanation and the reflecting arc that powers the entire sequence of influence above and below.

Consider that Shekinah is a presence that is resident within the body and it becomes activated according to specific energies concentrated there. When Shekinah becomes activated in such a way she "takes from the body" and becomes the Middle Pillar. This is the central activating force making the connecting link(s) above and below.

There is present within the body from head to toe, throughout the organs and especially in the brain a unifying force that ties it all together. This unifying force is composed of thoughts their likeness of which may be found in the counterparts of the organs of the body representing those pathways of refinement that naturally occur. This unifying force is Shekinah called the animating force of the universe.

Shekinah is the likeness of man in that she is in effect the template of man. Imagine a network of lights in the shape of a man and then superimpose the soul upon this template and color it in with life experiences…this is the Tabernacle which is man.

Man is indeed imbued with the 'way that things work.' It is the unifying template of Shekinah that he is superimposed upon. Therefore man is able to see through the eyes of the Creator with knowledge and insight and all manner of craftsmanship meaning that the finished product appears (the letter Heh) as the mind's eye sharing the Creators viewpoint envisions it.

The choices we make are reflected in the countenance of the person. It is as though the light will not go where there is confusion or doubt or where we haven't done the right thing. That template of Shekinah becomes fully realized through the Mazal of the face meaning the right choices we have made in doing essentially the right thing.

This Mazal is of another level of influence happening above all else. It might be compared to dew drops or heavenly vapors that are attracted by Shekinah.

The radiance of the body is Shekinah that emanates from within.

This radiance comes from all four sides flowing from the centers of brilliance that are the temporalities of the four angels. What this tells us is that these centers are indeed a part of Shekinah that exists as a nexus within. In a sense this nexus is a body within a body the one becoming the throne of the other.

The wise meaning the speech that is expressed by the inspirations received from the recognition of this body within the body have the purpose of defining or praising the King which is the hierarchy of brilliance that the source of these emanations.

The eyes are the perceptions of holiness that now with our inner vision activated we come to see the holiness throughout. This holiness comes to be understood then as the unity of all things in the universe comparing the planets, sun and moon to the levels of perception that are now accessible. The letters and vowel points are the signposts that reflect that inner holiness and show the interconnection that is Torah, which is the template of Creation.

This description of the planets, sun and moon and their relationships male and female refer to the relationship between the inner radiance of Shekinah and the physical body. This specific relationship is one of awareness or perception meaning that our thoughts must turn within to experience the nodal points of contact and through this contact we are then made increasingly aware of both the complexity of unity and its simplicity in that the entire universe is one.

(Daniel 12:3) *like the radiance of the firmament…*
The looking glass that shines

71

In mans face the eyes ears and nose and mouth
Conductors of his body and limbs

14a) The radiance of the firmament is compared to how our perceptions depend upon each other in both their vision and their meaning. One supports the other and one is the looking glass for the other. Again keeping with the inner radiance of Shekinah then it is both supported by and sustaining to the body. It then becomes a matter of service one to the other.

The five points are explained ultimately leading to Hei and Hei and the Ten Commandments via the Yud. The voices that the people heard in Ex 20:15 are the conversations of connection between Shekinah and the body or between our aspirations and our understandings. It is our awareness of the inner core of being.

A further relationship is drawn between the masters of action-scripture, the wise, and the masters of Mishnah, formation, in regards to the twenty-five letters of the SHMA and its answering verse "Blessed is the Glory of his Kingdom. Shekinah is compared to the twenty-four books of Torah. What this is saying is that the unity of the SHMA is discovered via Torah and its study comprising both the worlds of Yetzirah or the world of thought and the world of action, Assaiah, the world of form.

The tzaddik is the river between the two emerging from the higher Eden which by the way is the wellspring of Mazal via the connection of Vav that is the result of the union or unity of Yud and Heh.

Shekinah is a body of light that resides within each of us and is activated by prayer, deep meditation, Torah study, any life changing circumstance and is essentially already resident within us.

It is our awareness of Shekinah that initiates the holy conversation. This gives rise to the higher thoughts and their pathways of brilliance. Shekinah is a template of the life of the body.

Now we can extend this allusion by comparing the sun to the planets, the stars to the universe in general ad infinitum.

There is then self evident a body of light that simultaneously takes the forms of our awareness.

Whatever we may encompass, that is what we may experience.

This exile is an exile of our awareness which has become entirely engrossed in the material world not paying attention to the inner sanctuary that while remaining resident within cannot be accessed without active attention.

Herein it is stated the 'twenty-four letters of the Unity of Shekinah which is the answering blessing preceding the SHMA. In exile the connection between SHMA and its answering blessing are oppressed or blocked from their righteous connection.

The poor man is oppressed because of his lack of connection with his feminine partner, which is Shekinah. Solomon maintains this connection and is therefore blessed. To be blessed means to have the counterpart to the SHMA, the twenty-four letters of the answering blessing with you meaning you are connected to Shekinah within you. You are aware of its presence promoting this awareness at every turn.

"She filled the pitcher and went up" meaning she immersed herself in the five books of the Pentateuch making that connection that completes the unity.

It is the Torah that is the source of the holiness in the pitcher and it flows according to Vav, which alludes to the six words of the SHMA, which becomes ot or the sign of the connection.

The sea of Torah may be likened to the currents of consciousness composed of higher thoughts. From these higher thoughts a river of holiness signified by Vav comes through from the higher mother, the twenty-five or the SHMA seat of unity which then fills or reflects upon the twenty four or the answering blessing to the SHMA. All of this refers to the reestablishment of the awareness of Shekinah within. It is this awareness that she (Shekinah) drinks from.

She quenches his thirst for connection that is via the unity that is ever present symbolized by the 248 words of SHMA that mirror the waters that are the substance of Torah and from which the wise may renew their inner connection to Shekinah.

Every moment of the day is an opportunity to be connected to the unity within via the higher Shekinah, which is the SHMA, and the lower Shekinah the answering Baruch Shem Kavod...

A similar relationship that is between the Higher and Lower Mother is that which is between Halachah and Mishnah as one explains in effect the other just as Mordechai advised the King.

And She with many maidens, in the final decisions of law,
as it is said...
(Song of Songs 6:8) *and maidens without number.*

And She rises above all. As is written
(Proverbs 31:29) *and you are above all of them.*

And She is with them all, as it has been said
'the *halakhah* follows the majority'

(Daniel 12:3) *...and those who justify the public*
in Her may they be *...as the stars for ever*!

14b) The masters of Mishnah receive through Kabbalah the
halakhah that is like the many maidens that are the jewels of
Kabbalah. Those insights that come about through study of
Mishnah and Halakhah are through the same agency as the
higher Mother that flows through to the lower Mother. These
insights are also the product of Shekinah.

See how the Mishnah is an agency through which a righteous
person merits his own world. This means that via the
complex associations that occur in Halakhah the wise are able
to put together their own world that is uniquely theirs.

In the tractate of the Mishnah there is represented a kind of
thinking that takes place that by its unique exile causes the
mind to enter into a state of unity with its source of
contemplation. This is a metaphor for the way the mind
works in terms of its relationship to Shekinah. What we find
out through each insight is that Shekinah has been waiting for
us to lead her to her husband, unity. It is this unity that is
received or is the Kabbalah that is the result of the insight of
unity. The exile is when we see only the surface and not the
inner core.

During the time of Moshe the Queen rules meaning the direct
perception of Shekinah whereas with Joshua and continuing
forwards the maidservant ruled who is the means for the
perception of Shekinah. This is like the relationship between
the insights we have with Halakhah via Mishnah representing
a secondary revelation rather than the direct revelation that
Moshe taught. Metatro"n then is the messenger that runs
between the Queen and the maidservant.

How is the temple made and by extension what are the workings of Creation. Herein is explained the vehicle or chariot of Creation.

It is the flowing of Metatro"n that is the agency of Shekinah's connection above and below. There is a three fold operation of Creation. First there is the working of the chariot meaning the spirit of ELKY"M, Shekinah; this is the way that things work or come together. Then with this follows wisdom and understanding in the application of Shekinah called the Working of Creation. Then the third component is the knowledge of the unity called the Unique One of the world that brings the two others together via the chariot of Metatro"n that is the connection of Shekinah above and below.

It is the question that induces the answer. We ask what? Here we find the associations with "what" Shekinah, the Sephiros, and the mystery of the "Chariot of What."

These Sephiros what are they? They are the result of the connection of Shekinah. These links or associations called Sephiros lead us to the thoughts that are connected above and below. We see that these thoughts from high to low assume a definite pattern within Creation and are the substance of what Creation is forever becoming. It is then the chain of association or the histashelus that brings all into being. The core component in our understanding of this is Shekinah without which the Sephiros lose their meaning and connectivity.

Metatro"n the ark, the body of Written Torah, the Middle Pillar, the sacred table of Shekinah, the heart to the left the north. These associations are shown to implicate the same within our consciousness. It is the heart i.e. our feeling nature that puts us in touch with Shekinah within. Look closely into the connections of the heart that radiates the life flows throughout the body. It is a physical as well as a metaphysical location that we are called upon to discern and then B"H make use of.

The Menorah represents the light from within that illuminates the entire body as it states "the candle of YKV"K is the soul of man," meaning this is the animating force. It goes on to explain the oil, the wick, and the light in relationship to the levels of soul. Think about these soul levels occurring as various degrees of perception. In this way the body then is the vessel of these soul levels and within the body or vessel the oil is then our innate need to know. It the oil represents those eternal questions that have always been a part of our nature-the ruach of our being.

Our feeling nature is connected to the wick that partakes of the body or the oil that is the naphsha. The answers of those questions or the consuming of those questions is represented by the light that shines. It is further explained that the Tzaddik is the oil or in the case of this analogy the one who asks the questions. Then in response to those questions Shekinah is activated within the awareness. Subsequently the light that rises is the recognition of the unity that is established above and below.

The body is the servant to three sides meaning the operation of the way things work within the threefold wick, oil and light paradigm that is revealed here. To simplify the body is the servant of Shekinah meant to house the divine and meant to be cognizant of the divine via Torah study and the connections established by the Sephiros that awaken each node of connection within.

This servant, which is the body and by extension the awareness of connection called Metatro"n is the basis behind all the divine names which are symbolic of the higher associations that occur above. Now conversely those thoughts that are not unified should remain so because their attempted connection brings about a negative result. This separation of thought means that we do not tie one thought of negativity to another in order to prove that thought or to make it grow. We consciously refuse in effect the connection.

The work of Creation differs. It is not spoken with two
Then there is no separation. Therefore just with one
The Unique One (as a meditation on One)

15a) Two implies a reflection a loop of sorts and an odd number signifies a progression. When there are only two the idea loop together rapidly deteriorating. When there are one or three the idea may progress. This is why discussing forbidden sexual relations or anything of evil has to be done with two so that the loop is contained and not allowed to grow. Conversely discussing holiness is with the Unique One and its extension three signifying the progression that Creation most naturally takes.

And one does not expound the Divine Chariot (*merkavah*) individually, because the Unique One has no partner, which is Metatro"n; like the divine soul, which has no partner in the body.
And why does it the Mishnah say: unless he was wise and discerning from his own knowledge'?

The apperception of the Unique One cannot be explained to another because it is experiential in nature. It exists apart as separate influences on consciousness. This realization comes from being wise and discerning in the discovery of those mysteries that bring this experience of the Unique One.

Now this we understand, that *Ha Kodesh Barachu* a Chariot above, which is His handiwork And it is what?
It made up of chokmah and binah and daat

The chariot above is His handiwork, which is the fashioning, and the operation of the way things work. It is here that

YH"V Chokmah Binah and Da'at are the paradigm that Ha Kodesh Barachu maintains above. Then there is the lower Shekinah which is Malchus completing the work of the temple.

Only the wise and discerning may speak of the chariot because there is the given truth that Ha Kodesh Barachu above is one with His Shekinah. What this means is that even though in speaking of the lower Shekinah as separate in terms of the outcome of Creation there is no time in which Ha Kodesh Barachu is not present within Shekinah acting through and partaking of this energy of connection that is the unified essence of the whole.

Hashem is everywhere present. And yet when the awareness is not present meaning Shekinah is without her husband then She lies dormant so that the hosts do not recognize. She becomes in effect the maidservant who may only proceed when the awareness awakens wherein She becomes the Queen. Now Metatro"n is the current that connects King and Queen. This current also is not active until the awareness is awakened.

When a man sells his daughter for a maidservant this means that the awareness of Shekinah is subsumed. This maidservant is the epitome of materiality and the mother of the mixed multitude whose primary concern is always material. Still Shekinah is concealed there awaiting the awareness of holiness to be revealed.

In the Shemos the maidservant is freed but still does not come to the awareness of holiness so that when freed there is only the conception of escape and not of the impending freedom that the awareness of holiness will bring forth.

Now with the Torah, which is the template of freedom the daughter will emerge as Shekinah filled with the awareness of holiness meaning the opening to the perception of Ha Kodesh Barachu that is the definition of her freedom. She is free to become whatever she will because Ha Kodesh Barachu is woven into her being.

It is Torah and more specifically the awareness of the holiness within Torah that is what will free Israel from its exile from Shekinah and Ha Kodesh Barachu. This happens because Ha Kodesh Barachu will be walking with Her in Her glory.

Then there shall be the recognition or the awareness that never fades of the holiness within and unity without. This is YKV"K without concealment and freely associated now with all that is personally and experientially present in each moment.

Once there is awareness the connection need not be sought but is rather ever present. YKVK is the awareness and ADN"Y is extension of that awareness. What is this awareness? It is the unity of the way things work which is ELKY"M and its extension is EHY"H AND"Y which is 'the awareness of the way things work.

The six sides are described comprised of the letters of the divine name. So it becomes what it must be which is a cube of space that rotates on its axes of connection as described by the Sepher Yetzirah.

The right hand side YH"V is Chesed connecting above to Chokmah sealing it or rather intersecting it as one plane or dimension intersects another. It is the flowing of wisdom into Chesed that is the overflowing of thoughts that produce wisdom. One leads to another and then a cascade of connection ensues. In this flowing the above is sealed.

HV"Y on the left-hand side this is *gevurah*, sealed with it for wealth and of it, whomever wants wealth should go north

VH"Y moving to the east and taking the Middle Pillar, and there sealed *children*.

15b) The left HV"Y is sealed with Gevurah, this plane or dimension rises from below to above the north being above through the discernment of attention. In this way the above is recognized by its interconnection with the left hand. Wealth, *whomever wants wealth should go north* results from the material overflowing as the form comes into manifest its being in the North.

Vav Heh Yud seals the back moving east towards the right including the middle pillar that is the result of connection signifying children that arise from the reflection of right and left.

Vav Yud Heh completes the eastern quadrant moving from back to front comprising left and right thigh or the supports arising from below.

HY"V seals the below signifying nourishment in the sense that the below is the earth which gives forth its produce in response to the inspiration from above. These supports flow through to Chokmah that connects below through the persistence of meaning that arises even in the densest matter.

Arising on the top forward most plane moving to the west from the east YV"H passes through tzaddik as all are recognized together in their connection the Higher Mother which relates to Binah that is in effect the cauldron of Creation.

These descriptions of the spatial dimensions of the divine name triads are for visualization purposes and to reveal a deep secret, which is concentrated upon the way we look upon our world within in terms of what transpires without.

Thoughts move together in terms of the affinities they have for one another. Now this process of moving together is described by these various dimensions and by the mixture that is both its end result and the source of emanations.

Therefore the architecture of our inner space may indeed be ordered in a divine fashion instead of allowing a haphazard collection of thoughts we may indeed pursue their divine direction.

There is but one unifying force within and our attention to this force determines how in touch with it we will become from moment to moment. Much of this depends perhaps on personal affinities built up over lifetimes of experience but there still remains the qualification of learning something simply by moving towards it and surrounding our perceptions within its holy flow. These dimensions are ever present, however, it is our awareness of the same that is being promoted here in these verses.

These eighteen letters represent the eighteen worlds made up of the six three letter combinations and the twelve directions (lines) of the cube of space (four each above and below and then the four supports or lines connecting above and below. The unification of these called the righteous one animates all to simultaneously coexist.

The Higher Mother is the point of the realization of the awareness of the connection with Ha Kodesh Barachu that produces the emanation known as Shekinah. The Righteous One signifies that unity above, which gives forth emanations of life, that go through their myriad permutations shown as the chayot of the chariot. Yes Shekinah is a tree of life to those who grasp her significance and understand her purpose, which is to enliven consciousness in preparation for the experience of unity. Out of this experience of unity comes the appearance of Chokmah, which then rides upon this unity.

Malchus is the proving ground for Shekinah completing the perpetual union of above and below. These seven names by which she is called are the same name meaning that whatever circumstances arise there is always a unifying force.

These thirty-two paths of wisdom refer to the latticework of thought that makes up the template of holiness within. It is out of this template of holiness that Chokmah assumes its place.

Just like any other area that is explored you have to uncover for yourself the secrets that await you within. What are these chambers and depictions of the Garden of Eden? They are those pathways that we etch out by our meditations on the divine. Now there is an ultra special chamber that is hidden called Anokhi. This is the point at which your thoughtful meditation or intention intersects the awareness of holiness. At this point you are one and can therefore radiate all of the souls of the righteous since all are connected in a similar fashion. This connection though personally experienced is universally accessed as the spiritual realms compress in their unity to express the totality of existence.

The concentration of a meditative awareness is like a star that shines above expressing the above. This star that is a sun radiates by reflection or the Moon of its awareness.

Consider the idea that suddenly appears "a spark in the firmament." Then the idea attracts like thoughts, "a tribe has arisen out of Israel." The divided Aleph shows the reflection that takes place upon the moon from the sun.

Herein is also described the testing of higher thought as lower thought challenges for ascendancy (Samael from below) but finds that higher thought remains concealed above. Like the Kelippos lower thought can only exist by dint of the shells of higher thought. In effect she meaning Shekinah and her radiance of unity is literally unavailable to the lower thought.

The new moon is the first instance of reflection from above that now is started on its way below. See how the moon is covered by HVH"Y protecting her Shekinah from corruption from below. The new moon is the proof of reflection and emanation as felt in the body by Shekinah.

Beit then is the chamber for the conglomeration of thoughts. Above is the holiness-the firmament and is the patach in reference to the heavens that stretch above it. The Beit becomes also a Vav that is its unification connecting above and below.

Tzadi with it two heads come together as one with the vowel point tzeir"ei. These two heads are from above where it is called ayin.

All of these points that appear in the letters are in the context of this discussion bright lights in the higher consciousness. These bright lights are what surround the throne. The throne is the certainty of unity and its pouring forth from above to below. We can see in the example of Aleph that the structure itself is indicative of the shapes that thoughts will assume in the holy way. What we are referring to here in terms of chambers and coverings are the subtle awareness that is both built up and added to as we turn more within to affect our changes without.

ו six levels of the throne.
ס sixty wheels of the throne.

16a) Six levels, sixty wheels referring to the Sephiros from Binah to Hod each of which by extension contains its own set of levels ten each mirroring the Tree of Life as it must. These levels are interchangeable as is time in the Torah. What remains fixed inside of and outside of time is the throne, which is the unifying force throughout. While everything else may be in flux the Eternal is a fixed point around which revolves all.

These letters that come before the King are literally the shape of things to come. In addition these letters are the insights of the wise that also come before the King.

Whether letters or the wise there has to be a balance that assumes the proper order. This order relates to the way thoughts come into being and are paired with their correspondences. What is this like?

A King brings furniture into a room and then arranges it just so, however his ministers enter and the King sees that this furniture has to accommodate all who enters so he makes adjustments.

It is the compartmentalization of thought that is being expressed in this section here and is something to keep in mind as further esoteric passages are discussed. This is akin to knowing the end prior to the beginning. The Aleph and Bet set the tone for this compartmentalization of thought. We can see this clearly as the word Bereishis is broken up into its components and the Torah verses are similarly bisected and compared.

It is one thing coming from another. Take for example the verse "in whose hand is the soul of every living being," this orients the source-hand with its extension-the soul- and then the living being-the life that the soul experiences. These relationships are common not only to this current study but apply across the board to the Torah in its entirety.

This theme continues with the eternal building, the divine name as the source of all that is built.

It comes down to the letter Beit with all of its associations that give rise to the creation that develops. This principle of Beit as the choice of God to begin the Torah is not simply the start of Torah but rather the beginning that is eternity taking place. This principle of Beit embodies within itself (compartmentalized) the principle of ELKY"M which follows which is "the way things work." If we rephrase this using the discovered meanings we could say, "Out of Beit that is first to begin comes the 'way things work' applying this first principle to all of creation.

The meaning of the destruction of the first Temple is given in the context of the opening verses of Torah. The First Temple was destroyed and the world became as it was prior to the 'let there be light' phase of creation. What this means is that redemption is simply the following of the 'way things work' that brought about the transformation of void and chaos into light.

So we see that the door of transformation has been mercifully built into the structure of creation i.e. the word Bereishis so that even if there is a turning away from the 'way things work' it may be reinstated via those wheels of gold that bring forth the light irrevocably. This is to say that Creation is imbued with its own salvation regardless of the veils that man has placed between Him and His glory.

Jerusalem is the state of manifest being wherein 'the way things work' is in harmony with what has become and is becoming. It is a harmony of relation and transformation indicated by the door

What supports the door? It is Vav or Zeir Anpin the action of the intervening Sephiros in their continuous transformations rearranging towards the light.

Righteousness is the right way of aligning ourselves with holiness. Those gates only open in response to the proper key which is our innate understanding of 'the way things work.' These gates on a deeper level are cause and effect.

Once you realize the way things work you can never be lost, however it is this realization that comes from the histashelus of Zeir Anpin forming the central or core of your relationship to the divine.

The door or dalet that opens shows but two ways to perceive. One is to veil the perception and another is to be open to the perception of holiness. This holiness represented by the joining of arms and body or the connecting link between the letter Heh which is like a Vav is promise of the vision come true; its reflection like that of the moon.

The awareness of Shekinah (when He shines upon Her) brings about a full recognition of the way things work meaning that the hei and hei of the divine name reflect one another without a veil in their fullest shining form. Out of this full reflection the zayin representing a full cycle of creation makes up the rest of the divine name HVH"Y.

Now there is the realization one becoming the other so therefore remember this principle and keep it uppermost in mind and then remember once more to put into motion that cycle throughout your experiences.

The three roofs of Chet (Vav,Vav,Vav) determine the good dream. What is this good dream? It is certain knowledge that what has been envisioned will be manifested exactly as the vision appears giving substance to to the vision.

Yes there is a displacement from above to below and below to above because of the vantage point. When we start from Malchus or the substance of the vision we now have two points of convergence; one is the realization of Keter and the other is tracing back to Keter. Therefore instead of counting only one from Malchus on the ascending path we count two... ten, nine and then eight.

More symbols to ponder, Keter the crown the Yud
And Khaf the higher Keter. Yud, rises into Khaf.

16b) There is the passing of holiness from generation to generation in regards to the three patriarchs that represent three levels of awareness. Taken together Shekinah emanates or arises out of the Sephiros of Keter and Malchus one the image of the other... after a fashion there are ten reflections plus ten emanations or Khaf twenty. The two prophets of truth are the Righteous One (the choice to perceive and witness holiness amidst 'the way things work) and Shekinah (the certainty of that holiness is revealed in form.

Shekinah or the awareness of holiness appears above and below symbolized by the ladder (lamed) of Yaakov a mystical reference to the thought process that discovers and is enlightened above and prompted to action below.

The angels of ELKY"M are our higher thoughts symbolized by Mem i.e. the higher waters of consciousness.

There are thoughts that ascend via lamed, which is the ladder to unify above in holiness.

Thoughts also descend via nun and they are not worthy of the holiness above since they cannot unify themselves there.

Now samekh ascends since it is a part of the s"ulam (ladder) via lamed.

It is our perception that becomes holy above and below and this is symbolized by the letter ayin.

The recognition of holiness is through its open speech and acknowledgement of praise. This is a closed system where every correspondence has its counterpart.

Prayer is both the aspiration for and acceptance of unity. We give up our separation and accept unity. We praise the Eternal unconditionally since we desire fervently connection above that is encompassed in the divine name, in the Yud Hei of tzaddik and tzedekah.

It is the voice that is in prayer 'Kol' that merges with the Eternal and ascends together with all prayers as it is their innermost nature to ascend above.

Reish is a symbol for that first moment of holiness wherein all moments are dwelt upon. It is the certainty of awareness that is fulfilled.

There cannot be any connection without shin, shalom, peace since each thought has to let go of its own internal core to merge with the unity that it aspires to. Even those thoughts that are seemingly selfish in that they do not recognize their connection may still come from far to become one.

And the letter Tav symbolizes redemption or the end of exile freeing the thought for its higher connection.

Each of these letters and their symbolism tell us that the shape of things to come are an integral part of what goes on within vis a vis our thoughts. It is that careful attention to thoughts that gives rise to holiness and takes away-transforms chaos.

Our inspirations come from above*(Shemos 1:1) B-reishis bara ELKY"M...* (Daniel 12:3) *The wise shall shine like the radiance (k-zohar) of the firmament...*

17a) Everything comes down to that initial inspiration that comes from these insights that are offered here. Those who study Torah with this in mind are like the wise that shine with the radiance of the firmament. In fact the radiance of the firmament are those Torah insights that speak into the deeper meanings of consciousness.

The higher thoughts contained in the Zohar reflect that which is already present above.

It is by connection with these higher thoughts that the many are brought to righteousness of the recognition of holiness.

This recognition of holiness is the core of the way things work and this is an eternal principle.

Elijah in today's parlance represents the outsourcing of the revelation that voiced through him and is understood within our own thought atmosphere. In this way the unification of holiness is shared above and below regardless of the level of attainment.

There is unity high and hidden beyond thought since thought is secondary and descriptive and encompassing and You are without bounds.

The Sephiros are presented in their unity of concealment and yet by their awareness there exists the capacity for the direction of these hidden worlds both revealed and not revealed. This direction has to do with our focus in any given moment and the attention we direct towards that focus. The key here is that in focusing upon one we are focusing on all. We cannot therefore perceive the simple attributes of one without relating it to the entire panoply of the unfolding of what is to come.

The Sephiros are byproduct of the higher processes of connection that may only be initiated from within by the source that is the mystery.

Out of these Sephiros is the superimposed visualization of the body. The centers of awareness called arms, body and legs, and the organ of generation that completes this image serves to fulfill the oral Torah or the mouth which is Malchus the place where Creation speaks its intention-fruition.

The inner thought and the heart Chokmah and Binah are conversations of holiness that are hidden until our awareness rises to the level of recognizing them within.

The way of emanation or higher Keter contains the end in the beginning issuing forth holiness just as water irrigates a tree and then grows through the emanations of holiness. They grow in connection with the unity ever present rising from above. This is the spirit body unseen and is the framework upon which the body resides and is kept together by the unity of the holy name YHV"H.

The fountain that waters the tree is made up of all the insights, revelations, holy words, names, and higher thoughts that bring forth every blessing including the blessing of life itself.

Don't bother trying to fathom the depths of holiness it is unreachable and yet connection is always available.

So that you should recognize the organization above and below part is revealed to awaken your awareness. This awareness grows and perceives various levels and still cannot encompass the all.

Unified above and below. You are over all.
Imagine the sephiros and all their aspects
How they are called their names like the angels.

17b) It is the unity of emanation that is the driving force of creation. This is the supreme principle that animates everything and without which there is nothing.

Cause and effect are what we are taught by the sovereignty of judgment and mercy so that we may directly experience our recognition of the way things work.

Judgment is the effect that reaches back to the cause. This is something we may only see by reflection.
Elijah who has been speaking gives express permission to reveal the mysteries that come through Rabbi Shimon's innate understanding.

Rabbi Shimon calls forth Shekinah which represents the awareness of 'the way things work.' Only through this awareness may the righteous become enlightened.

Shekinah gives voice to awaken to inspire and to enlighten. Our response is to open, awake, and to give up our exile or our blocked perception.

Shekinah arises via our recognition and our reflection upon holiness.

It is the unity of being that sends forth Shekinah being quiescent in the holy name until our recognition draws her out of exile filling her from the fountain of all higher thoughts.

And so begins the seventy ways the word Bereishis is described-explained in this opening passage of Torah.

First Tiqun

בראשית, ב׳ ראשית. זה השער ליי׳ צדיקים יבאו בו.

In the beginning... (Bereishis)
made up of the letter *Bet* and *Reishis*
(Psalms 118:20) *This is the gate of the LORD; the righteous shall enter into it.*

This is the gate of the righteous, who have permission to enter there;
and those who are not righteous cannot enter from there.
In it are inscribed and depicted and engraved
the images of Higher and lower;

18a) Bereishis, Bet is the beginning of the start of the creation cycle. What is the gate of the Lord? It is the understanding that the end is contained within the beginning. This is the same understanding that the righteous must have to enter that same gate. It is the image making power of consciousness that gives it its eternal connection. Inside of this creation cycle the images that are envisioned above are the same as below, i.e. the end is contained within the beginning.

The central idea of the matter is Ezekiel's vision with the four faces representing the fixed signs of the zodiac suggesting the heavens are where he witnesses his revelation. How then does this relate to Consciousness?

The images that we transcribe within take on the character of these four faces. The lion represents the powerful emotions that go into the image making whereas the bull represents the tenacity of the vision, and the eagle represents the soaring capacity of the vision and its ability to connect on high. It is man that by definition directs the vision via his holy connection that comes about when he has the recognition of holiness that evokes Shekinah filling him with that holiness. It is Shekinah that connects him to the world around him.

Holy Shekinah there in the form of Adam
She is his image. She is his seal and about Her it is said:
(Song of Songs 8:6) *Place me as a seal upon your heart*;

Shekinah is the essence of man becoming in effect the superimposition of holiness that only comes from that recognition of unity within. It is out of this recognition that holiness is indeed the sign of the covenant in the covering of Shekinah through which there is revealed the hidden ways of Creation.

Shekinah makes its operations-connections via the love that is near and strong and is akin to the love Israel have for Ha Kodesh Barachu. The thing is that in exile God wants us back with him close to him and therefore provides Shekinah to be mindful of that love to guide us back to him. Anything which prevents the flame of Shekinah vis a vis idolatry and the battles against Amalek will be consumed by the flame of Shekinah which is the abiding connection above that occurs whenever we remember the holiness we are a part of.

It is Shekinah that is our connection that takes us back to the Master of the world because even the mere impression of Shekinah is enough to help us remember the way of return despite the limitations of exile.

Therefore we can see that Shekinah makes herself known the closer to unity that we approach. In this way we are provided the signposts for our return.

Tiqun 2

And this: The Second Tiqun

בראשית, פעמים הרב הם בתרו ראשית, וכל אהד מהפרש מקומו
Bereishis Bara (In the beginning created):
Many times in the Torah there is a beginning, and each one is explained in its place.

The first is: (Proverbs 8:22) *YKV"K has acquired me as the beginning of His way* and this is the Torah, in which there are cantillation notes, and vowel points and letters; and many positive and negative commandments which all depend upon the Name YKV"K.

It says (Shemos 3:15) *this is My Name for ever. My Name* שמ״י (350) together with ה״י is (365; *My remembrance* זכר״י (237) together with ו״ה (11) is 248; 365+248=613, 365 from the left, from fear of gevurah they were given, the terror of Isaac.

In order to ascertain the meanings of these first verses the mind has to be open to YHV"H together with addition of the vowels, cantillation marks, dots and letters. The mitvzos totaling 248 and those totaling 365 that show the awareness of that is called by Yitzhak or the fear of Hashem. This fear is the awareness that our actions have consequences and we should therefore be mindful of them.

It is the desire of Ha Kodesh Barachu to unity with his Shekinah; it is our purpose to unify with our feminine nature.

This is how creation comes about or this is 'the way things work.' Shekinah needs to align itself with Ha Kodesh Barachu in order to connect.

This alignment is referenced by Ezekiel's vision of the wheels and their turnings. In order to get anywhere in such a situation man must have the intention to connect and this sole intention is the aligning force that makes connection possible.

Tiqun 2 (Tiqun 3)

בראשית שמ ירא״ת. מה נשאר מאלו אותיות, ש״ב
Bereishis The word fear of (yirat) is contained there;
what is left *Sh"B*,

Then the mystery of the word *Shuv*
is return in the fear of Y"Y.
Without fear, there is no wisdom,
as they have established:
'if there is no fear there is no chokmah;'
because fear is the treasure-store of wisdom,
it is its storage, its hiding place, the house of the King

Tiqun 3

And this is: **Tiqun 3** like this:

בראשית, רא״ש בי״ת, ודוד הדבר בחכמה יבנה בית
Bereishis (In the beginning)
RoSh (head) *BaYiT* (house);

And the secret of the word:
(Proverbs 24:3) *In wisdom will a house be built…*

18b) Fear is the secret repository the treasure house of wisdom because it reminds us of the consequences of our thoughts and actions which are determined directly in the house of the King.

Rosh the head the initial insight builds the house. When we remember this we recognize that wisdom is only there in its own house.

The Middle Pillar becomes evident when we become aware of it through ADN"Y filling us with the awareness of YKV"K.

Shekinah expands itself to fill its container and then contracts consolidating its connections. Then there is a further expansion depending upon the expansion of consciousness that is affected by listening within and responding to the designs of Ha Kodesh Barachu. This container is of course Beit also known as the chamber.

The seven lands, seven chambers, seven heavens all refer to this filling aspect that takes place within Adam or the archetype of man. There is a flowing the consciousness of which is the holy connection or the Ba Kodesh. The covenant is the conscious recognition of this flowing that continuously takes place within

Our grasp however never exceeds our reach meaning that what we may conceive of (our grasp) never exceeds our ability to become the container (our reach) wherein consciousness flows into the expressing itself as itself.

Tiqun 4

בראשית, כתוב פתחו לי שערי צדק אבא בם בם אותה יי"ק

Bereishis: : it is written…
(Psalms 118:19) *Open to me the gates of righteousness; I will enter into them, I will give thanks unto Y"K.*

(Shemos 25:20) *And the cherubs shall be spreading their wings upwards* two cherubs of the eyes; spreading wings this refers to the eyelids

What is there that must be opened? It is the gate of righteousness symbolizing our direct access to Ha Kodesh Barachu. This passage here sets up what is the primary purpose of this discussion which is opening ourselves up to the inner voice that is one representing the unity of heaven.

This is how we acknowledge Ya"K." When we open up we let go of the blockages shown here as the "crooked serpent." This tells us that because of this blockage it is only death that releases us from the serpent unless we open to the one true voice within.

The mystery of Bereishis is that we are the daughters of the one through our acceptance of that inner voice. You may only enter this holy place via the 42 letter divine name meaning that each letter must be thought of and focused and then recognized for the pathway to the divine. Without this recognition the name loses its meaning.

(Shemos 1:2) *And the earth was formless and void...*
"I will come in..."

19a) Rabbi Shimon refers to the 42 letter name of God which references the first 42 letters in Bereishis up to formless and void. We can go into detail here concerning the Ana BeKoach or 42-letter name of God. These holy names are descriptive of the ten Sephiros and the thirty-two paths that make their internal structure. Each phrase of the seven verses of the Ana BeKoach is also considered to be a name.

These names are the recognition of the holiness that is present throughout the seven corresponding Sephiros relating to the seven below Binah as described by the phrase "daughter of seven." All seven Sephiros partake of the holiness sent from above meaning they include the awareness of all that is through the way that things work themselves in and through Creation.

The completion of Unity is the understanding that the end is contained within the beginning just as the end also proves the beginning.

We go into detail concerning the Ana BeKoach or 42-letter name of God. These holy names are descriptive of the ten Sephiros and the thirty-two paths that make their internal structure.

The daughter of seven is Binah because below her emanate the remaining seven Sephiros. Here in consciousness Binah represents the distilling of the higher emanations of the initial thought, its brilliance and then its course of action. Binah contains the seed that unfolds.

Your wisdom is then only as strong as your immediate understanding of this process whereby the flow of consciousness comes into manifest being. This is the quest to be mastered. There is no other.

Tiqun 5

בראשית ב' ראשית. נקודה בהיכלו. וזו הנקודה היא מחשבה סתומה.
Bereishis, *Beit Reishis*
The point of this temple
This point here is Hidden Thought מחשבה סתומה.

In the meantime, Elijah by chance to Rabbi Shimon.
He said to him: "Rabbi Rabbi,
Beit is open.
How then is the Thought within it hidden?'

It is hidden because the nature of thought that is being impressed upon consciousness is that its attachments run deeply into the nest that is your inner being.

So there is the point within the Beit and it is the Yud that blocks the light that becomes the AU"R once removed. This is the defining light. It is mentioned five times because Heh is the defining characteristic of the divine name including both outflow of the first Heh and the resulting Malchus that is the second Heh.

Yud is the limiting factor while Vav is the expanding connecting influence and the two Heh's are the reflections of one upon each other producing the impressed vision in unified symmetry.

So how is this question answered about the hidden thought that Elijah asks Rabbi Shimon about? It is this. The hidden thought is the seed that is enclosed in darkness which then responds to the light, which is its inspiration.

This hidden thought becomes revealed as the extension of its intention. This is the Vav, the seed growing into the sprout and then the sapling and at last the Tree. Our thoughts follow similar extensions and transformations of state.

And there are five mentions of light in the act of creation;
and they are Hei 5.

And about them it is stated: (Isaiah 40:12) *Who hath measured the waters in the hollow of his hand...*

These five levels of light, the Heh of the Divine name are akin to the five soul levels, nefesh, ruach, neshamah, Chaiyah, and Yechidah. Always in one there is the reflection of the other increasing in complexity until becoming unified in Yechidah where the complexity resolves into simplicity revealing the hidden thought and its intention as the idea is reproduced through transformations of the thinking cycle.

At first you have the inkling of an idea which may not be available to you on the surface but through meditation and deep need it comes through and bursts through the soil of your imagination growing with your attention and then becoming through the process of 'the way things work' the thing unto which it was intended.

At every step along the way there is consciousness that acts as the guiding pathway to the inner discoveries that reveal themselves.

and hills considered in the balance two pillar of truth
this hei that is shining through five colors five times (revealed) the light

Yud is the measure. Hei on high the Higher Hei five (mentions) of light;
below Hei five colors light shining through five.

19b) Within Consciousness nothing comes to light without the awareness of that something that is going on. This is the basis for the entire progression of Creation that is depicted here.

Vav immediately spreads itself towards Her.

How do we measure this awareness? It is with Yud that is the initial spark of awareness and Vav that is the connections that are made between the Yud's that are shining there in the darkness. Through these connections what happens?

A curtain is formed by the extension of Vav via the five Heh's shining from the awareness of Yud that comes through. The Yud is bejeweled because it is the point of manifest awareness within. The Husband is the progenitor of all that comes from the seed of inspiration nurtured by the awareness or Shekinah.

Therefore the קו של מדידה line of measure is the verification of that awareness accessible everywhere now as the reference to the Husband or Ha Kodesh Barachu which is the holy name that is recognized above and below.

Specifically these measurements of cubits are the points all along the Vav where the awareness attaches itself above and below.

The lower Hei called broken matzah or bread of poverty because it is farthest from the awareness and yet ironically it is the most accessible. This alludes to an insight we can understand simply which is the reflection of something much higher that is not immediately available to our breaking it down into areas of clarity.

Again within consciousness this handful that the priests take is the blocked Mem or hidden thought. What is the priest? The priest is that area of connection that raises our awareness on high to give us the insight necessary to make the higher connection.

Now in this pregnant place of connection we find the chayah the transmitters of connection from above to below into malkhut symbolized by the lower half of the Aleph.

The tzadiq is this firmament or the one who makes the higher connection and then earths it in the transmuted meanings of every day. Netzach and Hod mirror the pillars of Chesed and Gevurah above in that they establish firmly and root the connections made from the Vav via the five Heh's of light shining forever in the created firmament or the place of becoming.

Continuing this allusion there is the higher connection also called chayah - Higher Thought.

Higher thought is takes place via the higher crown with the mirror of the higher Vav, forming the 'crown of glory,' and as Higher Thought weaves itself simultaneously along the pathways now of discovery.

Herein what takes place is a joining of Father and Mother. Yet we refer now to the feminine aspect of creation, which is its Shekinah or mirroring relationship.

This relationship appears the same as each Yud or point of inspiration whereby the flowing of Higher Thought awakens the Hidden Thought and the process unfolds in the mystery of the letters, the cantillation notes even to the tip which is the mystery of the vowel points. This is a deep mystery that takes on the qualities of holiness fulfilling itself along the way.

See now that these feminine waters below are the rising of a fountain that overflows in the firmament above partaking of the higher masculine waters that make their connections via the Vav, the five Hei's and the symbolism of the higher and lower Aleph. These waters are called so because they collect both the Higher Thought and the Hidden Thought and out of their collection and overflowing the firmament of becoming is forever awakened and then is resting.

The debate that is for the sake of heaven may be compared to our prayers that seek unity above. They are crying for that Higher Thought to awaken the Hidden Thought so that the firmament will in turn be awakened bringing about the flow that is the awareness of Creation and the cause of all causes. This is the King. What our prayers do when they are successful is to align themselves with the Cause of all Causes mirroring the above and then overflowing below so that as like follows like prayers are answered only from above.

Look and see the two great luminaries for they are the symbols of your own creation that takes place within consciousness and is the way that things work. The light of the moon may be compared to our thoughts that have not yet awakened to the awareness of Higher Thought and therefore their light is dim.

The light of the sun conversely represents the light of the awareness of Higher Thought, which emanates via Ha Kodesh Barachu. These two the sun and moon or our limited thought and Higher Thought become equal when the moon rises to the sun and shares the same space or understanding of the way things work.

Unlike the moon or sun, which are physical objects, our consciousness is only limited by the awareness of our perceptions. When our perception is unleashed then our thoughts become one with the Higher Thought giving us the awareness now of the way things work.

We become aware of the lights of Higher Thought by our contemplation of them recognizing their orientation in the space of holiness. In this way like an architect we envision the plan of Creation and as we do so we learn that we are at the same time active participants in its ebb and flow.

And the mystery of the word:
(Bereishis 37:7) *for, behold, we were binding sheaves in the field, and, lo, my sheaf arose, and also stood upright; and, behold, your sheaves came round about, and bowed down to my sheaf.*
It is Aleph with cholem above all by Joseph dreamed and rose.

20a) It is clear that thought inspires. These words evoke a certain meaning within and it could be said that they are opening doors within to brighter pathways of discovery. Look at what it speaks of here in Shemos 37:7 "for, behold, we were binding sheaves in the field, and, lo, my sheaf arose, and also stood upright; and, behold, your sheaves came round about, and bowed down to my sheaf."

Here in Joseph's dream we find the elements of connection that evoke that special focus within. The binding of sheaves in the field refers to the gathering together of thoughts of like mind so to speak. The sheaf that arose is the higher thought and the sheaves that came round about are those thoughts that are unifying with the higher or highest thought

Kabbalah asks this question continuously "where are you going and where have you come from." When you learn the symbols of Kabbalah they are like guideposts helping to establish a vantage point and a sense of direction. This sense of direction is focused upon holiness.

Therefore what we have is the completion of the thought that establishes the holy connection. If we take this passage in

(Shemos 28:12) "And he dreamt and behold a ladder was set in the earth and its top reached the heavens." What we find is that the ladder represents every point of connection in between heaven and earth.

Every vowel point is a point of connection that emphasizes this attention and sense of direction.

In our daily lives we build this ladder by our attention to the unity that surrounds us in each moment of introspection. It is here that we may acknowledge the holiness that exists in those thoughts that have returned fulfilled to their maker. Then in their acknowledgement the holy connection is established via this internal continuing recognition.

Shekinah is the rising flow of awareness from its base level until its elevation above, thus the stone that could not be used because it was not ready or raised. Now once ready this stone or building block is utilized in ways (without hands) that are the architecture of the above. This place that is not above is the coming together of holiness wherein the praises are then called forth from.

The conceptualization of the lower Shekinah is what arises into the higher emanation or Atzilus. It has been formed by the consistent rising above and surpasses all that is below. Once in its resting place above it becomes the ruler of all below assuming its sovereignty containing all Sephiros within its all-encompassing ideation.

Now see that this stone is the foundation of the worlds, the unique knowledge of which confers upon consciousness the Kingship of all that surrounds it. Through this kingship is derived the momentum of consciousness including the emanation of the Chayot, Seraphim and Ophanim, the speech of above and below and the knowledge of all things

This stone is transformational in that as it arises it becomes the central emanation that is the conceptualization of Consciousness. At every point of understanding there is this stone that acts to awaken the substance of every thought via its connecting point of reference. Therefore the water mentioned by Rabbi Akiba is not just water but the water of the stone. See into all things this stone of relationship whereby all is interconnected.

What is it that we have to discern within? It is the realization that thought transforms itself going from below to above and back again.

The heavens refer to consciousness in terms of its outer perimeters and its inner dimensions. This is why the tips of the letters are the key to the mysteries of above and below because these tips or Vav's touch both above and below completing the circuit of holiness. The letters with their tips are the connecting links not only above and below but also as well between the letters themselves as they form the holy words.

The 'bird of the heavens' is the higher thought the voice that speaks above. Now in our contemplations of higher things we awaken the heavens via our prayers and our speech on high. What is prayer and speech but an intention that is expressed. Specifically for Isaac in the field this is the time of connection above.

We are obligated to pray the morning and the afternoon service and the evening service is optional. In the morning we make the initial connection and in the afternoon like Isaac who went into the field to pray Mincha we ground this connection above and below.

In the evening our prayers are a summary of both morning and evening, which is why, they are not required since a summary is a kind of rehashing of that which we have already experienced. In like manner we discriminate between above and below acknowledging both and then summarize our results in the conscious awareness of the connection that takes place between the two to make it one.

The main purpose of prayer is to establish yourself within the field of your Maker. This is what the text is speaking of when it refers to 'encountered the place.' Who is the master of Her-Shekinah? It is the place of the maker, the realm of Ha Kodesh Barachu that awakens when She is in her place, the place of the maker. Therefore it is imperative to establish yourself in the field of your own making, your own thoughts and their intentions.

Shekinah is always present evoked by the recognition of Ha Kodesh Barachu. In the night she is the connection our soul has with the above and during Sabbath our recognition of holiness brings her forth.

Just as the sun calls forth the life that is within the earth including man so too Shekinah evolves out of the recognition of the unity of consciousness. This is the same unity that is present in the afternoon prayer of Eternal connection.

See how the symbolism of the Tephilin of both arm and head are both the recognition of and the remembrance of Her who is unified irrevocably with Ha Kodesh Barachu. It is as though the rising of one is the recognition of the other and visa versa.

Because of this binding, this unity the ancient words now become crystal clear. Seek Shekinah and find Ha Kodesh

Barachu. Stated otherwise, seek the lever of thought and find the outcome of experience.

There are levels to thought both higher and lower and the comparison here is to the vowel points and the letters. Just as these vowel points color or provide the level for its expression so too are our thoughts placed accordingly. These higher and lower thoughts occur simultaneously.

What we have to establish then prior to letting go of our conscious awareness while awake is the place above where holiness resides. We do this because we want to identify with holiness, which produces order and abundance rather than our lower thoughts that produce chaos and lack. The Vav is what we attach ourselves to it is by definition the place of connection.

(Proverbs 1:28) *Then will they call me, but I will not answer, they will seek me earnestly, but they shall not find me..*
(Psalms 132:4-5) *I will not give sleep to my eyes…*
Until I find a place for YKV"K.

20b) There are levels to thought both higher and lower and the comparison here is to the vowel points and the letters. Just as these vowel points color or provide the level for its expression so too are our thoughts placed accordingly.

These higher and lower thoughts occur simultaneously. What we have to establish prior to letting go of our conscious awareness is the place above where holiness resides. We do this because we want to identify with holiness which produces order and abundance rather than our lower thoughts that produce chaos and lack. The Vav is what we attach ourselves to it is by definition the place of connection.

It is through connection or the Vav that all transformations take place. This is something that must be pinpointed by our awareness. It is the unity of this oneness that our awareness

108

is intent upon recognizing Whether first or last without this recognition there is no holiness no conception of god.

(Ezekiel 1:16) *The appearance of the wheels and their work was like unto the color of a beryl; and they four had one likeness; and their appearance and their work was as it were a wheel within a wheel.* (Bereishis 1:16) *And God made the two great lights: the greater light to rule the day, and the lesser light to rule the night; and the stars.*

What are these wheels within wheels? They are thoughts within thoughts; higher thoughts and lower thoughts together in the grand design of consciousness. As you become of aware of these multiple levels you experience the two great luminaries and learn the differences and the means by which each is propelled above and below.

Each spark is a point of recognition the moment when you become aware and what are you aware of? It is the field of consciousness wherein every thing that is made was made and will be made. For it is here in the firmament that all connections (Vav) take place as the breeding ground for the awareness of the way things work.

What is it that is desired? It is the awareness of being that we recognize via our attention above and since nothing happens that is not reciprocal this same awareness is awakened, enhanced and glorified by the expressions of man in his acknowledgment of his divine nature.

There is that which comes to be out of that which is the supremacy of being. When you consider the source you recognize the degree of holiness that had to be there in order to come up with Adam. Adam is the highest form of the expression of the thought that cannot be expressed.

This is a paradox yes but that is because of the particular attachment we have to our own frame of reference. We are being asked to step outside of this frame of reference to encompass as Ha Kodesh Barachu the whole picture of being.

The secret wisdom unfolds with the symbolism of the hand. The hand signifies control, guidance, and minute adjustments. The allegory here is to how we mould our thoughts and their relationships to the limbs which are simply the anchors of this moulding that delineates the facets of our lives all within the field of consciousness called firmament.

These Sephiros symbolize the tracking mechanism keeping us in touch with the holiness above as it transforms itself level by level Sephirah by Sephirah until in the finished product we can easily witness the initial design.

We go past the details here of vowels and letters turning straight into their alluded meanings. Thoughts without doubt may be colored. They may directed and they may also be transformed. No matter what we call this or at what stage we recognize it there is still the voice the Bat Kol that is directing, transforming and coloring.

Consider what happens to thoughts. They too become stretched going to and from only operating according to whatever instructions have been given. If there are none at all chaos results. When however, direction is given to thought it attaches itself to these directions and acts as directed depending upon our level of focus._

Each symbol that is given, the letters, the phrases, the quotes from scripture, the vowel point and the cantillation marks are for the purpose of giving us somewhere to place our attention. Thoughts that have both the structure of Sephiros and the visualization of place in terms of firmament can only rise and become a part of the holiness their source. This has after all been the plan all along.

Tiqun 6

בראשית, קם רבי שמעון פתח ואמר לאליהו. אליהו בשבועה עליך במלצות
הקדוש שהיא נפלה בגות. קח רשות שלא תזוז מאתנו. שהרי השכינה וכוחותיה
שומרים אותך.

BereishisRabbi Shimon calls out to Eliyahu:
It is prayer itself that is in exile. Bring back Shekinah that is with you
To receive our prayers.

21a) There is a higher connection that runs throughout the heavens. These birds of prayer are carried on the wings of thought and await their disposition on earth. These angels are the means of carrying thought to its holy place.

Consider the home of thought that arises in connection above. This is the home of all that is, all that is coming from the source. The recognition above this is wisdom, which only comes with awareness.

The nest is the interwoven thoughts that bring forth the chicks. The Temple is the consciousness of heaven of Sinai of the freedom to awaken in holiness.
Thoughts beget other thoughts, the chicks compared to the appearance and awareness of Zeir Anpin. As a result of special prayers yes but these prayers take us to another level of listening.

These prayers are in the egg stage when they are not linked with holiness. Once linked with holiness they can assume a holy direction. This is why we do not take the mother symbolizing holiness, Shekinah from her chicks because until the Mother resides with her chicks the holiness cannot be born within the thoughts that are now coming together.

The permanent place of prayer is our constant awareness that prayer abides within and is aided by Shekinah rising and lifting prayer infusing it with holiness. When we have the realization of a bird's nest; within this is the kernel of prayer that we promote daily and groove it into its place.

The throne is the seat of the Mother in union with the Father or Shekinah with Ha Kodesh Barachu or even better still our thoughts infused with holiness that are actively aware of the unity of their being.

Rachel's tomb a crossroads

(Jeremiah 9:1) *Oh that I were in the wilderness, in a lodging-place...* Therefore the two messiahs, redeeming Israel.

This is about the awakening of consciousness. Rachel's tomb is a symbol for transformation of Israel or the mundane thoughts that are part of the system while as yet underneath the awareness of holiness. When these are interconnected Messiah appears in our recognition of rebirth and our sense of the unity of connection.

It is by our consciousness that we grow in the field, in the firmament, inside of consciousness since striving to discover the mystery leads to the awareness that the mystery in equal measure is discovering who we are.

The Sabbath is the quiet place within or the simple awareness of the truth of unity. It is here that all these transformations take place fed by our realizations (rivulets of water) so that on Sabbath eve souls are reborn in terms of their awareness of holiness.

Chicks, sages, symbolic of thoughts that are infused with their own capacity to discern not only one another but also the direction of their flow are crystalized by Shekinah giving them the pathways above of Eternity. Each time these realizations rise up on the wings of Shekinah unity is experienced which enlivens the entire thought atmosphere transforming below and rising above.

The mother that is lying with her chicks is Shekinah so that the eggs which are hatched are the new thoughts, the new souls, that are the result of Torah study, Talmud study that is accomplished by those masters who understand the purpose of that study which is to create new thoughts and unify the tree from bottom to top.

Ha Kodesh Barachu is the Torah, Shekinah is *mitzvah*
Worthy one who unites both together.

21b) When you see into the heart of Torah you recognize the way things work and act accordingly.

It is the unification of your understanding of becoming aware (Remember) and acting in the fashion of the way things work (Observe) that you fulfill the unification of Ha Kodesh Barachu and His Shekinah.

All of these examples given speak to the same principle. Unless you have the feeling of what is right (Shekinah) unified with your highest purpose (Ha Kodesh Barachu) you will not bring forth the holiness that is your calling.

You are bound to this holiness because it is by its signature nature that your soul is attached. How much more then could your thoughts and actions also be similarly attached?

Because Shekinah resides within you and only comes forth when you do the right thing, mitzvoth, Torah study, all inquiries into the nature of things, etc., you cannot reach above until you connect within.

It is as though Shekinah once awakened is destined to rise above and that is your connection. Therefore first awaken

Shekinah and be guided in your ways by Her. This is the pathway to holiness.

Without Shekinah the inner space is darkness and void. With Shekinah there is light. What does this mean? It is the knowledge of the way things work that lets you accomplish your heart's desire. First however there is the mastery of the way things work which is Shekinah.

Shekinah is then a spiritual state of being that we may only bring out within ourselves via our intentions to do so in all the moments of our lives. Shekinah is the opening through which the passage above or the unity of purpose and design are realized.

(Psalms 27:3) *Though a host should encamp against me, ... In this I trust...*

(Psalms 103:19) *...and His Kingdom rules over all.*
(Shemos 7:23) *...neither did he lay even this to heart.*
(Psalms 92:7) *A brutish man knows not, neither doth a fool understand this.*

22a) Shekinah rises above reaching the King. Thoughts in their supplication stage are raised into their manifestation stage meaning here is where prayers are answered. This b'zot (*in this*) is the Kingdom, the realization of purpose.

These six days of the week and the Sabbath are not speaking of actual days but rather the levels of awakening that consciousness goes through. Thoughts have a gestation period call it a period of growth. Once this growth reaches the level of maturity thoughts rise up.

This rising up this is Shekinah. Now we see this in detail in the fifty gates of freedom-levels of maturation.

Work in the context related here refers to cutting ourselves off from Shekinah since we labor under the assumption that it is our efforts alone that accomplish our ends.

Arouse for me the fifty gates, fifty times Shemos from Egypt in Torah
Fifty letters of SHMA twice a day they recite.
(Deuteronomy 6:4) *Hear O Israel (2 times 25 or 50)*

It is through contemplation of SHMA that Shekinah is realized. This is the arousal spoken of here.

Our thoughts can only take us so far and then it is up to Shekinah to travel those nether spaces into unification. Indeed whatever brings us to Shekinah is our healing of the vagaries of non-focused attention.

This hidden light is the light that fills us, the feeling that awakens us. It is the higher Mother because of its effect on our consciousness bringing the sense of unity in moment

What we are praying for ultimately is that connection with Shekinah no matter what physical outcomes we are striving for. Until we have that connection those physical outcomes are out of reach. Once in the flow of that connection with Shekinah nothing can be denied to us since we are one with all.

Truly what we ask to be forgiven from is indifference; the indifference of thinking that we are alone in this world. Without Shekinah we are alone however when we use our attention to seek Her this is when we reach Unity called Ha Kodesh Barachu.

There are those that live in this world without regard to the consequences of their thoughts, their actions, etc. They are unaware of Shekinah and Her relationship to Ha Kodesh Barachu. Their fulfilment is an incomplete one subject to ebbs and flows or not at all. Through the contemplation of Torah, your mother, you awaken Shekinah and are given the truth about the way things work and your relationship to Ha Kodesh Barachu.

This is 'the covering' of tzitzit, and its wrapping.
and *tephilin* of the hand, of which it is written:
(Psalms 102:1) ...*A Prayer of the afflicted (prayer is a wrapping of thought)*

22b The aspect of thought that is prayer is what covers us via the tabernacle or through insights into the deeper nature of thought. The three colors in the eye, the burning bush, the covering of Tephilin, etc., all of these refer to the veils of thought that must be awakened to insure their transparency.

Shekinah is the expression of holiness that rises above. When it begins to rise this is the function of Higher Thought. When it touches the Principle of Ha Kodesh Barachu it immediately flows below fulfilling the imaging process that must take place.

This is the ensouling process whereby forms coalesce around thoughts giving tangible meanings to their ethereal counterparts. Shekinah is the expression of holiness that is received above and via this reception the entire consciousness is transformed unless there are blockages in which case the process is cut short until these blockages may be transformed into transparency.

The means for doing so is called the tabernacle of peace. Here is where the flowing of Shekinah fills consciousness with unity so that there may be the recognition of Divine Principle Ha Kodesh Barachu. In this way thoughts are prepared for their transformations via the unification that takes place in the expressions of holiness. This is compared to the tabernacle above and the sukkah below.

At that same time: the children are under the authority of Ha Kodesh Barachu,
and a voice came out it said: *do not take the mother upon the children.*

Immediately comes *Remember* and *Observe* Shabbos,
and the night of the first day of Shabbos
a second voice came out: *Send Out*!

23a) Consciousness is a labyrinth of mysteries. It is fluid and always hard to pinpoint in the way a moving object is difficult to predict where it will start or stop or just keep moving. The same thing is true when trying to discern the meanings in this passage. "Do not take the mother," refers to the general precept and the "children" refer to specific instances.

The Sabbath is the meeting place within and is where the exchange of thought takes place as connections become easier during this hiatus of movement, i.e. thoughts become stationary and subject to connections.

The nest is the place of connections where thoughts interweave themselves into this stasis. "Remember and observe" is the recognition of the Sabbath, or that special place within, or the nest that is the stasis field.

Israel is in exile in order to find that stasis point to bring itself back together. When it does so Shekinah returns.

The female does not surround the male but is rather open to the male. In the same way are thoughts in the nest allowed to mature and then are accepted by the female. This acceptance is one of the mysteries of consciousness that gives form to thought. It is one thing to have an intention and it is a progression of that intention to recognize that it is accepted above or within.

This acceptance is a letting go called "giving thanks to the Lord," and without this the process is one way. Now once the

stasis is achieved and accepted you have "And he travelled..."
"And he came..." "And he stretched..."*the passages of the
seventy two names from Shemos 14: 19-21 which is where
the concept is born within itself and "do not take the mother
upon the children." This means it now has it own mother or
overriding concept.

What is applicable in thought also speaks to the nature of our
souls and how they are put together. The "first born of Israel"
is the experience of Sinai that is the unifying factor that is the
actual first principle or Ha Kodesh Barachu.

Unity takes place continuously even when Israel rejects it and
experiences the loss of both temples and the diaspora. The
allegory is also true of consciousness that even having
experienced a high state of unity may choose to reject this
high state and live the life of fragmentation.

Second Temple was destroyed
and darkness upon the face of the deep...

And because of those souls were created before the world was created,
and no bodies to have mercy over them,
they set up for them this precept.

He said to him: Father,
then a scholar who is from that thought,
of which it is said: Israel went up in thought to be created,'
then the Torah is a son to the scholar,
why should his wife levirate marriage...

23b) The Levirate marriage is mentioned in terms of holy
thoughts that might in fact be combined with those less than
holy. What takes place is that the nests where these holy
thoughts reside are open to the mundane thoughts since it is
their purpose to lift them up.

While it is true that transformations take place between the
sacred and the mundane it is also true that we cannot take
from the tree or nest that is evil meaning where thoughts are

so predominantly chaotic that sacred thoughts would be scattered there. Therefore the process of transformation is always, good promotes good and yes evil promotes evil.

In terms of souls in reincarnation that process is ameliorated by a holy soul taking on those souls that did not have a chance to incarnate and needed the opportunities that are offered by a holy soul.

If we extend this allegory to consciousness we see that our holy thoughts in a sense build up in their preponderance and thereby are able to subsume the lower thoughts transforming them and their nature into a more elevated reality as shown by the various levels of soul discussed here. The end result is that by such connections or grafting the entire person meaning the all of consciousness is raised in its entirety.

24a) Consciousness contains within itself the means to create and to destroy or rather the means to amplify or diminish depending upon the circumstances. This is what the significance of 'fear of shame' represents. Imagine that you are fully cognizant of this function of consciousness. You would therefore tread lightly in all of your actions and would do everything you could to participate in the progression as opposed to the degradation of being; your being and welfare included.

Tiqun 7

בראשית, יר׳א בש׳ת. אוי לו לסמאל, כאשר הקדוש ברוך הוא יבוא לפדות את השכינה ואת ישראל בניה.

Bereishis fear and shame. Woe Samae"l when Ha Kodesh Barachu comes Shekinah and Israel Her children to bring into redemption.

There is momentum in consciousness. This momentum can carry you towards or away from heaven and can indeed seem to block your entrance there. When Israel, which is the mass mind of thought and all of its connections, gets caught up in a negative flow the doors to heaven are obscured and the recognition of heaven via Shekinah is veiled or degraded.

Despite these self-imposed veils heaven is continuous. Higher thought always resides by definition above and the voice of higher thought can be heard once we let go of the illusions that the momentum of negativity has brought about. The shame from Shekinah is our realization that heaven is there and Shekinah is that recognition reoccurring time and again to remind us.

Tiqun 8

בראשית ש׳ שמים ורי״א בו״ת, שלו שהוא רא״ש בי״ת.
Bereishis - fear of His house, He is רא״ש בי״ת
Have fear of Him in His house.

When we disregard higher thought our thoughts degrade into spirals of negativity going lower and lower reaching the bottom called Gehinom. The sun and moon representing the overt physicality of human actions must be replaced by the recognition of higher thought. This can only occur through the agency of higher awareness which makes materiality itself ashamed or degraded to the higher influence of the heavens.

The lowest thoughts (Samae'l and his partner) are only sustained by our attention and belief in them. When we return to the heavens or higher thought these lower garments dissipate and are worn out through lack of attention.

Tiqun 9

בראשית יר״א שב״ת. שהיא השכינה. שעליה נאמר מחלליה מות יומת
Bereishis fear of Shabbos which is Shekinah, about Whom it is stated:
(Shemos 31:14) ...*every one that profanes it shall surely be put to death*
...

24b) The Sabbath is likened to Shekinah and her resting place, called the holy of holies. Now to make this clear we have to understand the workings of Consciousness. There are higher thoughts and lower thoughts and then there is the space in between called the holy of holies, the firmament in between, the place of Shekinah. This space in between is the realm of no thought or no mind.

Tiqun 10

בראשית שי׳ר תא׳ב. והרי הוא שיר משובח מכל השירים
Bereishis ShY"R TA"eV (song of desire)
and this song of all the songs is the most praiseworthy desired above all songs;

The song of desire is the raising of the harmony from the potential to the realized.

This song is naturally occurring when the lower thoughts had dissipated or worn out.

It is the song of the recognition of Shekinah, her place, the space that is holy wherein higher thoughts absorb the lower emanations and transform them.

The raising of thought is its comprehension of the various levels of thought. Moshe is the key because via Torah we have the means to pinpoint and be made conscious of these levels.

The singing of the song is harmony that knows itself and because of this has become self evident within becoming the cornerstone of all thought.

It is this cornerstone of thought that vanquished all evil since evil cannot attach itself here and without any roots to multiply evil perishes. This is the place then of glory simultaneous with the recognition of Shekinah and the holy of holies, the place of heaven.

All thought ascends via its connection with higher thought. Higher thought having been established below there is then the coupling of heaven and earth. He who recognizes this for himself crowns himself with Shekinah meaning he has established the holy connection above and below.

And from where is rose and stood in the middle the crown on his head
When rising the crown on his head is
Like a woman of valor is the crown of her husband.
'one who exploits the crown shall die.'

25a) One who exploits the crown without the knowledge of her connections shall perish meaning be unsuccessful uniting above and below.

The analogy of connection above is explained via the qametz below like the lower half of aleph. It is how connection rises above discerning the link between thought and form. This link or chayah between them is the Eternal attribute of mercy that is continuous via the omnipresence of higher thought. The Chayot represent levels of awakening which when reached (their wings lower) the meaning then ascends above.

Her ascension is for the purpose of transmitting the prayers or intentional thoughts from below. The wings are the levels of ascension whereby she connects above. The sustenance may be seen as the answering call or the imaging of thoughts into their subsequent expressions. Out of this imaging the transformations are called good things since they literally abide with the original intentions that brought them forth.

It is most certainly the Vav that is the pathway of ascension telling us that it is only through her connections that she rises up above.

The wings symbolize the openings in thought that reciprocate level by level within our awareness all the while touching the Infinite culminating in the unified awareness that makes the above mirror the below.

The SHMA is the statement of unification around which the connections above or the Vav which is the Song of Israel which follows the SHMA in prayer. All the while then the soul which is the heart of thought itself or rather our particular focus in connection which is bound to the one SHMA with the other; Tephillin. Here is the binding of above and below shown in this symbolism.

The unity is explained through the symbols of the vowel points that unite the letters mirroring the unity of the crown on the head with the rest of the body, the feet the lap, etc. Also through this unity the shells of negativity or husks are shattered including the idols of materiality.

Vav is linked with Yesod, which is the connection of generation on the Tree of Life so that we may use this imagery in our prayers including the Amidah with its 18 blessings. The wings drop to allow the divine emanations to pass through mirroring the avenues of prayers answered above and passed on below.

It is in recognition of unity that prayers ascend above. It is with also with recognition of unity that they descend in fulfillment below. Each time another gate is opened on the way up and subsequently on the way down.

The mezzuzot symbolize this up and down acceptance of intention and fulfillment of prayer.

It is in the silence of our hearts that prayers ascend and descend. The holy place spoken of before may only be accessed via this way of communing within.

Therefore in this silence where the chayot raise their wings or lower them in openings to the gates of heaven then and only then are prayers received and blessings sent forth.

The blessings of the bride refer to the unity she has with her husband to mirror Shekinah and Her Ha Kodesh Barachu.

The holiness that can be no less than ten refers to the Tree of Life and the unity of Intentions and Blessings that are met coming and going. These Sephiros transmit the totality of the Intention and the abundance of the blessings together not as ten but as one entity operating in unity. The aspect of ten in this case does not have to do with a minyan because the holiness we are seeking is only that which may be realized by a person in communion with Shekinah via Ha Kodesh Barachu.

והם ארבע פני יקו״ק. ארבע כנפים אדנ״י. בחבור אהד יאקדונק״י.
And these are: the four faces of YKV"K; the four wings of ADN"Y in one composition: YAKDVNK"Y

25b) There is the question and the answer, the thought and its outcome, the four wings and four faces, the ties and the knots, the 248 words of SHMA, YAKDVNK"Y, Torah and precept, the raising of the wings and their lowering, A'DAM and Ha Kodesh Barachu. What is the body if not a garment that houses the soul? Where is throne on high if not the place from where Mazal emanates from? A house is built from the outside in. First there is the frame and then the inner structures have something to attach themselves to.

There is a process and yes it is a two step. If we take all of these symbols and discover the common meanings that exist amongst all of them we come up with frame of holiness in which resides the soul of being. Think about this. There cannot be any discoveries without the all important context.

What is this about these symbols and the all, context and attachments? It is about the conversations we have within called thoughts raised to the level of holiness called in unification Ha Kodesh Barachu.

These conversations can be rambling or directed. When they are rambling they lose their connectivity. When they are directed every moment becomes an opportunity to raise itself higher and higher. Take the special case of prayers. In the best case these prayers, our prayers are directed above and connect as we have learned via Shekinah with Ha Kodesh Barachu or the unified field of awareness.

Prior to their connection above a framework must be established. This framework includes your prayers and the intentions behind the prayers. This is alluded to by the repeated reference to the 72 names which is a specific prayer for making the pathways along which Israel (your prayers) are led in their upwards journey of connection above.

The verses in Torah Shemos 14:19-21 from which the 72 Names are derived from represent the point of departure for Israel (your prayers) from the confines of the status quo (Egypt) through the Red Sea (the mass consciousness of body and the outward appearances) leading to the deliverance which is the connection with Shekinah that will establish the Promised Land.

These are seed concepts that are presented here which will be used to magnify and amplify the lessons of being in its encounters with the unified field of awareness.

And Heh versus Heh is what binds the string of David's violin
And the 'wings of precept' the fringes...

There is a secret there are four faces four wings
Corresponding to the divine name YAKDVNK"Y
These are eight strings as well

26a) In the symbolism of prayer the eight strings are the
Chayot both wings and face. Imagine or construct your
prayers according to this fashion.

The Ana Bekoach or AVGYT"Tz is a shorthand for the
unification of prayer rising above while being bound with
Tephilin and directing the attention during the prayer. _
The unification of bride and groom or Ha Kodesh Barachu
and Shekinah occurs during mindful prayer.

Music symbolizes the opening responses to prayer calling
now from one to another like the Chayot call to each other.

What prayer in its purified form does is to take our wayward
thoughts and focus them upon the intentions of prayer. The
people of Israel are those wayward thoughts that need the
focus and unification of thought YKV"K.

When we say the SHMA with the consciousness of the unity
that is contained therein we are in effect speaking the holy
name that is the unification of thought. This also takes place
via Torah study and the insights that are discovered therein.

The SHMA is the definition of Ha Kodesh Barachu as we to
acknowledge Him in hymns songs and praises. It our then our
conscious acknowledgement that causes the Unity to come
closer to us since we are defining it moment by moment by all
we intend in the prayer. For the wise this is an opportunity to
commune on high, for the average a way to ground their
everyday fears and seek above and for the wicked it is also a
place of refuge to find forgiveness and a better way.

This is also an opportunity to heal past errors and to both acknowledge their sin and to accept upon oneself the yoke of heaven meaning the awareness that every action has consequences. Once we deal with these past errors and repair them it is time for the Unity to reveal itself by ADN"Y entering into YKV"K or YAKDVNK"Y the unity of thought and form.

As we have been leading up to it is the framing of prayer or its organization that helps us stay on track with our intention. We are seeding the heavens and then we are making a receptacle to receive those asked for blessings that fulfill themselves in Malchus, the demonstration of thought.

These intermediate prayers are where we make the connections Vav, Vav, higher and lower linking our prayers to the framework of prayer that we have been repeating. Once prayers have ascended and are met we turn away, the three steps backward letting go and at the same time letting the unity absorb our thoughts.

Tiqun 11

בראשית הר״א שיי״ת. ומה הוא. ששה היכלות. וכנגד ששת ימי בראשית אלקים. אימא עליונה עליהם. שהיא היכל שביעי.

Bereishis, or BaR"A ShY"T

What are these six halls? They are the six days of creation.
ELKY"M is the highest Mother which is the seventh hall,

And as higher Mother issues six, the lower Mother issues six.
And what is *the heavens and the earth.*
And those six words spoken in six days in which God made the heavens and earth.
The lower halls are instruments for the higher halls.

26b) Think of these six days as halls and as holding patterns for the conceptual realizations that are ongoing in the continuous processes of connection both above and below. The Higher Mother is the overflow from Ha Kodesh Barachu that is the natural order of things. What this means is that Creation builds upon itself endlessly. This is the underlying pattern that makes possible the awareness we experience. Therefore the flowing that takes place is one the higher in the other the lower. This is the imaging aspect of Creation that differentiates as it transforms.

Each hall opens in response to prayer when all are aligned in harmony. In exile there is a shift so that the harmony is misaligned. The angels are the connecting links above and below.

The way to alignment above and below is through the Master of Tears meaning the process of overflow. Once you are able to realize this overflow the keys to the various gates are made available for use.

Tears symbolize the overflow and their operation has always been a part of fervent prayer since the intensity of tears brings about an emotional response that triggers the opening of the 'eyes' which are the gateways to both above and below.

Now what passes through is the imaging of above which heals the below and makes it into its own image of perfection.

All of these chambers that open in response to tears, music, righteousness, fear, poor are all part of the special connections that must be in place for the alignment of above to below. It is this alignment that is made possible via their agency (tears, music, etc.) so that the continuous flowing of above is not interrupted or misplaced or ignored but is rather set into its proper place.

Exile is the property of ignorance that prevents a person from the awareness of the above. It is truly a blockage that is maintained either by a person or a culture that directs their attention not above but to the outward effects, In this case they never recognize the inner core of Creation that goes on all around them.

The waters that are divided are done so in order to make clear the relationships between what is above, the heavens and what is below the dry land, or in other terms the thought or Higher Mother and Lower Mother the essence of the Land.

The hidden meaning then of BeREiShY"T is that within these flowing tears is the salvation of Israel. This is the salvation of mundane thought that does not seek above. It is the salvation of reactive thought that does not seek above. The daughter is the recognition of the above in the heart of appearances that indicate Ha Kodesh Barachu.

Note: In prayer it is the process of overflow that both initiates and promotes the pathways both of the prayers that flow above and the blessings that flow below.

What is this like? A King built a garden with many streams but he first built a lake that would feed these streams. Now the streams contained the waters of Lake, which were constantly being renewed from the Lake, which was situated above the streams. However, the Lake itself needed to be renewed so the King built a series of channels, which eventually flowed back into Lake. In this way both Lake and streams were then continuously renewed.

Now if there were blockages at any point along the way the Lake would cease to overflow and the streams would dry up. In order to prevent this the King devised a plan of watchful sentries to patrol the both stream and Lake removing blockages from storms or excess build up of silt.

Our prayers are the channels that fill the Lake and blessings are the streams the Lake sends forth. The Lake is Ha Kodesh Barachu and the sentries that work together to remove blockages are collectively known as Shekinah or the Divine Presence.

You might think that we have described separately the operations that are taking place. It is however true that all of these operations are a unified field of awareness. Your prayers and the answering blessings are part of the same thing just as the water that flows above from the Lake is the same that flows back in channels to the Lake from below.

This is perhaps difficult to understand after all how could both prayers and blessings be exactly the same? Surely one is asking and one is answering. The paradox is resolved when you realize that what you are asking for could not be answered except in exactly the same way that you have asked for it. If you ask for rain, rain is then your answer.

Your prayers are the framework of the blessings that it elicits. All is one in the same thing.

Tiqun 12

בראית, מאמר ראשון של הכל, כלול מעשר אמירות. והיא ל״ב אלקים של מעשה בראשית של (ברי׳ת א׳׳ש), ומצד השמאל ניתנה שהיא גברה אש אדומה.

Bereishis – the first of all included in the ten statements, and it is thirty two (mentions) of ELKY"M of the act of Bereishis ברי׳ת א׳ש (covenant of fire), and on the left he was given red fire-gevurah,

For this reason: (Shemos 3:2) ...*And the angel of YKVK appeared unto him* (in a flame of fire בלבת)... And Moses was on the side of the Levites, from his right side.

27a) _ What is the red fire-gevurah and what is the heart of the flame and what is Moshe from the side of the Levites? All of these symbols are speaking about the refinement of consciousness. The initial utterance is sent forth in purification acting upon the darkness and void and bringing into view the something out of nothing. Moshe had the same task with Israel to reveal the whole the unity while purifying them of their Egyptian experience of separation so that they would be able to leave. The heart of the fire is its essence, which is the utmost in terms of refinement of purification.

Shekinah is the epitome of purification because when She arises all around are cleansed of impurities. Israel is the sum total of our aspirations, our thoughts of holiness. Now in exile these thoughts are in the midst of the mixed multitude meaning the kelippos or shells of awareness that remain disconnected from the sense of attachment to the unity. What the wicked or errant thoughts do by oppressing Israel is to drive her towards Shekinah, which then gathers up the dispersed of Israel.

Now when Israel is not sorely pressed they become absorbed by the mixed multitude and are unaware of their exile.

Therefore what Moshe must do is to remove the body of the mixed multitude prior to approaching the burning bush or his connection with Shekinah and subsequently Ha Kodesh Barachu.

The temple being spoken of is our awareness of the unified field within our own vantage point of consciousness. All outer temples pale in comparison to this inner temple that is built to be our own recognition-acceptance of the Eternal.

So Adam or man is built by chokmah by the wisdom of his awareness of the unified field. The rib, which is the bride that is Shekinah, is man's identification with spirituality.

The boy is crying because of the lack of connection. He is seeking the unity. It is only through Shekinah that their cries are answered and their supplications listened to in order to open the gates to the unified field even to triumphing over past patterns that have blocked this access.

The chayot represent the connecting links. It is they who prepare themselves for the connections wherein the entire flow is integrate above to below via the ten Sephiros. The sanctification takes place because all ten are united as one, which is the result of the first instance of unification, which is the image and its reflection.

These seven blessings prepare or frame the way for holiness. The place of union between bride and groom is the sending forth of blessings in this case from below from Malchus to up to Chesed these seven Sephiros which then arouse the above or Higher Mother Binah so that She vibrates in sympathy with these blessings from below. This in turn enervates the entire ten Sephiros to unify as one. All of this is therefore the action of Bereishis.

Tiqun 13

בראשית, שם אשר״י. וזה הוא אשרי האיש.

Bereishis: There is *ASHRe"Y* (as part of the letters of Bereishis)
And this is: (Psalms 1:1) *Happy* אשרי *is the man...* and this is:
(Shemos 3:14) *I am that I am* אהי״ה אשר אהי״ה
And this is the head of all heads.

There it is in the essential building block of Creation BeREiShYT the happiness of man is his own acceptance of "I am that which I am." How does this happen? As suggested by the text above this takes place via the transformation of consciousness via the connecting links established by Shekinah. In this sense Shekinah may be considered an innate response to holiness that is awakened when man approaches the unified field.

And it was said: (Shir HaShirim 7:6) *Thy head upon thee is like the Carmel.* And it is the tephilin of the head,
and the hair of thy head like purple...this is the tephillin of the hand.
And therefore is the daughter praised with happiness (AShReY)

27b) The raising of the daughter is the acknowledgment of the flowing of Shekinah. There is the connection between head and hand whereby our actions proceed from our intentions and both are bringing forward Shekinah into our awareness.

In order to connect with Shekinah our thoughts literally have to exist above the mundane thoughts of others. They have to be free in order to have the 'wings' to rise above in their connections. Anything which detracts from this freedom brings down the level of awakening to the point where our perception is then limited and cannot perceive holiness.

Our thoughts become like a tree that always has access to holiness when we cling to the Tree of Life or the perception of holiness that it represents. Our sustenance is then continuous and indeed endless

This song is one of aspiration whereby the melodies make the pathways above for the words to ascend through. Even there in the Divine Name this holiness shines forth then in harmony with the aspirants songs of praise.`

Praises are the pathways of holiness that we ascend by. We learn that there are thirty levels corresponding to thirty degrees or one tenth of a circle whereby the daughter-Shekinah ascend to the Father Ha Kodesh Barachu.

The harp of David's that plays by itself sounds out its praises and affirmations with each of its five strings in demonstration of the unity that exists in the harmony of song.` Each string vibrates in sympathy with these praises.

It is via the essence of vibration that the ten Sephiros are to be understood in terms of how they relate to one another and how Shekinah travels up and down mirroring the wheels of the chayot and outlining Zeir Anpin, which describes the steps to the throne. This is the operation of thought.

See how thoughts are the connections via which the wings of holiness are brought about in the acceptance of thought and the unification of holiness.

It is Vav that is the connection throughout the Tree of Life. This Vav is a symbol of the six words of the Shema that is the ultimate realization of connection and is its primary source of awakening.

It is the channel of holiness that comes into being left and right guiding thoughts into holiness using the both the anchors of thought and their points of connection to rise up level by level.

When this song ascends with six it is the unity that is proclaimed and when it descends with six it is the unity that is established.

The six levels rise in pitch or vibration designating levels of attainment. Likewise when the pitch lowers these levels are lowered meaning their vibratory levels are tuned lower giving now the appearance of more and more substantial form.

The wheels represent patterns of awareness as the harmonies are struck or strummed. These six steps create a variety of harmonies all based upon Vav or the connections between these steps or Sephiros.

Every level that is ascended or descended comes by the hand of David who masters the notes on the harp and yet it says the harp was playing by itself in another part. We rise by the intention to rise in the awareness of holiness.` In a sense it is Ha Kodesh Barachu that plays through David.

Each step is via connection and the awareness of the highest (Yud) arises by the harmony that relates one level to another.

The menorah now becomes the symbol of connection its branches the Sephiros and its central flame holder being Vav with the candle on top becoming the Yud. The six branches symbolize Zeir Anpin, with its six Vav's or connecting links.

Therefore find out how the Shema places itself within consciousness to become the central connecting link just as the candles connect above so too does the Shema in its letters and inner symbolism utilize the harmony of intention with holiness to produce the unity being sought after.

These are males and females are those of the Shema.
which Moses established, are male. These females are of Solomon.
And the house is full of those levels that are a receptacle of Solomon and of Moses.
And when all are joined together,
When connecting (both words together) one as the form of another
Solomon became Moses.

28a) What are the levels of Solomon and the levels of Moshe? We find out that Moshe represents the Shema, which is the declaration of unity. Solomon represents the receptacle for unity. This is the receptacle of thought or the place where thought is then transformed in the garden of Solomon into the abundance of manifestation or the fulfilment of prayer.

Each verse in the Shema contains an idea that is related to the whole. Everything is of course related to the idea of unity, that God is One and there is no other. What this means here is that God is the both the intention and the demonstration of prayer and its subsequent transformation.

Specifically saying the Shema with intention now with your prayers overlaying the words opens up the receptacle that by understanding the meaning of the Song of Solomon transforms your prayers into their intended outcomes.

Now if the essence of Solomon is transformed into the essence of Moshe meaning that the thoughts that are Moshe are seen in the building of the temple or the intention of Moshe is demonstrated there then it is this same song that is established via the Sephiros of transformation throughout the four worlds and the four letters of the Kabbalah of Creation.

See who is in charge of it all. It is man that guides the transformations via the choices he makes with his thoughts recognizing the chariot of YKV"K as that which drives those thoughts into the life experiences he is irresolutely a part of.

The lips that speak the intention or the man whose intention is spoken forth via this chariot of YKV"K is perfect. It is beautiful with the happiness or the certainty of completion and the song of the joy of the expression of that completion. The third part of Intention is the higher Shekinah that facilitates the answering blessings. The soul is the image of above experiencing via its experience the holiness that is the unity above.

The third welcomed this is called the Higher Shekinah.
(Tehilim 103:1) *bless the Lord oh my soul.'*

So the Holy One blessed be He (HKBK) sustains the whole world,
As the soul sustains the whole body
So HKBK sees is not seen
As the soul (not seen) sustains the whole body
In the deepest chambers HKBK
Like the soul in the deepest part of you.

And the secret of the soul which is on par with HKBK
(Yishayahu 40:25...*To whom then will ye liken Me, that I should be equal? saith the Holy One.*

We learn the association of the soul to the body is the same as the association of Ha Kodesh Barachu to His creation. In addition we learn the mystery of the chambers of the Holy One blessed be He is the image of the chambers in which the soul dwells.

This understanding or Binah of the mystery of the reflection is shown clearly here and is the substance of what we ask when we say 'who dwells here' meaning who is inside, who is our soul and what its relationship to the above?
Now we see 'to whom will you liken me?' The answer is the image of that reflection which is our own unique soul.

Another mystery is thought that resides within the heart and issues forth the essence of the soul through speech and voice and utterance. This describes the connection or Vav that radiates from the heart, thoughts that radiate in their various ways and levels of meaning. These thoughts are guided by the intention that is behind them. Intention is the King, which is the reflection of the image of above.

In order for spirit to flow the analogy of the lungs is given to show that there is a transformation of spirit that must occur according to the vibrational levels of thought of the strings of the harp called the five nodes of the lung. Our souls then are 'played' via movement of spirit within sounding in harmony to the Intentions that are expressed upon and through it via the heart which is the Intention of the Image of Reflection that is Ha Kodesh Barachu.

The actions of the lungs are to temper the holiness of spirit so that the body does not disintegrate. This action is called Yud or fire and it is the rising up of thoughts from the heart as it is explained via speech. `

The hymn is the definitive intention of the right hand that occurs by directed attention. It is the recognition of combining our intention with the songs of David letting their words be the guiding principle so that our thoughts attach themselves to.

Our thoughts remain in exile (from perception of Ha Kodesh Barachu) even though we have the intention to connect above meaning we always are supporting that connection or Shekinah in our prayers.

When we continue to reach up for unity the connection is strengthened and is the key to our redemption or return to the state of unity.

Just as we image the above so too does the soul image itself throughout the entire body. Here the hand, arm with the symbols of Tefillin in the morning raise up our awareness of Shekinah and connection.

The seed thought of this particular section is that Ha Kodesh Barachu lives within us and we are the image of that reflection. It is an eternal Name for us allowing us to 'split the waters of Torah' meaning to discern the meanings of holiness and also simultaneously of what it means directly in our lives which are allegories of the above.

ומדוע נקראת זרוע יי. מפני שכך היד בוי׳ (יו״ד) חמש אצבעות ה׳. קנה הימין
שהוא זרוע ו׳. כתף בו ה׳, וזה עמוד האמצע שנקשר בימין, להקים בו השכינה
בגלות, ומשה שהוא דיקן עמוד האמדע, נאמר ו מוליך לימן משה זרוע תפארתו,
והוא בוקע מי התורה לגבי זרע אברהם שהוא ימין להיות לו שם עולם
And why is it called the arm of God?
From the hand of ten are the five fingers of God.

The shoulder support in the middle bound to the right column setup by the Shekinah for Moses who was in exile and made the middle column, it said.
About how Moses and the right arm is the glory
that is coming to Torah through Abraham's seed were left to him in the world.

And calling to the God of Abraham which is the five books of Torah.
Where Moses completed (with the Heh that is in MoSHe and AVRaHaM)
And immediately the right hand is revealed
(Isaiah 53:1) ...*And to whom hath the arm of the YKV"K been revealed??*

28b) The right hand the arm of YKV"K is the revelation of intention and the way of the transformation of the above into the below. It is this knowledge that is the perfection of the name since by its perfection conscious awareness of the way things work is initiated and perfected

The northern wind is the accumulated actions of unified thought that strikes the harp of David that then in sympathy with unified thought expresses the intention. This intention is as the musician has played since the musician always seeks harmony

These thunderclaps are the rhythms contained inside of the music that results from the pulsing of intention

The rhythm aspect is then punctuated with the staccato, the penetrating, and the broken up sound made by the shofar. These sounds are for the purpose of removing blockages and promoting the prayers in their intended directions

The transition from one state to another is described. The end of days meaning the end of the status quo and the awakening of the new paradigm.

The sixth type of music is '**Halleluyah** Halleluyah
and this is Hei"Vav.
About that is said: (Shemos 12:42) *It was a night of watching unto YKV"K, And this is the Middle Pillar.*

This sixth type of music shows the rising levels awareness uniting with each other symbolized by YH and HV in the awakening consciousness that recognizes the holiness in which it is surrounded thereby giving off Hal-luyaH

Yes these wonders are the recognition of holiness in which all good things may be discerned. Through this holiness all thoughts are gathered together within this holiness even those called 'the remnants of Israel.

The Middle Pillar is the avenue of connection. This is established through this conscious awareness of holiness akin to Moshe and his acknowledgement of the above. It is here that Moshe does establish his point of view or his seat above.

It is important to keep in mind here that thought is the central allegory here. There are joining's of thought raised level by level. At first we absorb-the fourth hour, then thoughts are in suspense-the fifth hour meaning they are mingling together awaiting their rising. And then at the rising of thought the dross is burned away in the sixth level or hour, leaving the purity of intention.

It is important to understand that the mixed multitude represents kelippos or shells of awareness that are the abridgers of chaos. They arise to turn the focus around towards their own numbers instead of holiness. It is in reality inertia that is at work here within consciousness. This mixed multitude is then absorbed as a result of the connection of holiness that completes the seven times cycle.

Imagine the sum total of all thought that is gathered in the sixth millennium only for the purpose of once and for all transforming their essence into the holiness that is the intention of the seventh millennium. Now this transformation goes on continuously within the thoughts of sages, seekers, the wise, and the righteous.

The purpose of all of these transformations is to bring about the unity of thought and the awareness of that unity meaning that Shekinah is reunited with Ha Kodesh Barachu.

Shekinah was incomplete because her connection was interrupted by the mixed multitude or those thoughts of chaos that challenge the unity of Creation. It is described as prevented the mitzvos from taking place. The complete matzah is the transformed Daleth, which adds the Vav to become the Heh.

The incomplete Matzos and complete Matzos are allegories for the unification of thought or its fragmentation.

By the same analogy the bitterness that is experienced is because of the fragmentation of thought. Just as water is embittered by impurities so too is the unity of Ha Kodesh Barachu made inaccessible by fragmentation. This unity it should be noted is always present but it is our fragmentation that prevents us from experiencing it.

The cause of this fragmentation then was the circumcision of the mixed multitude. What is this like? Imagine you have a mikveh purified initially and then introduce impurity into the mix. This is essentially what happened in terms of the mixed multitude and Israel.

Moshe by including the mixed multitude with Israel corrupted the purified Israel, which by its release from Egypt cleansed them of their chaos, their slavery and their adherence to Egyptian ways. What is this like? Imagine a jar of quarters. It contains only quarters that are declared to be the currency for all higher functions. Then you introduce pennies and nickels and dimes into the jar. When you mix these other denominations the purity of the quarter mix can never be fixed. The only way to make it pure again is to separate out everything but the quarters.

This is a significant revelation since it speaks to the basic principles of holiness.

The Eternal is the epitome of holiness. This holiness is brought about by the truth of thought being in harmony with being. This means that specifically what we are thinking maintains its harmony with the world around us. This seventh type of music speaks to this harmony in the way in which each note relates to another vis a vis its composition.

Thanksgiving is the acknowledgement of the above. This is the miraculous experience of unity whereupon we realize that this is where we are meant to be all along. Praise is our way of mirroring the above and is the understanding that Moshe was given of the action of holiness that ever sends forth its abundant good.

These eight days of circumcision described as the eight kinds of music speak to the joining of the above or the holiness of Creation with our innate comprehension of the process of the way things work. The circumcision symbolizes the disjoining of unity and chaos leaving only unity to demonstrate the divine will.

the Yud of circumcision is the tenth of the ten sephiros.

And this hod is the eight days of the festival of *Chanukah*
Four and twenty days (Kislev) they are...
'Blessed is the Name of the glory of His Kingdom for ever.' (24 letters)

But of netzach it is stated
(Bereishis 8:4) *And the ark rested in the seventh month...*
because netzach alludes to Noah the righteous.

29a) Hod and Netzach represent the stability of the emotional and the intellectual in regards to the holiness in which they are surrounded. This holiness is either accepted or blocked. The circumcision is the quality of separating yourself from whatever is blocking the holiness. The nations of the world are those many thoughts of chaos that are seeking your strength your energy to survive. When chaos or these nations thrive holiness is blocked.

The only way to keep us in the flow of holiness is to firmly establish Netzach and Hod, which represent in another way our victory over the chaos, and our recognition of the splendor of the glorious kingdom represented by Malchus. This kingdom also is symbolic of our heart's desire, our prayers answered and the unification of Ha Kodesh Barachu and His Shekinah.

Now herein is explained that Netzach and Hod represent the middle pillar, which is only complete when both inside and outside are complete, or when Jacob and Moshe are unified. The extension of this is when the raised Jacob called Israel listened to Moshe unifying Israel with the Divine Principles of the way things work.

The house that is built is the dwelling place of YKV"K which is the rib of Adam and the joining with Shekinah.

Another example of this joining is the concatenation of YKV"K with ADN"Y forming YAKDVNK"Y. This is the animation of matter by spirit. The life force is given a body in which to operate and experience the unification that is ongoing around them.

The weapons of war are your discernment and ability to choose what is right. If you retain these weapons you will always win the war over evil.

The body is described in terms of its mystical counterparts. Now beyond the symbolism there is the lesson of what takes place within and how we are unified in connection. "The One who rides upon them is YKV"K refers to our ultimate connection with unity on both a spiritual and physical level.

Consider who animates the body and its wholeness. These descriptions of the implements and symbols of the Sukkah are significant. The Sukkah is the dwelling whereas the body is the dwelling of YKV"K. The spine is the pathway whereby this dwelling is connected above. See into these parables and descriptions the truth of being which is the movement of spirit throughout the body.

It is Shekinah that offers the body its sense of connection with holiness. The combination of lulav, etrog, myrtle and willow symbolize the combining of Shekinah with the body of righteousness making it suitable for unification.

And one needs to arrange, with them,
the circular march, like the altar (the circular march with the Torah scrolls around the bimah).

29b) This (perambulation-rotation) is the renewal of consciousness like the rotation of crops in the fields that keeps the fields fresh.

The man is encompassed by the female meaning that intention is surrounded by gestation.

What is it that renews Creation? It is the Oral Torah or Talmud or rather the exposition of the practical meanings of Torah.

There is the pattern of Creation that replicates itself via the renewing waters of Consciousness. The tree that is planted arises from this water and then produces the seed, which completes the circle of life of Creation.

Joy is the expectation of the certainty of renewal that comes as we recognize our part in the scheme of things. It is then this joy that is the life force or chai that moves thought into its realized expression

It is a long process that is being explained. It is the law of opposites. There is the taking of one from the other and a sharing of the impetus that shapes the outcome. This is the fiery law.

The covenant is herein described as a connection that takes place between Shekinah (daughter of the King) and Ha Kodesh Barachu. Three drops or three Yuds arise or descend to form the channel of that connection. This connection is the experience of unity.

Connection is the extension of the 'arrow' that comes from the realization of unity that is close. Because of this the connection is extended in the manner of the large pazer.

This snake is subversion of the power of connection that takes it into areas not designated for unity but rather represent the dispersion of the energy there. When the snake is blocked or neutralized or even killed this means that the way is made clear for connection.

It is prayer that slays the serpent with the large pazer with the arrow of the Righteous One, its rising and falling notes symbolizing the flight of an arrow.

Prayer is made up of the words of the mouth formed by the tongue. It must be aligned above and below always mindful of the unity that is its connection.

Negative thought or a negative state of mind (the serpent or Samael) may only be pierced by righteous prayer. Righteous prayer has as its target the awakening of Shekinah which then envelops thought into its rising arms of connection. In this way prayer is made holy or made unified with the One, the Eternal or Ha Kodesh Barachu. Shekinah is awakened or rather the pathways that exist between prayer and holiness are enlivened so that connection takes place bringing about the experience of unification.

And to whom it protects, it is stated:
(Psalms 91:5) *Thou shalt not be afraid of the terror by night, nor of the arrow that flies by day*

30a) What happens to thought when we let it go? It is under the protection of above as long as we connect therein via the holy name and its meanings. How do we connect? It is by contemplating its mysteries. This is the building of the structure of the holy temple that is the name.

Now in our contemplations we connect above and experience the connection below or rather the integration of our thoughts with holiness. As we let go of the dross of thinking mundane thoughts the higher and lower Shekinah are united bringing out the connection we are seeking.

On the one hand we remove the negativity, the chaos of non intentional thinking and we think about Torah, which opens us up to the world to come and protects us in this world.

Tiqun 14

בראשית עליה נאמר ראשית בכורי אדמתך תביא בית יי׳ עלקיך לא תבשל גדי בחלב אמו.
Bereishis. Upon it is stated:
(Shemos 23:19) *The choicest first-fruits of thy land thou shalt bring into the house of YKV"K thy God. Thou shalt not seethe a kid in its mother's milk.*

Come and see Higher chokmah:
About which it is said: (Shemos 13:2) *Sanctify unto Me all the first-born*
For all 'firstborns' are what is called (first fruits)

The first born refers to the inspiration that you encounter when studying Torah or thinking about Ha Kodesh Barachu.

It is a sacred area of study.   This is how we make our connection the Vav or Middle Pillar.

This oral Torah is that which we learn from our contemplations.   It is what is whispered in our ear meaning what our holy thoughts are telling us.   This is the way in which the Tree flourished meaning it is watered by contemplation and grows via inspiration.

Yes the watering is our meditation.   It is the wellspring of our connection to holiness.

You cannot connect above unless what you intend is holiness. You will not rise above thinking mundane thoughts. You have to have context to begin.   Therefore mixing mundane and holy is forbidden.

You cannot put one inside the other. A discussion of holiness deteriorates if non holy topics are interjected. The mother's milk and the kid are of a type. The cooking destroyed the type and therefore the soul of the thing making it not holy.

Each thought has its counterpart in terms of unification above.   If a thought is linked to the unholy it cannot rise above and another thought will take its place the true place for unification.

מפני זה ראשית בכורי אדמתך תביא בית יי' אלקיך לא תבשל גדי בחלב
אמו. שאותו בן הוא ערבוביה כלאים

And because of this The first fruits of your land you shall bring to house of YKV"K your God, you shall not cook a kid in its mother's milk, that mixed child is a mixture.

30b) The child is the thought that results from a merging of two thoughts. When they are not suited to each other there is a forbidden mixture

When two thoughts merge together that are connected to Torah their union is completed in this world and the world to come.

Otherwise the mixture is produced which causes a degradation in both worlds, to come and now.

However repentance meaning returning to Torah study is finding the wife that is tov so that the image is made in a perfect reflection above and below.

Tiqun 15

בראשית זו ישראל. זה הוא שכתוב קדש ישראל ליי' ראשית תבואתה. ראשית בלי
ערבוביה אחרת.

Bereishis – this is Israel. About which it is said.
(Jeremiah 2:3) *Israel is YKVK's hallowed portion, His first-fruits of the increase,*
First without any other mixture. And because he is holy, he is not made up of any different kind.

Thought is the first appearance of order, of connection and of intention. Israel is the intended of Ha Kodesh Barachu.

Just as Yud which is holiness or Ha Kodesh Barachu and Israel is the intended so too is Hei the intended for Yud. The King produces the perfect fruit, the first of Hei.

Thought seeks to reign within itself in relationship with the corollaries of thought. This fertile thought joins with the infertile thought (matzah) and produces holiness.

When our intention follows through to holiness all are joined. When we defile that holiness by losing our focus then the bread of affliction is produced caused by a wandering mind.

These drops described here are of course referring to thoughts.

This takes place in terms of the chain of association that is established by thought. Wives refer to the refinement and elevation of thought. This means to only give your best to your wife because what you intend for her is what you will receive in return. This is also related to the aspect of growing thought in that the wife accepts the seed of thought first. In other words it is acted upon there.

Chaos is the result or the trial by fire and knife when we are not circumspect with our thoughts. When we are mindful it ameliorates the results of this.

Israel is the nation that clings to YKV"K containing within them the intention for holiness. It is this that reminds us that our thoughts always have a center of attraction and that center for Israel, for that which is the first born of YKV"K is Ha Kodesh Barachu.

There is a distinct way of perfection that admits of no other. Thoughts cannot bind with any that are not their own kind. Holiness reveals itself to holiness both above and below.

(Devarim) 33:28 *And Israel dwells in safety, the fountain of Jacob alone..* Entitled-worthy is the person who guards the covenant.

31a) Guarding the covenant means that we are always mindful of the relationship between our thoughts and Ha Kodesh Barachu especially in regards to their unity. Israel represents our thoughts but more specifically our holy thoughts. Surely these are the children of the King.

Tiqun 16

בראשית, זו חלה, זה הוא שכתוב ראשית ערסתכם חלה תרימו תרומה

Bereishis: - this is *challah*. This is what is said:
(Numbers 15:20) *Of the first of your dough-challah ye shall set apart a cake for a gift;*

Adam was the *challah* of the world.'
And how do we know that *challah* is first?
The verse proves it – this is what is written:
Of the first of your dough-challah ye shall set apart a cake for a gift.

Adam is the soul, which has been made flesh just as the dough in its original state is flat and then rises, so too does the soul rise throughout the flesh. The first (reishit) of your dough refers to the praises we send on high in acknowledgment of our holy state.

The letter hei might be compared to the yeast which gives the dough its rising quality. Without the hei it is sin chet alluding to man whose intention of holiness is bound to sin, to death.

Since we know that Shekinah is the connection between our thoughts and the thoughts of holiness what must be removed is the lack of awareness of holiness. This is the offering to Ha Kodesh Barachu. Therefore the offering which is that drop and then also the seed composed of both Ha Kodesh Barachu and Shekinah bringing forth the Vav the symbol of Connection. In this way the circuit is fulfilled. The challah is the awareness the recognition of the process that makes it possible.

Adam died because he lost that awareness of unity. of the connection. This is why by way of return the Challah is extracted in order to return the awareness to Adam.

She the female refers not to the woman but to the focus that is reactionary. It is outward seeking. The focus therefore needs to be inward seeking with love and fear of the awareness of holiness bringing forth the son of holiness.

Her blood refers to the effects of reactionary seeking which cannot renew itself and ends up in destruction.

The woman again represents the focus internal and with care that focus separates the Challah...the awareness of holiness, is careful of the reactive state of consciousness, and lights the Shabbos candles to awaken the Divine Presence and its connecting links above.

Therefore the mystery of ChiTa"H by allusion refers to the letters of Torah in their combinations as we flow through them in our expressions of that holy awareness.

Tiqun 17

בראשית, עליה נאמר רזשית מעשר דגנך (תבואתך) וזו מלכות שהיא מעשר.
והיא עשירית לעשר ספירות
Bereishis: It is said: (Devarim 18:4)
The first fruits of the tithing.
And this malchus that is *the tithing,* and it is the tenth of ten sephiros,

Tithing is the recognition of the outcome, the Malchus of this world. It must be free from the mixture mentioned earlier which includes the husk and straw. Since the Hei which is part of Challah is to be kept this Hei awakens the lower Shekinah with the Y'ud that is from Keter linking the thought with the now realized form.

Similarly two souls come together to bring another soul into this world via recognition of holiness between them.

In the world to come the twenty-two letters of Torah are completely holy so that all that is produced or expressed cannot but have a holy outcome.

The blessing of hamotzi is the meal offering that is consumed then with a conscious intention for pronouncing the Hei just so to link it with the holiness spoken about in this context here of Yud, Vav and Hei.

The tithing that is given to the priest is the holiness from below. The tithing that is given to the Levite the first tithing is from above. Both are given that they may be connection one to the other.

In summary the offering is Torah, the two tablets that awaken the awareness of holiness via the ten Sephiros extended by tens throughout the four worlds (the forty days - four tens)

Through malkhut we know the completion or fulfilment of the above. Out of this fulfilment we take our lessons from the three patriarchs and the two prophets of truth all signifying the tens.

ובה נעשו ספירות כולן עשרונים. שלשה אבות
שלשה עשרונים נביאי אמת הם עשרון עשרון
And through it all the sephiros are made tens
The three patriarchs are three who are two
the two prophets of truth are: (Numbers 28:21) A tenth, a tenth... _

31b) What are these tens? See them as the extensions of the Sephiros visualized within. They are ten dimensions of Consciousness accessible only via our recognition of their presence. These are the visions that are described throughout Torah. Ten Sephiros each with its own Tree of Life making one hundred or ten times ten. This is say that creation replicates itself ten times ten as well. For the wise the seen are unseen.

Tiqun 18

בראשית ברא אלקים בר"א שי"ת. הן שש דרגות הנבואה

Bereishis or (BaR"A ShY"T) (Created six): these are the six degrees of prophecy,

The six above reflect from Yesod which are Zeir Anpin in return. They are sixty since each Sephiros represents ten as mentioned previously.

Shekinah is the awakening of the awareness of unity which in Malchus or the lower Shekinah is verification of the above. It is the hand which fashions the Creation. This is then the imagining of creation. As such it is a proof of the preceding verses that what we are speaking about here is the visualization of Creation.

These sixty wheels are the Sephiros or Zeir Anpin that section which contains the levels of operation. As these wheels turn their aspects are presented one to another in such a way as to enhance the vision with holiness from above and verification from below. The throne begins as its point of focus, As the throne is perceived at first fleetingly and then in more and more detail the imagining of YKV"K is realized.

In the way of the visions of the prophets whose faces are what their thoughts, their words are composed of, we then have subsequently the imagination which is brought forth.

Here are we in Malchus seeing through the aid of Shekinah the visions above in this sense within and this is how Ha Kodesh Barachu becomes known to us. As we question we see and when we see we learn to build rightly.

With eyes shut, it is called 'vision in a dream.'
This waking vision is the simultaneous thinking above and experiencing below. We ascend above through the windows of Shekinah opening the core of our being.

And there are two who are appointed there:
Sagro"n and Patcho"n are the two keys to the waking vision with their higher component Metatro"n. Imagine the triangle the right and left and then the top from the aspect of the Middle Pillar,

Mouth to mouth is listening to the internal that speaks through you as if coming from you at its deepest source. The vision that is beheld that Moshe beheld with of YKV"K is entirely self contained.

The righteous are made aware of this vision in a dream the quality of which is the understanding of the thought form in all of its phases.

What are the appearances of these thought forms from the aspect of Tipheret or the Middle Pillar? They are the visions that are taken together from both sides where they are stored temporarily until their combining.

The active force or impetus of Creation comes from this vision that changes in aspect, the lion, eagle, ox and human regarding the interior body meaning the visualized forms of thought. Of these four Chayot it is the human that is in recognition of the process and therefore that recognition forms the connection awakening Shekinah energizing and filling the entire movement with the cha'y almin, life force of the worlds.

The prophecy or the realization of the vision appears in the perceiver according to their understanding or level of awareness in which that vision is depicted.

Ultimately it is Shekinah that provides the pathways for the comprehension of this vision making them into prophecies.

It is one thing to envision a thing or even to prophecy a thing, however the understanding of the operation of a thing belongs to a wise man who sees into the heart of a thing. This is the more than human who is described.

And it is Moshe who is the light, the inspiration for all openings that reveal the light. Moshe is aroused to shine the light and to be a channel for the light. In likewise fashion everything that comes from light, the planets, stars are all aspects of this bringing forth of the light which Moshe mastered.

There is no prophecy like that of Moshe that he brought into the world with his faithful listening and revealing to all Israel.

Therefore through Moshe through his connection we open the supernal treasure house of above to reveal the hidden things of the Most High King. For just as a son walks freely in the house of his father so can we walk in the house of treasures that Moshe revealed to us.

The Higher Mother is Shekinah that reveals through Chokmah or Wisdom the son of the house above imaged in Tipheret. This is the internal house of discovery as above so below.

And you were like one of us of the same house
The Bet of Bayit (house) higher mother,
The yud is chokmah or father,
The Tav is Tipheres at home above.

155

For in that house, a prophet has no permission to enter there except by permission.

And you would enter without permission, just like a son of the King where no gate is closed

32a) It is through Moshe who had permission that the door is always opened. Moshe brought us Torah and through our study of its lessons we may come to understand the way things work.

What is it that opens for us? It is our sense of connection and our participation with Unity. In this way each step becomes connected to the greater whole as understanding builds and becomes more accessible.

We are speaking of Moshe here and also of the Torah scholar that rises to the levels of Moshe.

Those who are able to "see" usually can only see but dimly or through one faculty or the other symbolized by the limbs of the body.

Moshe could see with the unification of the body throughout all of its parts. In a sense his soul level extended itself into the awareness of unity therefore bringing about that unity within his being.

Each and every limb has its vision via the awareness of unity called YKV"K that is within the chamber ADN"Y.

The awareness of both gates and chamber are what are required for the permission to be given. This permission is the recognition that what we are asking is specific to what we hope to focus upon.

Therefore bring forth the imaging intention of Moshe in order to open these doors to the chamber ADN"Y. For first the place must be prepared, the chamber and then the gates may open within the setting of the chamber.

It is via Shekinah the queen that we enter into the bayit of holiness, the chamber where Yud has its home. It does no good to boast of the understanding of this secret because it is only through a certain level of vision that you will get the permission required to open the holiness within.

What you are asking for is for Moshe or the level of Moshe to ascend upon you saying "ADN"Y open my lips." Patcho"n opens and Sagro"n closes. These are levels of awareness that are signs of the recognition of the focus or level of Moshe.

Just as the vowel points open up the meanings of letters, of words so too do your specific focus determine the permission you receive to be open to the level of Moshe.

I shall give thanks to Y"K, Who is keter above all.

(Psalms 118:20*) This is the gate of the LORD; the righteous shall enter into it. ...*
(*zeh*) this is tzeir"ei,
and they are 'the two pillars of truth;'
the righteous shall enter therein this is the Righteous One,
the sign of the covenant in both of them.
It is chireq under tzeirei, and it is the shure"q the connection of both of them. (Shure"q with Vav is the connection of male and female).

32b) For every thought there is a connecting thought which links together one idea after another. There are supporting ideas like the chireq beneath the tzeirei and there are binding ideas like the shire"q that links to the holiness above.

The binding of Shekinah is the connecting link of the tzaddik by whose actions the world is corrected and made anew.

These descriptions are allusions to the internal process that takes place in consciousness. Things are added together based upon this right and left arrangement of truth between them meanings like associations that are binding.

In building the way within the appearance of Shekinah is the beginning of the realization of connection.

The souls that rise are the thoughts that are of holiness that we have attached ourselves to. These rise according to the level of our awareness of Shekinah which once perceived becomes the channel for the fulfilment of these thoughts.

The image of the Maker sees through the eyes of the Maker meaning what we envision raised to holiness becomes the thing unto where it is sent.

What we realize then is the truth of a thing through its performance and our awareness of being aligned with that awareness.

These angels are the doorways through which our prayers ascend. The prayers are then aligned with holiness. What is this holiness? It is unity of Ha Kodesh Barachu. There is the recognition of prayer and blessing being a part of the same thing.

This image called face is the reflected impression of holiness upon the prayers that have risen causing them to become imbued with this face according to the intention that is the prayer and its alignment above.

These spirits and fires, spirit winds are the pathways upon which prayers-thoughts travel in their seeking unification above. In this way the smoke and scent of the sacrifices is transformed into the thought forms that represent their intentions.

Higher thoughts brought about by the image that speaks through them are called the birds of heaven and their wings are self contained in the wisdom they embody above.

The body is then an instrument for the transformation of substance (the body) into prayers that rise above in the symbolic acts of the sacrifices. It is the breath that propels the word and it is here also part of the transformation process.

We guide the prayers above through what we think about during their speaking. This guidance or our hands is likened to a man that is carried up by wings.

The body of perfection is built by the masters whose intention realizes the levels of awakening and prays with the unification in mind.

These signs are the inner dimensions of Shekinah meaning that She is perceived both outwardly and inwardly.

The complete realm of consciousness is included as the dwelling of Shekinah.   The masters of feet have this knowledge throughout.

These first three blessings of prayer symbolize the openings above wherein we enter into the holiness of the cause of causes or more practically into operations center above.

Everything is in its proper place. Blessings are then above while prayers are in the middle and the fulfilment is below. This is an analogy for the transformation of intentional thought-prayer into the intended outcome.

As we ascend above those prayers become the realities of consciousness moving with the power of the cause of causes. What is accepted above is what transforms below.

See that in Torah there is the study and its many precepts. Also see that there is its exposition that is applicable to every day life.

Call this written Torah then the theoretical Torah central to the understanding of above where there is wisdom.

The Oral Torah is what we understand about its meanings and what we are able to relate to in terms of pursuing our worldly affairs and the world to come.

The final thought in this section is Malchus the completion that makes the connection to the Higher Mother above. This is the Book of Life meaning this is the way that things work within consciousness.

Sagron, and called ADN"Y his name is as the name of his master
And they say to him: Tell him, ADN"Y, open my lips'
Open the gates of the temple.

33a) There is the juxtaposition of prayer and the opening of the chamber of prayer. This process could be seen as separate in that the one who prays is praying to the one who listens, however the right way to look at this is to see this as part of a single process. In this case during the Amidah, the standing prayer it is the connection above and below that is being opened.

Once the gates are open meaning the connection is established then there is the interchange between above and below.

There is the identification of soul connected to that which is embodied in soul, the Divine Presence is awakened and the connection is established.

The Divine Presence the Queen acts as the conduit through which travels the prayers from below and the blessings from above.

She is the opening and the entreaty that not only awakens the perception of holiness but also seals its connection making the two prayer and blessing one.

During the Amidah the focus is attenuated above and the mechanics of prayer are explained.

At the end of the Amidah the proper form of closing the prayer-blessing operation is explained. Another kind of more advanced prayer wherein there is more of a spiritual opening is performed symbolically by Patcho"n.

The unification of Ha Kodesh Barachu and Shekinah occurs via these eighteen blessings with attention to the level of Yesod-Foundation-Generation. It is a further narrowing of focus here.

These are the levels of blessings-prayers that are being shown. A prayer becomes everlasting when placed in the context of its corresponding blessing. These vowel points and cantillation notes color the letters they enhance and in this way Shekinah arises out of he combinations of letters vowel points and cantillation marks that circumscribe the holiness in the heavens.

Consciousness frames itself in terms of the righteous, those who ask questions, masters of signs, of tefillin, of tzitzit and of charity. All of these qualities knock on the gates above and are answered accordingly. There is always a corresponding blessing for every prayer. The opening and closing of the gates refers to the alignment that takes place between the two.

We also have the idea of angels that accompany the prayers. This is like having a carrier for each prayer reminiscent of the electromagnetic waves that carry various forms of communication, i.e. radio, television, internet, etc.

In order for all of these communications (prayers-the righteous, those who ask questions, masters of signs, of tefillin, of tzitzit and of charity) to align or reach their destination above they must be guided. What they are guided by is the existing holiness which becomes the pathways along which they travel.

Now these pathways are set into their proper alignment by the blessings we send above along with our prayers. During prayer we sent our thoughts-our prayers along with those blessings from the daily rituals. In this way we provide our own carrier waves that then align themselves with the angels and in this way prayer is transformed into the blessings above that radiate then below following the permission of above. What is this permission? It is alignment above of prayer and blessing that releases the fulfilled prayer.

If we view these permissions from above like a circuit that is only tripped (opened) when a specific amount of current passes through we will see that when that current opens the switch prayers turn into blessings.

Another analogy might be like priming an engine prior to starting. The priming are the blessings which accompany or act as a carrier wave for our prayers. We send holiness above as like attaches itself to like. In this way our prayers also attach themselves becoming imbued with holiness so that as they ascend they ultimately trip or start the circuit that opens to descend with blessings.

At that time, hands of man go out...
they are gedulah gevurah, and they receive their gift.

And this is written: (Ezekiel 1:8) *And they had the hands of a man under their wings...*
What is man? He of whom it is stated: (Isaiah 44:13) *...like the glory of a man...*

33b) The 'hands of a man' refers to man's acceptance of the blessings. This acceptance occurs first above in the spiritual representation of the man that is always linked above.

What this tells us is that we must always have our spiritual counterpart linked in order to receive the prayers-blessings from above.

The prayer must also be accompanied by the accompanying blessings. This is the acknowledgment of the alignment that must take place.   Without this alignment the prayer is not fitting.

Those who are spoken to outside receive their blessings but in not as complete a form as those who are masters of prayer.

Those who understand or contemplate the knowledge of the way things work are engaged in the study of creation. This is a specific study that builds upon itself and draws the student into the study of the teacher. What they are studying is the operation of holiness and its applications above and below.

You don't have to however be a student of the 'way things work' in order to experience its effects meaning that Ha Kodesh Barachu always answers prayers no matter if those answers are understood or not because it is in the nature of the 'way things work' to answer prayers with blessings.

Those who discount the prayers or ask for that which is unseemly profane the process and are turned away. It is as if they don't believe in prayer or at least do not pay attention to its message of linking prayer with blessing.

The levels of prayer are many as are the blessings that accompany prayer that include the food and drink of sacrifices.

When you pray before you eat you give thanks for that which you have already received but in another sense you are acknowledging the process that has brought you sustenance in the first place. Without this acknowledgment you lose your sense of connection with 'the way things work,' and risk being cut off from that which you need the most.

All prayers contain within themselves the keys to the gates above knocking on them yes but also affirming the presence of these gates above as well.

It is one thing to stand and pray and another to be aware that you stand in the chamber of King. This cannot be explained except by experiencing this. It is further explained...

ADN'Y is the chamber in which YKV"K resides. "Open my lips" refers to awaken the capacity that I have for union above and let me speak within that chamber and to that unity that is ever present.

Think of it this way. When the mouth speaks prayer it assumes a place above letting go of worldly concerns and operating now in heaven or in the chamber of the above. When the intention reaches the lips it is confirmed.

Shekinah is the awareness of the knowledge of 'the way things work.' This is how prayer must begin with this perception awakened within and the sure knowledge of our communion above. If this is done properly meaning with intention, gratitude, certainty of unity and an awareness of all that is happening at once then the prayers are answered immediately and acted upon in the moment of their conception.

Here we find what the chasmal of Ezekiel are all about.
This is the glowing awareness of being inside the chamber or ADN"Y with YKV"K interspersed throughout.

Again Shekinah is the realization of connection and when this occurs then the prayers are moved along and through until they are one with the above. There is an ascension of thought that makes this possible but only with the accompanying realization of the holiness of unity.

Without the connection of Shekinah there is no entering the chamber even by a third party messenger. Shekinah, the realization of the 'way things work' must always be present to enter the chamber of Ha Kodesh Barachu.

And if the Shekinah does not rise in the same prayer as the mitzvah then HKBK cannot receive this prayer even if a messenger brings it.

And is not worthwhile of entering the chamber of the King;
and about him it is stated: (Deuteronomy 24:11) *Thou shalt stand without..*

34a) The essence of prayer is Shekinah. It is the feeling of prayer and its certainty of acceptance. You cannot enter above nor can you connect on the outside even though you say the proper form of prayer. The Divine Presence is a subtle condition that is only entered into by experience with holiness.

With Shekinah the holy name is awakened; the connection is established.

It is the awakening of Shekinah with deeds-precepts that causes Her to come forth from within. There is only one thing worthy of speaking of and that is Her awakening, or 'this.' Therefore it is from a center of certainty that there arises Shekinah as if by Herself she appears. Prayer must be based upon what it good and right so that the opening will be established making the connection above.

Prayer spoken with the earnest desire for connection that is at once mindful of holiness and yet spontaneous is the prayer that is accepted. Prayer by rote or ritual without connection is 'torn up.'

We pray to Ha Kodesh Barachu and our earnest desire to connect reveals Shekinah announcing our prayer and connecting above with the blessing(s) that are the answer to prayer. When we recognize one we receive the other.

It is the unity of Israel praying together that awakens Shekinah making the connection stronger and recognizing the progress that is made.

For these things Ha Kodesh Barachu is awakened within each of us. It is the purpose behind all that we do (our steps).

The Shema is the recognition of the unity of Shekinah and Ha Kodesh Barachu. On the level of prayer it realizing that our thoughts become one with Ha Kodesh Barachu only by the agency of Shekinah. Throughout TKZ Shekinah is defined, illumined and discussed. This may be described as the meeting of our thoughts with the unity of thought.

Once our thoughts approach the level of unity with all thoughts the unity of thought descends in that it accepts our level making it a part of its own level.

What is the inner gate of the chamber-court? It is Zeir Anpin and this is the influence of the awaiting of the word from the chamber above. This is continued next.

The chamber above is ADN"Y and it is through here that YKV"K descends in response to the unity of the Shema spoken with intention. This is a key phrase 'declare your praise.' It speaks to the idea of seeding consciousness with the ability for its own transformation. What praise does is to give prayers access to the blessings that they are calling forth.

The elements of prayer are like the levels of a thought that is unfolding. It unfolds to the left or is the lower Shekinah meaning that it seeks connection above and below and right and left. The Levites in their sanctifications cause all to come together providing a common linkage. During Shabbat is when all of these levels are available for connection.

The place between borders is that which is the domain of the higher Mother the rising of Shekinah out of which the definitions arise that are the twenty two letters that define Torah.

The words of Torah evoke Her as She comes to listen and connect above with below.

Likewise too is YKV"K evoked by the middle Pillar uniting Shekinah and YKV"K.

The extra soul is the evoked soul that comes about through Their union.

Therefore in connection is there the receipt of these extra souls on Shabbat.

The *musaph* service –this is the Righteous One,
includes all prayers which they say prayer.
And it is in the additional prayer that they say:
'A Crown (keter) they give to you YKV"K ELHYN"U…'

And the 'crown' is Higher keter, Y"Y ELKYN"U Father and Mother;

(Isaiah 6:3) *Holy, holy, holy,* the three patriarchs.
Y"Y of Hosts –covenant of circumcision
two 'thighs of truth' ...*the Earth is full of His glory* – this is Shekinah.

34b) Imagine the placing of this crown that includes the summation of all prayers defining and making you aware of the holiness of One

Now seen altogether become conscious of the maker and his prayer and the blessings and their results. All is one here.

These lips awaken the gates of the chamber for prayers to pass below and blessings above. These are two places within for the wise to ponder and know.

For there are the gates of righteousness below and YKV"K to answer from above. See them in the mind's eye.

Concatenate the letters. Make the connection the distinction between father and mother, the one inside the other.

What you make is the feeling and the impression one. This is the Tree of Life as it comes into its evolving play. Thoughts by their nature are ephemeral going right and left and yet by the unity that is YKV"K thoughts are brought together in a commonality of association. The connection between them is always One.

The Tree of the Knowledge of Good- in which there is no evil connects within itself right to left and back again the middle pillar is YKV"K meaning this is where all of the connections emanate from.

Out of these emanations of unification the image is engraved within the lower Shekinah or ADN"Y. When you read of chasmal know that this is the creative force for good that is self contained and is the breath of life, the fire of the soul.

Herein described is the cycle of thought that is always coming into being. During prayer we effectively link together thought and intention with unification meaning we have the recognition that the two are always becoming One. In bending the knee at Blessed...we acknowledge our place to be standing in unity.

Again there is the recognition of the flow of being into conception, Shekinah in operation throughout.

What does it mean to elevate prayer? It means to have in mind the consciousness of unity, the construction of the connection between Shekinah and Ha Kodesh Barachu. It is the feeling of knowing and the letting go into the unity of being.

Thought seeks to impress itself throughout the image of its making or it seeks connection until that image is made. There is the looking glass that illuminates- sending the image through. There as well the image that does not illuminate-it sends the thought through in connection with another thought and then there is an image produced.

In prayer the image is affirmed by Amen.
Amen is the affirmation of the unity and is the answer to 'let there be light' becoming 'and there was light.'
The unity expresses itself throughout the various names of God depending upon where your at in the moment

What is pertinent is that in the middle pillar the unity is always expresses singularly as YAKDVNK"Y in the merged name.

These four names are in the four parts of the tephilin (houses and scrolls) of the head to the left and right and above and below.   Imagine these as your thoughts in their flowing awakening and unifying.

A prophet is one who would seek a higher vision. By rising up with Shekinah, that is with the awareness of the feeling of connection then this prophet would be open to the unity that speaks above.

It is the aspect of holiness that the seeker of a higher vision perceives as in the four compartments of Tephilin, the four faces of Ezekiel, the four names that are unified as one. All of this comes with the awareness of the feeling of connection that must proceed the actual merging with the unity.

Therefore become acutely aware of what these four sanctifications are meant to be thought of, i.e. as the unification of the four names, the four chambers, etc

It is in the blessings that a person is like a servant receiving a reward from his master.

35a) The sequence of blessings and prayers are shown to provide the context in which these two that are one take place. We stand, we acknowledge the Supreme, we ask in the middle of Shekinah who resides there and then it is done, we receive. Following this the cycle is complete or is it? For wise yes but for those still learning it continues.

There is deepening of intention the knocking on the door, the direct link with ADN"Y the chamber of blessings

Within this chamber of blessings resides Shekinah that gives those who stand the connection of unity above.

Prayer is then the arising of Shekinah by our recognition of the name and all that it means in holiness.

It is our prayers that erect Shekinah. It is the awakening of the inner spirit of unity. Call it the soul connection.

Yes the goal is unity. It is the unified awareness that consciousness in one way or another is constantly seeking and finding. It is by our efforts, our standing meaning our active recognition and then a letting go into the unity that evolves out of this

Prayers provide the pathways of righteousness, of holiness but there must be an answering recognition otherwise Shekinah is never called to witness the transformation and therefore be its catalyst.

The lesson here is to pray with positive intention otherwise prayer is meaningless. The wise pray with intention the fool doesn't pray at all or simply goes through the motions.
The mother is affected because She is the great transformer. She is Shekinah initializing connection; She is Binah reflecting the blessings below. She is malleable. The Father only is active through connection.

Wisdom, the south and the right hand side-chokmah are positive precepts, things that we act upon to do. The south is the place of mysticism and is actively pursued. The meanings come forth only after trusting in the process of enlightenment that comes simply from trying to understand.

The negative precepts, from the left hand side-higher Mother-Binah are the things we must not do represent the filtering process of consciousness as it flows itself into being via Binah.

Repentance is the adjustment of the filter that allows consciousness to flow into form. We correct the filter recognizing that our actions have been wrong and must be adjusted for the good to appear.

On the one hand there is a letting go representing YHH"V and on the other hand a contraction a filtering YVH"H.

The place of the filter is described, the tephillin of the head. There is the permutation of the divine name rising and descending declaring itself in its various aspects. This is the understanding that one should praise above all.

Without the knowledge of these permutations and the images they convey then the proper alignment is not possible. What is sacrificed and what is offered are both levels of knowing.

The mother and the daughter refer to the process of filtering thought from above and then from below respectively.

Therefore the Higher Mother releases its transcendence while the lower Hei is its image channelled by Vav.

What is caused is the flowing into Vav, which we already learned is Shekinah. The elevation is the transformation of thought.

Intention resides in Chokmah and connects with Shekinah and continues in reflection, the brain of the son from the brain of the father. The written Torah a source of contemplation always the control in the experiment of consciousness

The oral Torah is its exposition that must be filtered with the truth of the way things work.

The prayers are meant to evoke these chaylinn that are the channels for Shekinah to flow through and connect with.

It is the consciousness of this connection with Shekinah that affects the unity with Ha Kodesh Barachu.

Israel represents the totality of our thoughts the reality of our consciousness.   This consciousness is dependent upon Shekinah to flow with the connection of Ha Kodesh Barachu.

(Proverbs 6:22) *When thou walks, it shall lead thee, when thou lies down, it shall watch over thee; and when thou awakes, it shall talk with thee.*

35b) Shekinah is the consciousness of connection ever present. She ameliorates the judgment by unification with Ha Kodesh Barachu. She stands with us in Judgment. What is this like?

A King sends the prince as emissary to a neighboring country but cautions him not to get caught up in their ways. He tells the prince to travel with his most trusted minister and to never leave her side. If he becomes separated from this minister he must seek Her out and join with Her because this is the only way he may return to Him.

Shekinah is always the precursor to the unification of thought. It is Israel unified with Ha Kodesh Barachu.

It is Shekinah that intersperses every level of thought. Now there is the aggregate of thought called the six hundred thousand. There are the six levels of prophecy and the sixty six wheels that surround the throne.

What are we to do with this? We are to envision thoughts that occur in cycles bonding together according to the level of awareness they have attained. In this sense thought is then as you imagine it to be and is indeed the sole instrument of the imagination. Taking this into account then Shekinah is also a vehicle for the imagination in terms of its connection to the unified awareness that is inherent in our design.

There is such a thing as the life of thought that is awakened via Shekinah. This life of thought blossoms and flourishes in that connection rising in levels of awareness the closer in proximity to Ha Kodesh Barachu that we are able to realize.

Now consider the actual levels of prayer described by those who enter and those who exit. What is this referring to? Those who enter are those thoughts that have raised themselves to the level of holiness and have unified their substance their meanings with Ha Kodesh Barachu. When they are complete they exit and other thoughts perhaps of lesser intensity of meaning enter but all the same they are enveloped by unity and so on it goes.

What is it then that guides these comings and goings? It is Shekinah. We envision and She enlightens meaning our pictures are sent above and then shine through Her operations of making them accessible above.

There is the image that is taken from below and placed above. This placing is Shekinah who signs in accordance with Ha Kodesh Barachu. Then there is the image that is signed that is reflected below in the form of the blessings that issue from prayers. Here the signature is Ha Kodesh Barachu.

(Psalms 51:17) *ADN"Y! Open my lips…*
And they are the masters of the sign which is the Life-force of the worlds.

36a) What is the life force of the worlds? It is the force that holds worlds together and pulls them apart akin to gravity in the universe. The sacrifices are all about the transformations of the life-force. What this suggests is that through our prayers we learn to unify and guide this life force.

The references here to Mazal speak of the higher relationships that take place in terms of the aspects we are born under. The higher Vav and the lower Vav relate to the connections we are joined with vis a vis Shekinah

The twelve zodiacal signs determine the sign for each hour and what its aspect is.

These zodiacal signs described here allude to the overarching effects of the heavens and their relationships to what we are planning and what our actions are. What is this like?

Imagine a King that has built many pathways for the water to flow into his garden. These flows may be aligned together or at right angles or in opposition to each other. When they are aligned the flows are uniform and increase their power and range. When in opposition they negate each other and when at right angles or any angle they divert the flows this way and that. The same may be inferred from the pathways of our lives and the hours of each day, the times of the seasons, etc.

All of this is according to the plan of Ha Kodesh Barachu. From above to below these signs are potentialities. From below to above they planets, or the resultant of the forces that are in play.

These signs relate to the physicality of a thing in its outward expression.

What is it that lives in the blood? It is Shekinah. For She travels in relationship to the aspects that are understood, awakened and suffusing your awareness.

What we do depends upon the consciousness we have built up from our prayers and our studies. What we awaken either moves towards judgment or beneficence.

175

At the center of the nogah is Ha Kodesh Barachu. This is where our attention has to be focused. The surrounding glow or Nogah represents the chaos, darkness and void out of which the world is made into order, light, and substance. These aspects are not the focus because they are like it says husks or flimsy representations of the holiness. When seeking Ha Kodesh Barachu be mindful of the holiness and not its outward appearing precursors.

All the while those husks are not removed from the rainbow, the rainbow is not in its illuminated colors.

36b) The rainbow without the husks displays the signs. These husks are removed by conscious viewing meaning we discard them in our seeing. In this way the holiness within is revealed. This is the holiness that accompanied the revelation of the covenant and this is the capacity for Israel to become one with Ha Kodesh Barachu. At one point man at another Ha Kodesh Barachu and at even another the two are eternally One.

The Eternal is awakened within the consciousness of man.

The navel is the point of passing a center of the power through which Shekinah passes along. It is where will is centered that is the reflection of the above through its connection with Shekinah. It is from here that all manifestation proceeds and is processed.

So it is that Shekinah spreads Herself in the four directions infusing with being all that is.

The sign of the covenant focuses the power in the navel radiating outwards for good and turning to thwart evil in the opposite direction.

The voice or Bat Kol is speaking from Shekinah to awaken the slumbering soul through its daily activities. It is the light that shines upon the mirror and reflects what is good.

The image called Jacob receives the will of Ha Kodesh Barachu and receives it purely without alteration.

The image is called to mind by its representation/reflection in the body. It is shaped there in another place as stated and it comes forth alone imbued with Ha Kodesh Barachu, the Divine will expressed.

This is the purified unmitigated Divine will.

Every thought has a center a point of reflection from which the image is shaped. Now if this center is pure and focused upon Ha Kodesh Barachu it is called Israel. If not it is called convert. Converts are those thoughts that started out initially as opposed to unity but then by the sheer weight of thoughts around it became linked to unity. However, they are not linked in their centers and are thus called refuse.

Now there are also thoughts that were linked initially with holiness and then were diminished. These thoughts like the moon that was diminished are to be renewed; their husks taken away and new clothes of holiness will surround them just as the purified thoughts called Israel exist in this similar state of being.

As soon as She Shekinah is established within the body in the totality of her Presence then the unity of purpose is revealed, the prophecy or the ability to see the clear results of all thinking will be upon all of Israel.

The body of the King is the body we make with Shekinah awakening our awareness to the holiness of Ha Kodesh

Barachu. This holiness reveals the five lights or levels of awakening.

Torah the five books are the connection Vav that opens the five lights of Hei with their Sephiros in conjunction for the expression of each adding to the fifty gates of freedom.

The masters of stature are those that recognize the awareness of the body and Shekinah. They pay attention to the bowing and the significance of the connection to Ha Kodesh Barachu brought about by Shekinah.

It is the bowing in prayer and the eighteen blessings that awaken the life force within.

37a) There is the opening of the pathways through which Shekinah flows throughout the body. This is the life force a subtle reference to the connection potential we always have with Ha Kodesh Barachu

The spreading of the leaves dilutes the flow causing a lack of focus.

The flowing of prayers and blessings are likewise affected by a dilution of focus.

The snake symbolizes the lower life force that can interrupt the thoughts that rise on high. These lower thoughts are to be ignored.

Interruptions may only take place when circumstances dictate they must.

Here is the context in which prayer takes place. We include the ten Sephiros by thinking of them during these blessings in the manner described above regarding Keter, Chokmah, Zeir Anpin and lower Shekinah or Malchus.

The sephiros are included in the body that bows which opens up the pathways for Shekinah to flow through.

Because of these actions Yosef merited this dream.
When Shekinah is flowing so too is the spirit of prophecy.

So prophecy is the opening up of the flowing of Shekinah from which it comes or arises. The reward is the sense of unity that is experienced because of this operation of bowing or opening the spine with intention.

Another example of the focus of prayer is the wrapping of Tephilin.

Now we learn that Tephilin represents a covering of the evil inclination.

The evil inclination uncovers our nakedness or rather makes us aware of the chaos that is there. The covering up acts to shield this awareness so that we are not tempted to succumb to its attraction.

Those who perform acts of kindness are opening their hands similar to the opening of the spine. All gifts are to Shekinah to open the way for Her to flow.

It is prayer that flows along the pathways established by Shekinah and the gifts to Her of opening the hands.

At that time, several *chayot* open their hands,
It is said: (Ezekiel 1:8) *And the hands of a man beneath their wings...*
They give a gift to the soul of that person, a few good gifts , from several levels of prophecy.

37b) The gift that is given is the gift that is offered. There is recognition of the way things work above and below.

Herein Shekinah awakens the capacity for even greater awareness. This is 'his portion.'

As we act we are acted upon. Our gifts above then descend below like a farmer seeding crops that yield its produce.

With the gift of Shekinah the unity is established. This is the purpose of creation to suffuse itself throughout consciousness.

In every case it is the gift of becoming open to Shekinah that awakens the unity above with Ha Kodesh Barachu by means of the vehicle of the entire body dedicated in holiness above.

At all times we ask 'what is it we are making' for what is being made is the gift that is given above and what turns into blessings below.

In the beginning there is darkness because we have no recognition of the King and His Will.

See how the primordial light of creation is described. It is related to our awareness first as a point of recognition meaning let there be the light of our awareness of the unity between thought and action.

Once we become aware of the unity of thought and form our understanding grows, i.e. it becomes colored so that with the wisdom of this insight the house is built. What is the house? It is the creation that follows that awareness.

Therefore through our increasing awareness it becomes possible to measure the expansion of creation that evolves from the single point into the five colors that determine various aspects of what comes into being.

Imagine measuring the breath in the body where it goes and where it comes in and how it not only sustains the body physical but also always infuses the body spiritual with its light.

These revolutions in their four aspects that amount to ten represents the inner connections of holiness that bring forth all that is to come to be.

They immerse themselves in the primal substance burning away the dross and perfecting the image of above.

Seven heavens are presented as levels of attainment as plateaus of fulfillment. Sephiros from Yesod to Binah and then back again. They are filled with five hundred years of coming to be bringing forth their outcome.

Look at the firmaments stacking up as bits of mica in flakes yet transparent as quartz inter penetrable as liquid and always resolving into the unity that is the image transformed.

The Sephiros are shown as a point radiated by three on each side.

With these nine points on a side you look at one inside the other the empty space being possibility that always reveals and becomes and yet remains empty or open.
Only the wise may visualize and know the meaning. Saba asked for clarification now of this meaning.

The Rabbi or the teacher within comes out of the chayot, the breath and the inspiration and reveals more.

<u>Interlude</u>

If you're looking for a sea of perfection look for it here where the night winds blow.

Seek it too in the river valleys near the edge of morning.

Sometimes if you wake up and remember there it will be out of the corner of your eye.

It rises within you even sometimes when you call.

Remember when you seek it with all your heart you will find it.

She resides within you yet her tendrils like a quickly growing vine reach all the way into the unknown and becoming world.

She is never still yet her quiescent rest is the epitome of all stillness.

Haven't you noticed that she brings forth all that you are?

When anything new appears she announces it moments before with a sense of feeling.

This sense of feeling is the making of something out of nothing.
She connects with your thoughts aligning them with holiness according to your focus and attention.

Did you know that you live inside her? Your purpose is to complete her in connection with holiness above. From the moment you were born you are in her hands.

If she had a face it would be more beautiful than anything you could imagine or ever see. Her name can only be described by those whom you love and that which you love the most.

Since she is always moving you will only see her in passing and then only as a feeling of profound Bliss, peace and indescribable harmony. Think of anything you could be and she is already there opening the door.

Tiqun 19

בראשית שם ב"ת. וזו בת נקודה סתומה באויר. עליה נאמר שמרני כאישון בת עין.

Bereishis –daughter is there.
And this daughter is the point hidden in (the word) the air אויר
This is what is said: (Psalms 17:8) *Keep me as the apple of the eye..*
She must be concealed in the light אור in which is made air אויר.

And why, it is said: (Shemos 3:2) *And the angel of the YKVK
appeared unto him in a flame of fire out of the midst of a bush.*

Five times bush סנה is mentioned and likewise five times light is mentioned in the act of creation;
and they are: (Shemos 1:3-5) 1)*Let there be light, and 2)there was light &
3) the light for it was good, 4) ELKY"M divided between the light, 5)And
ELKY"M called the light...*

38a) The daughter is the image that has been conceived, the point within, the empty space surrounded by dots and out of her is made the air which flows through and into everything animating life and synchronizing it with the above.

What is the five times light? It is the series of emanations that progressively build the nexus of creation that is making itself continuously. The answer lies as always between the lines. The first emanation, the first light is the recognition of the pre-eminence of light; it is the effusion of inspiration, the thought that is the image.

Next 'there was light,' is appearance of light, the image that is the reflected light.

Then 'light that was good' is the confirmation of the light analogous to Tipheres on the Tree of Life that confirms the emanations that have gone forth.
Subsequently the light is divided into the firmaments above and below.

Finally "called the light" Above represents day or appearance of the constructed form. Below represents the primal substance, the darkness out of which the light is continuously reborn.

These five from Chesed to Hod are described once again with Tipheret in the middle. Look inside the divine name to see Hei and its mirror image, the four out of which the ten are seen.

Yud from the air or Higher Keter animates the Sephiros, as the image keeps on becoming more of itself.

These five hundred years introduce the time span into the imagination expanding the thoughts so that in their depth they may then become compressed into the matter of becoming.

Always there is the image, that which the imagination holds on to and lets go. Details of the inner structures too are imagined even to the place where these imaginings take place.

What are these kingdoms? They are the various images that are to be reflected. None of these reflections impinge upon each other because of the thread that separates them.

This thread is also an imagined thing and yet it is super important for the entire process to remain in its proper place.

Were these images to intermingle yes there would be chaos because then Ha Kodesh Barachu would be veiled inside these images and chaotic associations would take place. Every image is the dwelling place of Ha Kodesh Barachu.

Likewise does a thread separate the written Torah and Oral Torah. The understanding of one is separate from the insights one receives about it. These insights then have a life of their own making up the holiness that surrounds Torah, the Chayot so to speak. One is the source and the other the Oral Torah is the outcome.

The locked garden is the closed focus around which we study the Torah bringing forth in the moment the Oral Torah which are our thoughts about Torah.

On Shabbat our understanding is opened to share with Ha Kodesh Barachu our insights in awakening Shekinah that is always present.

It is the organization of the hierarchy of levels of imagination. Imagination as in the ability of the images to bring forth the reflections of their intended form. On Shabbat those extra souls are indeed helpers for the process to maintain the thread of separation while expanding the awareness of each level individually.

These levels are closed to those who do not become one with those extra souls opening and receiving the addition that is added to them.

It is the extra soul that connects the levels in unity working together while keeping the distances coherent meaning the integrity of each is kept intact.

On Shabbat the extra soul is added, however when it is not then blessings do not result.

38b) By denying the Shabbat extra soul the flowing of Shekinah is static and the inspiration of the day is missing. Out of this nothing comes and what has been added are taken away and blessings do not come through.

By promoting the Shabbat and accepting the extra soul, the garden is tilled and the plants flourish meaning our thoughts that are now on these various levels of unfolding to receive the blessings of reflection promoting them into being the warehouse of our good.

Every seed of thought produces souls of its own making that are nourished by Shekinah until the time is right for them to express themselves, which they do on Shabbat and the festivals.

The opening that occurs is the palette upon which the image that first awakens is colored with the particulars of the first inkling of connection between the thought and the form. These openings and closings are links themselves attaching to each other and then separating.

The letter Yud is symbolic of Keter representing the first awareness of the way things work. My sister is the complement, the image that is capable of reflection on the second day. The third day 'my beloved' represents the inspired proof of the image, and then 'my dove' who is the companion of 'my beloved' goes out to announce the image.

Then the entire world is imbued with the image declaring 'my perfect one.'

There can be no other response to the way things work other than an acceptance of the blessings that this enables.

Therefore on the sixth day this acceptance is shown. Man who appears is both the recipient and the offspring of this acceptance. Man is by extension Israel or those who have accepted the covenant for themselves.

The seventh day the recognition of Creation the hidden Yud becomes the revealed Yud within the Beit or its dagesh.

Consider that the dew of Torah is the awakening of Shekinah. Here especially during her time called Shabbat via the insights of the week Shekinah is there to revive and connect these meanings with their unified home in Ha Kodesh Barachu.

All of this takes place throughout the seven firmaments each mirroring the other cascading in effect the distillation of holiness understood each to his or her own discernment.

It this qualified discernment that enables the Tzadiq to apprehend the differences between the levels especially in this highest heaven of Raqi'a. The waters above where the image is born and the waters below where the image is animated and lives and moves and has its being. It is a thread of difference that distinguishes them and this thread is the study of the Righteous.

So yes this thread or strand of hair is the connection of holiness above. It is the Vav or connection that ascends above and below each without end.
This measure of the body is for the awareness of the body as light is changing the perspective from the material to the spiritual.

So we see how one dimension of ten is applied to every part of the body. Each part may be measured by Yud.

In the opening of the hand or qame"tz the levels are clearly delineated and time is constant, a five hundred year span.

When it descends meaning when the thought that is contemplating this matter seeks within, it seeks through the various dimensions of Sephiros. When it ascends finding a meaning and then relating that meaning above it is called stature because we are attaching the known to the unknown standing level after level one based upon the other.

In the counting of the Omer there is contemplation and meditation. Meanings result which are the purified levels of the higher and lower Shekinah.

Which purifies the lower Shekinah through which the lower Shekinah is purified regarding Her husband, through the mikveh (this): (Jeremiah 17:13) *The mikveh of Israel is YKV"K.*

39a) The only purification that ever takes place is the immersion into YKV"K.

The form is purified in terms of whatever dross has attached itself to it during its period of unfolding from inspiration or initiation into the actual thing itself.

The alignment of a thing is not fully established unless it is able to flow effortlessly from above to below and then again from below to above. This is what is meant by stature. It also relates to the alignment of the spine, which determines the flow of Shekinah.

The forty-nine faces of purity refer to the process of the image making that is made passing through into form

Therefore the two faces, Oral and Written are one inside of the other, one being born out of the other continuously.

All first born or the initial image that is represented by Keter above fills within itself the holiness that is coming to be.

This holiness is flowing via the Sephiros one opposite the other balancing the flow and purifying it at the same time.

How else could this be? The relationships between the image and its unfolding reveal progressively more and more as one passes on the attributes of the other.

There is a sharing of substance, which must be because all is one substance and what appears comes out of the transformations that molded above and shaped below.

Here are the channels of flow centralized in the middle Pillar via which Shekinah passes Her essence out to every part of the body.

Shekinah is there because every movement is a direct result of Her unity with Ha Kodesh Barachu. Her unity is symbolized by the Vav of connection coming from the Yud the wellspring of the image making and then Hei which is its extension.

The nine channels in the garden of Shekinah each portion of Torah representing another insight, another tie to the whole. She arises with the nine channels, the nine Sephiros from Her to above.

Shekinah remains true to the image above passing its reflection above as a fountain returns the waters that it receives continuously in a loop of flow. She is the crown of Vav because She is the connection that is continuously taking place with Ha Kodesh Barachu.

The six channels representing Zeir Anpin and Ana BeKoach are the forty two divine letters

There is no division of unity. It remains the same as crown or as lower Shekinah from beginning to the end.

How are the heavens stretched? Consider your thoughts that awaken after they have been first brought forth. Each moment opportunities for connection occur expanding the original thought focusing it more and more, distilling it. As this happens thoughts fill the consciousness like stars in the heavens. These thoughts are arranged and expanded upon.

She is above She is below. Learn how to see her everywhere.

She exalts from above and sustains from below like the vowels do in terms of the letters they color.

From chokmah is called chole"m, and on the Middle Pillar is called shure"q.
It is called...(Yirmyahu 2:21) *Yet I had planted thee a noble vine, wholly a right seed;*
As it is said (Michah 7:20) *Thou wilt show faithfulness to Jacob*

39b) Consciousness becomes of itself what it has made from its highest intentions. Therefore YKV"K arranges things so that man may complete the divine nature.

Each definition of the Divine word is a truth that is revealed just as the vowel points reveal the true nature of the word.

It is here in the middle pillar where Shekinah arises and flows to every part of the body unifying the image with its reflection. This searching-unifying is Shekinah in its movements.

The mystery of shire"q is the discovery of Shekinah within knowing Her movements and recognizing Her intentions for unity.

Therefore the light of Shekinah is that which is revealed in insights that are the result of Torah study and all contemplations of the Divine.

The unity of the expressions of the vowel points shows the unity that Shekinah reveals in Her movements in connection with Ha Kodesh Barachu. One is an allegory for the other.

Now in the consideration of the possibilities there is always judgment and mercy in terms of how an event should turn out. What we learn here is that it is out of the mixture that we obtain the truth of what is to be.

Malchus is the event that has come to be and She who is Shekinah after another fashion. Her coming to be is a fluid occurrence albeit seemingly solid in nature. The wine barrels symbolize the aspect of time, the aging process and the dimension of time as another variable.

In Tipheret the thing that is to come to be gives off the scent of what must become. Her destination is the barrels via the Middle Pillar which is the Intention that carries Her (Shekinah) to her resting or manifestation place in Malchus.

She is made into a segol meaning she is made into the mixture of what is coming to be -the apples that are formed by the focus of Intention-Connection-Vav.

Here is the confirmation of the previous supposition i.e. 'YKV"K ELKY"M formed.'

It is via the continuous flowing of Shekinah that the ground is both seeded and bears fruit. Her love in unity with Her husband is the Intention that becomes a flow in effect spiritualizing the unformed into the forms of love.

If there is any blockage of this flow the ground becomes dry and does not give forth its fruit.

These wellsprings symbols of flowing and the vowel's that open and close are their counterparts in the expressions of words and phrase and the concepts of Creation.

The running and returning refers to Shekinah in its flowing to and from. We are given the vowels as pictures for the imagination to contemplate in order to understand the deeper significance of Shekinah in Her flow.

The crowns depend upon thought, the vowel points on speech. When you have a thought it arises to join with unity depending on your Intention and the accumulation of holy thoughts produces these crowns. The vowel points are what colors what each word and phrase takes on and they are the precursors to the action of the outworking of form.

Here the distinction is between the thoughts of the heart and mind and then the speech of the mouth symbolized by the taginns. Everything is a symbol for something else. In this way we learn of the way Shekinah connects above through symbols that go all the way from thought to speech to action.

The repeated visualization of a thought produces this hidden throne about which it is said Atah. This becomes the object of focus and because of this it becomes imbued with holiness that at a certain point radiates that holiness. It is concealed because what takes place happens of itself as the awareness changes state from active Intention to hidden mystery.

The power of what relates to the connections that take place whenever we look deeper into the mystery. We keep asking the questions and with the proper focus we raise level by level the awareness of the mystery.

It is the higher unity of YKV"K ELKYN"U YKV"K
This is the higher King. If this power is withdrawn…
(Lamentations 1:6) *they are gone without strength before the pursuer..*

40a) The higher unity is that which goes beyond the limits of the current reality. It is the ability to think and act within the context of the divine.

You have the strength of creation when you are able to place yourself there at the moment of its inception.

"You" is the moment of creation. It is your realization of both the act and it's continuous nature.

"Established" is the realization of unity, which is continuously with the matter whether he was standing or sitting down. This refers to the act of prayer which is a standing and sitting down operation.

It is as if you are in the midst of the divine. Because of this you understand the way things work. Then acting accordingly the Unity is complete.

You are the One. You dwell forever. It is about You that is stated, Father, our King, Our father is You. Answering amen means you affirm the unity with the Eternal. This is the purpose of connecting above which is to acknowledge and to become one with that which you are seeking.

The Father is that which has been accrued for you and which then acts to produce for you the blessings you are praying for.

It is the result of the prayers and the seeding process spoken of above. It is the result of your contemplation of every word of Torah. The middle pillar which is Shekinah becomes active because of the Intention of the Father thus explained.

The throne is made generation-by-generation, meaning that our thoughts that seed consciousness go through transformations which bring about what is called the throne. It is the purpose of standing prayer too to keep this throne in place in terms of our awareness of the process that is going on.

When we reference the looking glass we are alluding to the awareness that is taken from the reflection of the throne.

Our thoughts begin to recognize themselves and the connections, which they are making.

Therefore with this awareness awakened the high priest enters the holy of holies.

The will that is extracted is the awareness of the part that Intention plays within Consciousness in terms of directing its influences

We act for YKV"K when we seed consciousness with Intention.

The time for Intention is during prayer when our thoughts are raised on high.

You approach the sacred wearing the high priest's garments which are your highest thoughts and then your Intention is for connection on high.

Our prayers reach on high via Shekinah which is the holy connection that is produced by letting go and listening and then moving along your Intention via her pathways called the Tree of Life.

David produced favor with YKV"K by his songs of praise. This was his seeding of consciousness meditating upon the Divine both night and day.

The heart of good is the realization of our Intention to do good. In this way we pray with an active direction in mind and recognize that every prayer is a seed that brings forth blessings.

So we see that all blessings come from prayers directed with Intention above.

Without awareness prayers are meaningless. They must be directed with awareness in order for connection to occur.

We make the name holy by our holy thoughts about the Name. It is 'this' which is being explained here in between the lines.

All of our prayers during every service have this end in sight to seed consciousness with good producing the answering good blessings.

The epitome of thought is its source because ultimately we are the reflection of that source. When thoughts arise it is up to us to color them with praises and strive for holiness transforming even the most base thoughts into their heavenly flights of return.

as David said: (1 Chronicles 29:11) *To You, YKV"K, is the greatness, and the power...*

And there is no action effected with those below but by malkhut,

It is said: (Psalms 103:19) *...and His kingdom rules over all..*

But while the need for Ha Kodesh Barachu to be righteous to the
Righteous One.
and to make it right the kingdom, which is malkhut below included in all
the sephiros
and they are called righteous by name.
YKV"K is called *the righteous one* as is said:
(Psalms 145:17) *The YKV"K is righteous in all His ways,*

40b) It is the proof of a thing that testifies to the sovereignty
of its source.   Malchus is the proof of Keter and the
stabilizing link that brings everything into perfect operation.

Ha Kodesh Barachu is righteous when all is in alignment
above and below. This is the alignment of all the Sephiros.

The righteous are the reflections of YKV"K mirroring in their
actions the source above.

It is via prayer that we set up all the blessings that are to
come. We see that in the word Tzedekah the various elements
of prayer. The Tzadi stands for the ninety amens. The dalet
for the 4 sanctifications, the quph for the 100 blessings and
the hei for the 5 books of Moses.

We must take on the aspects of prayer as a workman takes on
the plans of an architect. These plans exist in the mind of the
architect but are not realized until the workman executes each
of the instructions that he has received to complete the
dwelling.

Righteousness is the ability or awareness to recognize that
every good action produces a good result.

The end result of righteousness is good which from the
standpoint of Hei is Malchus or the result of good. From Yud
it is what we carry with us.   Our awareness of source and
seeking of source are always with good intentions in mind

In terms of Vav it is our holy connection, the central channel of becoming all that is good endless in its measure.

All the Sephiros participate in the transformations that result in righteousness and it is indeed for this that we are awakened to the proper way to think about things.

The descriptions that are depicted in our imaginations are the results that the prophets bring forth as if by a mirror of reflecting that which is above on to that which is below which takes the form of the above and expresses it completely.

These operations of reflections take place throughout the holy hierarchy one mirroring the other unifying with each other always doing the will of the Creator.

Herein is described the levels of imagination from the highest on down one above the other endlessly.

The imagination of the prophets represents their discernment. The rulership of Ha Kodesh Barachu can be seen in the levels of awakening awareness.

Amen with all his strength represents the acknowledgment of this idea and its miraculous flowing into the various levels called forms after another fashion.

The infinite is spelled out throughout existence reflecting one to the other all partaking of the Divine Essence.

There in Malchus the evidence of this principle is where this unity and connection are constantly renewed.

In each of the Sephiros is this knowledge of the unity of Keter and Ha Kodesh Barachu in the way things work.

So here it is, from the potential to the actual describing what is coming to be in the processes of Creation.

The mystery of speech, the expression of thought all included in Shekinah the connection along which all travel amidst holiness.

We can see that throughout the study of the letters we also find the reflections above and below which are the cantillation marks and the vowel points.

In the middle there is Shekinah which is Ya"H from BYNa"H wherein this awareness arises from.

And it is the sign אות of the Righteous One, which is included in את. This is the lower Shekinah, which includes all the letters from Aleph to Tav.

41a) This is something that you should be aware of with each breath. All the letters provide the means for expressing the holy Righteous One.

Herein described are the letters and the way they patch themselves together one upon the other. In similar fashion our thoughts take from one and then the other to make up the conceptual reality that we use as a backdrops for our life experience.

The three Vav's of Hei represent the inner structure that is impressed upon consciousness via the eighteen blessings.

The middle pillar is where all connect to. The righteous maintains this middle pillar via these prayers and like minded actions.

Therefore what is being made as the body of thought is the promised fulfillment of thought symbolized by the covenant.

The Vav in between the Hei's of YKV"K is this dimension of stature which is the consciousness of the building of the holy temple within via prayers and right actions.

We see then the evolution of the letters out of parts of one letter making the whole of another. In like fashion then is consciousness made up of the same kinds of relationships.

See that this 'switching of the letters' refers directly to the body of thought that is being formed. Each connection becomes holy as it attaches itself to holiness.

Most certainly are the vowels included in this measuring of stature and they may be compared to emotions since emotions are what give thought their meanings.

We can take this further and describe the ethereal terms of consciousness as the parts of the soul, nephesh, ruach and neshamah, etc. Every description has its counterpart.

When we become self aware then we recognize that our light stems from above and that we are the candle, our soul is on fire from above in the three colors seen in the candle.

The olive oil represents the transformations that are consumed by the body referring to the experiences of life. Shekinah appears when this candle is lit and is fundamentally the operation of connection. The circumcision is thereby seen as the cutting away of the dross in order to purify the flame which is our soul.

This ga"d or coriander is what Israel ate. Their food was the spirituality of Shekinah or recognition of the Divine realization of the way things work. This is what sustained them during their travels.

Therefore the mystery of manna is Ha Kodesh Barachu telling us that what they ate of was the essence of holiness.

What is included in the ten letters that are YU"D K"E VA"V K"E
and this is the manna of the Torah, which indicates *what* 45 - מה
and he did not know *what* מ'ה.

And the mixed multitude asked for flesh, and He gave it to them; and what is said…
(Numbers 11:33) *While the flesh was yet between their teeth, ere it was chewed, the anger of the YKV"K…*

41b) The mixed multitude demanded to see the manifestation of the forms of their desire. If they desired holiness it was given if they desired less than holiness it was given. The manna that came down, the flesh was a gross exaggeration of substance. Seeing it as something to extract the holiness from it was fine. When engorged upon it brought decay to those who consumed it.

The core of the Holy Name is Yud and Hei deriving its essence from the two letters and their interactions. Compare this to two holy thoughts that come together in an awesome expression of holiness. Each of the holy Names are tied to a Sephirah according to their place on the Tree of Life.

The ten Sephiros bring out the Shekhinah which operates amongst all ten flowing up and down.

The crown and the thread; these are all allusions to the way that thoughts flow together.

The lip is the sling of the thoughts that flow into words spoken.

These five stones represent the levels of awareness one above the other that transcend the material into the spiritual.

The unification of these five stones or the five words of the SHMA resolving to Echad or One is purpose of putting our attention here. The SHMA attaches itself to each part of your thinking making your thoughts resolve in unity.

Now when the unification calls for gevurah then there must be this correction. When things get too far out of hand there is this correction that the SHMA implements

Likewise when the overflowing of consciousness in its perception of good reaches the saturation point there is abundance and likewise at the point of Tipheres, mercy.

What we see is how a subtle difference in placing the vowels determines the various aspects that are attributed to the Patriarchs. All of this points to the transformations of thought that are caused by the focus upon unity which acts as a magnet bringing all thoughts into a unified focus.

It is thought that is the wondrous and hidden designer and that which brings about all that we see. Abel brought about his death by first having the idea which Cain then picked up on and followed through.

The hidden of all thought is the awareness of the way things work. It is an insight into the big picture and the part that each of us plays. Once Adam lost his awareness of the way things work his actions were not connected to their consequences which is why he died because once you realize the significance of the way things work immortality in consciousness is the number one take away.

It the Name of Y'ud, is unsurpassable but He that created everything,and no one who creates it. That the Creator created such as as water and the herbs and grows them but itself it is not created.

42a Until you recognize the true nature of the unity which is the continuous nature of reality then any thoughts of directing this reality are unsuccessful. It is an intuitive recognition that relates to that hidden thought which is the maker of all things.

Therefore it is through Yud that the created comes into being with a process of creation that in and of itself reflects that Creator creating as in all things. By extension it is this Yud that is the connection with higher thought, i.e. hidden thought.

It is the mystery called Aleph that is presented to us here. Is this mystery that brings forth everything that is to come. The letters image themselves and become as one to both themselves and the above and below. One aspect of a letter as we can see is contained in another.

The Tree of Life is the result of the separation of light from darkness meaning the good from the bad. Now the bad was mainly theoretical construct or rather a misread sense of the good. When however this construct was followed instead of attaching to the good what happened was the exile of Israel the separation into the Shekinah and the nations.

The Name is intact. It is One. There is no other. It is way things work. It is the realization of unity that makes the Name what we can conceive. No letters may be taken away. Always it appears just as it will for its own meaning and our sense of wonder. Beyond this the letters are all taken together to produce the mystery that is One.

Tiqun 20

בראשית ברא עלקים אלקים, מ״י אל״ה. עליו נאמר שאהו מרום עיניכם וראו מי ברא אל״ה.
(Genesis 1:1) In the beginning, ELKY"M created

ELKY"M [is the same letters as] M"Y ELe"H (who are these?)
About that it is said:
(Isaiah 40:26) Lift your eyes up high and see Who (M"Y) has created
these (ELe"H).

Tiqun 21

ברשית. ירדו שם שהי זקנים. ואמרו התעסקנו במה שהיינו. שהייתם ואנחנו לא
היינו (ולא היינו וזה ב׳ שנים ראשית. הרי הזכן העליון ירד ביניהם. אמר הרי
אנחנו אהד. ושלש היינו), ועתה אנחנו אחד. אלקי״ם ודאי מ״י ברא אלה. מ״י
ברא באלו שלש. והיא רביעית ושביעית (וחמשית) (ותשיעית).
Two sages came to speak about the letter Beit and that there were two
Beginnings and the higher sage spoke about the one, the three and again
the one ELKY"M
See who created these? See who created with these three, and She is the
fourth,
and seventh (and fifth)(and the ninth).

42b) The definition of Creation is resolved by internal inquiry. You ask who are these in reference to the letters to discern their inner meanings and what lies behind them.

The two beginnings are one from the higher level and another from the lower level one the reflection of the other.

These sages are the working out of the thought process that determines the inner workings of Creation.

We are one, Keter, we were three, Keter Binah and Chokmah and then resolving to one which is above Keter unknown. The fourth is Chesed by extension there is the seventh, Netzach which also is the result of three the Triad Tipheres, Netzach, Hod.

We see the symbols of the Sephiros in terms of Creation and higher thoughts (the elders) what brings down their influence (the daughter-Shekinah) and the result earth or Malchus. The seven weeks of the counting of the Omer or the seven weeks following Passover to Sinai representing the revelation.

The enemy of the snake are the angels the prayers for good.

The snake represents the sins of Israel. They are victorious with gevurah meaning that they restrict the effect of these sins and reverse their consequences.

Imagine that sins are dense materials placed within a liquid called consciousness and these make it increasingly difficult for there to be a free flowing of above to below and visa versa. These angels, these prayers have the effect of dissipating this dense material dissolving it and adding to the free flowing of prayers above and below.

They fall meaning they dissipate from sins into nothing.

This sea is consciousness and because the Shema said twice daily in the morning and before retiring in the evening (and also in the evening Maariv service) serves as the backbone of consciousness. Into this backbone all sins are cleansed if there is teshuvah or repentance meaning nothing further is added to muddy those waters of consciousness or the sea into which those riders were thrust.

The prayer of the poor man is he who is poor in the wisdom of prayer so that even though he prays he cannot do so with the conviction of one who is rich in the wisdom of prayer meaning what is being added to consciousness all along.

Shekinah helps by uniting together the prayers of the "poor" so that they all ascend together.

The prayer of the poor cannot be interrupted by the sins that creep up within thoughts because the prayers must continue in order to take the focus away from the sins and place it upon the thoughts

There must be no interruption because it negates the purpose of prayer and might cause the sins to overwhelm the prayers.

Now in such a case that the sins rise to the level of a scorpion meaning they are poised to destroy the person because they cannot shake off the repetitive nature of the sins the prayer can be interrupted because we must not let holiness of prayer become contaminated with overwhelming sin.

The uprooting of Shekinah is the severing of the connection of prayer that occurs when the focus becomes directed toward the sin and not towards its abeyance.

The circumcision releases the attachment to sin.

He said to them: 'My father is one great fish;
when he is with thirst he opens his mouth and swallows the sea,
and for seventy (or seven) years the sea does not return to its strength.
And the mystery of the matter:

(Job 40:23) ... *he is confident, though the Jordan rush forth to his mouth.*

43a) The great fish is the awareness that swims in the sea of consciousness; this awareness swallows all lesser representations of awareness and out of this awareness is where we would gain the knowledge of the way things work. Rabbi Hamnuna the Elder is a character that appears throughout the Zohar as a sage that offers insights often astounding the students with his wisdom.

Rabbi Hamnuna the Elder is the appellation of revelation- the wisdom that is received on high.

The killing of the snake refers to the subduing of the evil inclination or the negative worldly thoughts that take away from the meditative state. The daughter that is the wife that is given for whoever kills the snake is Shekinah.

The oral Torah the zahav or gold are the lessons that are given on high from the standpoint of connection with Shekinah which is the connecting flow of the Sephiros.

The law that is decided is the operation of the way things work and this is being discussed-learned for the sake of the higher connection that is established by Shekinah or the daughter of the King.

Moshe - Shiloh symbols of transcendence. The snake or evil inclination is subdued and our thoughts rise above to another level of awakening that produces the state of mind that is unified with all that is.

The snake is killed by the realization of unity no matter where this takes place within our thoughts (the sea), our actions (the land) or at the highest point of our aspirations (unity).

The battle with the snake takes place within our thoughts.

When we learn to reject the lower thoughts we win. It is in Torah that is a microcosm of consciousness unified that shows us via our insights (the eyes) the way. Sometimes those insights go astray and must be cast aside like the horses and their riders in the sea.

Israel is the recognition of unity that passes over on dry land and does not get engulfed with the evil inclination

Just as the redemption takes place in the physical sea so too does it also take place in the sea of unity that is Torah. It is when we find ourselves guided by the precepts of Torah that this redemption or unity of purpose is realized.

Writing is a special form of focused attention in that we are able to go back over our words carefully editing them leaving out the snake or the evil inclination and revealing the arm of YKV"K. Writing also gives us the confidence of seeing our thoughts revealed and recognizing their divine nature.

The evil snake is removed by consciousness, awareness of the unity of being. The holy snake is the awareness that then instead of crawling on the ground rises up akin to the action of Shekinah.

The ships that travel in the sea are our thoughts and conceptual understandings that builds the world for us. The Leviathan that "you" have created is this world of cause and effect in which we do indeed play within.

It is the knowledge of the way things work that constitutes the Leviathan. The walls are that which we enclose ourselves in i.e. our bodies. Who do we look to? We look to the Righteous One who gives us our manna meaning who allows us to see the results of our thinking and to act accordingly to become more united with that thinking. The six days of Zeir Anpin are the gathering of thoughts from above prior to their transformation into forms below.

The Leviathan above is the Righteous One,

Higher Shekinah is the sea. Lower Shekinah is:
(Proverbs 30:19) *the way of a ship in the midst (heart) of the sea*, this is le"v
(32) mentions of ELKY"M in the act of creation.

43b) The sea is used as a metaphor for our thoughts and the thinking process itself. Presiding over this thinking process is the Righteous One meaning that which spreads a cover of unity over all that we may attach to it via the agency of Shekinah. Now the arguments of Talmud are for the specific purpose of finding connections within Torah to align with everyday life. These same arguments go this way or that and point to a unification that is being sent from above. It is being sent via the seven heavens, the seven within the seven, one superimposed upon another.

All of these heavens represent layers or levels of attainment that link again to each other via Shekinah which is the recognition of the realization of unity. For ultimately it is Shekinah that resolves areas of dispute by simply placing the harmony of unity above all along with the realizations of Torah that are the main reasons why these discussions take place at all.

These masters of defense are those thoughts that protect us from the evil inclination. They are the horses, the riders, the shields, the swords all of these implements of war which arrange themselves just so that the evil inclination does not gain a foothold. This is a battle that is ongoing until the time of Moshiach and yet each day we resist we open the door to the attainment of that state of unity that is the middle pillar to which all our thoughts may attach themselves to.

By definition the unity of thought requires connection. What is this connection? It is the tying together of a phrase in Torah with a higher principle that keeps growing until a spark raises it to another more sublime level. Why this constant rising above? This is because it is the nature of thought that the higher you reach the more sublime is its message and the more it applies universally. The deepest part of the mystery is its ability to connect one thing to another endlessly.

The stronghold of the Righteous One is the unification that is constantly taking place there with conscious awareness of every meaning and a constant learning of the deeper insights that have yet to appear.

and they are netzach and hod (the righteous ones), the mighty forces of the earth.

And this rock (It is said that there is removed from it
only drops , drop of the Torah in these section, because Moses smote the rock with his staff, two times. This caused just few drops to come out (of the rock)
(Isaiah 28:10) ...*here a little, there a little.*

44a) These mighty ones of netzach and hod are the pillars of the entire process of the way things work and are the rising of awareness that is sure based upon the truth of Torah. This is shown by in the switch of letters, tany"a which shows the progression of thoughts (statements) that have brought about the present reality.

These drops are those insights that evolve out of the connecting influences of Shekinah.

Now it is important in fact crucial that we make the right connections between thoughts between words, etc. This is because an improper connection like the water that comes forth because of physical strength and anger at Marah causes Moshe to lose his way spiritually and by extension affects all of Israel. The right connection comes as a result of Shekinah which makes the connection between above and below or in the case of the waters between the thought of water coming from the rock and the issuing of it thenceforth. "My word is like fire," meaning it penetrates everywhere and consumes everything including the mitzvah of the rock bringing out the water from within its substance.

Unless we understand that the word of HVH"Y is a word of transformation than our words will not have their true meanings and will become embittered, senseless and random in terms of our life experiences. When we allow Shekinah to guide our thoughts in terms of the connections we make then every word has meaning and these meanings conduct themselves in the holy work of the transformation of matter from ideation into actualization.

Therefore it is alluded that those sacred verses of Shemos 14:19-21 wherein the three Vav's are stated were the epitome of those transformations that took Israel out of the materiality of Egypt and into the spirituality that is Torah.

These are the statements that are the mighty ones, the foundation of all that is to come afterwards and the signal lesson that all of Torah is pointing us towards.

We are directly shown the sparks of inspiration that lead along the pathways of Shekinah via those drops that issue from the brain, the skull, and work their transformation throughout the body both locally or individually and globally the entire body of the universe that is also subsequently affected.

Shekinah sweetens the waters in that She is the presence amongst those drops that come forth. She is the branch also that is placed in the bitter waters to make them sweet.

(Shemos 2:6) ... *and watered the whole face of the ground.*
When it ascends, it does ascends through Mother, which is the aleph of ADN"Y EHY"H.
Who ascends? The Middle Pillar which is Vav for it is wound around it like a ring on a finger.

44b) The earth is irrigated meaning the body which in turn represents all the face of the earth.

This ascension is a curious event. It easier to understand the descending influence which is the result of insights learned from the making of connections above that share their essence, the drops, that filter below. However the ascension implies another kind of process that takes place.

This ascending influence is the expectation of unity. Call it perhaps the aspiration of unity. It is the rising up via the middle pillar partaking of the essences that are divine on the right and the left. What happens then is in preparation for the descending influence from above. How can we prepare? The answer is in our verses of praise that we say each day. This is what establishes within the template of our awareness the points of connection that will then partake of the descending influences. Like a puzzle the pieces must fit together perfectly and in harmony.

The examples of the Tree of Life are given to provide the mind with a focal point for the meeting of descending and ascending influences.

There is a calling from below which elicits the three drops from above linking thoughts below inexorably with those that are descending. It is a meeting of the mind so to speak wherein the various synergies of above and below are harmonized via the middle channel and the agency of Shekinah.

Now these three drops also symbolize the three Yuds as Creation takes place according to a series of reflections and imaging from above to below.

There is the higher yud above the letter Aleph, the yud in extension that is the diagonal in the middle and lower yud attached to the right hand part of the Aleph

What is the bow? It is the teachings of R. Shimon that reaches up to bring forth the drop that is descending, i.e. the connection of Shekinah.

Now visualize the lessons that ascend at first as a Vav and then higher forming the yud and then into the form of Zayin. This is all in preparation for the connection that is to happen from above to below, or the below meeting the above.

The directing of the bow is the conscious recognition that these lessons are for the purpose of making this specific connection so that when properly aligned the drop descends and finds its place amongst the lessons that ascend.

The symbolism of the sword and the sheath, the Shin with its crowns the three drops of segolt"a are for the purpose of allowing us to see the inner meanings that are attached in terms of how consciousness operates. It raises inspiration through these three crowns called Torah, Kingship and Priesthood by showing that the levels of awakening correspond to first the aspiration which is priesthood, and the will to become holy. Then there is the command of holiness meaning our inner acceptance of the process and finally its application to Torah which is the pinnacle of holiness.

Out of this the holy names one inside the other the sword inside of its sheath. There is the protection of awareness which is the knowledge of the way things work and the application of that awareness which is the sublime understanding of unity.

Shekinah is the connection between above and below. There is no avenue to holiness except through her or the state of being that she represents. In order for the flame to burn within the coal it must be ignited by Vav which represents Shekinah the holy connection. It is the middle pillar surrounded by Heh on each side. The five lights are Binah through Tipheres that are indicative of the five colors the five ways of looking through the lens of holiness.

The reality must be seen in its totality. You cannot have one without the other since one depends upon the other for its relationship. The connection when it is realized is the reminder of the holy covenant or the bond that exists between all things above and below.

Through this revelation Shekinah is shown to be the connection between above and below between the two holy names and in addition her operations are described as their effects below that are realized through the Sephiros.

The heart of the matter is Shekinah. She is the bridge to holiness, the crown upon the head of all our understanding. She resolves the argument she arouses unifying at the same time inspiring.

The husband of Shekinah is the knowledge of her works meaning the operations that she takes part in. She cannot be aroused except by that hidden understanding which seeks to unify phrases in Torah or to discover the hidden meanings within Torah.

The will is elevated with the knowledge of the way things work since it is through this understanding that the holy names are spoken properly and in the right context. In addition the sharing of this revelation, the writing of it comes through the unique place of listening within and transmitting that which has been received.

And the Names ascending like the birds and the chayot of the Chariot
They come towards each other and carry the essence upwards.

Shekinah in prayer
Ascending to HKBK

Like this...
(Psalms 68:14) When ye lie among the sheepfolds,

Shekinah rising in prayer to her husband HKBK

45a) Pre-existent and in fact Eternal are those thoughts of holiness that are represented by the angelic beings of the Chariot. It is these whirling centers of holiness that are the proving ground for new revelations and when they are accepted become a part of this holiness forever.

Shekinah is elevated with a conscious awareness of intention to unify with Ha Kodesh Barachu the unity residing ever present above.

There is a progression of holiness that takes place via the morning, afternoon and evening prayers. It is a matter of what we attach ourselves to. In the morning it is EL the awesome mystery of existence that is behind everything. In the afternoon it is ELKYM or the knowledge of the 'way things work.' In the evening there is the synthesis of EL and ELKYM leading to the unity of consciousness that unites day with night and awareness with the unconscious that is being revealed. It is only through these three that any sense of being may be established.

The prayer is accepted because it travels along the pathways of Shekinah.

A distinction is made between a man and a woman which symbolizes the overt action of speaking the prayer (man of war) and the inner response which is listening the accepting (woman) of the prayer so that it may be aligned properly to ascend above.

We must pray from the standpoint of being the receptacle for prayer i.e. its conduit. This is why with this state of mind that the prayer is answered even while it is being spoken. The sense of unity is invoked and the prayer and its answer become one.

Prayer is to be spoken with the understanding that it is meant to be linked to Shekinah so that in this connection it arises above for the fulfilment of the same.

The Queen is Shekinah and she is the feeling of connection that rises above to the King which is the sense of overall unity above the all encompassing mystery.

Prayer without this knowledge is ineffective for it is the feeling nature that connects with the above establishing the pathways of Sephiros called by another fashion Shekinah.

We are enjoined to love Her meaning our intention and focus is on Her so that the connection is established. There is no unity without this connection. Therefore we rise up in fear or awe of the holiness that we are hoping to encounter.

What we combine with our prayers in our mouth is the perception of one, the way things work and two that inside of the way things work is the the outworking of that plan set in motion by intention with connection and the rising up of prayer in unity above.

When you call it is to Shekinah to rise up to His court of Judgment. She is both the initiator and terminus of connection.

Yes she is the burnt offering the olah the ascending one. She is the one who carries prayers on high. Now she is a state of mind that ensues just prior to unification. She is the three drops that descend and then engage the soul elevating it to unity.

In all of these elevations Shekinah the connection that is established via prayer and intention must be the first place of rising just as we set up a ladder to climb on high the same is true of Shekinah and our awareness and consciousness of Her. She is the flowing that takes place both left and right and along the middle pillar of consciousness.

It is the knowledge of Shekinah, her presence that fulfills the dictums of prayer. Without this knowledge the words remain unfulfilled random and may descend into evil.

Now having established Her, meaning the presence of Her in prayer of all of the angelic beings, the higher thoughts of unity we rise as well with Her in harmony and song.

Israel like chicks asking Her for food that comes via prayer each to his own need.
She is the Higher Mother, the Shabbos prayer.

45b) We are the chicks that call to Shekinah to bring down the sustenance which is the connection above that sustains the body and the soul.

Shekinah the Higher Mother provides the connection to the soul of all life that is emphasized or brought to the front of our awareness on Shabbat.

This acceptance this qabalah is the oral law that is hidden from view and revealed according to each, their own level of acceptance or inspiration. The Sephiros are the shining examples of this flowing from one to another above to below and below to above.

It is the consciousness of connection that is ever ascending and ever descending which is why the five prayers are established for the awakening of connection and the subsequent linking of the above to the below in five steps of reverence and supplication.

The lower Shekinah comes from Malchus or the anchoring of our connection that takes place in the evening morning and afternoon service of Shabbat.

The archetypal daughter or Shekinah, the prime Shabbat is the template for everything that comes after and provides the spirituality for our immersion within.

Shabbat is both the receptacle and the linkage for the connection of the extra soul that takes place during these festival times. This can be likened to an extension cord that appears to connect two plugs that otherwise would not be long enough to establish the connection.

During the week another kind of hierarchy of connection is established. The prayers provide the focus of attention to the specific qualities of holiness that we are promoting.

The messenger during the week is the inspiration that produces the connection while Shabbat itself is administered by Ha Kodesh Barachu making the connection whole and complete.

Shekinah is the life force that rises and descends in accordance with our connection to Ha Kodesh Barachu. This connection is directed or linked to the awareness of holiness, the perception of what is right and the unity that is the goal of all life.

Think of Shekinah as a catalyst for the union of the lower consciousness with the higher consciousness. In both lower and higher Shekinah resides making the connections both above and below.

Where do these connections reside?   They reside of course within thought(s) that is the linkage all of us have with the unity of Ha Kodesh Barachu.   That unity is reached by intuition meaning the ability to flow from one voice of reason to another so that the highest may be reached.

The exiled are those who have no idea of the 'way things work' and although they are righteous their perception is lacking which is the key to making the connections that are offered by Shekinah.

Shabbos adds the extra soul to the poor man
And it done so because of Shekinah.

On Shabbos She descends along with the extra souls.

This is what is said:
The soul of all life shall bless Your Name YKV"K ELKYN"U...

46a) Shekinah is described here in terms of her going and coming, her arrival and her departure and its relationship to all we know.   Only when She is there may Ha Kodesh Barachu be present.   She is the connection that revives and proves the unity.   Conversely She appears only when Ha Kodesh Barachu is there.

In every thought that seeks connection She arises.   In each discussion that is for the sake of holiness She comes into being.   She moves according to the written and oral Torah and is associated with the Oral Torah that is within.   The Oral Torah is that which we receive via the contemplation of holiness.   It is therefore by definition the qabalah of the Oral Torah.   What we receive then is called Shekinah known by the various states of mind that the body experiences.

When She ascends it is called acceptance meaning there is an awareness of her presence leading to the unity that is Ha

Kodesh Barachu. Those whose work it is to bring Her constantly into being through contemplation of Torah are called craftsmen because they shape Her appearance intentionally and then when She appears they open themselves to the influence that She offers.

There are myriad ways for Her to appear whether through contemplation or discussion of holiness or through the direct perception of unity, which are the priestly garments that are worn. In effect they cover themselves with holiness.

She is called the law unto Moses from Sinai because what is learned is the 'way things work.'

Mountains and rivers and springs and all the flowing things are Her.
She stands between the above and the below and moves in making those connections rising and descending above and below.

46b) Shekinah is described in terms of rivers and waters and rising above and descending below. She fills her pitcher and the land which was dry becomes watered and becomes Israel. The letters themselves describe as well what is taking place here amidst the operations of holiness.

Shekinah is the realization of holiness the perception of unity and the touching of Ha Kodesh Barachu either from above to below or below to above. She is also the connection that makes this possible just as an canal connects two bodies of water so too does Shekinah connect the life force of the world with the all powerful Ha Kodesh Barachu.

Consider Shekinah to be the flow that takes place due to the realization of connection. This is a flow both palpable and yet esoteric in nature since the feeling of the flow takes place only after the spiritualization of the flow much like thunder (the feeling) follows lightning (the initialization).

If this flow, this connection, this Shekinah is not awakened the land meaning the physical body is dry, not spiritualized and therefore incapable of connection. Conversely when spiritualized or awakened and filled with Shekinah this connection is complete above and below generating and maintaining the flow.

She says to the Righteous One:
(Bereishis 24:18) *And she said: "drink, my lord..."*
(Bereishis 24:46) *I will give thy camels drink also* which are:
(Isaiah 28:9) *...Them that are weaned from the milk,...*

47a) What is this drink? It is the drink of consciousness the openings which allow the divine inflows.

In order for there to be any flowing of the divine there must be pathways into which it flows. These pathways are set up by the right aspects of consciousness that are described herein. The pathways are specifically between brain and heart or rather the intention and the impetus (emotion-certainty) that is behind that intention.

The connection of right and left evolves the pathways that Shekinah must travel; the pathways of holiness.

The unity that is called the day of Atonement takes place when thoughts are resolved, their antipathy dissipated and the awareness of above and below is clearly recognized conquering the lower pathways that enslave in the exile.

Here again the rivers are the pathways that are built and maintained via the prayers spoken daily which bring together the right and left.

These fifty gates are analogous to floodgates that open and close to allow the passage of water albeit in this case what is passing is spiritual knowledge, awareness that comes to replace the dross of the mundane thoughts. These arise via the middle path ascending towards the higher mother also a result of the daily prayers.

They call to Him, meaning these thoughts align themselves with unity and out of this unity is the recognition of holiness which descends upon the righteous one meaning the one who prays with the intent of unification and the awareness of the flowing of Shekinah via these holy pathways.

Through the actions of these prayers everything is conquered. Their smashing force cuts new pathways and obliterates the old negative pathways that are not connected above.

The windows of jasper offer perfect reflections and the pitcher is Shekinah that carries the prayers one after another. She carries these prayers in the rivers of holiness that are daily being set up and maintained.

Yes Shekinah carries the prayers and is the offering that is carried on high. On high represents the place of overflow where the prayers reaching their desired destination now overflow and are transformed from potential into actual demonstrations of being.

These pathways flow throughout the 248 limbs watering in effect the body with holiness. Our prayers upon reaching on high turn into the sustenance that is required below.
This is the covenant meaning what we think determines what we experience.

Therefore unless you pay attention to what you are praying for or thinking about you will be subject to the results that are contained in those prayers, those thoughts. Now it is always Shekinah that does the pouring. She is in exile because we do not always recognize her and Her relationship above. Once that relationship is fully recognized then the unity that is the covenant is reinstated.

The sign that is forever is the appearance of Shekinah and not only that but it is also the recognition of that appearance. This is so because her appearance is the completion of the thought that has ascended and descended becoming one above and below.

The seven rivers of Ana BeKoach are the Sephiros from Chesed through Malchus. It is through Torah study that these rivers are revealed in the following ways.

These voices of the Ana BeKoach are extracted from Torah and remembered. These voices are made into a prayer and repeated daily. They form the pathways of the seven Sephiros.

These cantillation notes evolve into points of reflection that are the actions of Shekinah.

And upon it is said:
(Psalms 93:3) *The rivers have risen YKV"K.*
And what are they?
(Psalms 48:3) *...the sides of the north...* that raise Her towards YKV"K who is Her husband.

47b) These wheels provide the connecting links that thought links to itself from other thoughts. These ten wheels called Sephiros contain the conceptual focus of Torah which is the 'way things work.'

The rivers that rise are the thoughts that revolve around each other in response to their contiguous nature and ability to share points of reference. Ultimately the Cause of all causes is the source of all references.

This covenant is the intimate connection between above and below or between the finite man and the infinite concept of God. This point or Yud is the central focus of that covenant which is our ability to communicate with the Creator.

Shekinah flows in response to the calls that are evoked by thoughts from within. She is both the river that connects above and below but she is also as well the central column that guides the influence of holiness that arises and descends.

There are two rivers that flow from each side respectively connecting via the middle path. These are rivers of connection uniting those inner flows in order to produce the awareness of holiness that is joined by the middle path.

The sounds of the shofar awaken the middle path and therefore subsequently open the gates from both right and left. On the right hand there is the momentum of mercy, the power of overflowing and on the left there is the restriction that channels the middle flow. To the wise comes the knowledge of such things.

(Shemos 32:18) ... *but the distress of them that sing do I hear.*

And all who have distress over the Shekinah who is the poor one in exile, distant from Her husband and calls to Him every day *Hear O Israel*, so that He may descend towards Her,
certainly, about him it is stated: *the sound of distress I hear*, the sound of distress of this 'poor one' *I hear*.

48a) Without connection via Shekinah there is distress since the process of unification is interrupted and chaos ensues. Because of this 'Hear Oh Israel,' is the calling of that connection into focus

The cantillation notes call into play the recognition of the awareness of Shekinah which is the path out of exile.

Even the mere inkling, the seed of awareness is enough to awaken the feeling that is Shekinah.

Shekinah harmonizes thoughts obviating the effects of negativity and providing a refuge against chaos.

This awareness of Shekinah is above below and in the middle meaning it is all around. The contemplation of the Mishnah is a means of calling into awareness this perception that is Shekinah.

Halakhah provides a straight path to the right to the ability to discern right from wrong. Qabalah gives the ability to understand the import of your prayers and how they work together to bring about the experiences of your life. Braita is the attraction call it the force that unifies you in the recognition of Shekinah, the proof that is witnessed from without by experiences.

The sling is Shekinah whereby the life-force of the worlds is sent forth via the three Vav's. Shekinah is within becoming sling and bow and the sign of the covenant understood intellectually as Chokmah Tevunah and Da'at.

The study of Braiita the alternative views of Mishnah allows for the discrimination of thoughts, of words and ultimately of meanings. These meanings coalesce in the unity of the SHMA.

Shekinah brings everything about. Her awareness built itself into the first and second temples and the first messiah (Moses) and the second messiah that comes after.

Shekinah is built up by the awareness of the countless who study Torah and the awareness that this brings frees thought from its mundane moorings. As thought is set free Shekinah travels freely and reaches the place of unification as naturally as a breath comes in and out.

And it is the purification (red heifer) that serves as the seed for the awakening of this perception that is Shekinah. Shekinah purifies that which is defiled because this awareness cuts through the dross and sets up the pathways of holiness.

And a priest who is pure, if he would strive to offer to Azazel, would purify Israel from all of its sins; and as it says: (Vayikra 16:30) *For upon this day it will atone for you to purify you etc.*

And whether he was pure he would become impure through Azazel.

And regarding the nidah the priest would be impure until evening time, and then would become purified.

48b) The symbolism is that all thought is purified by the thought of holiness that awakens the pathways of Shekinah. It is therefore by the separation of good from evil that the former is attached to and the latter let go of.
The principle remains the same with the priest through their taking on of the impurities and then becoming pure in the evening time through the process of holiness that continues awakening its attachment to good.

The world of form causes impurity through thoughts that are impure and through impure actions. The metaphor of Moshe and the burning bush reminds us of the sacred role of Shekinah in our lives. It is She who purifies us according to the recognition of her presence and the letting go of the negativity of the flesh. It is the pure body of Adam, the spiritual body and yet something else as well; the body that is spiritualized. This is what happens at the bush; the spiritualization of Moshe in the body of Adam renewed.

Once Moshe divests himself of the body that attached itself to him via the daughter of Pharaoh then Shekinah, the awareness of unity, the holy body of Adam, the divine connection returns to him.

The memory of leprosy or diseased flesh is then to be cured by the recognition of Shekinah, the ways of Torah and the truth of the above.

The symbols of cow and calf represent the transformed sacrifices that are now evidently spiritual referring to the pathways of Shekinah with their rising above and their ascending below.

Now this recognition of Shekinah and her pathways refer to the thoughts of holiness that remove completely all traces of Amalek and his seed. This means that the transformed person in completely in touch with Heaven resisting negativity and finally conquering it ultimately.

When the scholars argue they open up new pathways of Torah turning what may have been stagnant pathways into new living waterways of inspiration in effect their thoughts awaken Shekinah and push all obstructions aside. The secret here is that Creation came to be in an analogous, "in the beginning," manner.

The continuity of unity will always prevail over chaos.

The preponderance of evil will be vanquished never more to be found becoming devoid of essence, and ending up torn to shreds meaning that nothing can put together that which YHV"H had taken apart.

Therefore shall all evil and darkness return to the void forever.

This is the plan for complete annihilation of evil meaning those thoughts that speak of separation and only are centered in physical realms of endeavor must pass away. All these forms of death are described alluding to the Atonement where sins are discarded and life begun again anew.

At this time the pathways of Shekinah are opened all the way through above and below.

מקף is tru'ah – this is 'strangling'

49a) Negativity exists in loops of thoughts constantly repeating themselves. When the loop of negativity is interrupted or sliced through as with a sword or bound or interrupted; all these break up the massing of thoughts into fragments; which are then the kelippos that dissipate.

The "shouting of war" is meant to disperse the enemies or the negative self serving thoughts.

The strangling is the cutting off of our attention to negativity therefore returning to our soul's desire which was awakened with the "giving of the Torah."

The mixed multitude have no place in this world or the world to come and no portion with Israel. They represent confusion, the egocentric masses that cut themselves off from holiness.

Thereupon there is a gathering together of wicked and they are destroyed. What destroys them is the truth about the way things work, the truth that they in their ignorance have disdained but nevertheless they are still bound by it resulting in death as it were by their own hands.

Here the personification of evil is itself called into judgment by the way things work an incontrovertible truth that stands against all subterfuge.

Therefore Shekinah is awakened and the soul rises to its rightful place via tru'ah sounded in the breath, the soul of a person.

So here are the three notes of t-qi'ah, tru'ah, shvarim that represents the various levels of soul as it travels upwards to unity via Shekinah.

The levels of soul are seen as one soul arising out of Tru'ah containing within da'at (the knowledge of the way things work) both nephesh and Ru'ach.

It is within the Tzadiq that the foundation of the world resides because one light shining through the eyes of right perception is the basis upon which the world via Torah was brought into being. As then so likewise true now

The liver, spleen, the gall bladder all perform the functions of separating the good from the bad. Because of this it is said to be the realm of the snake and all that is associated with the snake.

These impurities that pass through these organs are eliminated via the sounds of the shofar representing the purifying force that evolves out of the recognition and awareness of Shekinah.

When we attach ourselves to Torah it is as though we were unified with Shekinah and this unity promotes and produces purification. Without this purification the animating force of Shekinah is not present weakening above and below.

The extra lobe of the liver is symbolic of what happens to impurities that remain.

The heart understands the heart knows, the heart sees.

For this is what must always be.
The heart is Shekinah, making the blood pure
Through prayer that is clean to Her husband offers the best of everything.

49b) It is the accumulation of faults or sins that turns the tide in terms of the descent into chaos or hell. When the liver cannot discern the difference between right and wrong the overflow of sin kills.

The heart works with what is natural to it; the purity that is the connection of Shekinah which rises above to present the offering of prayer.

There are two paths to go by. One leads to sin the other to righteousness. The pathway to sin is the left hand path. The extra lobe of the liver is a perversion, a misdirection of Shekinah. Instead of leading to unity this pathway leads to chaos.

The pathway of Shekinah follows what is right just as a stream seeks the pathways that lead to the sea in the same way are the pathways of holiness that lead to unity with Ha Kodesh Barachu followed. The perception of this 'good inclination' that is the guidepost for all prayers and subsequent blessings is its guiding principle.

For the wise the secrets of Shekinah are revealed in detail in relationship to the body, the location of the life-force and the process of the illumination regarding the ten Sephiros of transformation. These become revealed along with the pathways.

In the brain the Higher Shekinah, in the lungs there is Tipheres the harmonizing of the holy influence. In the right side of the heart there is the lower Shekinah and the completing of the circuit.

The Ne"R represents the initiating force between the nephesh and the neshamah. Therefore the wick is nephesh, neshamah is the oil. Therefore imagine these things within in order to experience firsthand the metaphor.

Torah provides the light that illuminates via the process described by heart and soul and lungs and brain all a part of Shekinah as she rises and descends.

The purpose of the liver and spleen and the gallbladder is a collection of impurities. These impurities are transformed by the mitzvos and also by the connection with Shekinah. Without this transformation chaos would result.

The soul that is enclothed in impurities will be released at the time of Moshiach. This is kind of like a trump card for the soul in that truly there is nothing that supersedes the awareness of Shekinah.

It is joy that breaks through the negativity and awakens the awareness of Shekinah. This joy is like a candle to the soul and is the direct result of connection above and below.

The coming of Moshiach is an eternal happening. What this means is that the appearance of Moshiach is both personal and universal. A taste of Moshiach is enough to dispel the negativity replacing it with joy.

Jerusalem is the heart the center of the flame of the altar which is the breath that arises from holiness that can never be extinguished. The breath calls forth Shekinah erases the uncertainty and inspiring Eternal connection.

It is Ha Kodesh Barachu that awakens within.

The soul that ignores the altar finds itself exiled much as the impurities are relegated to the spleen, liver and gall bladder. Yet even in the midst of impurity there is redemption because Ha Kodesh Barachu purifies even the most defiled.

And because of this, good the Righteous One, the life-force of the worlds is from the left-hand side, for it is the mighty one.
He who conquers his inclination, this is Samae"l.

50a) Reject the evil inclination from the left that is conquered by the life force the (cha"y) subduing Samae"l, clearing the way for the risen awareness that is Shekinah.

It is this awareness that awakens YKV"K that lives as the evil inclination lies down or dissipates until the morning of the awakening of Shekinah that connects above and below unifying Ha Kodesh Barachu with the soul.

The New Year is the time of giving up sins and Passover is the redemption of sin, the deliverance into the awareness of holiness.

We must learn to see not from the side of limitation but from the side of plenty, from the awareness of infinity and the possibilities that our lives may unfold endlessly good.

There in the heavens is the place of infinite darkness that also contains by the light by its connection to the infinite light that does away with the darkness. This is the purpose of the light of good to transform continuously the darkness into light into good. So therefore our thoughts flow with intention to the good. Without intention they are scattered and chaos is the result.

What is described is the effect of allowing the outside things to influence our thoughts rather then initiating continuously the thoughts that attach themselves to good.

By striving in Torah and precept you keep open the doorways of unlimited perception because it is through these doorways that Shekinah is experienced and via this experience that holiness is awakened which is of Ha Kodesh Barachu. Without this experience no sense of connection ensues and darkness is the result.

When you seek the inner visions of good Ha Kodesh Barachu opens up your perception of Shekinah so that your thoughts may travel along the pathways of good sending and receiving blessings.

Every soul praises Ha Kodesh Barachu meaning our entire thought atmosphere is infused with Divine light. This divine light is ironically of our own intentional focus that seeing the light that it is good continues to strive for more of the same until we reach the stage of endlessness which is the precursor to Moshiach in all worlds.

Once you turn to Torah, turn to the way things work then thoughts of darkness no longer hold sway and even the most hidden remnants of darkness are rooted out no longer having anywhere to attach themselves to they are dissipated and removed forever.

Yes I am small meaning I awaken the humility that is the cornerstone of the soul to receive the divine influx and the pathways are straightened so that following the awareness of Ha Kodesh Barachu and his Shekinah my thoughts flow along the pathways of holiness. This is a lesson that repeated over and over again in TKZ.

It becomes a matter of how you see yourself. What is your innermost perception of your being? Are you ruled by recrimination or by love? When the realization is that it is the overabundance of love that is your center then this love radiates from you around you and through you. All endeavors then unify themselves into the awareness of unity that promotes the good life.

There is this concept of a return to the beginning meaning a return to the state of being that concentrates on good and eschews evil. It is the concept that by attending to our good we awaken it within the world within Israel within the consciousness of the soul that is aligned in perfection above.

At that time the soul was held tight between the legs, this is what is written:

(Ruth 3:7) ... *and uncovered his feet, and laid her down...*
for she has returned to the heart like Jerusalem.

At that time: the heart sees.

This is what is written: (Isaiah 30:20) ... *yet shall not thy Teacher hide Himself any more, but thine eyes shall see thy Teacher...*
The heart hears, returning the cherubs to the Bet HaMikdash;

of them all it is said: (Numbers 7:89) ... *then he heard the Voice speaking unto him from above the ark-cover that was upon the ark of the Testimony, from between the two cherubim*

50b) The perfection of each moment takes place according to the harmony that is perceived. Without this harmony the pictures are muddy. Clarity of vision results from the way things work. It is as though there were a lifeline that is always available to you. This lifeline is Shekinah that always connects you to your higher voice, your higher self.

The holding tight is the attachment to the connection of Shekinah.

The heart which is the place of connection between above and below is a symbol also of the opening of the flow of Shekinah.

The clouds pass away. The obstructions to harmonious thought also pass away. This leads to the thoughts that arise in Mazal and re-establish the Temple within. As a result there is a direct connection between above and below.

The soul (Shekinah) prays to Ha Kodesh Barachu to raise Her up from the dust. The dust is the lower level of awareness and this raising opens up the higher levels of awareness.

There are levels of awareness indicated by the Sephiros but there are also levels of the body's awareness beginning with its base awareness between the legs the center of sensual feeling Yesod moving up through the awareness of spiritual feeling through the place of connection above.

It is the light of Shekinah that shines meaning the awareness is raised from the body into the spiritual. Stay the night means gets past the doubts that interfere and press on until the morning of the awakening of inspiration.

Anokhi is the awareness of Shekinah. This is the awareness that redeems you from a life without a spiritual purpose. Once this awareness awakens it becomes a part of the Higher Israel that is the husband of Shekinah or the connecting link that is Ha Kodesh Barachu.

Now the prayers are the intention to focus upon that holy connection and the opportunities as well to do so. By in a sense grooving this intention it awakens the connection that is sought after.

Here is a direct appeal to Shekinah that arises from the lowest levels and continues to the highest levels. Bring forth thy good thy great good that the connection and our relationship to that connection is continuous at every level of existence.

Herein the secret of the 42 names are revealed once again this time in relationship to the revenge that Israel takes over Egypt. This revenge is nothing more that the rising of Shekinah over all adversaries including the principle adversary of Amalek. We begin at the source between the legs, the foundation, the generation of Shekinah and raise Her level by level until the awareness is in the heart. Then from the heart we raise Her even more to the holiness She is destined for.

For it is from the heart that the raised awareness filled with its intention from below then sets out to become that which it is seeking which is the fulfilment of redemption.

The revelations that take place within the heart are the raised awareness that by definition can only take place there since the heart is the gathering of awareness prior to its unification above. The limbs serve however only as vessels to bring about this gathering of awareness.

Most especially in the heart there is gathered the awareness of the ways things work. It is an accumulation of events and reactions which defines the heart in its opening to the truth about itself. Via the written Torah all the wisdom is gathered into one place. This is the collected wisdom of the 72 names, and the seventy faces of Torah. Then from this place the exposition, the explanations are given that is the oral Torah.

We speak in terms of the body and its limbs and parts so that we recognize that everything that takes place happens within. Revelation takes place continuously in the heart where it arises by its own momentum.

The divided heart represents the various pathways that revelation takes on its upward journey of unifying connection.

And what divided their heart?

Yeast and leaven' - which are 'the mixed multitude.'

And the mystery of the matter (*sod hadavar*)
(Bereishis 1:6) ...*and He separated between the waters and the waters.*
For about them it is said: (Shemos 12:15) *howbeit the first day ye shall put away leaven out of your houses;*

51a) Choice implies intention and because of this is the first operation that takes place in creation. The first choice is between something and nothing. In effect through the separation that takes place a differentiation occurs. Out of the chaos of the multiplicity of design comes intention or choice which then completes the design in terms of "the way things work."

What is this division? It is the separation of negativity from holiness initiated and risen above like the sacrifice that released Israel from Egypt.

It must be noted that the first exile the sojourn in Egypt was directly the result of an attachment to negativity resulting from the assimilation of Israel inside the Egyptian culture.

These seven days mirror creation and the rebirth that is to occur within Israel.

The leaven is that in which something is mixed because on Passover there is no mixture no allowing of the bread to rise in response to the yeast so that the purification may take place. This purification is the light of the candle of Torah since its precepts alone are the unmixed purity of holiness.

The day of revenge could also be called the day of transformation when the darkness and blackness are turned into light. First however there is the light that sees through everything (the eye) and envelops the center of everything (the heart) all via the eternal unity that is continuously expressing itself.

Therefore the center, the heart is the unity of all things including the incomprehensible act of creation (32 ELKY"M mentioned in Bereishis) and the "way things work," (the ten utterances of creation)

The essence of being that which is called soul is the inner light that is the reflected light of above our recognition of the unity and our acceptance of our part in its purpose. At first it is the light, the luminous fire of prophecy and then in the final exile it is called the illumination of Torah the same illumination that radiated on the first day that was good.

The daughter of creation is what is derived from creation without which we would have no idea of creation. Since this is the daughter the reference is to Shekinah. The connection of one Shekinah is derived from the other Ha Kodesh Barachu just as the act of Creation brings about the perception of the "way things work."

A whole series of connections are reiterated here. The light that shines through creation via the 32 ELKY"M and the 10 utterances is the light of the soul of man since that light is the reflected light of YKV"K.

The waters of the flood represent those negative thoughts that build until they bring chaos to your world. With the wings of Shekinah meaning Her ever abiding presence you connect above and those waters either part aside as in the parting of the Red Sea of they dissipate due to the lack of your attention.

The chayot represent the higher thoughts which we may attach ourselves too. They are constantly revolving serving as the basis or throne for Ha Kodesh Barachu -- our conception of holiness and the above (the cantillation notes).

Herein there is the choice of thoughts. On the one hand of Esau, the accusatory thoughts that bring you down or the positive thoughts that allow you to attach on high. These higher thoughts are the delicacies that are given with the positive precepts.

In describing the shape of the cantillation note zarga a right descending half circle with a dot above it; this alludes to the positive precepts ascending over the negative precepts.
Ha Kodesh Barachu reserves for connection that aspect of holiness called Shekinah. It only appears in response to the positive precepts, the good that we do and think and say.

On Shabbat and the festivals including the New Moons, Shekinah stands alone and is accessible without any interference from the chaos that is present during others times (the week).

Ravi"a symbolizes the guarding of Shekinah from outside negative influences.

Shekinah is unblemished untouched by any negativity since by definition She is a part of Ha Kodesh Barachu and is the undefiled connection that resides within. Therefore when we turn to Her or recognize Her then we may by extension unify with holiness.

The mystery of Shekinah is that She is evoked by our prayers, they are the good food that reveal Her even when she is hidden.

At that time said Ha Kodesh Barachu to Israel: (Bereishis 27:4) *and make me savory food* and gave reasons for the will of Shekinah <u>such as I have loved</u> from the mitzvos and Shekinah prepares for Israel prayer foods (מאכליב של תפלות) which are the sacrifices.

51b) These savory foods are the inspirations that Israel receives via the study of Torah. The sacrifices refer to the upward motion of the revealing of these inspirations in that they connect the above with the below giving and proving the sense of unity throughout.

Shekinah offers up the pathways for connection whereby Israel (our thoughts-insights) travel setting themselves free from the darkness.

A Simple song may compared to a melody. A melody usually proceeds from the first note in the scale and then takes various routes until it eventually returns and resolves to that first note.

The Double song is analogous to two notes which form a harmony, called interval which is based upon the relationship of one note to another. Here the rules of harmony prevail in that there are consonant, dissonant and ambiguous harmonies which occur. In much the same fashion the harmony proceeds from its root notes making various combinations until returning to the original root notes.

Triple song is the triad, three notes whose relationship changes according to the intervals each not makes with the two corresponding others. Again there is the root harmony usually major or minor which proceeds until it returns once again to rest upon the root harmony.

Lastly there is the Quadruple song which proceeds from four part harmony. The combinations increase as one note is sounded in comparison to three others. Still the form remains the same in that the root harmony moves about and then returns to itself.

It is prayer that rises up and makes the connection above which is why it is called Shekinah which is connection. The pathways via which it travels are those of the Sephiros angelic qualities that display the attributes of the individual Sephirah.

The four worlds of Kabbalah, Assaiah, Yetzirah, Briah and Atzilus are represented in the four letter of the divine name, the four Chayot, the four faces and then the combined holiness of YAKDVNK"Y the dual divine name that is a kind of unfolding of holiness when the connection and the emanation, Shekinah and Ha Kodesh Barachu are revealed within it.

All of this takes place during rightful prayers. This also expresses the four-fold harmony one against the other that establishes the levels of holiness internally and externally.

When notes are sounded together in a certain way there is the suggestion of other notes which are complimentary tones called the harmonics of the notes. These harmonics are similar to the chasmal the result of the emanation of the four part harmony.

The sounds of ascending prayers have an organization based upon the music with which they are sent on high. This organization delineates the pathways of the Sephiros, the holy names, and angelic hosts and all the heavenly beings. They are heavenly because we have no other way of describing their ascent.

What this passage is telling us is that our prayers, the words and the thoughts, the intention behind the prayers make up figures, structures of thought, columns and spirals and edifices all resulting in a glorification of the throne upon which sits Ha Kodesh Barachu. This is our consciousness of the Divine. It is what we are constantly building.

At that time, all kinds of music will be evoked.
this is what is said: (Psalms 150:3-5)
Praise Him with the blast of the horn; praise Him
with the psaltery and harp.
Praise Him with the timbrel and dance;
praise Him with stringed instruments and the pipe.
Praise Him with the loud-sounding cymbals;
praise Him with the clanging cymbals.

52a) Music then is evolved out of its own harmonic relationships which are compared to the mystical relationships that occur below. Music is aroused because whenever there is a connection it produces music, i.e. harmony.

The Higher Shekinah is the connection between Ha Kodesh Barachu and the pathways that evolve below. The Lower Shekinah is the answering call that then arises according to its new arrangement. In exile that connection is dislocated like Jacob's thigh socket meaning it is out of the harmonious pathways of above.

In order to reset the socket, make right the harmony the son, which is the reflected form enters the heart which is the perfection of form alluding to a cheerful heart which rises upwards in glorification of holiness.

The wicked cause the harmony to go astray saddening the heart until they are destroyed.

Therefore through the harp is the light of Ha Kodesh Barachu, which is Shekinah made aware through mitzvos.

The redemption for him and her refer to the thought that is harmonized turned around by righteousness through the praise of Ya"H

The Amalekites are destroyed since they only thrive in disharmony, discord and chaos. Once the mind is established in its true place there is no footing for them.

The Satan is an allegory for the negative influence of chaos that interrupts the flow of holiness blocking the heart that passes through the influence of holiness.

Sins are transformed in the land that is uninhabited so they dissipate and are no more. In consciousness this occurs figuratively in the liver.

We're speaking about the darkness which occurs as a result of the lack of light. We are also speaking about the transformations to take place in the body via the liver, spleen, and gallbladder. The deeper meaning refers to what is taking place inside of your thoughts in any given moment. Thoughts achieve negativity or are of a positive nature. The purpose of the transformation for thoughts is so that they may be purified into their higher nature. The same is true of the transformations that take place within the body. Overall the metaphor pertains to Israel and the exile.

Because of the lack of a pure focus Israel has fallen into exile. It is up to the Torah therefore to purify Israel.

When the mind is not filled with substance it falls into exile. This exile takes place because of the mixed multitude meaning the mixture of impure thoughts with pure thoughts so that the higher connection cannot be maintained.

A Righteous person keeps their mind focused upon righteous things. Therefore they cannot be swayed since their entire focus is upon righteousness itself.

What is being demonstrated here is that righteousness has to be a focused and a continuous meditation. Then and only then will the mind not be swallowed by its own negative inventions.

Just as it is true for an individual soul so it is also true for the collective soul of Israel.

כאשר היא שלימה במיצות עשה, נאמר
She is complete with positive precepts, as it says: (Song of Songs 4:7)
Thou art all fair, my love; and there is no spot in thee.

At that time, the Name YKV"K there upon Her, and it is says,
(Devarim 28:10) *And all the peoples of the earth shall see that the name of the LORD is called upon thee; and they shall be afraid of thee.*
52b) She is complete so that the attention is directed to holiness and to its positive results. In such a case the negativity is transformed all around you.

In order for there to be a transformation of sin the positive precepts have to be followed. What this means is that the mind cannot contain any negative thoughts but must be surrounded by the holiness of prayerful intention.

The key to holiness is Shekinah the connection that is established via the preponderance of holiness making the pathways above and below. Once these pathways are established and maintained nothing may interfere in that holy connection.

When we establish the praises of Ha Kodesh Barachu there are seventy anointed ones that protect so that all the purifications take place as they are meant to be.

The purification of the body, of the mind is effected by the blasts of shofar symbolic of the direct routes of holiness that are established via Shekinah.

Man is equivalent to the spelled out version of YKV"K meaning that man by his efforts becomes holy burning away the dross of imperfections. The candle is the essence of Ha Kodesh Barachu the soul of man.

The colors of the candle allude to the transformations of the soul in aspects of holiness turning one way or the other or being enveloped by the higher voice all a part of a continuity of purpose brought about by the imagery of Torah awakening the Sinai experience over and over again. Here the black is transformed into those three colors.

The candle of darkness is described wherein the soul descends into black. It is an opposite process that darkens the soul when it is kept away from Shekinah.

מפני שהנשמה המקום שלה המוח יונה קדושה

Because the soul's place is in the brain, (called) the holy dove
The soul is an eagle, through which the dove is sustained,
with many prayers and services.

53a) What we are speaking of here is the resident awareness that is seeking on high. When this awareness loses its way it finds itself cut off from that which it is seeking

What prayers and services accomplish is the raising of the awareness on high because our focus is centered above in these praises.

There are the many voices that come together within. At first they are fragmented and then with study and mitzvos these voices coalesce until we hear the one voice the true voice that is the leader of all.

One may think of thoughts as being in the brain, in the mind but they are throughout the body in various configurations. What moves these thoughts is the breath, the spirits of 'great wind, wind of storm, and wind," that guides the thoughts via the lungs and the nose and lips everywhere that air is processed except that what is being processed in this case are our thoughts.

So you see it is truly wind that animates us in various ways lighting up our souls with divine influence according to our prayers and consciousness in the moment.

We are painting a picture here that is a mirror of the inner construction. What this is referring to is the way the letters combine together to bring out the sparks of holiness. "The spirit of YKV"K shall rest upon him" means that by contemplating these things what is built within is the holiness of Ha Kodesh Barachu.

This wind spirit is the action of consciousness in motivating the life experiences that we undergo. The boat is our head meaning our thoughts and our thoughts make up the heart of our being the essential nature of our soul the entire world that is built around us.

The Torah is called the soul enlivened by the inner essence the nephesh which provides the pathways for the spirit wind, our thoughts to rise up in between

Therefore it is understood in the parable of Jonah that the great wind is the power of thoughts and the harsh wind is the power of harsh thoughts evoking chaos, which threatens the boat which is Israel the boat the body interrupting the harmony of that relationship of body and soul.

Now in that light we see that Jonah descends to the lower Shekinah where he slept meaning he did not arise on high but rather was passive in his thoughts.

There is described in Jonah but also in general what happens when we do not engage in Torah and precepts. Our thoughts without direction descend.

In this chaos which is caused by the descent inside of the lower Shekinah our body suffers sickness and disease.

Now still pursuing the parable of Jonah the captain who is the sense of what should be happening as opposed to the current state of decay approaches Jonah.

This captain might be called our continuing awareness of heaven even in the midst of chaos.

There in the boat the captain that knows what's best calls upon Jonah to call to God meaning to rise up into the Higher Shekinah via the route of repentance so that the chaos will depart and the upper harmony will resume as should be.

Every blessing proceeds from above and the natural state of being is to be always in contact with the above especially on Sabbaths and festivals but in general the way out of chaos is to rise above via Torah and precepts that purify the thoughts that have descended.

Blessed are You YKV"K, who spreads the tabernacle of peace.

ובזמן שפורשת כנפיה על ישראל ונאמר
And when She spreads Her wings over Israel it is said:

(Deuteronomy 32:11) ... *take them, bear them on her pinions.*
As they have established:
(Shemos 19:4) ... *and I lifted you on eagles' wings... etc.*

And because of this: (Jonah 1:6) Rise! Call to your God!
which is Higher Shekinah, which is your repentance; and
return through to your Master who is Ha Kodesh Barachu.

53b) The tabernacle of peace that She spreads is brought about by the concentration of thoughts on the subjects of Torah and precepts.

Call to your God meaning let go of your lower thoughts and rise up into the awareness of and the concentration upon the higher thoughts. This is the way of return to your Master. Do not let the negative thoughts rule your thought atmosphere.

As long as you are mired in the chaos you cannot return to dry land since you are making the obstacles that prevent you in effect from returning.

The first exile depicted as the descent into Egypt the great fish that swallows Israel.

Even in the exile the chance of redemption the Higher Shekinah remains according to our efforts to rise above.

When Israel has descended as in the first exile then even their offspring has become polluted and cast aside. The king that rises up in Egypt to torment the Israelites comes about because the practice of Torah and precept has fallen into disarray.

The great fish is symbolic of the river into which the first born are tossed. What swallows Jonah however contains also the means for his redemption all the while nullifying the negative ways and offering a pathway for teshuvah.

It is via the prayers of Israel meaning the thoughts that praise and arise on high that Jonah makes his case even in the midst of the bowels the Egypt of the fish.

We tie together the spleen spoken of earlier with the great fish and recognize that here is the clearing house for chaos represented by the mixed multitude which is the holiness that has become mixed with negativity bringing down the whole part. It is out of this that everything then becomes embittered.

The great fish, the spleen, the mixed multitude and there the captain that represents the power of the mixed multitude to destroy and their part in bringing down the higher thoughts.

Coming out of Egypt the mixed multitude is destroyed since they are sustained by chaos and holiness is an anathema to them.

Those sons are the transformed of Israel by waters of light for even though they were cast aside and therein lies the pathways of redemption.

The sons are those that bring down the thought atmosphere whereas those that strive in Torah raise the thought atmosphere.

Jonah prayed amidst the depths of despair the poverty of the spirit that seeks its higher source.

Redemption comes through the prayers spoken on high that reach a point of raising the soul high above the depths into the places where now the soul may find its place above.

(Jonah 2:11) *And YKV"K said to the fish and it vomited Jonah onto dry land...*

And from that which was 'dry land' – Hei – is called earth to produce seeds and fruits; this is what is said:

(Shemos 1:10) *And ELKY"M called the dry land earth...*

54a) The poor man is he who is bound by his lack of Torah but since this is as good a place to rise up as any even this poor man may ascend on high naked and bare like the dove or Jonah.

When Jonah is completed the holy drop commences which is the nuqva or the Higher Shekinah that affects the holiness from above nurturing the dry land, the earth, which is our bodies and the world which forms around us.

These seas that gather are the result of the drops that form making the pathways of holiness that become the savior in times of trouble.

The small yud the Aleph, Chokmah that emerges flows through the Sephiros each with its portion and the tenth one the culmination is the world that forms itself around us. A deep secret is revealed here.

See how the middle Pillar is formed with the lengthening of the drop made into the pathway of Vav as all partake from Sephiros they partake from Vav because it is the pathway that is central to all the drops that are being formed and partaken of. The completion which is Malchus is the proof of the above, the witness to creation.

The arcane mystery of Noah's ark is revealed as the place wherein the drops are deposited until they come unto dry land the result of the deposits or ariq wherein the Righteous one is revealed. All of this takes place within and is purposefully managed.

Everything that was made via the drops that issue from above are revealed in the seventh month when the life force of the tzaddik of the world is bringing seed upon the earth.

Bringing the seed to dry land means taking the drops that issue from above and placing them into the earth, which is the understanding of the above and intentional awakening of the flow towards its fruition in Malchus. Any break in the pathways from above to below cause the waters to flood meaning they leave their places and subsume the pathways so that Malchus does not receive the directed flow. This is the intended flow from the drops that have been sending forth their essence from above.

The prayers we make on high accumulate and then overflow. These are the blessings from above that are the result of the filling with merit which then finds its place on the dry land and is the culmination of all that is coming from above.

There is a separation of the subtle from the gross, the higher thoughts from the lower thoughts. The two are the thoughts that harmonize one with the other. The seven represents a cycle of thought that then repeats itself on a higher level.

The mirror of the holy days and festivals, the two the seven and even the repetition of the eighteen all point to the harmony of thought that comes together as a result of the intention of raising thought on high for the purpose of holiness and unity with Ha Kodesh Barachu.

And because Qudsha Brikh Hu revealed all this to Moses, he requested mercy for them, and submitted himself for death; this is what is said:

(Exodus 32:32) ...and if not, wipe me out please from Your book...
And in his supplication he cleaved to the King, and he took hold of the right arm and said:

זכר לאברהם ואחר כך אחז בשמאל ואמר זכר ליצחק. ואחר כך אחז בגוף ולישראל. Exodus 32:13)
Remember Abraham! After which, he took hold of the left and said: Remember Isaac!
After which, he took hold of the body and said: ...and Israel

54b) There are those that let go of their wayward thoughts and others that cling to them. There is what is known as a complete and an incomplete letting go. The former follow the ways of Moshe. The latter are the mixed multitude.

Moshe represents the corrections to the mixed multitude. It is the continuing repentance that alleviates the wayward thoughts. Moshe took on the task of moving forward despite the chaos. Moshe was made mundane because he accepted upon himself the negative thoughts that were holding Israel back from their destiny.

Here is what happens. When you keep to the path of holiness that is all you will find in your life experiences because everything may be tied to holiness. You begin to see the world through the lens of holiness. However, if you stray off of the holy path repentance is needed to bring you back to the level of holiness that you have been pursuing.

It is and becomes a conscious act to strive for holiness via Torah and mitzvos.

We are charged to be like Moshe reminding ourselves of Abraham, Isaac and Jacob and their journey so that we may mirror their actions to achieve the levels of holiness they ascended to. Each moment a choice is there for us to rise ever further or to be distant from that which we are seeking which is the unity of Ha Kodesh Barachu.

the right arm to receive those who return,
and it lifts them up from their falling and takes hold of their hands,
and says to them: (Isaiah 52:2) ...*Arise! Sit down, O Jerusalem...*

ובשבועות יצאו בזכות משה שהוא מתן תורה רחמים. ומגלה להם ספר תורה ויאספו
לירושלים ותראה היבשה מלכות ישראל (הרשעה טרנונ עכ בניו, ובו כנשר יעיר קנו,
מהוא קנו ירושלים קנו לשכינה).

And on the Festival of Weeks they come out through the merit of Moses, who is 'the giving of the Torah' of mercy and he reveals to them the book of the Torah, and they gather in Jerusalem;
(Shemos 1:9) *and the dry land will be visible* ... the wicked kingdom, and He has mercy upon His children, for that...
(Deuteronomy 32:11) *Like an eagle arousing its nest.*
Who is "His nest?" Jerusalem His nest for Shekinah.

55a) There is the perfected state where and when Torah is given. It is a singular moment we return to following repentance. The cantillation notes represent directions above and below that are symbols of our spiritual pathways in regards to whether we are moving upwards and or away from holiness. In Torah the symbols of negativity or of the distance from holiness are personified in Esau.

There is the idea of repentance and of revenge, which are two sides of the same process. Repentance is when we decide to return to unity. Revenge is when the Ha Kodesh Barachu brings about that return eliminating the obstacles, Amalek and company, the nations that have opposed that unity. The problem of the mixed multitude also is eliminated since there can be no compromise with unity. All of these corrections are what are to take place in the sixth millennium.

The commandments, the precepts are the templates for unity and Torah study is the way we connect ourselves with that unity. What unifies then is the name YKV"K meaning that our understanding of the divine principle becomes elevated to the Sinai experience.

At that time smoke will be awakened to the left to remove Sama"el from there, and immediately another smoke ascends,
which is the smoke of incense it is the all of Torah; it is together the positive mitzvos to bind and bring close together the right in the left; for the pillar of smoke is the Middle Pillar, in love; and the negative precepts in fear the pillar of the incense.

מהי קטרת שלו שכינה תחתונה.
What is His incense? Lower Shekinah, ascending in many good odors and perfumes.
And when She ascends towards Him it is stated of Her:
(Song of Songs 3:6) *Who (M"Y) is this ascending from the desert?*

55b) What is being described in this section is the superimposition of the One. This means that whatever we are experiencing it is via the garments of the One and the action of the One. First we speak about the incense which transmute the dross and replaces it with purity. And again for example it is one thing inside another when speaking of the tephillin. Each of the specific passages of Torah are contained in compartments within. Again one thing is inside of another; Holiness that is in turn surrounded by its shell. The shells of Adam made of leather coverings for the skin and yet Adam as spiritual man needed no coverings until he ventured into the material and therefore needed protection and a containment for the life-force.

What is the point of this surrounding of essence by the material of the emanation of the essence? It is to point out that holiness always has a container a means of directing itself back to where it emanates from. Hashem is the peddler who offers his wares for the taking and what is taken is the self the soul that is bonded to holiness. This points out the awareness of holiness that we can enter into. It is something that occurs throughout every experience. Shekinah is symbolic of that awareness that opens us to the possibilities of unity and then keeps rising until we achieve that focus which is unity.

What is this? (Zot) It is the recognition of holiness and the part that is played by our own awareness, which is inside of the understandings we discover within Torah. This is the something that is surrounded by something else the one lower the former higher. The point is made that despite the compartmentalization of unity and its many instances, we may still arrive at a unified consciousness by focusing upon the essence around which our lives revolve.

Her three reincarnations are the three patriarchs, about which it is said…
(Job 33:29) *Lo, all these things doth God work, twice, yea thrice, with a man,*
She is His salvation, His redemption, because Ha Kodesh Barachu does not have permission to emerge from exile until She emerges with Him.

She is His prophecy made up of six levels, from the aspect of the letter Vav, which is the Middle Pillar.

56a) You have to recognize the pathway which is Shekinah before you can enter into the unity of Ha Kodesh Barachu. Once upon the pathway you are met and become one. The three reincarnations are the development of Divine Consciousness.

The six levels are Zeir Anpin, the Vav the middle pillar which attaches both right and left and represents the developing consciousness in its holy aspects.

Sleep represents the unconscious which is unified with the waking consciousness via the Vav the middle pillar the connecting links between thoughts and experience.

We recognize the pathway as being holy and do not stray from the pathway lest we lose our holy way. The awe or fear is the result if we stay or stray respectively.

Again the connecting link the middle pillar is Torah where we connect with the holy via the interpretations that come to us both individually and through the insights of the sages. We are meant to connect in this way referring to Torah as the meeting place above and below where holiness is the way, the pathways via the Sephiros between above and below.

It is our identification with Her that establishes the holy "I." By extension whenever we act in a holy way, kindness She is revealed.

It is to Her that we must turn for to chase after anything else is to diminish and block the holiness even to becoming turned to the snake.

Each holiday has its own point of connection and offers insights into the process of connection itself. Passover is the leap of faith that arises out of leaving the status quo behind. The broken unleavened bread represents the mixture of good and evil that is being parsed, the complete unleavened break the ascension to holiness that begins from the "north." Then the middle pillar whereby all is connected represents the cycle of seven, the Shavuos, the unity of the SHMA 49 letters.

The Torah is given as the realization of holiness takes the parts and makes them whole meaning the Torah, which represents the consciousness of the unified nature of everything.

The middle pillar of connection, the gates of Binah, and the Yud that ascends to Heh all point to the experience of Torah, the whole Torah and its deeper meanings of unity throughout the consciousness of the maker.

Also the forty years, the time preparation, of testing and the world to come all are alluding to the continuation of understanding that seeks only its own ascension, its own elevation. All throughout Shekinah is guiding us through these pathways of fulfillment.

Moses reached the heights of understanding, realizing the unification of consciousness via Shekinah his holy connection that allowed him to receive the Torah on behalf of all. It was his insight that allowed the Torah to become a living example of "the way things work." The lower Shekinah is the point of first awakening to holiness above.

What is given is the awareness, the verity of unity, and the lower Shekinah.

The fulfilment of Shekinah is Torah and the fulfilment of Yah.

The Sukkah represents the tabernacle of holiness that we build around our holy thoughts the combination of one inside the other as in YAKDVNK"Y.

The crown that is placed is the Higher Shekinah, the culmination of connection and the rejoicing of Simchat Torah.

...on the day of the 'Rejoicing of the Torah' (*Simchat Torah*).
(Vayikra 23:40) *And you shall take for yourselves, on the first day, the fruit of a hadar tree, date palm fronds...*
the *etrog* is lower Shekinah, and like the heart, is to the left, which is gevurah.

56b) What you take for yourself is the lower Shekinah meaning you choose this pathway of discovery since Gevurah is about making the right choice, the hard choice sometimes but the all encompassing choice as well.

Once you make your choice be sure it is the right one, i.e. no defect in it. Because of this it is the unified choice the beloved choice.

You put together your choice with the three myrtle branches to emulate the patriarchs whose choices brought about the nation of Israel, the holiness of Hashem and the connection between both.

Now the lulav corresponds to the life force, the 18 blessings three to each of the six directions and is representative of the middle pillar. Everything we see in the symbolism of Sukkos is tied back to the Sephiros, which are the archetypal forms of consciousness in connected unity.

Look and see the 72 representing the 72 names as well as four times eighteen, the praises that are the templates for the awareness of holiness.

See as well how these concepts are related to Shekinah, which is the singular focus of Tikkunei Zohar. See it in the body relating to the spine, the covenant of circumcision and the patriarchs joining with these concepts so that you may catch the higher drift of what is taking place above.

The symbols of Sukkos are linked to Shekinah and by extension Torah and through these connections we see that the overall purpose of thought is to have everything unified together in one seamless whole each relationship making sense to one another.

The central purpose in recognizing Shekinah and her place in the scheme of things is to join with Her in connection above and below. The alternatives are chaos, Samae"l, evil, and the uncertain outcome. Joining with her from the right side means choosing the good and the holy. Only in this way is this joining made pure.

אם זוכים לשמור שבת צריך לשנות אותו מימי החול בלבושים ומאכלים,
שהם ענג שבת

If you are to observe the Sabbath, you need to change from the weekdays, in clothing and foods,which are the 'delight of the Sabbath, for if he is accustomed to eat two meals on a weekday, then on the Sabbath eat three as it is written: (Shemos 16:25) *And Moses said: 'Eat that to-day; for to-day is a sabbath unto the YKVK; to-day ye shall not find it in the field.*

57a) The point being made is that the Sabbath is like no other. It needs to be special beyond compare with the additions one would not make during the week. Everything is for the purpose of glorifying the Sabbath.

We see that the Sabbath is symbolic of the union of Ha Kodesh Barachu and Shekinah. This is the union of awareness with holiness. When the two are one Ha Kodesh Barachu is in the perfect place and all is perfection. It is out of this perfection that Torah is presented and Torah is compared to the Sabbath since whenever we contemplate Torah we add to its marvel, its wonder and hidden discoveries are revealed. It is in effect a template for revelation always becoming something more than it was a moment ago.

Through Torah the mundane is raised to the sublime. Call it a change of state similar to what happens on the Sabbath where everything is more and the negative energies may not approach because of the immediacy of the creative atmosphere.

וכן שכינה תחתונה נקראת שופר, מצד השכינה העליונה שהיא שופר גדול.

And so, lower Shekinah called <u>shophar</u> from the aspect of Higher Shekinah, which is the the great <u>shophar</u> as in 'blow upon the great <u>shophar</u> for our freedom.'

57b) The shofar rises up and brings with it the specialized knowledge the notes single or broken or a combination that results in those aspects of holiness that resolve the inner connections.

The knowledge that rises comes from Shekinah that is the activation of our holy connection. The depths that are split are the tofu va bohu that represents the inner awareness until it is tapped for integration unification.

The shofar opens up those areas of enlightenment that we need the most making the pathways for Shekinah.

The result of the Day of Atonements is the re-imaging of the inner connection whereby our prayers serves as the garments for her arousal and she becomes a garment for our prayers.

Once we are adorned with the garments of Shekinah we are ready for the holy connection.

It is via Shekinah that the transformations that reawaken divine consciousness take place.

In this way the consciousness is renewed and surrounded within the holiness of redemption.

There have to be basic steps of contrition and opening towards Shekinah. Without these steps our prayers are in vain. These steps are caused by Torah study and adherence to the mitzvos. Without the unification that takes place between Ha Kodesh Barachu and Shekinah this holiness does not occur.

She is protected by words of Torah. This means that in the concealment of holiness that must take place there is the opportunity to reveal the holiness via the unity that Torah offers in every phrase, passage or letter. These combinations are what link us to the above. Without minds focused on Torah nothing can detract from holiness.

The brother that hides Her is the rising flow of Knowledge discussed previously connecting with purpose and keeping the flow going all the while.

for She (Shekinah) is the unity of Ha Kodesh Barachu.
And instead there rules over him a *demon* ש'ד
who is אחר another.

The specific Yud of שד'י is the tip of the Dalet of (one) אחד and if he is false, the tip of the Dalet of ECha"D is taken away with אחר that remains.

And because of this, the verse says:
(Shemos 34:14) *For thou shalt bow down to no other god;*
And at the time when the demon who is 'another god' rules over a person, he becomes enslaved with all kinds of troubles. And this sin causes Israel to become enslaved by the nations of the world.

58a) Mind is either focused or scattered with the Yud focused without the Yud scattered. The focused mind or thought is unity, the scattered mind is the other meaning caught up in other than unity, settling for illusion.

The attraction of evil cannot come to one who is focused above in unity and conversely when not focused above it is attracted to the other and becomes enslaved.

The covenant is the connection between us and Ha Kodesh Barachu made possible by the intermediary Shekinah.

Our thoughts focused upon holiness will always rise above all afflictions and trials.

Esther symbolizes Shekinah in all Her glory becoming the epitome of holiness, which is the manifest unity of above and below.

It is via this unity that surpasses all chaos that brings chaos into its proper place of annihilation.

There must be a receptacle for holiness. That receptacle is called 'charity.' We are poor in that we may only receive holiness when we are open to charity. In this way Ha Kodesh Barachu is the conceptual receptacle to receive our aspiring holiness via Shekinah so that all are in line receiving passing from one to the other.

The dry land is watered by holiness, which cannot flow without receiving all along the line. Israel sinned because she tried to receive for herself alone and did not pass on the flow thereby causing the 'dry land.'

Charity is related to the flowing of unity of holiness since to give to another is to emulate that gift we receive continuously from above. By our emulation we then take on the aspects of holiness that have engendered this process from the start.

Shabbat is simply an extension of the act of receiving for the purpose of passing it on. On Shabbat we pass on freely the holiness that is in abundance becoming suffused with its...delight. To interrupt or ignore this flow is to become transformed by plague since that which flows must overflow and when it doesn't it dries up.

The poor woman, Shekinah, is Qabalah when she receives and Halakhah when she sends forth what she receives. Holiness from above denotes Qabalah.

The endless flow is repeatedly endlessly overflowing.
The middle pillar designates receiving from both right and left.

קבלה היא מצד הימין. הלכה בשמאל לגבי בעלה, ומקבלת ממנו בימין ויורדת מלאה לגבי צדיק

Kabbalah the right-hand side, halakhah the left side in regards to Her husband, and receives קבלת from Him, via the right hand, and then descends full on towards the Righteous One and because of this: (Psalms 37:25) *yet have I not seen the righteous forsaken,*

And when and with what? She descends full towards Her husband, who is Vav...the river that is drawn out of Eden -
Vav enters Dalet and becomes Hei;

ומה שהיה צדק נעשות צדקה, לגבי עני שהוא צדיק

and that which was is made into *tzedakah* (charity)
towards the poor man who is the Righteous One.

58b) Kabbalah is the opening that receives from above in response to the inspiration that is the making of another connection. Halakhah on the left side makes the choices that determine the ensuing flow. Inspiration flows to the left in order to channel that energy of above into the practical forms below.

Specifically She is the one who is descending meaning Shekinah increases the awareness of the connection with Ha Kodesh Barachu. The connection is Vav which is the connected flow of Zeir Anpin that evolves into the righteous man and also redeems the poor man who is desirous of Her flow.

She is the river since she contains the abundance of the flow, its continuous nature and the passing off of that abundance all along the way.

Shekinah refers to the connection between above and below. Our thoughts have to contain the higher perspective in order to awaken her to flow in her own way. When She rises our thoughts are of holiness and when she descends our thoughts are corrupted. Shekinah awakens according to the inspiration that She is offered.

Good deeds are part of that inspiration that raise Her to Her place.

When Israel reveres holiness She is active and awake. When Israel sins She departs because She cannot coexist with sin. Taken as a whole consciousness must be open to holiness and aspire to holiness otherwise it will descend into chaos.

The children are the products of holiness, of holy thoughts and of following the mitzvos and performing acts of kindness and compassion.

Israel sins by becoming self absorbed with wealth and materiality and not with holy things such as the commandments positive and negative.

The Torah is the central focus that produces holiness via her contemplation. When you wander from Torah contemplation into the things of the world then She leaves since She is only concerned with matters of holiness.

Just as the days of the week are diminished in terms of the Sabbath in terms of wandering away from this holy interval, it is like when Shekinah wanders away from Israel because they have lost their holy focus.

Shekinah returns as the New Year makes us return in repentance or as the evening is the return of the day. The waters that subside are the waters of chaos, of negativity, and of not reaching for holiness.

The key presented here is that via Shekinah the image of Her Husband Ha Kodesh Barachu is found or impressed upon the consciousness. Until this time the ark which is symbolic of the potential for holiness floats upon the waters but when She meets Her Husband the ark is not necessary so She doesn't return here.

Bring forth everything that you can about her. She is everything because she is connection. You leave the original focus of your upbringing. Then she will join with you because she is in Him and He is in Her.

The opening may only take place when we become aware of her. When we give up our old ways of thinking and turn to thoughts of holiness she appears. When she appears we are lifted up so that we are once again connected above and below.

Shekinah is called festival because there is an overabundance of her because our minds are focused upon the holiness that we celebrate during the year.

(Shemos 23:14) *Three times thou shalt keep a feast unto Me in the year....*
and why is this so
(Shemos 23:17) Three times in the year all thy males shall appear
(Shemos 20:8) *Remember* and (Deuteronomy 5:12) *Observe*
Remember and maintain for a male and *Observe* for a female;
all those who go to gaze at Shekinah should give Her a present

this is what is said:
(Deuteronomy 16:16) *...and they will not be seen before YKV"K empty handed.*

59a) The present we give to Shekinah is our attention. The awareness of her presence is enough to make that holy connection. Therefore a male 'Remember' which is the active study of Torah and for a female 'Observe' this is the recognition of holiness that is brought about by Torah study.

The purpose of Shekinah is to establish the holy connection in order to remove the blemish of negativity, the descent into materiality and the active awareness of holiness. Sadness cuts off the connection.

When you let go and allow Her to become a part of you there is the awakening, which in itself becomes the gift that is hidden and then suddenly is there. It is the gift of the awareness of ELKY"M or 'the way things work.'

The blessing from lower Shekinah is when we make the connection with holiness bringing it (the blessing) forth from the right hand side and as it flows it changes state from blessing to gift. In this way we continuously pass along our blessings as gifts.

At every moment holiness reigns calling itself the various cosmic events which line up the templates for holiness called new moons, seasons, Mazalot, etc.

Living a life without awareness you become ensnared by death called carcass, beasts of the field, Sama"el. In order to prevent annihilation by your own negligence we are given the means to become aware of Shekinah allowing us to continue to partake of the holiness that is connection.

ועוד, השכינה היא מצות אסיפת דגי ים התורה, שנאמר בהם דגים וח גבים אינם טעונים שחיטה.

And furthermore: Shekinah is the commandment of the meeting of the fish of the sea of the Torah, of whom it is said: 'fish and locusts do not require slaughtering;'

59b) Consciousness recovers itself via holiness and this recovery is described as 'my corpses will arise.

Consciousness takes on the properties of what it focuses upon. If it muddies itself then it is overcome by its own deitrus.

The sea of Torah represents the continuous flow of holiness that is entered into and increased via Torah Study and its ensuing inspirations.

Shekinah is compared to the blood which flows since it is holiness that flows because of Shekinah.

The continuous prayers of those who connect with holiness lift up thoughts for connection above so that Ha Kodesh Barachu examines what are in essence the thoughts that are His own.

We are included in the part of awareness that knows itself and that has the ability to seek its own causes and effects. We are not only cognizant of our own being but also of the unity in which that being functions as an integrated part.

We are immersed within cause and effect and are responsible for our actions and their results.

Consciousness can become cluttered with fragmentation called tohu va bohu which occurs because our thoughts react to the world around us rather than impressing upon the world the aspects of holiness that we ascertain from our study of the same. The burning is the clearing of consciousness by the realization of unity the divine name of One.

All of these forms of death are alluding to the death of the conscious awareness of holiness. Without this awareness the body cannot survive, i.e. without its holy connection.

Recognition of unity of the name results in life whereas the converse is also true.

There is only life via connection. All else is to live in the world of the kelippos feeding off of others but never experiencing the dimensions of holiness provided by Shekinah. The woman that we love is Shekinah, the connection that we love since we are attaching ourselves there.

One who diminishes the Sabbath and treats it as an ordinary day; this is one that is without a special holiness. When you return to holiness the Sabbath regains its rightful position.

If you lose Shekinah you lose that which bore you, the mother and therefore you cannot partake of the essence that continuously emanates from her.

(Vayikra 5:23) *which he took by robbery*
Restore the Shekinah to Her place;
or the thing which he hath gotten by oppression, this is Ha Kodesh
Barachu, שפריש ממנה Who becomes separate from Her.

השכינה נקראת מצות עשה מצד הימין, ומצות לא תעשה מצד השמאל
For Shekinah is called a positive commandment from the right
and a negative commandment from the left hand side;

and She is called Torah from the aspect of the Middle Pillar;
and anyone who steals or oppressively withholds funds in the Torah,
whether in a positive or negative precept, is as if he had stolen Shekinah
away from the arms of Ha Kodesh Barachu.

60a) Shekinah is a continuous flow. When She is blocked it is our awareness of Her that is blocked. She is restored when we return our awareness to Her in which case She is united with Ha Kodesh Barachu.

Shekinah is symbolic of the flow of holiness which is our connection with Ha Kodesh Barachu. If we in any way block this flow we block our connection.

The connection must always be maintained otherwise what is made is alien or negative causing holiness to depart leaving the shells of awareness to flourish which is a degradation of life.

It is to holiness itself that we ascend and not to some other contrived vehicle that is temporary in its allure causing idol worship. Idol worship means worshiping the effects rather than the causes.

When we repent we reawaken that holy flow returning it to holiness. It is the joining of Yud with Heh.

There is a place that rises above wherein the unity of the divine name is the pattern for the higher awareness. Within this pattern everything that is to come to be takes place.

We describe this pattern as thought although it is not just any thought but the thought of Creation.

We overcome our evil inclination by rising in thought attaching ourselves to holiness as the Masters of Mishnah establish, 'who is might? One who conquers his inclination.'

We become aware of both the evil inclination and our control of it as a dog that is tamed and bound by the hand of a person

We return when we recognize the holiness within that surpasses all confusion. In this way we return to the joining of the divine name via Torah and precepts.

When we recite the SHMA we renew the fire that is holiness that acts upon the chaos to inhabit the realms that produce the blessings from above. We can never let that fire go out.

We maintain our position within holiness recognizing that here is where all good is generated from and to. Like the Vav that is the symbol of connection so too are our thoughts the substance of connection that produces Yud or the pinnacle of holiness.

It is our world to fill with Creation. It is our world to fill with good thoughts and to attach ourselves to the holy thoughts that are produced via Torah and precept.

The Tree of Life refers to the primary symbols of holiness called the 'fruits of the tree.' In addition everything that is from this Tree of Life, which represents the thoughts of holiness, the insights of Torah and precepts and the connections that are in between go into making the continuous flow that is Creation.

The lower Tree of Life is the antithesis of Torah meaning that instead of connection there is separation. It is the separation of life, the disjoining of meaning and the realm of chaos.

Shekinah is the kingdom meaning that our sense of the awareness of connection is what we are guided by. It is our template for the life experiences we undergo. Therefore it is the place of highest awareness, our King, the Lord the awakener to holiness.

For there is a no king without a kingdom;
In exile: (Proverbs 30:23) ...*the maidservant shall inherit her mistress.*

And at the time when the messiah will come, it is said:
(Esther 1:19) ...*and her kingdom, the king will give to her companion who is better than her...*

היא מלכותו, היא כסאו, היא עטרה שלו
She is His kingdom, She is His throne, She is His crown.

But now, when She is far from the King, it is said of the King:
50:3) *I shall clothe the heavens with darkness...*
and of Shekinah it is said:
(Song of Songs 1:6) D*o not look at me for I am blackened.*

60b) Thought rests upon holy thought meaning our thoughts rise to their holy place. The maidservant is the potential of thought whereas the mistress is the inspiration of thought; therefore one shall be the precursor of the other.
Imagine that thoughts build themselves up in layers, one layer the kingdom another on top of that the throne and another still the crown. The unification of all three is the messiah.

Every time we focus upon Torah we produce that special vessel that is beloved by the King, Ha Kodesh Barachu. In every aspect of contemplation Torah delivers holiness above and below.

When Shekinah is denied or blocked she is distant from the unification of above in which She is meant to be attached to.

The enlightened see the deeper meanings that build up the inner worlds uniting them with holiness.

What we wear is what we are attached to and when we throw off the chains we are free to soar to the heights experiencing the light, which is our true nature.

When you are clothed in garments of chaos, negativity, or anything which blocks the light you are cut off from the benevolence of Creation.

Everything that we are is self contained and when we bring forth the light we are attaching ourselves to holiness and when we hide from the light we take on the appearance of darkness mainly through our own ignorance at repeating what is not in our best interests. When we look to Hashem, our highest awareness and allow the light to come shining through all things become infused with that light.

Make it your highest intention that you will put on garments of light each day, every moment checking them and refining them to reveal more and more brilliance. Such is the role of Torah to awaken our own innate intimate connection with holiness through pondering and speaking of its secrets 'when we are lying down and when we are rising up.'

It is via our attention to holiness that the angels rise up and sing their music (nigun) because of what we are centering our attention upon.

Praise signifies that you are knowledgeable of the divine presence. It is through this awareness that you are able to attach yourself on high. It is a knitting together of all disparate things into one divine unity.

The house of Shekinah is an unbroken chain of connection. It is where every choice is a divine choice.

Whatever we build is to be built out of this unbroken connection. Because of this we will recognize that it is the work of the holy one blessed be he.

The temple by definition may only be built from our highest thoughts that resound with the unity of Creation giving forth the colors of brilliant light that illuminates Jerusalem without and within

It is always the higher conception that illuminates and sustains what is below.

The sun and moon will not cycle meaning they will be ever radiant. The Song of Songs will give forth its higher meanings as the light of oil gives meaning to the wick of the candle. The purpose of higher awareness is to unity Israel; to unify the disparate thoughts. It is Torah that provides the inspiration, the oil that is the fuel that lights the wick resulting in the connection and Shekinah that rises above to Ha Kodesh Barachu.

The unification of Shekinah causes Ha Kodesh Barachu to be revealed, 'without his shoe,' meaning his veil.

There will no longer be a need for connection because the realization of unity, which is by definition oneness in every part will be already present within all.

Even sin which crouches at the opening is destroyed because no entryway is ever provided since as a whole thing there are no places for sin to attach itself to. All that will be is surrounded by in and through Shekinah.

It is via Shekinah that all flows into being from above to below, the higher Shekinah, and from below to above the lower Shekinah. In terms of consciousness thoughts are exchanged for actions, which in turn produce the affirmation of thought and complete the cycle reinforcing it from above and below.

ומפני זה למטה הוא תמורות אותיות יקו'ק בודנ'י. אבל לעולם הבא אין תמורה,
כמו שהעמידוהו בעלי המשנה לא כשאני נכתב אני נקרא.
And because of this: there below the exchanges of letters
YKV"K and ADN"Y; but in the world to come, there is no exchange as
the sages of the Mishnah established: *Not as I am written, am I read.*

61a) The exchange is always of thought because thought is our acceptance of holiness choosing the right thought and being aware of the holiness contained therein. In this world thought degrades or may be suggested but in the world to come there is but one thought and that is of holiness.

The pronunciation of the divine name is masked in this world to illustrate the illusions that may present themselves while in the world to come illusions are none.

It all becomes a matter of place in terms of how we see ourselves in respect to holiness either with the connection (Shekinah) that arises or descends or is the middle of connection.

Therefore what we exchange one for another is our aspect in these 'places.'

The garden is only locked until the awareness of Shekinah is realized. And then the fullness of the connection, the ten sephiros are awakened.

We then cleave to holiness and let go of (divorce) chaos by attaching our thoughts to the Sephiros.

Just as there is the transmutation of YKV"K into MTZP"Tz via atbash (the replacing of one letter by another) so too the shifting of one form of divinity into another may not take place on the day of atonement since there is connection (Shekinah) unification (YKV"K) but not in conjunction with one another

There can only be a joining when the door is opened on the Sabbath wherein Shekinah is united with Ha Kodesh Barachu

The cup that requires ten things is filled with Sephiros because this signifies the connection above and below

It is the unification that is 'this' being spoken of. Because with the unification of thought and form there is a singular unity that is the truth of the universe.

The chamber that is opened is the chamber of connection wherein Shekinah is reunited with her husband Ha Kodesh Barachu.

It is the one thing that is spoken of through these passages. It is called Zot. This refers to the unification that is the purpose of Moshe, Prophets, and the young one, Solomon, the King, Ha Kodesh Barachu and Shekinah. It is for the protection and glorification of this one thing that all purposes must divert to. This is the magnum opus of Creation, the raison d'être for all that is was or will be.

When we realize this we are the master of the sling.

הדרך שלו להיות קלע אתו לזרוק אבנים אצלן, להיות הצאן שמור מחיות רעות
His way to have a sling with him to throw stones towards them,
so that the animals are protected from evil beasts.

קום טול קלע בידיך
Stand fast, take the sling in your hand.

He began and said: Zarq"a - The Holy Shekinah. You are the holy sling shot of Ha Kodesh Barachu, It is said:

(Psalms 118:22) *The stone which the builders rejected is become the chief corner-stone.*

61b) The stone, the inalienable article of faith is the unification of above and below via Shekinah, the Sephiros from crown to kingdom. The cantillation notes are the essence the crown of that unity representing the intention that produces its result.

Unification is that stone. It is the mind that unifies with holiness.

That wisdom is the revelation of holiness and that is what overcomes all obstacles. It the Father that gives mind the daughter...dominion over matter...the footstool.

All the permutations of mind that lead to holiness represent the stone that is thrown; the stone that is the end contained within the beginning just as a thought contains its demonstration in its initial conceptual realization.

This place is the realization of unity; it is the glory of the Holy One.

The sword is the SHMA representing the two edged unity of Ha Kodesh Barachu. Within thought this is the unity of realization and its demonstration. The Egyptian that was killed are the lowers thoughts, the incomplete thoughts, the thoughts without holiness as their goal and the sword that is the SHMA that superimposes itself destroying the lower thoughts and raising the higher ones in recognition of the unity of Ha Kodesh Barachu.

The sword is the essence of unity.

It could be inferred that the entire purpose of the Torah was to produce the SHMA and all that comes after is either adherence to its precepts or a falling away from those precepts. YKV"K answers Moshe in the moment of his highest realization.

The entirety of the SHMA likened to a spear. It is a most powerful thought form. Arousing above and awakening below the SHMA stands as a testament to unification and is thereby an Eternal template for such.

The word that is Binah or Beit and Chokmah wisdom linked to Reishis-beginning as if to say understand first that it is wisdom that brings everything into being.

נאמר בעשרה מאמרות נברא העולם
…the world was created with ten utterances.

What is Beit? It is the wire that spins around it.
And this point has a head, middle and an end.

ואמצע וסוף ונעשית שלש יודי'ן י' י' י' שעולות לשלשים
And it is made into three Yuds Y'Y'Y' – that count to thirty.
And together with that wire Beit are thirty two.

And through them, act the forty two letters of YKV"K.
And the mystery of the matter:
(Psalms 118:19) *Open to me the gates of righteousness; I will enter into them, I will give thanks unto Y'ah.and all are included in* בבאר שבע – *this is AV"G YT"Tz (Ana BeKoach) and its companions.*

62a) There is a hierarchy of fulfilment. Thoughts cascade according to their affinity to holiness one above the other. The organization of holiness whether it be the thirty two paths, the forty two letter name of God or the realized potential of connection, the stone that is poised or the keys to Torah, all of this comes under the influence of Shekinah. Shekinah is what enervates the entire creative process. It shows the links between above and below and then once the awareness is awakened it rises via these connections to become one with Ha Kodesh Barachu. As a result of this the descending flows take place completing the cycle.

She is the precious stone.

For with Her did the first ones bind the hand strap of Tefillin in the Shema,with *And you shall love* in the mercy of love,
which is (Deuteronomy 6:5) *And you shall love YKV"K ELKY"Kha*
so that there would be love by her husband, and they would stop.

62b) The SHMA the symbol of eternal unity is the basis for the linkage of all thoughts that are holy arising via their attraction to the unity.

Within the unity there is the expression of the unity the part of the SHMA in order to signal the holiness of divine connection.

These letters Sh'ATNZ GTz are symbolics of the crowns that offer connection one to the other within Torah but also between our holy thoughts that seek their unification above.
In particular within Zeir Anpin these connections are emphasized suggesting the means by which connections are established in the first place.

For Malchus establishes the covenant Sabbath and the sign of Tephilin the source of connection from below to above and above to below.

For the priesthood must also connect in the same manner via the prayers.

Now are the sacrifices each given their respective connections that are made to bring one into another. It is to prevent the unholy from entering into the prayers or sacrifices that what is offered is in a sense given to the unholy not in appeasement but as a filling up from below so that they are not an impediment to prayer.

מחשבה, זה אדם. יש מחשבה טובה של חיות טובות.
Thought this is man. There is good thought of the good animals

and there is the evil thought of the evil animals and the good thought he
is the good man and bad thought this is the evil man,
(Psalms 144:4) Man is like a breath...

Thought, this is man, riding above them all
like his chariot they are like horses are for people.

63a) It is the nature of thought to be everywhere throughout the body presenting itself according to its level of elevation. Higher thought assumes holiness and lower thought the lesser animal forms. The point of this is to show how the awareness awakens and is grown from within via its attachment to Torah and to the essential holiness that is inborn.

It is thought that conceives and holiness that provides the substance and the mold for thought to flow in and through. In this way our purpose is revealed in speech, which is none other than the reflection of thought. Because of this reflection we can organize thought to become elevated at every turn. Thought becomes elevated by speech, which is its reflection. It is then this reflection that arises higher and higher becoming the mirror of holiness. In Torah we polish that mirror to a gleaming surface and venturing within the clear path of righteousness is revealed again and again.

Tiqun 22

בראשות ברא אלקים
In the beginning ELKY"M created...

בראשות אחד הוא שלו גלוי. ובra שנים
Bereishis one that is not revealed; and He created two.

These two are Beit and they are two undefined worlds.

And with what did He create them?
With one undefined point, called *reishis* and about it is stated:
(Psalms 104:24) *In wisdom hast Thou made them all.*

And the two undefined worlds were not revealed until
He made for them two garments. And what are they, the heavens and the earth...the heavens, (this is) a garment for the Higher world, created with the Higher point, and the earth (this is) a garment for the lower world which was created by the Name Elokim, the Higher Mother.

63b) Before anything there is One that is not revealed and yet He creates two that are hidden and then revealed once the vessels are prepared meaning the heavens and the earth.

Elohim is the process, the 'way things work.' There could not be anything without this underlying concept which is why this is what brings everything else into being.

One is not revealed and yet of course this must be the basis for everything. We cannot describe it except as One. It is the self awareness that is present in all things and of all things is it self aware. The One can only identify with that which is singular and yet encompassing all. Our conceptions no matter how exalted usually come from a framework of how we each relate to the unity. What about how the unity relates? How does the singularity express itself other then by awareness and then begin that awareness with a reflection, the two that are hidden made into vessels and revealed in this way as a process and its fulfilment.

This one that is the singularity expresses itself via the awareness. The awareness is Shekinah the connection that aligns the limited self with the singular self expressed in multiplicity. It is only our distinctions that separate. The singularity is always One. Remember Archimedes principle of the lever when he said that if he had a fulcrum he could move the world. That fulcrum is the singularity.

Now you can say that in mind we may choose to stand anywhere in relation to what we are thinking about. This choice however masks what is actually taking place every moment we think. It is the singularity expressing itself through us and pointing to itself in ever so many ways to recognition which is the unity via Shekinah.

The divine name HVH"Y ADN"Y and its permutations all center on the singularity in its expression. The higher and lower referring to the relative flow that takes place within the channels of holiness called Shekinah, the Yud and Heh connecting and developing the Vav and Heh below all demonstrate the particular process that the singularity is expressing. Just as in any knowledge we learn from afar we cannot make sense of this until we make it our own.

ויש תורה עליונה שלא נקרא בה בריאה אלא אצילות שלו, והא והא הכל אחד
And there is a Higher Torah, which is not called creation (briah) it is emanation (atzilus) and it and He are totally One.

And every son of Adam who employs themselves in Torah, the Name of Ha Kodesh Barachu is there. Let alone, let alone is this so of the holy lamp.

And the holy lamp! Certainly your mouth this is Sinai.
Seven voices come out of your mouth and Shekinah rests upon them which is Bat Sheva. These are the seven Names of the Shem Hamephorash which is the Name of 42 letters.

64a) The continuity of the One voice is supreme inspiring awe and fear and the weaving in Torah analogous to our thoughts doing the same.

The secret of the Name is contained within the connections we find within Torah in every place where there is linking of ideas, words, phrases that describe a particular aspect of holiness. It is from these aspects of holiness that the Voice issues from Sinai.

The higher Torah is the place of entering into being. It is this aspect which is paramount above all. In this place we find Ha Kodesh Barachu not as something to be described but as the continuity of all that has ever come into being.

It is through a discernment of this place that the holy lamp, R. Shimon is able to make those connections we find below including the seven voices, the seven Names and the Name of forty two letters. It is the coming into being that is the key to understanding what we learn from here.

R. Shimon ascends to the place of Sinai. It is a state of being from which his words are communicated universally. It is the realization of the totality of connection.

Unless there is this complete connection unifying within and without there can be no unification of above and below. It is the breath that carries the voice meaning it is the essential nature of holiness never to be polluted and always remaining pure. This is the purity of thought, intention and action.

There are two speaking's which occur at Sinai. The two speaking's are the overt and subvert meaning that one voice is thought which is the overt voice which we can clearly hear. The covert voice is that which prompts thought into being and is but a far away glimmer until with discernment it too is heard as a rush more than a whisper.

Now so that you do not dismiss Sinai as a historical event step inside the vision where Sinai happens simultaneously as a state of mind. It is the awareness of the unity of holiness.

It is through this unity that the ten speaking's are understood as the evolving of the Voice as it flows through our awareness rising level by level until Unity is ascertained both left and right, front and center, back and forth, up and down and within and without. In short all there is ... this is the Unity.

All of Israel was disposed towards these two speaking's that are ten according to the levels of connection each experiences. Now to make clear there is just one voice that encompasses all and yet still there are interpretations call them the colors of holiness that line up the individual parts of Israel into their unified whole. Therefore Hei represents the two speaking's since it divides the ten. It is a way of looking at something by highlighting this or that aspect.

As the two speaking's arise out of the ten utterances the Yud, the central column is formed via the Vav by which the aspects of holiness called Zeir Anpin are colored in their way and then via the Heh Hei of those two speaking's add up to make twelve and then together make 72.

The state of being called Sinai happens when all is one. This means that the two speaking's, the ten utterances come forth from all places simultaneously from every level of the unfolding of the both the greater and lesser reality.

וזה הוא ופני אדיה אל הימין לארבעתם, ואחד כך היה יורד בחיה ששמה שור, כמו זה, קוק'י .ה' בראשו, ו' בפיו,ה'בכנפיו, י' בזנבו.

and this is: (Yechezkiel 1:10)
and the face of a lion to the right of the four of them...
After which, it descends through the *animal-chayah* whose name is ox like this: KVK"Y; Hei in its head, Vav in its mouth, Hei in its wings, Yud in its tail.

And this is: (Yechezkiel 1:10) ...and the face of an ox from the left.

After which, it descends upon the *animal-chayah* whose name is eagle like this: VKY"H; Vav in its head, Hei in its mouth, Yud in its wings, Hei upon its tail. And this is: ...and the face of an eagle for the four of them.

64b) Throughout Ezekiel's vision the whirling faces tell of the aspects of holiness that each of us may turn to in our efforts to embrace the divine. It is the unity that we are seeking either in the 72 Name or 42 name of God that represents the templates for the awareness that are available to us by means of our Torah study.

Each letter then describes itself according to its aspect to the other letters in the unity and to the particular veil that we need to lift in order to enter into that unity.

The covenant is our eternal connection to unity. All of these symbols coalesce via the substance of our thoughts. It is to heaven that we must cleave. Heaven represents the holiness that is continuously being emanated from the source.

Because the heavens are all encompassing we need only reach up to make those transformations necessary to fulfill our lives. As it says if you seek wealth go north, wisdom go south. These are spiritual verities that are outlining the states of mind that we may unify with.

ואף על פי שאותיות השם הקדוק בו כלולות סתומות הן בו
And even though the letters of the holy Name are included in it, they are not defined in it;

and because of this it is said:
(Psalms 25:14) *The secret of YKV"K is with them that fear Him; and His covenant, to make them know it.*

And if they are undefined, with what do they become recognized.

Through Shekinah, who lights up t when YKV"K descends to the Righteous One, to shine specifically through Her, and from Her they are recognized.

65a) Shekinah comes to being and awakens via our actions in which She is the looking glass that shines. When Shekinah shines meaning when she is active Ha Kodesh Barachu is revealed although only to those whose actions are righteous meaning in the service of Ha Kodesh Barachu.

When Shekinah shines the outline of Ha Kodesh Barachu may be seen within our souls. Call Her the active force that awakens when we do good deeds. Out of Her awakening the image of holiness forms within and produces its corresponding effects without. These effects are called 'the likeness of a human.

In a similar fashion too the holy Name outlines the form of Ha Kodesh Barachu throughout each of the four letters and their connections via the many instruments of Kabbalah.

We are developing a sense of Shekinah that appears throughout Torah. This is as it should be because Torah's purpose is to connect us with holiness and via that holiness to the unity that is Ha Kodesh Barachu.

(Ezekiel 1:5) *...and the likeness of a human, they had.* This is the impression (roshem) of ten letters, they are YU"D K"E VA"V K"E, that add to man (אדם =45). The image of man, certainly this is Shekinah, who is His image (the image of man.) And of Her it is stated:
(Numbers 12-8) *And the similitude of YKV"K does he see* and this is from the side of the garment.
but from the side of the body, She is the unity of the Middle Pillar.

הוא(היא) החותם, אומרת השכינה לגבי יקו'ק שהוא מבפנים,
שימני כחותם על לבך. שאף על פי שאתה תסתלק ממני בגלות
, החותם שלך נשאר עמי ולא יוסר ממני לעולם
She (He) is the seal of the aspect of the body and because She is the seal, Shekinah said in relation to YKV"K, from the inside right,
(Song of Songs 8:6) *Place me as a seal upon your heart*
for even though you shall withdraw from me in exile,
Your seal stays with me, and will not leave me forever.'

65b) It is clear here that Shekinah is the impression of Qudsha Brikh that is there even in exile or in a place where seemingly there is no sense of unity. This impression rises up according to our efforts to awaken Her including mitzvos Torah Study and tzedekah.

This impression that is Shekinah is the revelation, the realization of holiness that we are eternally linked to. It is there in remembrance via the tephilin in each of the phrases generated by contemplating the Divine Name.

Think of this impression as something that grows from within and fills the soul so that it arises in connection. Shekinah as stated before is the absolute vehicle for connection. Everything that we do in terms of the daily prayers is to awaken and reveal this engraving that is the seal of the King, the indelible spark that is holiness carried by each of us or denied by each in turn.

The angels of ELKY"M are raised, but at the time that he stands in
judgment, they all stand and teach him right; *and descending*
at that time that they his adversaries are victorious over him in judgment,
and he descends below, they all descend with him, as they established
about Jacob:
(Bereishis 46:4) *I will go down with thee into Egypt; and I will also
surely bring thee up again*

66a) What are these angels if not the thoughts of unification
that arise by our awareness of Shekinah and descend
accordingly?

In life we acquire circumstances but not without a purpose
that is built into our plan for that life.   We enter into
experience in order to come out of that experience with a
higher knowledge of unity.

When She is aroused by our fervent intention called prayer
then He becomes accessible.   She is the animating influence
that pulses through the world in all of its directions.   What
She animates are our life experiences unifying them above so
that what we experience is in line with what our intentions
have engraved upon the holiness that is the awakening of
Shekinah.

The world flows into being via the awakening of Shekinah
which causes the various images to be produced, engraved
upon the faces of the earth.   It is like a mold that is filled with
the animating substance called Shekinah.   All creatures, all
life itself is the effect that comes about through the openings
that Shekinah flows into.   The various levels of awakening
are described by neshamah, ruach and nephesh as the stages
expand and fill the expressions that are what we perceive in
the world around us.

If you consider that thought is the prime maker and mover of
the universe consider also that thought arranges itself in
specific patterns according to the affinities that are first

presented by the initial offering of Bereishis. When thought degrades or assumes a negative posture nothing that is built upon its foundation can last since by definition it is a tearing apart instead of a building up. Therefore do we endeavor to think on high relating on high so that all of our intentions are made holy and therefore may serve as the vessels of holiness.

It is a level of holiness which the soul enters in connection with Ha Kodesh Barachu. The ShD"Y on the outside of the mezuzah the Shin and Shekinah allude to the gate that separates between the mundane and holy. We must go through Shekinah in order to reach Ha Kodesh Barachu.

It is via the active awareness of Shekinah that death is removed and does not come near the gate because this gate leads to holiness. This relates to how our thoughts have come together. If they come together for holiness that gate is accessible. Conversely if our thoughts arrange themselves to defile then they produce the death since the outcome of evil is always death, dissolution. There must be repentance, a letting go of the defilement and a turning towards holiness in order to break this cycle of death.

And the secret of the matter:
(Vayikra 14:42) *...and he shall take other mortar, and shall plaster the house.* Because for the snake, dust is its bread. until it becomes sustained from that flesh and does not move before it.

66b) You cannot build upon a foundation that has cracks in it. It has to be repaired or sustained. When your foundation is not truth is not the intention for connection then there is a general dissipation. The analogy to the poor refers to the principle that when you are thinking of blessings and praises you are filled with the same. The converse is also true whereby when you dwell upon negativity, lashon hara, and all manner evil then the result here is also the same.

Our health or illness depends upon our state of mind. When we are conflicted then the effects occur as illness, sickness in the body.

Once Shekinah is restored to Her place according to repentance She flows and is the elixir of life healing the sickness whatever it may be. The poverty that is experienced is shutting down of Shekinah, the blocking of the elixir of life.

Torah study provides a means for connection for awaking Shekinah and therefore is instrumental in keeping the flow of life connecting above. Think of Torah as a catalyst for Shekinah in that via its study Shekinah is made to flow again.

The image of man is expressly awakened by Shekinah. The seal is that point of connection that flows through the soul of man for the purpose of his higher source, his constant ascension. The Sabbath and festivals are opportunities to connect above illustrating the importance of the blessings and praises and the flow in the life cycle of Shekinah.

The divine names ShD"Y and YKV"K are templates for the flowing of this elixir of life. It points this out to us so that we may become increasingly aware of it, through the histashelus of the flowing of the Sephiros..

Think about how things become made, how there is the appearance the image within and then the actual substance without.

We are created in the image of man that has the soul of life breathed into it. What is this soul of life? It is Shekinah called the elixir of life, called Torah, explained through the Sephiros, and yet Her presence is not mysterious since it can always be felt. We know Her by how we feel. Truth brings

her forward and dishonesty blocks Her becoming. Our image
is a mere shell without Her.

(Shemos 1:31) ...*and it was*
evening, and it was morning, the sixth day; for this
Hei of הששי (the sixth day) is malkhut, the seventh;
and it is called *a cloud* (עב =72),
and in it rides Vav to redeem Israel, this is what is written:
(Isaiah 19:1) *Behold YKV"K rides on a light cloud (עב).*
Because malchus includes the three patriarchs, from whom are suspended
the 72 Names and they are included in it.

And corresponding to the three Names, it is said in the passage starting...
And they were completed... ויכלו *three times the seventh.*
And this is the mystery of השב"ת
ש ב"ת (daughter of Shin) of which these are:
(Shemos 14:19-21) *And he travelled, and he came, and he stretched...*
which are included in Ba"T (daughter).

67a) The cloud that surrounds us is consciousness born of the
realization of the unity of being that is generated and uplifted
by the purposeful meanings of connection. From this
connection the 72 names are the operational standards of
coming into being.

In order for something to come into being it has to be
assumed. This means that its completion is contained within
its conceptualization. This is the meaning of the 72 names
that saw the deliverance of the Jewish people. The Sabbath
likewise is the completion of the week seen at the beginning
of the week as a crown for its ending.

The key to redemption is the awakening of the 72 names,
their meanings, and their operational standards. As this comes
to be the world is fulfilled once more.

Here we are given a clue to the unravelling of the mysteries
of Torah. Every story contains a beginning and a resolution
and like the 72 names each beginning is the precursor to that

resolution. One is found inside of the other. Likewise we are to view all of Torah in such a manner.

The right hand is the hand that recognizes the end contained in the beginning. Call it a foreknowledge of the follow through. The sea that is split makes the channel whereby Shekinah may flow.

This Hei of Abraham is the promise of completion that takes place within Moshe. It is all one thing. What redeems the children? The children are our thoughts that issue from that initial focus of unity, and the awareness of connection via Shekinah provides the completion that redeems and fills with wonder.

It is thought that produces joy arising out of the level of thought that moves itself within connection. This is a focused thought which seeks the above via Shekinah. We live in a world of thought so that the patriarchs are symbols of various levels of attainment, levels of awareness all leading to that which is the master of thought, ADN"Y.

The flow that is lost is of Shekinah. The bread that is eaten and the wine to drink is thought immersed in the flow of Shekinah.

Shekinah ascends in a filling that is called Great activating the creative flow akin to the process that awakens the knowledge and operation of the 72 names.

Herein you will discover the secret of the 72 names, which become operational to redeem or re-establish the flow of Shekinah throughout Israel.

The savior therefore is Shekinah which re-establishes the flow of connection that awakens the eternal connection above and below.

חותם לא כתוב, אל כדותם, כאותו חותם הסבעת שהוא חותם אמת. ובה וזה חתמנו
לחיים. ומה הוא ז דחותם שהו חיים, שלא זה עץ החיים, שבה נוים חיים ומזונות
יוצאים. עץ ודאי אותו שנאמר בו עצ ההיים מהלך חמש מאות שהנ.

It is not written 'a seal,' but like a seal
like that seal of the signet ring which is the seal of truth;
and with it (this is) seal us for life.

And what is this seal in which there is life?
But this is the tree of life in which children and life and sustenance come
from specifically a tree, that of which it is stated:
The tree of life distances five hundred years. This tree is Vav.

67b) There are the children, life, sustenance, Adam, depictions of the seal, life, wisdom, Abraham the morning and the light, the sixth and seventh days of Creation, the 72 Names and completion. See how it all comes together, their relationships and the aspects of the letters, which combine into holiness. It is this process of coming together that makes the internal justifications that produces the outer demonstrations.

It is this combination of the flowing of Shekinah and the joining aspect of Ha Kodesh Barachu that is the catalyst for Creation. In order to flow it has to be Eternal. This represents a paradox to limited perception however, once that perception is enhanced via its yearning for holiness the way becomes clear to actively participate in that Creation.

וממנו יותשים בני ישראל בנים חיים ומזונות. חיים מצד של אבא ואימא שהם יי"ק.
־נים, מצד עמוד האמצע, שאל ועל שמו נקראו יראל, והוא ו'. מזונור, מצד הה'
שהיא המוציא לחם מן הארץ

And from it the Children of Israel inherit children, life, and sustenance.
Life from the side of Father and Mother who are י"ק
Children from the side of the Middle Pillar,
Upon (and upon) whose name Israel are called below.
(Shemos 4:22) *Israel is My son, My first-born,* and it is Vav.
Sustenance' is from the side of Hei which is the One who brings forth bread from the earth.

68a) The first born son called Israel is Vav the connection. A channel must be in place wherein we receive our sustenance from above.

There is a building a filling and an overflowing these are the levels, called Israel, the children of Ha Kodesh Barachu, and the awakening of consciousness to its Eternal connection.

Everything we place into the consciousness via our perception and the choices that we make affects the outcomes in the world around us. When our thoughts are directed in connection to the above then the source of our children, life and sustenance realized. If we are separated from our connection then there the circuit is broken.

There is but one directive and that is unity between Ha Kodesh Barachu and His children. When His children block that unity they experience separation, which is death.

It is this primary function of Creation to build upon itself, build upon the good that is already present. This is where we take our cue from. It is established as a given and yet when we do not take heed things go against us since we are in effect going against our own better nature. Unless Shekinah is aroused there will be no connection.

The restoration of good takes place through the active awareness (male) and the connecting awareness (female-Shekinah) when they are in line with each other. Simply put our intention must be for the good and for sharing that focus of good throughout our life experiences. Anything contrary to that which seems to rule will always be trumped by the good intention.

A seal is like a valve that keeps out unwanted air maintaining the pressure. This seal is Koach the Higher Shekinah that regulates the connection above, the perfect connection, Israel Above, the ideal state.

By adhering to the truth above and striving in Torah meaning striving to study and understand her secrets we maintain the connection. Conversely that connection dissipates through disuse like the air from a leaky valve breaking off the connection.

All around is chaos and yet we thrive when we build up the relationship that consciousness has with its prime mover Shekinah. Through that our mazaleh rises instead of fails and we can prevent the descent into chaos.

The mystical chamber of YKV"K ELKYN"U... is formed by the strength of our intention, the ability to become aware of Shekinah and Ha Kodesh Barachu in effect to participate actively in the processes of Creation with our awareness always raised on high.

וזה כח הוא סוד של יקו"ק אלקינו יקו"ק, כוז"ו במוכס"ז כוז"ו

And this is the power of the secret of כוז"ו במוכס"ז כוז"ו (which is happens when you replace the letters of יקו"ק אלקינו יקו"ק) and about that it is said all who answer Amen, may his great Name be blessed with his power which is the power that is enclothed in the two arms which are chesed and gevurah.

And one needs to raise it the power towards Yud which is the High One of Heaven and to lower it towards Vav which is the heavens, about which it is said: (1 Kings 8:32) *then hear Thou in heaven...*

When he lowers towards the Middle Pillar, thereby redeeming Israel His children, he raises it towards the High One of the heavens, which is Yud, to take vengeance upon Amalek.

68b) We are speaking of the power here specifically the power of what. This is the power of consciousness to build upon itself by constantly developing its good aspects and increasing them infinitely. It is out of these good aspects that all of our blessings come through erasing the chaos that is Amalek once and for all.

Raising of the hand is symbolic of building on while high maintaining the creative flow step by step. Within consciousness we redeem our wayward thoughts; they are the children of Israel, the children of the chosen of the Divine.

Now part of the process is that the redeemed thoughts, the children, arise to the level of mother meaning that they themselves become the womb for the creative flow to bring forth more good.

View these two Heh's as symbolic of the forms of our thoughts how they arrange themselves and what they make from that arrangement. All of this comes from their ultimate connection above.

Herein the plan for the destruction of Amalek is laid out which represents the chaos of consciousness. This allows the purpose of above to be realized below transforming all before it.
Now there is built up within consciousness the hierarchy of Kabbalah, the sephiros in order to operate from the highest levels in producing the holiness of the Divine Name.

The lower sephiros called binding complete themselves in malkhut meaning the union of above and below. All of these symbols are aids to consciousness in depicting holiness and having the construct from which to work from.

The completion arises out of itself and therefore cannot be fathomed since the process involves the mystery itself.

Therefore how can you encompass that which has no end since it is ever expanding and always goes beyond the moment's understanding.

The holy connections are established; chesed with netzach and gevurah with hod in establishing the balance that comes with the foundation that follows. In this way does Torah through its phrases draw out the holy name.

It is the conception of the Infinite that is hidden even as thought which comes into being instantaneously is hidden.
This conception reaches beyond and also permeates the four elements of the body symbolized by YKV"K

There are three levels that unfold the reality of vision. First there is the initial conception the thought that is the holy soul from which flows all into being. Then there is the expression of thought, its ramifications, and connections that is the ruach of utterance. Then the mirror of thought produced in form called the animating soul, the nephesh that brings forth the image in its fruition.

Tiqun 23

בראשית, ברי״ת א״ש. ברית זה צדיק. כל נקרא. כשר כל אברי הגוף
Bereishis,
ברי׳ת א׳ש (covenant of fire)
Covenant is the Righteous One. Everything it is called כל,
The connector of all the limbs of the body.

The letter ה is the eight days. They are the measure of the Sabbath
that is two thousand cubits in each direction, with which to keep the sign
of the Sabbath.

כמו כן הם שמונה ימים תחום לקבל בהם אות ברית, ולשמור אותו בהם, שלא נעשה באות
ברית
Also they are the eight days of the field with which to receive the sign of
the covenant, and through which to observe so that desecration of the
sign of the covenant is not committed.

69a) This refers to rush of influx characterized by Shekinah which is the everything that connects all the limbs of the body.

These are the eight days of the covenant which describes the link between the recognition of unity and Shekinah and refers to the connection that is increased during the Sabbath.

There must be no separation between the awareness of holiness and holiness itself. It serves as a protection with Shekinah continuously active.

The world of thought is always the image of this world. Also the world that is come envisioned by thought is the image of this world. In this we have to ask how is the making of man the eight days prior to the circumcision or covenant equal to Shabbat?

Tiqun 24

Bereishis

בראשית ירא שבת. (ובה) שבתותי תהיה ירא

ירא fears Shabbat. And of it of *My Sabbaths* be fearful;

Fear ירא'א the Torah; fear (YR"E) the covenant.

Just as one is required to guard the covenant, so as not to enter into a foreign domain, also a person needs to keep the Shabbat so as not to take out an object from a private domain and enter it into a public domain. 'A private domain' is Shekinah, its width is four, and they are YKV"K; and its height is ten: YU"D H"E VA"V H"E.

It is during the Sabbath that we focus upon the kind of self reflection that is the contemplation of the divine. During this contemplation we come face to face with the realization that our thoughts, and the direction that they take has awesome and fearful consequences. We are to be mindful of this

There in this circumspect state of mind we need to remain in this reflective stasis and not enter into the public domain but rather remain within the private domain of Shekinah. The examples of the four letter name and the name of ten letters spelled out are given as the source of that holy contemplation.

The public domain is the world of reaction where there is no thought of holiness. It is by definition profane operating solely by physical laws that offer the decay, which is the poison of Samae"l.

It is during the Shabbat that our encounter with Shekinah takes place. Consider that there is a place within called Mikdash that is the gathering place of blessings called Sabbath and is the meeting of upper and lower Shekinah. In order not to profane this place we do not bring anything here that is not holy. What is holiness? They are the blessings and they are the domain of Sabbath the time of reflection above and below.

What we meet are lower and higher Shekinah, the gathering of blessings above and below. One meets the other together in holiness they are one.

Therefore the blessings are said to awaken and acknowledge the holiness that is Yud which brings forth the connecting links to the tree of life. Now this unholy connection be it wine or wheat is other than the sublime, the gathering place spoken of previously.

Nothing can be made that does not include holiness otherwise it is by definition profane. We must be mindful of holiness in all things therefore the blessings.

Shekinah is a gathering of good as in an orchard only the best fruits are gathered.

ישראל המוח ביניהם. כך כמו כן השצינה היא פרדס בגלות. והיא המוח מבפנים.
אגוז אנו קוראים לו, כמ שאמר שלמה המעלך אל גנת אגוז ירדתי, והיא השכינה
הפרי מבפנים זה הוא שכתוב בת כבודה כל כבודה בת מעלך פנימה ממשבצות זהב לבשה.
Israel is the fruit (brain) on the left. So also the Divine Presence is in
exile in Pardes, (orchard) and She is the fruit of the inside
the nut אגוז they call Her, as King Solomon said:
(Song of Songs 6:11) *To the nut garden I descended*
and it is Shekinah, the inner fruit this is what is written:
(Psalms 45:14) *All the glory of the daughter of the king is inside,*
of latticed gold is her garment.

69b) There is ever present the inner fruit of connection
represented by Shekinah. This connection opens you up to
the all encompassing unity of the king. The latticed gold
represents the shining points of light that are the connections
to unity.

What we connect to on the Sabbath is our holy connection
and what we divest ourselves of are the attachments that we
have to any foreign domains. All of this occurs in order to
promote the highest connection.

We irrigate the garden with every sense of inspiration
connection that we experience. It is the Vav of connection
spoken of here so that we bring about the holy union of
Shekinah and Ha Kodesh Barachu. We leave the status quo of
what comes before for that in which we are actively
engaged...leaving father and mother and cleaving to "his
wife."

The tree of life is revealed once we let go of the reactionary
flow and bring our thoughts in line with the holy flow. It isn't
enough to know that we have a choice; it is important to
realize that this choice must be for good to promote always
the principle of good throughout all the worlds.

We cast off leave behind our reactive nature opening
ourselves to the inner good that is always resident.

Every effort must be expended in connection. Otherwise Shekinah leaves or does not descend upon a person

Fire symbolizes the inner longing for connection therefore all outer fire is extinguished to give precedence to this inner fire

The workings of purification in the body take place via Shekinah; it is the connection to life. Without it death and decay maneuver themselves into place

Let not your thoughts turn to sadness or arouse disputes since this blocks Shekinah especially in the heart where Shekinah gathers to fill the entire body with grace.

These guests, these angels, the extra soul and the higher Shekinah all arise out of the abode within the dwelling place of holiness.

There is no place defined within unless there is a recognition of Shekinah. There is no place for the abode of holiness unless it be made from within via the recognition of Shekinah.

We travel south for wisdom and north for wealth. It is the flowing of one thing into another that brings about these holy aspects.

This gold is the discernment of truth of the presence that resides in response to our calling in a special conscious way.

The bed is the place of rest recognizing that where we rest is the dwelling place of holiness. This is where we have to focus.

On Sabbath eve the extra soul has a place to come otherwise this is not a dwelling of Israel.

השבת לעשות את השבת לדורותם, לדרתם כתוב חסר, מלשון דירה.
...the Sabbath, to make the Sabbath for their generations.'
It is written: לדורותם לדרתם (*for their generations*) כתוב חסר, מלשון דירה without Vav, saying a dwelling.

70a) Therefore you should know that the dwelling is a place you make within by your thoughts in their connection mirroring the Sabbath forming the sign of the circumcision.
Our enemy is anything that blocks connection. We give that enemy bread and water so as to occupy them with the mundane and not the holy things we are partaking of.

For ordinary people the symbols are clothed in flesh in the sacrifices, the burnt offerings. These are then the vehicles for an ordinary connection.

For the righteous connection is the place of holiness and that holiness is within the place of God in the blood where the movement is life and the awareness is Shekinah.

Removing the blockages, the captives in the pit restored holiness.

Tiqun 25

בראשית זו התורה, זה הוא שכתוב יי' קנני ראשית דרכו קדם מפעליו מאז.
Bereishis: this is the Torah; this is what is written:
(Proverbs 8:22) *YKV"K made me as the beginning of His way, the first of His works of old.– from that place of which it is stated:*
(Psalms 93:2) *Thy throne is established of old; Thou art from everlasting...*

I am the acquired one the beginning of the way wherein is established the throne. My cooperation in these matters is critical to their success.

Via Torah the connection is promoted and sustained and grows progressively.

ספר תורה מדוע למלך. מפני שאין הוא מלך אלא מצד המלצות, וצריך להיות לו עמו בכל מקום ספר תורה שהוא עמוד האמצי, להתקשר בו הקדוש ברוך הוא עם שצינתו.

Why does the king have a scroll of the Torah, because he is king from the side of malchus, and there should be with him, in every place, a scroll of the Torah which is the Middle Pillar, connecting Ha Kodesh Barachu with His Shekinah.

The king is the master of his domain, the body. It carries the Torah, its secrets and its inspirations with him to bring about via the middle pillar the holy connection that is Shekinah and Ha Kodesh Barachu.

Just as the Torah needs to be perfect so too does man in his aspect above and below recognizing Shekinah and then living the life of God.

Consider what is being said in terms of the lungs and Torah and the number five and six. Connections are being made. The subtle process of breathing and the subtle art of studying Torah are being compared together. There are transformations taking place in the body just as in the spiritual realms of discovery within Torah. If we choose to take these paths of inspiration we are renewed if not there is decay, Samael. Allegory is raised to a supreme level here.

The heart is the consumer the expresser of life that fills the body with its intentional force. The lungs temper that expression by transforming it via the oxygenated blood and pathways symbolized by the lobes of the lungs. Hashem moderates via the soul and the mind that expresses its connection and the transformations of inspiration that occur via Torah study and a focused intention.

Therefore the connection with fire and air with heart and lungs and with intention and spirit is established. What is important here are the pathways and their various assignments. We see how the body mirrors the spiritual universe and therefore have a map for proving our thoughts into expression.

And the heart, when the *spirit-ruach* ascends via it, and separates from the animating soul-nephesh which is Vav a fire burns on the blood, it is stated of the animating soul (*nephesh*):
(Song of Songs 5:2) *I sleep...* and when the wind/spirit (*ruach*) comes towards it, it is stated: ...*and my heart is awake.*
And this: (Isaiah 26:9) *With my soul have I desired Thee in the night; yea, with my spirit within me have I sought Thee earnestly;*

וכאשר יבוא הרוח אצל הלב ששם הנפש, נאמר בו קול דודי דופק
And when the spirit comes towards the heart,
where the animating soul is, it is stated of it:
(Song of Songs 5:2) *the voice of my beloved knocks*

70b) Start with what is this 'dew' for it is the culmination of the movement of nephesh-and ruach. It is what is passing through at the gate of the heart and then radiating throughout. This accumulation is apparently the trigger that opens due to its overflowing.

It is when you become aware of the nexus described herein that you are simultaneously made aware of yourself as a spiritual being. The avenues of entry are described as BaRa ShY"T each letter an entry point analogous to the entry points of the heart.

There is a subsequent filling throughout the body again in synchronicity with the spiritual six directions, the heart and lungs flow and now the sephiros all designating the same thing albeit in different aspects like watching a ballgame from the field or in the bleachers; the same show only a different perspective.

It is shown with sounds that derive from the frequency that each level represents. And each sound represents a pathway that arises upon the concentration of this sound.

When these pathways are formed the angels ascend and descend. It is the opening of the spiritual pathways. The life force of the heart beats in tandem with the release and flowing of the spirit through the intentional pathways.

Once you become aware of these movements then there is the direction of movement taking the beat of one to accentuate into another as in transforming to chesed from gevurah. Every sound is a node that repeats the flow.

There is the extension of the heart, which is the place of accumulation and the sending forth of the intention. The sick one represents they who are without Torah, without a sense of meaning in their lives and without the flow of unity that ensues from both.

וכולם דופקים לגבי השכינה שהיא סלם שבו שש דרגות
And they all knock towards Shekinah
Who is a ladder, in which there are six levels.

And this is the heart, and through it angels of ELKY"M
ascend and descend, which is the beating of the spirit (דפקי הרוח)

The knocking comes about because of a sense of the impending flow. When it is frequent and seems to be oppression then there is the release. The release is the flow of meaning that comes to heal the 'sick one.'

The 'sick one' is also like the darkness of the deep which did not respond to the spirit that hovered over until light came; the light which was the meaning which dispels the darkness.

Shekinah is fed with meanings that are derived from connecting the pathways within. These are spiritual pathways that are eternal.   When they are activated by our awareness Shekinah flows through them.

When you restore the sense of meaning everything else makes sense.   Shekinah is restored to her rightful place as the connecting link above.

Meanwhile בינתים an eagle came by the great eagle with great wings... and gave three voices, and then ascended to the mountains.

Rabbi Shimon said to his companions:
Favor is certainly present above, and mercies are found in Shekinah and Israel in exile,
שודאי שלש חיות הן במרכב
for there are certainly three chayot in the Chariot, lion, ox, eagle, and none of them have mercy like the eagle.
And because of this, He has said to Israel: (Shemos 19:4)
...*I bore you on eagles' wings, and brought you unto Myself.*

71a) And this healing is the healing of meaning itself restoring it to its holy place.

Thought on many levels here described as three all pertaining to rising above for the meanings of unity

The eagles are the highest voices. They ascend to and connect with the unification via the agency of Shekinah

Again the highest voice symbolized by the eagle.   This is mystical presence that is associated with Shekinah who also rises and ascends as the connection is experienced.

'Go up' meaning to ascend to the higher voice and translate, transform what is being said to what symbols we have inferred.

This ascension takes us into the highest heaven beyond even the sight of what is going on.

The eagle brings us the meaning so that it may be filtered through to them, the higher voice to him, Ha Kodesh Barachu.

The temple is thereby restored via the symbolic roses giving access to the holiness that resides there signifying a complete recovery. What is understood is that our access to the wisdom of the temple above is granted without question. So begins the discourse of meaning.

Rabbi Shimon began speaking and said:
(Song of Songs 6:3) *I am to my beloved and my beloved is to me,*
the shepherd in the roses.
What is the meaning of *the roses*?

But Higher rose is Higher Shekinah, and She is the saying of SHMA in the morning service, and the second rose, is the saying of SHMA in the evening service the lower Shekinah; this one to the right and this one to the left; the shepherd in the roses, this is the Middle Pillar.

And Higher Shekinah of the recitation of the Shema in the morning service, which is morning the right hand, of Abraham has five words and they are:
(Deuteronomy 6:4) *Hear (Shema) O Israel* יי׳ אלקינו יי׳;
and thirteen leaves inside (alluding to) אח׳ד six red, and six white, together with the rose, which is comprised of them, they are thirteen the number of אח׳ד

The rose symbolizes Shekinah both higher and lower rose connecting with the SHMA in the morning and evening respectively. What guides our thoughts is the shepherd which is also in the roses and is the Middle Pillar of thought, that which connects all rising and descending thoughts to each other and to the unity of meaning.

Just as the words and letters of the SHMA come together as one so too do our thoughts arise and link together in the holiness of unity. These symbols point the way towards the temple and our connection therein.

The worlds are thereby created Bara with meaning via the two roses, Bereishis, and the two houses Beit placing one inside the other focusing on the connections that result in this instance of the fifty that are spotlighted.

Tiqun 26

בראשית ב׳ שושנה. המשה עלים שלה ראשי״ת. בראשיי״ת לחשבון קטן של חנוך שלש
עשרה תיבות מן אלקים ועד אלקים

Bereishis is Beit the rose שושנה

Its five leaves are the letters of ראשי׳ת.

בראשית *in the small counting of Enoch,' is thirteen;*
its thorns are the thirteen words from the first ELKY"M to the second ELKY"M,
and they are:
(Shemos 1:2-3) *...the heavens and the earth;*
and the earth was chaos and void
and darkness upon the face of the abyss
and the spirit of ELKY"M…
Five other thorns: *...hovering upon the face of the water and He said...*

Continuing now with the meaning of rose related to Bereishis.

The connections are between the phrases now starting from the first ELKY"M to the second ELKY"M. Bring these words together for the light that is to shine upon them. Wherever our attention is it is there so that the meanings come forth.

With the temple destroyed the higher meanings are masked by chaos and void.

Redemption is inferred from the higher and lower Shekinah to bring about the light that resolves the masking of chaos and void.

Therefore the rose is revealed with her five petals and the five mentions of light that are synonymous with the redemption, the revelation of meaning.

Here within the roses respectively higher and lower show the unity of meaning that establishes the Middle Pillar making the connection above and below with Shekinah the agency that is both ascending and descending.

(Song of Songs 2:16) *...the shepherd in the roses*;
and His number is EChaD (13)

שושנה תח תונה בה יראה והוא יראה. שושנה עליונה אהבה של אהבאם טבג
באנר אן תעורט ת אנ תעטררט עת האהבה עד שתחפץ.

The lower rose, in her is fear, and it is fear (awe).
The Higher rose is love, and it is said,
(Song of Songs 2:7) *...that ye awaken not, nor stir up love, until it please*

71b) Meanings come through only when our intention and attention are directed their way. Then via our attention they come of themselves linking togethers thoughts of holiness one with the other.

Our action is what arouses and only when the connecting link is aligned in unity, Echad.

She is aroused with combinations of holiness such as the holy letters and the deeper mysteries that are revealed there. When the spirit of ELKY"M hovers or the knowledge of the way things work enters our consciousness which is the Messiah then there is a synthesis of thoughts that brings about the connection which is Shekinah being healed from Her neglect and awakened by intention and attention to holiness.

She is only aroused by an equal portion of the love she embraces via the meanings that are now coming together.

The pillars of truth are the reflected images that we make once we understand the import of Her connection. This is done by instinctual feel or called here the 'scent of your nose.'

We align with what we are made of.

Unity, is where She comes into being and is harvested by holiness called Ha Kodesh Barachu in the place of Her becoming known as the nut garden.

The different ways of combining the letters and their numeric values lead to the sublime connections that awaken Her in Her garden of becoming.

The unity is represented by these connections are made within via these symbols of representation that they mirror in mind and in the thoughts contained therein.

There is the connection of ten that shows the meaning of ten, the soul of Shekinah and the mystery of the letters derived one from the other endlessly.

It is 'Place' or the abode of the most high whose mystery comes from the connections between the letters. Everything points to where you are looking. Holiness is in the moment of revelation.

What doesn't change is that we are always looking for meaning and what never changes also includes that this meaning is finding unity in all things especially viewing the sacred text for its mysteries. The literal interpretations are superficial while the deeper meanings are sublime.

Solomon sought out wisdom even amongst the superficial things. It was here in these husks that he was able to gather even their shells of meanings in order to know what it meant to find these coverings that contained the kernel of truth.

The four sides of the nut are the canvas out of which is painted the divine form. Out of void, chaos, darkness and the abyss come form, order, light, and fullness. All of this is because the awareness of the way things work has been revealed by the way shower who is ADN"Y, which brings together the unifying awareness that is One.

Transformation occurs according to our actions including the changes that are for the good, for bringing forth of connection, and uniting Shekinah with Ha Kodesh Barachu.

פעמים נגלה להם בדמות אריה, זה הוא שכתוב אריה שאג מי לא יירא.
Sometimes He is revealed to them in the form of a lion;
this is what is written: (Amos 3:8) A lion has roared, who will not fear?

פעמים בדיוקו שור, זה הוא שכתוב בכור שורו הדר לו וקני ראם קרניו
Sometimes He seems in the form of an ox;
this is what is written: (Devarim 33:17)
His firstling bullock, majesty is his; and his horns are the horns of the wild-ox

ולפעמים בדיוקו של נשר, זה שכתוב כנשר יעיר קנו.
And sometimes He seems the portrait of an eagle; this is what is written:
(Devarim 32:11) *As an eagle that stirs up her nest...*

ולפעמים בדיוקו אדם זקן, כמו שנדמה לאלו שאמרו זה א"לי ואנוהו. שהוא היה נדמה להם בדמות זקן
And sometimes He seems the portrait of an elder man,
as it might sound by those who said:
(Shemos 15:2) *This is my God...*
He seemed to have the form of an elder;

72a) Each of these four faces man, lion, ox and eagle represent levels of perception according to how we interpret the unity related to what we are discovering in the moment. These are all versions of the moment of inspiration that ensues from such discoveries.

However having been through these discoveries we recognize them for the unifications that appear and . and is This becomes an eternal realization.

These exchanges are the model for seeing unity everywhere one thing inside another even to the greatest or smallest of details.

On the one hand the removal of the shoe (as in the Levirate marriage) before Shekinah represents a purity of vision while the patriarchs all had the covering of shoes signifying respect of holiness. This is a deep secret about the mystery of revelation in that nothing can be revealed unless we both discard the blockages and retain the awareness that unity is ever present.

The patriarchs understood the power and workings of Blessed Holy One but did not comprehend the 'way things work,' in that within Hashem is the meaning of Y'H and that the name is the thing itself that is to become after another fashion, the image of its maker.

The woman removes the shoe because She removes the husks of uncertainty so that the snake of doubt will not bind up the consciousness. She is the certainty of unity.

That drop is the initial realization of holiness and of the unity of the word taking form of the conversation between above and below and their subsequent advancing creation.

The sin is the misstep, the errant thought that was taken to be real and then all that came after was a result of the error. And then the removal of that misstep allows that first drop to descend and the error is repented and the unity restored.

In order to ameliorate the error of thought it goes through transformations, which take the thought into a better outcome teaching along the way and reminding of the synthesis between above and below.

Man is the realization of the image of thought and as such is constantly perfecting itself to be the progenitor of thought by choosing the right outcome prior to witnessing its fruition. What this means is that we are able to tell by our thinking what that outcome will like and it follows that we will arrange our thoughts accordingly seeking above for the unification that is inherent within us.

What Jacob earned that changed him into Israel was the unification of thought. He fought with the angel until he became unified with it and realized his unity was with heaven.

What is it that we bind ourselves with the outer forms or the inner realities. When we leave Shekinah all else is illusory and leads to error and is by definition sin or hell.

Isaac represents the awareness of the other and keeps us from binding with the other

Through Jacob meaning the transformation that becomes Israel we are able to let go of the transitory forms and realize the divine presence.

The soul is renewed via transformation. This transformation is of the thought atmosphere, i.e. the consciousness of a person that is renewed and revealed so that self awareness becomes awareness of Shekinah. In this way spirit and lower and higher soul are united.

לבו ששם נפש רוח בכנפי ריאה, נשמה במוח וכולם אחד בקשר אחד
Heart-mind-spirit wings where lung, brain and animating soul al one single connection

72b) Call these the pathways via which Shekinah flows via heart lungs and brain unifying in thought word and deed. In each location there is connection that is raised accordingly. Levels of meaning are therefore transcended in this way.

The hunters trap is the trap of our reaction to world and not to the inner dwelling Shekinah. The knots are what keep us from rising above the circuitous thoughts that lead to decay. The soul breaking free unifies all of its separated parts.

Tiqun 27 (part of the introduction Tiqun 6-7)

Tiqun 28

בראשית בו שלש מצוות. אחת יראת יקו״ק, כמו זה בראשי״ת יר״א בש״ת. והר העמידוה.

Bereishis – in this word there are three commandments:
one is the fear of YKV"K, like this: BeREiShYT – YR"E BoSheT
(fear of shame) that has already been established.

שני בדית, כמו זה בראשי״ת ברי״ת אייש.

The second is covenant, like this:
BeREiShYT – BRYT EiSh (covenant of fire).

שלישי שבת כמו זה שב״ת יר״א.

The third is the Sabbath, like this: ShaBaT YR"E (fear of Sabbath).

What is the meaning of this fear and why is it so important?

First fear presupposes a thought process that does one thing and then another according to what is right and avoids what is wrong because following a wrong thought process leads to negative events bringing about chaos.

The second component of fear is awe, which is the reverence for the holiness of connection; the connection that we seek to maintain with Shekinah. It is the connection that is the linking of all three parts of the soul.

What is this wellspring? It is the flowing of the waters of realization that are the purpose behind Torah and why we study it and what we make when we do so. These waters of

310

the wellspring are the flowing of Shekinah through our bodies and through our lives.

The wine of Torah is sealed for those who do not fear HVY'H or who do not recognize the relationship between cause and effect.

Torah is partaken of by those who are able to make that connection with Shekinah in order to reveal her secrets subsequently making new pathways in Torah. It is a kind of user manual for connection with Shekinah and by extension YHV'H although both being joined together there is in truth only one.

In order to purify the heart it must be cleansed and cleared of the evil inclination.

The heart that is pure is the beginning of wisdom where it arises to permeate all throughout every conjoining connection.

Thoughts that gather without holiness as their center decay and produce death. This is the chaos and the breaking down of order.

This wine that is spoken of is the gathering fruit of holiness which derives by definition from the precepts of Torah.

Tiqun 29

בראשית. ברא עלקים ב נקודה בהיכלו, עליו נאמר גן נעול אחתי כלהגל נעול מעין
חתום. מי הוא מעין חתום, זו נקודה. מי הוא נעול שלה זו ו', שסותמת את ההיכל
ובה נעשה ם סתום היא ם גדולה מלסרבה המשרה.

Bereishis BaRA ELKY"M
Beit a point within its chamber (Dagesh) about it is: (Song of Songs 4:12)
A garden shut up is my sister, my bride; a spring shut up, a fountain sealed.
Who is the spring shut up? It is the point. What who is her lock?

It is the letter Vav which shuts the chamber,
and through it She is made into a closed Mem, which is the large final
Mem of: (Isaiah 9:6) To him who increases (מלמרבה) authority.

And about this point it is stated: (Job 28:21)
Seeing it is hid from the eyes of all living,
and kept close from the fowls of the air.
and this point: from the right side, is called 'love (*ahavah*),'
and from the left side is called fear and from the aspect of the Middle
Pillar it is called Torah, and it is *mitzvah* for the Middle Pillar includes
the two of them, because it is Vav, including Y"K, which are to the right
and left, and it is Vav in the middle, including both of them.

73a) The flow of Shekinah is released via the aspects of love,
fear, Torah, and Mitzvah. It is the connecting link between
above and below. The mystery of the name is therefore
included as to its contemplation producing the equivalent of
connection, the Vav between the two Heh's.

It is this knowledge of the perception of Shekinah that is the
beginning of the way since this alludes to the flowing of the
sense, the awareness that produces the meanings that are the
basis for wisdom, Torah, and the middle pillar.

The purpose of precept is to awaken Shekinah which is why
the relationship between M"TZ and YH is shown via atbash
to be the same. There is where we find the flow from
connection to unification.

When ELKY"M is paired with Y'H there is the transformation
of change. The realization here is that consciousness is the
canvas upon which all of us work upon and within. ELKY"M
is the 'way things work,' the operational variant paired with
YH the intentional variant that produces the hearts desire.

The flow of essence arising from mercy is another
transformation that works on letting go of the negative
aspects and allowing the positive to dominate.

The constant fire on the altar is Shekinah the fire that burns within and consumes the dross of the mundane consciousness and presents the place of holiness continuously.

Throughout this Tiqun She is showing you the way that She moves. She is showing you Her pathways and fulfillments. She is residing within Torah but is also as well within the revelation of its hidden passages that travels along in a consistent continuous fashion. She is included in both negative and positive precepts for the revelation is always there according to its level of discernment. She resides within man to enlighten him and to keep that holy fire within constantly burning.

This is Her purpose and it is the design of our purpose to become one with Her. When R.Shimon is inspired to speak the words of revelation it is because he is speaking through the burning light that resides within and which is particularly the emphasis at this point in the discussion.

Tiqun 30

בראשית, מי היא ראשית, זו חכמא, זו נקודה שבפנים שנאמר
Bereishis who is called *reishis,* It is chokmah, this inner point
of which it is stated:

(Psalms 45:14) *All the glory of the king's daughter is inside*;
and it is fear (*yir-ah*), which is the first commandment,
and about which it is stated:
(Proverbs 1:7) *The fear of YKV"K is the beginning of knowledge*;
and it is alluded to in the word Bereishis.

We are speaking of a conceptual beginning a place from which thought evolves. This place is called wisdom meaning we are aware of the consequences of thought. It is also called fear since we must be careful not to promote thought that will come back on us and destroy us.

This point is symbolic of that place where thought comes from so that cutting off the errant thought is critical to evolving from that place of choice into holiness. There is a progression and the symbolism of the Sabbath, Festivals and Tephillin is to remember that place of choice and to keep it holy.

Do not allow the errant thought to evolve by giving it your attention because it will block you from the light.

The meaning of Bereishis contains fear, Shabbat and Creation meaning that in order to set yourself free to partake of holiness with no strings attached, you must recognize the fear and let it go.

Bereishis therefore indicates a divine principle the three contained in the one word.

Again we have the beginning of the way, wherein the thought that comes from the source is the pointer to all that comes after.

This space spoken of is where the thought takes form concealed within the closed Mem and then opens as the added spirit or soul of Sabbath comes into being.

What is being described here is the coming into being of thought as it grows within its space and awakens its potential during Shabbat.

נקראת סתומה באות ו'. וזה ערלה ופריעה הן כמוץ ותבן של חטה.
She is called blocked 'stumah' with the letter Vav.
And this foreskin and membrane likened to the chaff and straw of wheat.

בימי החול נקראת ה"א שהוא הב"ל לה"ב המזבח לשרוף מוץ ותבן.
On weekdays She is called Hei, which is HeVeL (breath /vanity)
whose letters form LaHaV (flame) of the altar, to kindle the chaff
and She remains as clean fine flour.

אבל בימי שבת וימים טובים נקראת י׳ עטרה על הכל.

But on Sabbath Days, and Festivals, She is called Yud,
the crown upon everything, and Her house (throne)
is the 32 mentions of of ELKY"M in the act of creation.
And She is Beit ,that includes the ten sayings on every side.

73b) She is blocked in terms of having boundaries. These boundaries foreskin and membrane separate the creative thought from the chaos of thinking. Weekdays are analogous to thinking about the mundane things while Sabbaths and Festivals denote holiness wherein the crown is upon everything. In the Creation story there are details and there is the action of holiness or the 32 mentions of ELKY"M.

The rays of Shekinah permeate Torah via the precepts connecting from all sides the holiness that we aspire to offering a realm of connection in every conceivable location.

The first path is that of awareness or the recognition of unity and the connection of Shekinah the two that are one.

Shekinah is always present even though there are those who hide from her using various 'public' devices. No matter what veils are in place Shekinah surpasses them all meaning that our aspiration for holiness will always allow us to have a guaranteed point of entry.

Those who would deny holiness are themselves denied its protection. The spirit of holiness once blocked cannot operate unless we reach up to connect with it with a conscious action of the intention of connection.

This connection occurs by a direct experience of Shekinah in in all of Her fullness and connection. Even the study of Torah without the awareness of Shekinah is simply intellectualizing truth and not its actual experience.

There is a type of fear of Ha Kodesh Barachu that exists 'in order to receive reward,' so that circumstances will not overcome you but in truth what is more proper and fitting is that fear which distinguishes good from bad.

The awakening of this love that seeks reward misses the point entirely. She awakens, she watches, and she is ever present a thread that seals together the above and below. This continuous flow She awakens is end result of holiness.

…is of the maidservant:
(Proverbs 30:21-3) *For three things the earth doth quake…*
For a servant when he reigns…
…and a handmaid that is heir to her mistress..

עלקי״ם זה מן ויאמר אלקים יהי אור הוא נתיב שלישי יהי אור. יי״ה אויי״ר או״ת י׳.
This ELKY"M of:
(Bereishis 1:3) *And ELKY"M said: 'Let there be light'* is the third **path**.
YKY AUR (Let there be light) forms the words
Y"K AVY"R; is composed of *AU"R, (light)* Y';

and when this point is wrapped herself (spread) in this light
and is made air, from here are continued all beings.

74a) When you rise to the level of the 'slave who rules' you are cognizant of your unity with Shekinah. Initially we are slaves to circumstance, a maidservant to the power that resides within us via the mistress Shekinah.

The extension of light that is made air is thought that is wrapped in ethereal substance and takes part in the flow of continuous creation. This presupposes that thought always has a place in context with all that is. It is never separate.

Let there be light and there was light are phrases that discriminate time. Let there be light is instantaneous while there was light references a time delay. This time delay is that which brings judgment for the whole world.

The light is the instantaneous transmission appearance of thought into form while the darkness obscures this transition giving rise to doubts.

Moshe talks about the fulfilment of creation in its instantaneous aspect whereas Korach vies for the time delay essentially causing a rift in Creation. This rift is referenced when Korach and his followers were dropped into the bottomless pit, the rift.

This darkness is analogous to a time delay, which we experience in this world due to an limited understanding of the continuous creation. We as finite beings can still work within the framework of separation but we are called to witness the light meaning the instantaneous Creation in order to show us the way forward.

This distinction is found symbolically in the hierarchy of the typical man who contains both light, darkness, instantaneous continuity and time delayed results.

Continuous Creation is configured to work together with the time delay of darkness merging the two aided by the agency of Shekinah the connecting link, the middle Pillar and day and night together.

The precursor to inspiration is a series of unifications denoted as positive precepts. These camps are the thought forms that arise in response to these unifications. The Queen is Shekinah the thread that runs through these unifications. The King is the all becoming one.

Compare this to a kind of docking maneuverer where the connection is lined up, established and then initiated just like our intention is prior to prayer.

The connection of ascension makes ready all of the compliant thoughts that orient themselves in such a way as to make for our simultaneous unifications. Therefore what happens is that disparate thoughts come together in amazing ways to unify with the holiness above.

This throne that is the pinnacle of the middle pillar is the essence of being and its central focus is called Anokhi the 'I am' the identification with holiness combined with the connection of Shekinah.

The commandment is our intention and that which performs is the result of that intention taking shape.

Shekinah is the primary focus for contemplation since it is the connection that establishes the linkages between thoughts. If we realize this then everything else becomes secondary. This is the initial realization of holiness.

The middle pillar is the connection of Shekinah between the highest, the head and all that comes as a result of this revelation "the which."

In order for there to be any interaction we first have the king the highest point and then the Connection or Shekinah which provides the next. It is She who opens the womb meaning She sets the stage for the gestation of the next step. She is forever tied to the King in that her sending flowing is based upon the initial impetus, which is the King.

ואימא זה הוא שכתוב ויאמר אלקים יהי אור ויהי אור
And Mother, this is what is written:
(Bereishis 1:3) *And ELKY"M said: 'Let there be light;' and there was light;*

And He said, from the side of Father, who is Yud;
let it be – from the side of Mother, who is Hei;
one *saying* אמירה and one (*level of heaven*) הויה
I did both of them, *let there be light.*

318

74b) ELKY"M is the combination of Father and Mother. It is the creative process. There is a sending forth which is Father and a state of being called havayah. The combination occurs as one is compacted into the phrase 'let there be light.' To explain this further this is what happens when a thought appears first at the level of intention.

We have many thoughts each day but not all rise to the level of focused intention. When intention is realized in its proper form, which is ELKY"M then the understanding this produces evokes the becoming which is a natural outgrowth of this understanding.

It is because of this thing, which comes next that everything is brought about. It is the end in the beginning and the continuation of creation that is brought from this beginning that is the end.

The slave is the ignorance of the truth. Therefore when that truth appears it is never to be forgotten for it is the essence of our being and what we are called to remember.

We are asked to live in the light of creation to know and procreate from this knowledge. This isn't the procreation of physicality which brings forth new life but is rather the procreation of ideas that brings about new connections and increases the awareness between thoughts.

The Sinai experience of connection above and below and the special quality of attention that is given each of us by the divine is the awareness of our unity. It is our ability to work together with creation and to recognize that we are not only acted upon but are also the conscious actors of creation.

We work in concert with the above since we are ever mirroring the divine expression.

Where is it that we have the most intimate connection above? It is within where we listen to our thoughts. There are thoughts and there are thoughts meaning some thoughts are reactions and others are filled with intention. Learning the difference is the property of the higher sephiros. It is the voice that encompasses all and is the basis of everything.

What we see therefore is the connection that the middle pillar, Shekinah enhances and shows us that voice and insight into our own intimate reflections of the above. We are in turn called to listen to make that voice our own to identify personally with it and hear it for what it is showing to us.

Therefore we enter into the becoming of creation, the mist the connection, Shekinah the bringing together of sound and light, the imaging of the voice and the becoming of creation.

Anokhi is your identification with the word. It is the realization that ELKY"M is the active force in your life. This is the highest of your comprehension that you are indeed part of creation and that it responds to you in detail completely.

The first commandment is the recognition of the divine source, the initial intention and the becoming of that intention that runs throughout all that we touch and experience in the world.

The first commandment linked to Remember and Observe as well as the recognition of Divinity that is in unity with the self.

Tephilin is symbolic of connection. It is the middle pillar between head and hand, source and outcome, father and mother, Ha Kodesh Barachu and Shekinah. All of these point to the basic premise of the above and the connection below.

The third commandment, the third path, prophecy comes about because we expect or rather imagine the outcomes based upon our intention and the way things work. Now initially above these imaginings are not revealed. However, in the fullness of the outcome they are revealed according to the awareness of the prophet within and to the degree in which they have become awakened.

Shekinah is seen in Her various aspects all relating to the connection of above and below. This is what shows in terms of the spirituality of a thing.

נתיב רביעי ויבדל עלקים בין האור ובין החשך. זכר ונקבה הם חשך לילה, זה הוא
שכתיב ולחשך קרא לילה. ויש חשך מצד הסהרה ולילה מצד הטהרה, זה הוא
שכתוב גם חשך לא יחשיך ממך ולילה כיום יאיר כחשכה כאורה.

The fourth **path**:
(Shemos 1:4) ...and ELKY"M separated between the light and between the darkness, they are male and female.
Darkness is night; this is what is written:
(Shemos 1:5) ...and He called the darkness 'night'

And there is darkness and there is night on the purity and the purity of the other purity; this is what is written:
(Psalms 139:12) Even the darkness is not too dark for Thee, but the night shines as the day; the darkness is even as the light.

The light that darkness receives is female.which is which is masculine from the sun.

75a) The darkness is the pure undifferentiated substance out which all that is comes into being.

The aspect of darkness is female in that it evokes the light out of its substance like the moon reflects light and like a mirror emanates light and the mirror that doesn't reflect the light.

When there is separation it is the darkness of the other side that is the false light or the impermanent light.

When Shekinah enters secrets are revealed. It is the connection of Shekinah and Ha Kodesh Barachu that awakens and transmits the revelation.

A comparison and an alignment is shown; The Masters of the House of the King-the looking glass that shines-YKV"K-love-written Torah are conjoined.

It is at the time of these unifications that the masters appear. They have risen in their own realm to the perfections of unifications. All of these masters come together before the throne since the singular unification is Ha Kodesh Barachu.

The prophets speak of things that are to be but have no hand in their becoming while the sages presuppose that becoming influences events via the unifications of thought.

The false prophets seek to superimpose their prophecy for what is to become. The difference is that they ignore the divine will causing people to stray from the divine path. It is this division of light and dark that is not clearly adhered to and causes these false prophets to assume a role they haven't earned.

When the source and its connection are together only then is there the distinction between light and darkness flowing naturally as the result of an endless becoming that is good.

The light that is day is subdivided into masters of Scripture, Mishnah and Talmud. All of these masters reveal the concealed on the surface, in midrash and in commentary and allegory.

מצוה רביעית לעכוק בתורה שבעל פה ולהבדיל בה בשש דרגות באסור ותתר וטומאה כשר ופסול.

The fourth **commandment**:is the practice in the Oral Torah,
and to differentiate within it six degrees of
prohibition and permission impurity and purity, valid and invalid
This is what is written:
(Shemos 1:6) *And ELKY"M said: 'Let there be a firmament in the midst
of the waters, and let it separate between the waters and the waters*

There is a basic tenet in this fourth commandment of Oral Torah to discern its meanings no matter what circumstances are present. Everything can be traced to its original source and indeed this is the purpose of Oral Torah to make unifications where the appearance of chaos rules or where harmony is the prevailing tone.

Firmament in this instance represents discernment, the ability to make something out of nothing or out of chaos. It is the ability to see beyond the surface into the interconnected nature of things. When we reach this level of intuitive knowing we are reaching for holiness.

החיה רקיע

chayah – a firmament;

and about it is said, (Bereishis 1:7) *And ELKY"M made*
And about this is the sixth path.
and there is a firmament above the firmament, and this is the Righteous One, who separates between female and male waters, in order to become known through it; and about that it is said:
(Shemos 1:7) *And ELKY"M made the firmament, and He divided between the waters that were beneath the firmament,*
and between the waters that were above the firmament...
and this is the seventh path, the Righteous One.

נתיב שמיני ויקרא אלקים לרקיע שמים. ויקרא אלקים זו אימא עליונה. לרקיע זו עמוד האמצע שהוא בין ימין ושמאל וכולל שניהם, זה הוא שכתוב ויהי ערב ויהי בקר יום אחד. והם ערב של יצחק ובקר של אברהם.

The eighth path: (Bereishis 1:8) *And ELKY"M called the firmament heaven...*
And ELKY"M called, this is higher mother, *to the firmament*
this is the Middle Pillar, which is between right and left
and includes both of them; this is what is written: (Shemos 1:5) ...
and it was evening and it was morning, one day
and these are: the evening of Isaac and the morning of Abraham.

75b) The firmament above the firmament is the Righteous One that which comes in and that which goes out. It is the taking of nothing and making it into something. ELKY"M in its making effects the source in connection with its outcome.

The division of waters is seeing creation from both sides of inspiration and becoming

Firmament equals connection the source and its outcome called the middle pillar.

Tiqun 31

בראשית בר"א שת"י. ועליהם נאמר ותלכנה שתיהם וגו', והם שתי תורות תורה
שבכתב ותורה שבעל פה.
Bereishis composed of בר'א שת'י
and about them it is stated: (Ruth 1:19) *And they went, the two of them.*
And they are the two Torahs, the written Torah and the oral Torah.

There is what has been revealed the written Torah and what is about to be revealed through inference and meditation, the Oral Torah.

Seeing the voices asking… this is Naomi meaning this is the connection between source and outcome. Also this is the deeper inner meaning of Torah, and its pleasantness.

The Torah which is full is rejected by the sin of the people meaning their vessels were impure so they could not fathom its depths. They were dumb as to its secrets.

What is body and soul? It is the connection of the thing itself the source with its outcome. They are inseparable except with the dissolution of the outcome the source remains the same.

The discrepancy comes when the body dissolves however considering that outcomes always arise what becomes of the initiating thoughts? They become attached to higher thoughts and reside within that which has promoted the progress of thought either in positive commandments which are the momentum of thought or in negative commandments which is where the impetus of thought ever resides.

It is the voice of connection that establishes us on high. Without this voice or this connection we face exile. When Naomi follows Ruth she is saying that she will listen to this voice of connection.

The result of not listening to the voice of connection is destruction because anything that is built up comes about because of this voice. The opposite of this voice is the yetzer hara which seeks to supplant the voice of heaven..

At every point the soul chooses its direction and part of that choice is to cut off the evil inclination and to remain steadfast and connected to the higher thoughts.

Connection is what must be established from above and below. Israel sins and connection departs. Without connection there is no conversation and no intimacy with holiness.

The animating soul passes along with the body since it is the sustaining force of the body. This is however a transmutation in which the animating soul takes upon itself the purpose of the body and seeks to refill that purpose if it has fallen short.

(Proverbs 6:22) *When thou walks, it shall lead thee* – in this world;
when thou lies down, it shall watch over thee; – in the grave;
and when you will wake up – for the resurrection of the dead
(for the world to come)*it shall talk with you,*
This is the animating soul (nephesh) in relation to the body.

And, holy lamp, if the body has not returned in repentance,
and has 'turned the neck' towards repentance, then the soul is separated
from it and it is called ערפ'ה, and this body is lost to both worlds.

76a) R. Shimon tells us that nothing is ever lost not the souls
or the body since Ha Kodesh Barachu made both and this
represents perfection. What seems to be lost by ignorance or
stiff necked opposition is dissolved and reconstituted
according to the next use which promotes the good of the
Creator.

The wealthy are in exile because they partook so much of this
world that they lose sight of the next whereas the poor always
seek good and find it in the world to come. The perfect world
dissolves the wealthy and promotes the poor yet all come
together on common ground in the world to come. The
written and oral Torah are offered here depending each upon
their level of understanding.

Moshe rose above the body taking his shoes (lower nature)
off to commune with the highest.

The Tree of Life represents eternity of life the expression of
which is our destiny. The image we are made into in turn
images on high causing a back and forth learning that derives
from both written and oral Torah.

Even though the body becomes sullied its aspirations are
always on high amidst those couches of silver and gold.

Tiqun 32

בראשית מאמר ראשון לכל. והוא כולל שני דבורים
Bereishis the first statement of all, and it includes two speakings,

אנכי ולא יהי לך שנאמרו בדבור אחד
(Shemos 20:2-3) *I (Anokhi)... and There shall not be...*
that were stated simultaneously in one speaking,

ושניהם הם רמוזים במלת בראשית

And both of them are alluded to in the word: Bereishis.

Because of this, Bereishis
is composed of א'ב (father) רשי'ת (beginning);
א'ב Aleph is אנכי
Beit is 'There shall not be... and all through one letter, Beit;
and this is the Beit of Bereishis.

The distinction between 'I' and 'there shall not be' is that the former represents specific a intention while the latter is the absence of anything except that intention. This is how the container becomes filled with intention or there is the beginning Reishis of the container Beit or the father.

אמר לו רבי שמעון, כך הוא ודאי. אבל כאן לא משבח הקדוש ברוך הוא עצמו
שהוציא אותם מן הגלות

Rabbi Shimon said to him:
That is certainly how it is, but here, Ha Kodesh Barachu does not praise Himself that he brought them out of exile.

But the fifty times, in which are mentioned the יציאת מצרים (Exodus from Egypt) in the Torah, make known the level at which he took them out, which is the level of jubilee of which it is stated: (Vayikra 25:11)
It is a jubilee, the fiftieth year and they are the fifty gates of binah

76b) There are fifty levels of the Shemos called the gates of binah which is why it was mentioned fifty times in the Torah. All but one was transmitted to Moses at Mount Sinai. Now these fifty gates are symbolic of the levels of attainment that lead to becoming free of the earth bound thoughts and rising up to the higher heavenly thoughts.

This is accomplished in various ways but each of these gates of Binah are like those images that used to be captured on the large photographic plates in the early days of photography. Your progress and your intentions are all collected here over the stillness of time.

Call these gates then the imprinting of consciousness in ever increasing levels of holiness. This last gate however, is only accessible when you have the awareness to piece all of these various levels together in a unification of thought.

It is a vast conception worthy of Ha Kodesh Barachu and yet it remains presented as an attainment that eluded the master Moses. The reason for this is that consciousness has to evolve to the point of being able to contemplate its own images for what they are; a reflection of holiness itself, Hashem.

The Torah becomes a bulwark against the evil inclination represented by the seventy nations and Samae"l. This refers to the choice of thoughts that one may adhere to.

The choice of Torah rules over the evil inclination. Torah has God as its primary focus. Therefore studying Torah is the study of God.

Your thoughts may stray and therefore pollute the body, which is then given a chance for repentance. If repentance meaning returning to Torah isn't taken the body deteriorates.

Repentance clears the white horse, which is the body of sin.

Even when the red horse is what the body has become it too is cleared by repentance.

The green horse a further stage of degradation is also cleared by repentance.

Repentance is the clearing of sin so that the soul is free.

Evil inclination has no part in the upper realms. Only holiness reigns there.

When you act as a catalyst for thousands you earn for yourself the equivalent of thousands of reincarnations.

Those who do not return in reincarnation descend into dissolution.

Even the righteous descend as agents of reincarnation for the wicked.

Tiqun 33

בראשית זו מצוה ראשונה שנרמזה בל״ב שבילים שהם ל״ב אלקים של מעשה בראשית.

Bereishis, this is the first commandment, which is hinted at in all 32 paths, which are 32 of ELKY"M in the act of creation:

22 letters and ten statements that are included within them.
The first *tiqun* is fear and about it is said:
(Psalms 111:10) *The beginning of wisdom is the fear of YKV"K*
for there is fear and there is fear.

Fear of the Lord means you must be mindful of the consequences of your actions, your thoughts.

יראת יי׳ ו השכינה מלכות קדושה. יראה רעה זו רצועה להלקות הרשעים. ומה היא סם המות של סמא״ל, הנקבה שלו.

The fear of YKV"K, this is Shekinah, the holy malchus. Bad fear is the strap with which to whip the wicked. And what is it? The drug of death of Samae'l his female.

The fear of YKV"K is the reward for who keep the negative commandments. bad fear is the strap, the whip for those who pass them by.

Rabbi Shimon rose and said: "Elazar, my son. there are those who fear Ha Kodesh Barachu, but only so that that his children live and his wealth prospers in this world, and if any of this is missing he does not fear Him. This kind of person does heed the fear of YKV"K as the main principle, but one who does fear Ha Kodesh Barachu whether in good or bad, heeds the fear of YKV"K as the main principle.

77a) The fear of YKV"K is the awareness of consequence and it is proven by the wicked.

The main principle is consequence therefore be mindful.

Shekinah the middle pillar is the illumination of the light of fire, and the awareness of the manifest into being from conception to completion. Having free will and understanding leads us to pathways of holiness.

Light is established on the first day as the first principle of creation meaning that the awareness of light, holiness is the direction we are to take. We see that the light is the precursor for all that the good that is to come. Shekinah represents the continuous awareness of that light or that first day light.

There is the idea of fullness or completion that is indicated by the light however it fails to complete its course through misdirection as in the misdirection of a thought.

Through Moses that completion is given or rather the understanding of that completion about which the light was brought into being to show us.

Tiqun 34

בראשית ב' נקבה פתוחה לקבל מימין את אותו שגומל חסד עמה
Bereishis Beit is female open to receive the right,
to that (from that one) who bestows chesed to Her.

ומדוע שאות י' על ראשו כמו כן ג',ומפני זה הרוצה להחכים ידרים
And why? For the letter Yud is upon its head like this: ג
and because of this, one who wishes to become wise should head south.

Creation calls upon itself to become all that it can be. It is a bestowing of kindness to walk inside of the vision and become one with it. The Yud shows the way of becoming and supports the female in her giving.

The light cannot be brought into being unless holiness is its direction. Therefore if a man takes his sister...the entire set of consequences degrade as in the letters turning away from each other.

ומדוע מחזירות פנים זה מן זה
And why do they turn their faces away from each other?

Because of the עריות (eryos- forbidden sexual acts) that correspond to them: Aleph corresponds to ארור cursed (arur)
which correlates to an 'ervah (forbidden sexual act), and about it is stated: (Deuteronomy 27:22) Cursed be he that lies with his sister

77b) The sexual perversions represent incomplete or disjointed couplings. The way of unity is blocked by disunity. What you make is either all holiness or not. The point is to be consistent in your thinking.

Tiqun 35

בראשית בתשר׳י נברא להיות בראשית, זה אדם שנברא בתשרי
Bereishis, BTisShReY have the same letters
The world was created, missing Aleph to become BeREiShYT
This Adam was created in Tishrei, and because the earth was prepared to be cursed because of him this is: (Bereishis 3:17) ...cursed is the ground for thy sake
Aleph was removed from Tishrei, and the Torah began with Beit, which is Bracha (blessing), so that the earth may be blessed, and to take it out of the curse.

Adam is made and is destined to sin because he has free choice, which also means that he may choose holiness since the Beit that begins Bereishis signifies blessing which is the precursor to holiness.

Tiqun 36

בראשית שהוא שבת בראשית. שהרי שבע שבתות הן. ולכל אחת יש לה ששה ימי המעשה.
Bereishis which is the Sabbath of creation, for there are seven Sabbaths, and each one has six working days.

וכל יום של הקדוש ברוך הוא הוא אלף שנים

And every day of Ha Kodesh Barachu is one thousand years;
this is what is written: (Psalms 90:4) *For a thousand years in your eyes...*
And the Sabbath of creation, its six days are:
two thousand years of chaos, two thousand years of Torah,
two thousand years of the days of the Messiah.

'Two thousand of chaos,
(Bereishis 1:2) *And the earth was chaos...*

Two thousand of Torah:
...and the spirit of ELKY"M was hovering on the face of the waters
and there is no water but Torah; the face of the waters – its two faces,
which are:
positive precepts and negative precepts, white and red,
right and left; and they are two thousand of Torah.

The waters of Torah are the building blocks of Creation containing the two faces or waters above and waters below. This represents the holy thoughts (above) that are transforming the images below into the object of your heart's desire.

The light of good that appears is the harbinger of the Messiah and the proof of the presence of Messiah even amongst those worldly things since it is a continuous creation that is manifested.

The two luminaries refer tangentially to the reflected light that is mistaken for the actual light of heaven. Therefore 'it was' indicates a non continuous creation of something 'bad.

Be mindful of your thoughts and their expressions. Father and Mother are the precursors of thought bringing about all that is witnessed in each moment. Therefore fear means to stay away from errant negative thoughts since they will come back to trouble you.

Upon him it is stated:
(Numbers 19:20) *...he has defiled the sanctuary of YKV"K,
and he will be cut off...*

And this point is the sign of Sabbath,

the sign of Festivals, the sign of tephillin,
the sign of the covenant of circumcision,
the crown of the covenant, we call it the crown of the scroll of the Torah,
'the crown on the head of every righteous person.'

נקודה, שעליה נאמר אדם וחוה שהיו שני פרצופים,
ועליה אמרה הלבנה אי אפשר לשני מלכים שישתמשו בכתר אחד

It is the point, of which it is stated: Adam and Eve were two faces,
and about it the moon said:
'it is impossible for two kings to use one crown.'

78a) The holy place i.e. the sanctuary of YKV"K is where thoughts arise into holiness becoming transformed into the mind stuff that permeates and creates the universe. When this is profaned by negative thoughts the sanctuary is closed or cut off from entry.

There is the gathering of the mind stuff, the transformed thoughts that face each other as in Adam and Eve. The lesser light can, however, join at this crown which is the pinnacle of mind stuff. Both the greater and lesser lights make up the all encompassing light of the crown.

Bring it all together we have the thoughts of light framed by lesser and greater light made into the all encompassing light.

The point of this is the association of light symbolized by the crown where the thoughts of holiness make up the perfection that is the soul seeking internal and external unity. The working days are the assimilation of thoughts that are brought together in unification on the Sabbath.

This opening that occurs is analogous to the free space that causes the new thoughts of holiness to abound. These in turn creates the Crown or point that is the culmination and purpose of Shekinah.

These symbols or letters represent the various ways of joining that produce holiness. They are a completion of thoughts coming together and then rising up. The examples of the 42 names and the 72 names show that intricate levels of holiness are arising out of the structures of Creation in Bereishis.

This fear is the awareness that what we are working on produces results, which we must be careful of in order to produce the holiness of the Sabbath where there is an opening and a fulfilment of the promise of those thoughts. It is fear that tells us to be careful and watch out for what is coming.

It is love that shows us the right way to proceed for this is what is good and it is fear that stops us from sin because of the harmful results. In this way the positive and negative commandments are explained.

Tiqun 37

בראשית הוא ברי״ת. ודאי כאשר הוא בלבושי אלו כקליפות שהם ערלה ופריעה,
צריך שם יראה. ועליהם נאמר לא יהיה לך אלהים אחרים אל פני.

Bereishis is BRY"T, certainly when it is in the garments of these husks which are the foreskin and membrane, one needs fear there and about them it is said, (Shemos 20:3) *You shall have no other gods before me...*

And only Israel inherits this sign, for there is no sign of the covenant until the husks are removed, which are the foreskin and membrane,

When surrounded by that which would block holiness we must use fear to navigate through these muddy waters. The BRY'T covenant is the promise that if we do navigate correctly surely all holiness will be ours.

The inheritance of the covenant is the awareness of what it signifies.

These three layers or husks of chaos, void and darkness are what we are born out of and subsequently into. It is this process that awakens us to the holiness that is our birth right. It is this that we are called upon to remember.

The time of redemption is for those remembering the covenant since all three of these husks, chaos, void and darkness will be removed and only holiness will be revealed continuously.

There is the casting off of these husks, the nations, the false idols, the false ideas and liberation akin to the revelation of leaving Egypt.

The rainbow of luminous colors represents the enlightenment of the soul that is set free and the star is the igniting of that soul with the unification of holiness. The scepter is the passing of that unification along to others who have embraced the covenant.

Why do we place the foreskin in a bowl of earth?'

אמר לי שמעתי ביע״יבה, שערלה הוא נחש. וכיון שמעבירים אותו ממקומו צריך לתת לו מזונו.

He said to me: I have heard in the Yeshiva, that the foreskin is the snake, and since we remove it from its place, one needs to grant its food,"
this is what is written: (Isaiah 65:25) *and the serpent, dust is its bread.*

78b) Nothing is ever lost. All that exists is in a state of transformation so that even though the husks have to be discarded they are not forgotten and they are subsequently transformed by the quality of light that is always making these transformations possible. The fact remains that out of something there is something but also out of nothing there is something. This is the grand cycle of creation. Otherwise why mention it in the first place. The pattern of Bereishis is this.

There is a concept of the creative force. Then there is the chaos the void, the darkness upon which this creative force works. In consequence through the interaction of the chaos void and darkness with the creative force the light comes in; the light that is good. Everything that comes after is simply the result of these interactions

Tiqun 38

(Shemos 1:1) *In the beginning Elokim created...*
He began a discourse and said:
(Song of Songs 2:2) *Like a rose between the thorns...*

שושנה יש בה חמשה עלים מבפנים. וחמשה עלים מבחוץ.
A rose has five leaves on the inside. And five leaves on the outside.

And they are ה' ה'
Its stem' is Vav. Its 'apple' is Yud. And all is ELKY"M
Its five letters are: Hei, five leaves on the outside,
Hei, five leaves on the inside,
Yud the apple . The word (מל'א) Vav is the shoot.

The action of ELKY"M is to transform the darkness the chaos and the void. This is the natural flow of creation into being. However when this natural flow is blocked there is the exile.

When the chamber is opened prayers ascend. This is the chamber that opens in response to our thoughts of good, of a desire for connection and of our one pointed focus on Shekinah

The SHMA symbolizes unification. This is also another way of saying the chamber opens since it is unification that is the goal and the key to the door to Ha Kodesh Barachu.

It is when the two names ADN"Y YKV"K are one YAKDVNK"Y that it is the 'time of favor, the thought and word, speech and voice, conception and action; these comprise the unity of divine reflection, as above so below.

It is the joining of intention and action that fulfills the Torah. It is the joining of Shekinah and Ha Kodesh Barachu that transforms the nations into a pure speech.

(Tzephaniah 3:9) *For then will I turn to the peoples a pure language and this is the mystery of:* (Deuteronomy 27:26) *...and all the People said: 'AMe"n.'*

And until Israel emerges from exile, they will not be of one pairing, and when Israel shall emerge from exile, they will join as one.

At that time, (Shemos 15:1) Then shall Moses sing; and immediately: (Shemos 1:3) And ELKY"M said: 'Let there be light!' which is the going out of exile.

באותו זמן שהמלכה רוצה להכנס בהיכל שלה. הקול עולה במרומי רקיעים ויאמר כך.

At the time that the Queen wishes to enter into Her chamber, a voice ascends to the heights of the firmaments, and says like this:

Many camps, of holy souls, were preparing for the Queen who comes to be made ready to redeem her children from exile.'

79a) The unification of consciousness is its higher calling. The exile is the veil that is preventing this from happening. Going out of exile represents the awareness of Shekinah and the beginning of the divine connection 'let there be light.'

Whenever you come together in connection with higher thought She makes the connection between the higher and lower yeshiva of holy souls who are surely holy souls. In this way She is enveloped by higher thoughts and their arrangements above.

Here is an indication of where thought comes from via the combinations of sounds and lights made discernible by the communication of Moses with ELKY"M. Moses transforms the light and sound into the holy thoughts that are made known to him.

The voice of Moses is the distinguished voice taken from the connection above via Shekinah who is the middle pillar answering with the voice that becomes one. As Moses speaks so says the Lord.

At Sinai there is one who speaks and one who hears and both arise from the same place, the middle pillar above and below with Shekinah riding in between, the ancient sound is the voice that speaks through to hear Ha Kodesh Barachu.

Therefore in Ps 62:12 'God hath spoken once, twice have I heard this.' This refers to Keter bringing forth Chokmah and Binah and all three become one. Another way of seeing this is that when ELKY"M speaks he empowers us to understand the 'way things work' thereby transforming our thoughts from the mundane to the sublime. We can compare this to the extra soul we receive on Shabbat that enhances our connection. The same is true via the flow of holiness from above and its return flow from below to above unifying the Tree of Life via the middle column.

Out of this is explained that the person has three bindings, the soul, nephesh, spirit, ruach, and the animating soul, neshamah. These are the connections subtle in nature that are the result of our higher voice. The nephesh resides in the throne of glory. It is the place of the coalescing of thought.

Here the ruach or spirit is developed called Metatro"n. The people saw the voice because the voice instantly became clothed in the holy forms with each saying. The levels of transformation are built into the nature of the six sephiros comprising the middle pillar

Man is the microcosm with the animating soul the nephesh in every part so that he will always be tied to holiness and so that the voice will continuously speak to him.

Tiqun 39

בראשית שם אש'ר, שנאמר

Bereishis Ashe"R is there, of which it is stated:

(Shemos 20:2) ...*that (asher) I brought you out*...
(Shemos 3:14) EKY"K (I will be) ASheR (that/which) EKY"K (I will be)
The name Asher: (Shemos 30:13) ...*'Happy am I! for the daughters will
call me happy.' And she called his name Asher.*...
and this is Higher Mother.

79b) ASher (which/that/who) is the connecting link between
words and is a metaphor for the connecting link we have
above. Therefore it is Shekintah that is arises in connection
to holiness, the mother so it is called.

Consider the Torah as a template of thought. The evolution of
man in terms of thought takes a marked turn with the
introduction of Torah. Prior to this discovery, this revelation,
the spirituality of God or the sense of God was limited to a
few. These few had their own ways of communication and
perhaps could not describe adequately the process they
underwent to make the connection. Now along comes Moses
who is the latest in a line of Jewish mystics who has not only
discovered how to communicate with God but also can
provide a book to share that communication. Included with
this communication is a language, a way of speaking and
listening to God that explains not only the nature of man but
also as well the nature of God.

Thoughts are what are being built up here. Consciousness is
being raised. The entire Sinai experience is for the purpose of
raising consciousness. It is the raising of consciousness to the
level of holiness so that for all intents and purposes we
become as Moses, one with God. Prior to Moses' time the
level of thinking never reached a unified level. There was
never a people who were so unified as were Israel at the
giving of the law on Sinai. This could only be made possible
by planting seed thoughts, which grew until they blossomed
together with the Sinai experience.

Therefore when we speak of sanctifying what this means is
that the seed thought is placed into our consciousness making

us holy, as Hashem is holy. Anokhi, the I Am begins all of this. It is the first thought so to speak which carries the seed of holiness to infuse all of Israel with its essence.

Ha Kodesh Barachu is the seer meaning that Hashem or the thought of holiness has built into it the fulfilment of its design. Hashem sees and it appears, or the prophet sees and the events occur. All of this takes place via the build up of thoughts starting with the seed thought of sanctification.

One grows out of the other. From the middle column come the offshoots of Sephiros. The interaction of Mother and Father, Shekinah and Ha Kodesh Barachu produce the revelation of light, 'let there be light.' It is the process that we are being taught here.

Thoughts come together inspired by the same light of inspiration from above and fuse their essence arising to the throne, which is the collection space, the crown that sits on the throne.

There are transformations along the way that are a part of the essential nature of thought. These transformations are what produce the holiness that we experience as a result of the various steps that are undertaken, the fifty mentions of ELKY"M, the fifty gates of Binah. All of this Torah has built into it. Torah is a sea of holiness inspiring holiness to all who partake of its sacred waters.

ובמה היא חזון, באות ו'. בו נעשית מראה שמאירה אדון שלה
And with what is She called vision?
It is with the letter Vav, through which She is made into the mirror that shines, her master.

80a) This mirror that shines is the result of the connection that is ever present called Ha Kodesh Barachu transformed via Shekinah.

Tiqun 40

בראשית, שמעי בת וראי והטי אזנך וגו'.
Bereishis
(Psalms 45:11) *Hearken, O daughter, and consider, and incline thine ear;*

In the word B-REiShY"T are alluded the following words:
there is שמעי (hear), there is ב'ת (daughter), there is רא'י (see),
שמע'י (hear) is the ש of B-REiShY"T;
ב'ת (daughter) is made known through the beginning and end of the word.
רא'י (see) is made known, there, in the middle, like this: בר'אשי'ת

And when She shall be joined with Him like this: יאקדונק'י,
He says to Her ...and forget your people and the house of your father,
for: (Shemos 2:24) Therefore shall a man leave his father and his mother
and cleave to his wife, and they shall be as one flesh;
(Psalms 45:12) *...for He is your Lord, and bow down to Him;*
(Psalms 97:5) *Lord of all the earth,* certainly.

What we are to recognize, 'see' is the image of reflection.
What we are to 'hear' is the coming of that reflection as it
appears as 'daughter.' Contained therefore within each
thought is its own reflection and the call of its coming into
being.

Thoughts of holiness turn one to the other leaving behind the
mundane thoughts. When you pursue holiness, the Lord, you
sublimate everything to this direction. There is then a
gathering together of the concepts of 'the way things work,'
and the concept of 'rulership,' the Lord.

When the connection is established she shines when she is
with Her husband. Otherwise she does not shine or rather
make the link that produces the fire that shines.

At the time of the opening of the chambers meaning the
chambers of perception, many will be able to prophecy to see
and hear things that hitherto were powers that were dormant
but will then be aroused. Imagine that there are two thoughts
each containing the seeds of holiness and yet both need the

inspiration the connection in order to rise fully into bloom via Shekinah the middle pillar. It turns out that each joins in turn one helped by the other via the connection that is established between both.

It takes three men who want to cross a river whose current is strong. It takes two men to row in order to overcome the current and one to steer. Without the two men the boat stays in the center but with the two men and the one steering the boat crosses. So it is with two thoughts and Shekinah between. Each of the thoughts provides its impetus while Shekinah provides its direction the ultimate destination of holiness.

ולא עוד אלא אתם תסכנו עצמכם.
Moreover, you will endanger yourselves,
because those stones, of the tree of knowledge of good and evil, are in separation, and these stones, of pure marble, are in unity, without separation at all.

And if you say that the tree of life withdrew from them and they fell and there is [now] separation between them...
(Psalms 101:7) ...*he that speaks falsehood shall not be established before mine eyes*– for there is no separation, there, Above.
And they that smashed were of those (vessels).

80b) Thoughts that are false meaning they are destructive are meant to separate and have no place of attachment.

Do not associate the things of the Tree of the Knowledge of Good and Evil with those of the Tree of Life otherwise you would be promoting God forbid a separation in the unity.

All is one unity. These stones originally seen as Sapphire stones must not be mistaken for marble for that perception is a false one. Aleph is composed of a Yud above and a Yud below with Vav in the middle describing the connection that unifies above and below. All is one unity.

אמר רבי יצחק כל אלו מתי ארץ טשראל,

342

יחיו ויקומו בראשונה בזמן שיחיה הקדוק ברוך הוא המתים.

Said Rabbi Isaac, All the dead of the Land of Israel will be revived and resurrected first at the time when Ha Kodesh Barachu will revive the dead.

81a) The raising of the dead is discussed. Remember that nothing is ever lost. Holiness is the goal of all thought to link up together with Ha Kodesh Barachu to have the awareness of unity permeating their entire being. Think of death as a temporary interruption of the flow of a center of being. Either that being is self-directed towards holiness or it is not. A self-directed being that chooses holiness is reborn or rather the thoughts that have become its center are placed back into the form of their last demise. When thoughts are focused around a center that is wicked the antithesis of holiness then these thoughts are not revived and they are left to become non-existent as if they never were.

If you think about it if all the souls were resurrected that died or rather even if only those Jewish souls were resurrected the world would be too densely packed so that the idea of reincarnations must take hold here. In this way only those souls that promote the unity are saved or brought forward as it suggests in their latest body. Even this calls for a greater than literal interpretation. Thoughts come together in life centers to increase the progress of the line of holiness that it is pursuing. So there is a culling process that keeps the good and makes the bad or evil as if it never were.

Tiqun 41

בראשית שם תשר"י. וזה זרוע שניה יום שני. השנה,

Bereishis, the month of TiShR"Ei is there,
and this is the second arm, the second day,
(Psalms 18:12) *He makes (YaShe"T) darkness His concealment..*

יש"ת חשך סתרו, נשארה ר' היא ר'אש השנה, ושם הבדלא בין טוב לרע.

After YaSheT is taken away the Reish remains, then there is
Ro"sh Hashanah (New Year), *and the division between good and evil is there.*

81b) It is in the making that we choose good and evil. This is the beginning of all that comes to be.

Shekinah is the connection to the King as She rises via the Sephiros. Those who rise with Her are included in the holy flow.

We are the result of our choices, the negative and positive commandments and the synthesis of both. We are part of the stream and cannot escape it except by choosing the heavenly flow, the middle pillar of connection.

Tiqun 42

בראשית, שם איש, שנאמר בו ויעקב איש תם.
וזה יום שלישי. שהרי שלשה אומנים היו אד כאן.
יום ראשון ויום שני ויום שלישי.

Bereishis IY"Sh (man) is there, of whom it is said:
(Bereishis 25:27) ...*and Jacob was a man...*(*ish*) of perfection
and this is the third day, for there were three artisans here,
the first day, and the second day, and the third day
each one produced its artist.

The appearance of man occurs within BeREiShY"T called the third day, the perfect man and yet prior to this are day two and one all fashioned by the artisans. This creation then is an artistic expression.

He spoke to that first day to impart the artistic direction that is the creation of something out of nothingness. This nothingness contains within itself the three sephiros out of which all possibility could be formed.

There is built into this process its self same fulfilment. This action of let there be light is followed by there was light. It may be called a principality. It is this artistic expression that is also imparted to the next two.

Moving out of the nothingness, Aleph is air and produces the light that is all encompassing. The Yud contained within the same but now released produces the firmament and finally the Nun of Ayi"n produces the dry land, the waters that are gathered under the heavens so that in this place, this specific place the dry land is made visible.

The waters that gathered via the principle of ELKY'M (the way things work) demonstrates unity and the procreation that is the coming forth from one thing to another. This is central to the complete process.

In unity the waters are gathered giving rise to the Sephiros that are gathered in their place.

The idea of place is once again introduced this time. Its central meaning becomes clear. Place in terms of the SHMA, the unity, the oneness and the sense of being that we each identify with this. This is place.

Ha Kodesh Barachu establishes a place and yet acts from an all-abiding presence. Still this place is what we have to work with as it is our body, our world and the sense we have all around us. While we are in this world we act from above filling the world and yet remaining open to all that is.

The recital of the SHMA twice a day is the equivalent of establishing a place. It is also identifying oneself with that holiness that is the unity we are aspiring to.

Consider that the hundred blessings are the walls that are built into the foundation of place.

Through Vav the connection is shown in the wings of the Seraphim and the six words of the unity adding to forty two

alluding to the forty two-letter name. What is intimated is
that the unity may be perceived from every location or place.

בזה השם שהוא יקו״ק צריך לכנס דרגות היחוד ולהכליל בו עשר ספירות בצורה
זו, יו״ד ק״א וא״ו ק״א, שהן עשר ספירות בלימה.

With this Name, which is YKV"K, one is required to gather the levels of
unity, and to include in it the ten sephiros appearing like this,
YU"D K"E VA"V K"E, which are 'the ten sephiros of *blimah*
(containment).

YKV"K is the place of YU"D K"E VA"V K"E,
which is hidden and concealed; and because of this,
It is called *'olam* (world) from the root *elem* (hidden),
for one is required to hide it from the whole world for He is called *elem*.
And Shekinah is hidden.
This is what is written:
(Job 28:21) *And it is hidden from the eyes of all life...*

82a) YKV"K is everywhere, every 'place' in the heart of the
sea and even in the stumble of justice. This shows the unity
of Torah derived by the comparison of the letters that add up
to YKV"K.

When we contemplate the nothingness YKV"K is the place of
the nothingness. In itself the contemplation of the Sephiros
represents the imagination that establishes a place within.

The place that is hidden is your consciousness and within this
consciousness we find Shekinah that represents the
connecting links that establish as place YU"D H"E VA"V
H"E or the expressed nothingness in short, YKV"K.

Consciousness is YKV"K. It is the recognition of this
something from nothing, the conceptual understanding of
deity that is what is gathered in every place. It is like
describing a point on a sphere from any other point on the
sphere. The vantage point may change but the description
remains the same because what we 'see' never changes.

We cannot encompass a description of deity, the nothingness that is alluded to, however, via the connection, Shekinah we are able to see that unity that is called YKV"K. There is no place unless we establish the connection.

When you have the realization of unity of one then you see the sephiros as one and know that to become a thing is to think a thing and see it through until the Kingdom, the realization of a thing.

Without the unity there is no fulfilment of the thing, the thought, the intention, or the desire.

The cycle of being is intention and connection leading to reflection. As above so below. Imagine your thoughts gathered by their relationships with one another and then imagine the birthing process whereby thoughts become the images they went sent unto.

By ignoring the covenant or abusing it the demonstration does not take place. She, meaning the connection that brings the above to the below is dry. There is no reflection. This is what causes decay and destruction because the power of renewal is the central core of Her, of Shekinah and of the power to bring forth something from nothing.

So we see that it is renewal which flows from the Oral Torah or those insights about Torah that are passed on via Kabbalah that is irrigated by the written Torah which serves as inspiration in each of the 53 portions of Torah.

Tiqun 43

בראשית שם את'ר יב'ש. וזה הוא ונהר יחרב ויבש.
באותו זמן שהוא יבש והיא יבשה.צווחים בנים למטה ביחוד,
ואומרים שמע ישראל. ואין קול ואין עונה. זא הוא שכתוב אז יקראנני ולא אענה.

Bereishis את'ר יב'ש (a dry place) is there; and this is:

(Yishayahu 19:5) ...*and the river is parched and dried up.*

At that time, when He is 'dry' (יבש) and She is 'dry land' (יבשה),
the children below cry out in 'the unity' and say:
(Deuteronomy 6:4) *Hear O Israel!*...
(1 Kings 18:26) ...*and there was no voice and no answer...*

Without Kabbalah and its wisdom the inspiration dries up.
The insights are parched. Without the deeper meanings the
entire purpose of Creation is subverted and made mundane.

One who does not go deeper into Torah does not add to the
inspirations that are flowing and causes the dry parched earth
returning to chaos and void.

You bring forth from these inspirations and insights that
which is called vegetation, the growing of Torah yes but
deeper still the growing of the unity that expresses itself.

Once you begin thinking about Torah in a deeper fashion you
renew your sense of unity, you bring about everything that is
taking place in the beginning to irrigate the land, to prosper
the entire world you are living in. The analogy for your
thoughts is that you keep finding new ways to describe the
unity, to affirm it and to realize that you are always at the
center of it.

אלו נשמות שנגזרו מכסא כבודו, ואלו רוחות שנגזרו ממלאכים, ואלו נפשות
שנגזרו מאפנים כל אחד מוציא למינם לכל אחד כיאות
Those souls (נשמות) are hewn from His throne of glory,
and they are spirits (רוחות) that were hewn from the angels,
and they are animating souls (נפשות) that were hewn from the Ophanim;
each one produces according to its type, for each, that which is
appropriate.

(Shemos 1:11) ...*fruit tree...* – this is the scholar,
making fruit – this is his female partner;
for each, that which is appropriate, each one produces to its type

And furthermore: the *tree of fruit* – this is the Middle Pillar;
the *making fruit* – this is the righteous person;
that which seeds with it upon the earth – this is Shekinah,

for all seeds are included in Her.

82b) What are these souls? They are the thoughts that we take hold of and send forth to be fruitful and multiply. Specifically they are our higher thoughts that connect with the unity. They are the essence of our being, our core representation of the unity.

Our purpose is to be mindful of those thoughts that they should be good and serve the purpose of the unity. We are the co-creators and we exist to pass along the inspirations from above.

Conversely if we simply react and do not attempt to rise above, chaos and void result since without the impetus of our thoughts going high there is a dissolution of the perception of the unity.

Tiqun 44

.בראשית, שם תר״י שם א״ש

Bereishis: TR"Ei (two) is there;
Ei"Sh (fire) is there;

and about them it is stated:
(Bereishis 1:14) *And ELKY"M said:*
'Let there be lights (m-orot) in the firmament of the heavens...
מארת is written without a Vav this is the written Torah;
What is the meaning of *luminaries*? It is the oral Torah.
And even though they have established
that מארת *(lights)* missing a Vav is Lili"t, there are seventy faces to the Torah, and therefore *lights*, as discussed is that which it is said:

(Proverbs 6:23) *For a candle is precept, and the Torah is light...*
the Middle Pillar, and about them it is stated:

(Bereishis 1:16) *the greater light to rule the day, and the lesser light to rule the night..*

We see how from the beginning, from Bereishis is generated the lights in the firmament of the heavens. One thing by relationship comes from another.

Even so there is the distinction of small light and large light representing sun and moon.

Taking this further one borrows from the other light from the greater to the lesser. There is a unity between them a conservation of energy in which the transformations of the light are continuous.

So truly we see that "they receive one from the other."

Again it is by relationship and the continuous nature of creation that all that comes to be takes place.

Shekinah is the image of reflection, the connection that exists for our own sharing with Ha Kodesh Barachu participating in the continuous stream that is Creation.

The inference is that all learning takes place by sharing, by relationship with that which has come previously. There is a continuous light that shines represented by Moses in his giving of the oral and written Torah. Our light comes from that reflection, the meditation on that light producing of its own device the lesser light that mirrors the greater light.

Tiqun 45

בראשית ברא אלקים א"ל הי"ם. ים התורה.
(Bereishis 1:1) *In the beginning ELKY"M created...*

ELKY"M is God of the sea the sea of Torah, א"ל הי"ם

And about it is said:
(Shemos 1:20) *And ELKY"M said:*
Let the waters swarm with the swarming of living things,
and birds shall fly over the earth...

כאן המצוה לעמול בתורה, שנאמר בה הוי כל צמא לכו למים.
Here is the precept to engage in Torah, of which it is stated:
(Yishayahu 55:1) *Ho, every one that thirsts, come ye for water..*

ואלו עוסקים בתור יורשים נפש חיה מהשכינה, זה הוא שכתוב

And they that are occupied in Torah, inherit *a living soul (nephesh chayah)* from Shekinah;
this is what is written:

Let the waters swarm with swarming of living things.
...and birds shall fly – this is spirit (רוח), of which it is stated:
(Ecclesiastes 10:20) *...for a bird of the heavens will carry the voice,*
and one with wings will tell a thing; and this is YKV"K, the Middle Pillar.

It is the Torah that swarms with living things called precepts that invite meditation and discussion and inspirations that are the birds that fly over the earth.

The way of Torah study that is written here shows the 'living things,' those insights that we can discover and the pathways that lead on high including the bird that can fly, and the spirit that establishes the middle pillar of connection Shekinah.

The symbolism of Metatro"n who also acts as a connector between above and below given in the same allusion as the bird with two wings representing the middle pillar with Yud Heh Vav Heh at its center.

The breaths that rise and fall gather the insights, those inspirations from above and return with them below placing them within our understanding producing the fire of learning.

Creation mirrors itself in myriad ways, the sea running and returning, the breaths rising and falling, all point to the same principle of reaching up and coming back, transforming and endlessly acting out the cycle of continuous Creation.

and they wish to return the world to *chaos and void*;
but when they look at Shekinah,
who is the domain of the sea,
they return to their place.

בא ראה, י' היא אמירה ודבור וקריאה.

Come and see, Yud is ten.

Saying' (*amirah*) and 'speaking' (*dibur*) and 'calling' (*qri-ah*);

Vav is voice;
Hei Hei is: breath descending in speech, breath rising in voice;
voice rises, speech descends; and when it rises and descends,
the angels of ELKY"M rise and descend with it, for they are His camps
and armies. And this is the mystery of:
(Proverbs 30:4) *Who has ascended to the heavens and descended?...*

83a) Without our conscious intention the world tends to chaos and void meaning entropy. Shekinah epitomizes this conscious intention, which is the connecting force that brings about the unification of above and below.

All through the many impressions of thought, (speech, calling saying, voice, and yes even the breath) there is a rising and a falling, a becoming and a taking stock, an image and a reflection.

All the while there is a transformation that is taking place. This descending in speech is the expression of thought. This rising in voice is the prayerful connection with the higher thought. Who has ascended is prayer and who has descended are blessings.

What is rising is the sense of connection from below to above and what is lowering is the answering, the reflection from above that answers prayer via blessings.

What are called angels are the vehicles of connection operating both above and below.

Our thoughts determine the quality of the reflection. Therefore the completely righteous can only have righteous thoughts going up and coming down as righteous blessings

She is suspended meaning Shekinah. She is the connection that arises with the sum total of thoughts and descends with the reward, which is a transformation of the sins and merit to be experienced in this world.

Whereas the wicked having only wicked thoughts can only expect wicked outcomes as a result. This is because the voice carries true throughout the heavens returning only that which is sent unto it.

The face of the firmament, this is the reflecting pool above wherein those who are worthy in Torah receive those living souls of inspirations that they have helped to build above.

In this way partaking of Torah is equally a partaking of the blessings of Torah.

Therefore whatever our thoughts dwell upon send that focus above to be reflected each according to the quality of their thinking.

Lower thoughts will therefore produce lower outcomes

Tiqun 46

בראשית ברא שית (פי' שש). ואלו שש כנפי החיה שנאמר בה ועוף יעופף אל הארץ אל פני רקיע השמים.
Bereishis: is composed of the same letters as BaRA) ShYT (six), and they are the six wings of the *chayah*, of whom it is stated:
(Shemos 1:20) ...*and the bird shall fly over the earth, upon the face of the firmament of the heavens.*

שש ספירות שכולל זה העוף שהוא עמוד האמצע.
Those six wings are the six sephiros that comprise this bird, which is the Middle Pillar.

The Middle Pillar is the activation of reflection. The all-abiding flow that we take part in as a sense of our being here. Envision these six as encompassing you all around so that your thoughts find their way above as in the bird that shall fly over the earth. You are representative of the earth.

From the divine presence of holy thoughts there is emanated a spirit of holiness.

Also the same attention the quality of thinking refers to the basic animal nature of humanity, its needs and basic wants. In all cases this spirit and the others mentioned happen simultaneous to each other.

Tiqun 47

בראשית ברא שית (פי׳ ששה) וזה יום הששי, שנאמר בו ויהי ערב ויהי בקר יום הששי.

Bereishis Bara the sixth day
(Bereishis 1:31) ...*and it was evening and it was morning, the sixth day*.

The second group of those who make three. The fourth day one artist made light to see. From above to below coming through the light.

And then a second who makes from water swarming things
(Bereishis 1:20) *Let the waters swarm*;
Again from above to below the second day
The firmament placed to stand in its way.
(Bereishis 1:6) *Let there be a firmament in the midst of the waters*
So water is made from one into one.

Now on day three a third one who makes on the third day
The following verses to correspond in their own way.
(Bereishis 1:11) *Let the earth put forth grass, herb yielding seed, and fruit-tree bearing fruit after its kind*...and of the sixth day:
(Bereishis 1:28) *Be fruitful, and multiply, and replenish the earth*.

The sixth day includes all of the other days within it.

Once light came into being it was eternal (suspended) capable of producing and reproducing itself in every transformation including the reflection of the first day taken up now by the fourth day.

Again the reflection of day two is day five transforming from one type of water (spiritual) to another type of water (earthbound).

The third day reflects the sixth day. This is the transformation of earth from ethereal dry land to actual earth.

When His glory fills the earth it becomes transformed from the dry land into the earth that gives forth its abundance. His Glory is Shekinah the connection between day one and four, two and five and three and six.

Blessed be the Name of the glory of His kingdom for ever and ever.
(Isaiah 6:3) *Holy, Holy, Holy, is YKV"K of Hosts...*
and this versus (Bereishis 1:9) *Let the waters under the heaven be gathered together unto one place, and let the dry land appear.' And it was so,* and this is contrasted to *all the earth is filled with His glory.*

ביום ששי נתקנו שש דרגות הכסא.
On the sixth day, the six levels of the throne were arranged דרגות,

and on it, Adam was created in His image,
for he was made ready to sit upon the throne;
this is what is written:
(Bereishis 1:27) *And God created man in His own image.*

83b) Blessed is the connection that produces the Kingdom, the demonstration, the life experience continuously without end.

By giving us a way to relate the verses of Torah to each other we can see their correspondences in a new light. In this case the glory is the gathering of the waters meaning the points of connection which are the domain of Shekinah providing links wherever we are (the earth) making accessible the divine flow of being.

The image of ELKY"M is the self aware actor on the stage of life experience. This actor is cognizant above and intentional below.

For the convert there must be a taking away of the negativity and a recognition of the divine above.

For the convert must follow the pattern of recognition otherwise he cannot fulfill what is necessary to become that image of above.

The image of the human is drawn from the angelic state above taking the divine attributes that are one with Ha Kodesh Barachu. Therefore, 'Holy, Holy, Holy, is the answering calling from one to the other.

The idea of place and the gathering of holiness is then recognized below so as to unify with the above. Again one calls to the other…

What better way to assure the continuous creation than to have it reflected endlessly in the form of holiness above that takes on the appearance of the earth below. It is in its ideal self-aware state embodying the qualities of the angelic image, and the image of higher thoughts. There is a loop of holiness ascending and descending in the pattern of the awareness of the human. We have the image 'Holy Holy, Holy,' and the reflection 'Blessed is the glory of YKV"K from His place.' In this way the idea becomes embodied by the imprint of the intention of its image-making source.

There is the idea or the conceptual reality of a being that mirrors the divine perspective acting as an on site inspector of form. This is one way out of myriad ways of looking at Creation. Because man asks the questions he receives the answers and yet it appears as though in the beginning man already knew his purpose in the divine scheme of things. Still as the story progresses he (man) wants to know more which is as if only by a kind of regression can he truly appreciate the divine nature he is ever apart of.

What does it mean to inherit spirit? It represents a capacity to receive on high and also an opportunity to expand that capacity increasing your ability to learn even more. It is a specialized kind of sustenance that the scholar takes in, or takes on that is akin to the manna in that it is self sustaining and always enough for the purpose of enlightenment. The ignorant do not feed on this rarefied elixir and cannot prevent the wise from their just due, which are the positive precepts of heaven.

The house that man dwells in is Shekinah. In this way man has built within himself the stepping-stones to heaven.

It is therefore the relationship between that which surrounds (Adam) and that which is surrounded (Shekinah) that makes up the Middle Pillar of connection.

It is the meeting place between these worlds of connection and intention. This interaction is the play of consciousness within itself evolving the higher concepts and theorizing the new worlds to come.

The unity above is reflected below. Ha Kodesh Barachu and Shekinah, Adam and his wife each represent the unity through which the expressions of the sephiros are found in Malchus.

Four dimensions Dalet, ten dimension of the private domain the tip of the Yud describing the interpenetration of consciousness continuous and interchanging depending upon the perspective we stand upon.

One is composed within the other.

The image of donning tephilin upon head and arm is linked to the angelic beings providing a template for the understanding of both image making and acting inside of the image, and the creation mirroring the creator.

שעליו נאמר ויברא עלקים את האדם בצלמו בצלם אלקים ברא
ותו בצלמו בתפלין של ראש, כמו התפילין של אדון עולם,

...in His image – with tephillin of the head,
like the tephillin of the Master of the Universe;

that is the Higher Shekinah,the tephilin upon the head which is the Middle Pillar, for She is all of the first three sephiros.

And the Middle Pillar has all of the six sephiros;
while Higher Mother is the tephillin upon His head;
that is the tephillin that Ha Kodesh Barachu dons every day.

...in the image of ELKY"M is the tephillin of the hand;
this is lower Shekinah, for She is His binding,
and about Her it is stated:
(Bereishis 44:30) ...his soul is bound up with the lad's soul;

שניהם ביחוד אחד בקשר אחד
Both are one single connection.

84a) In your awareness the raising of the Higher Mother is the equivalent of the tephilin that Ha Kodesh Barachu dons. The head, which is the Middle Pillar, is symbolic of the pathways through which the Sephiros flow bringing to the front the first three Sephiros. All of this happens within by way of imaging process.

Further explained is the imaging process that begins with 'in his image' the inspiration that is sent forth. Then in the image of ELKY"M, the reflected image and the working ground for the manifestation of form is found. It is the recognition of the unity that is the ring around the finger uniting lower Shekinah with higher Shekinah.

The blessings that are inherited from the higher mother are the result of 'in the image of.' This is the reflection from above. The seven mirror the cycle of creation. There is a continuous sending forth and an affirming back.

We are called upon to unite heaven and earth. This means we unite the higher mother with the lower mother. This is the covenant. Unite the inspiration you have received with the understanding you have developed. Take what you receive above and make sense of it below. Complete the great work.

We are sanctified with holiness therefore we must express holiness. There is no completion without the part each of us must play.

It is the connection of consciousness that unites above and below. There is the principle in general and its expression in detail showing the many facets of Creation.

The divine principle is expressed via the seven lower Sephiros. It is the completion of what has been sent forth from above and is now expressed below in detail.

Therefore the praises are the affirmations of holiness, and the recognition that all are included in the one.

Everything from the beginning is driving towards the completion, the seventh day, wherein all is sanctified meaning holiness has run the gamut from above to below.

It is presented as the principle of completion that is embodied in the Sabbath(s). It is the completion as well the extension of the Sephiros.

The extension of the upper Sephiros into the ten emanations that derive from each of these three as well as from each Sephirah continue the cycle of creation.

All the Sephiros as called sevenths to denote the completion of the seventh day.

Completion is end result of the beginning and the purpose of the continuous creation.

Shekinah is arranged according to the aspects of holiness that are engaged by the consciousness. North and south arrange as the Sephiros that bring illumination and sustenance, bread.

And the secret of the word:
(Ezekiel 41:22) ...*This is the table that is before YKV"K.*

ז'ה בחשבון ו' ו'.
This ז'ה *is 6 and 6 in numerical value,*
which are the six parts of the two arms and the six parts of the two legs.

שהרי השכינה נעשית גוף למלך בכל תקון
For Shekinah is made 'a body' for the King in Her entire makeup

and with those twelve parts of the female and twelve parts of the male, the angels say: *and they call one to another* זה אל זה *and say: 'Holy, Holy, Holy*...

Ze"h (12) together with Ha Kodesh Barachu is ECha"D (one =13);
Ze"h (this) with Shekinah is ECha"D (one =13),
and all is one YKV"K =26, uniting the two of them.
And corresponding to *one to another* זה אל זה,

84b) Torah must be joined to this table, meaning to relate the unity of Ha Kodesh Barachu to the analogy described, to see the correspondence between breaking bread and the guest that blesses, the righteous person. It is like this.

Our inspiration derives from holiness via the Middle Pillar Above, which is Shekinah above in its connection to Ha Kodesh Barachu. Consciousness receives inspiration and immediately must recognize the source keeping the connection intact so to speak.

The Master of the House, Ha Kodesh Barachu is blessed by the Righteous One Shekinah. In terms of consciousness we bless or recognize the unity and therefore are blessed by the unity since we can never be apart from that unity.

These blessings may only move above or below by the agency of Shekinah the Middle Pillar, otherwise the Righteous One.

There is a merging that takes place between the blessings and Ha Kodesh Barachu. The former is subservient to the latter. You have to allow the elevating force of the latter to permeate the former. There is a God space. Call it the ruling transforming influence. Just as the rivers all flow into the ocean so do all prayers flow into the eternal.

Crowning...Keeping your higher thoughts enclothed in prayer linked forever with Ha Kodesh Barachu.

Wrapping...It is the spiral flow of prayer that rises up via the agency of Shekinah.

Rinsing and wiping...This is the purification the removing of the dross elements making the prayer acceptable before Ha Kodesh Barachu. This is also arranging the Certainty of Prayer.

Living...Being open to the answering blessings, the way of return, and the expression of prayer through your life experiences.

Shekinah overflows when She is full. This means that the connection that the blessings are mirroring occurs when the overflow is active.

The right hand symbolizes letting go to allow the blessings to come into being to flow through you in order to interact with your world of being. We accept the truth that we are one with Ha Kodesh Barachu.

שתי ידים הן ה' ה'. אחת שמאל ואחת ימין. ומפני זה צריך להנתן בחמש אצבעות משום כוס ישועות אשא.

The two hands are Hei Hei one left and one right, and therefore it should be given held with five fingers, because of:
(Psalms 116:13) *I shall raise the cup of salvation.*

85a) Raising the cup...This is what happens to those thoughts that have come together in holiness and then reach up in the unity of Ha Kodesh Barachu. The two hands one to the other also unifies passing together.

The focus keeps coming back to the Middle Pillar where the flow of Shekinah is concentrated symbolized by the Vav of Zeir Anpin.

He raises it (consciousness) off the ground and delivers it as a gift; it is the gift of insight, the connection that is the portion that is derived from Torah.

The cup is the place of filling and until YAKDVNK"Y is joined (ADN"Y & YKV"K) the cup is empty without the Vav. When filled ELKY"M results meaning the operation of continuous creation is established.

Tiqun 48

בראשית שם תרי״י (פי׳ שנים) שם שב״ת. כמו כן ב׳ראשי״ת. ב׳רא ש׳י״ת (פי שש). והן שתי שבתות. עליהן נאמר שמרו בני ישראל את השבת לעשות את השבת וגו׳.

Bereishis TR"Ei (2) is there; ShaBa"T is there,
like this: Beit =2 Reishit, BaR"A (He created) ShY"T (six);
and they are two Sabbaths, about which it is stated:
(Shemos 31:16) *And the Children of Israel kept the Sabbath,
to make the Sabbath..*

שתי פעמים הזכיר כאן שבת. כנגד שכינה עליונה ותחתנה.

Sabbath is mentioned twice here, corresponding to Higher and lower Shekinah. *for their generations* –what is *for their generations* (לדרתם)

But worthy is he who makes a habitation (*dirah*) for them on the Sabbath in the two chambers of the heart, and removes the evil inclination which is the desecration of the Sabbath from there.

The place within that we make is the expectation of connection. This is where both higher and lower Shekinah reside. Our thoughts reside in this place both arising and lifting themselves up along the connection of Shekinah.

The Sabbath represents a special kind of thought that is the fulfilment of a cycle. This cycle is represented above and below. Unless we become aware of both Lower and Higher we lose the connection.

The delight is the river. It is the connection, the flowing of Shekinah, and the ancient brook. It is sustained by Torah insights and brought together by the two Sabbaths.

What emerges from the Higher Eden is the essence of all that is emerging from Ayin Soph. It is the operation of the 'way things work' the essential production of something from nothing that is continuous throughout Creation.

The five hundred years represents the dimensions of Sephiros five each representing one hundred years or ten times ten. This is five from Binah or the seventh whereas the upper flows are transformed into the lower flows watering the garden blossoming into the lower Shekinah.

Make yourself a place of becoming which is the Sabbath and resist the chaos that is represented by the spleen, by the gall bladder. Keep your thoughts on high and seek to travel with them ever higher and higher.

No judgments are carried out on Sabbath to also avoid the sins or the cursed things that conceal the true nature of Shekinah

The admonition is to dismiss or stay away from the chaos since nothing can be transformed in this state of mind. Chaos brings all these negative things, hunger, thirst, etc.

וצריכים ישראל לעשות לה שנוי בכל והרי העמידוהו. והוא דבור חול שהוא אסור בשבת.

And Israel needs to make a change in everything, and thus they have established it. And it is the mundane weekday speech which is forbidden on the Sabbath.

85b) Thoughts of holiness need to be the focus on Shabbat. Shabbat is the symbol of holiness wherein we are given an extra boost each week to help us remember the higher pathways. It is these higher pathways that take Israel from indifference or the status quo-exile into the place of return the age of Moshiach.

Once you are immersed in holiness there can be no turning back.

Keep the Sabbath by attaching yourself to the holiness that is imbued in the day. Make use of the extra soul, the holy soul, and cleave to this.

Tiqun 49

בראשית ברא עלקים שאו מרום עיניכם וראו מי ברא אלה.

(Bereishis 1:1) *In the beginning ELKY"M created...*
(Isaiah 40:26) *Lift up your eyes on high, and see: who hath created these?..*

מי*(who)* אלה*(these) is the same letters as ELKY"M;* מי *created these.*

Lift up your eyes on high... first letters from the word SHMA this is the recital of the SHMA.

The first letters are SHMA with which Israel unifies Ha Kodesh Barachu twice, and you will find there מ"י which is the generality of the fifty letters of the verse of the SHMA twice.

Who created these' translates to ELKY"M meaning the mystery of creation lies in 'the way things work.'

Shekinah emerges because of the connection of the SHMA that provides the pathway to unity both in the morning and in the evening. It is the appearance of light (insight-inspiration-the stars appearance) that establishes the pathway that brings forth Shekinah.

The rising and falling of Shekinah is the flow of connection that continuously resides within and makes itself known in the presence of the unifying influence of prayer, of the SHMA, and of the blessings that rise above and return below.

When you bring forth insights then you create the space for more insights to be sent from above through you. Forever you are mining the fields of awareness opening new areas for habitation from the most high.

Adam called them all by name since he dwells within the Holy One most blessed on high. It is your perception that you respond to, your building you construct brick by brick and it is your holiness that comes to you through your unified connection.

So too may you mirror your thoughts each to their place referring back to the source and then coalescing in the unity level by level awakening to unity.

The river is thought and the place is unity. The source produces the inspiration, which unifies with that from which it was taken.

Ma'on Kadosh. It is the holy place. Here the unity asserts itself in concepts that encompass the whole. The essence of man and all that is sent through him to be expressed is in this triad of Sephiros.

Man is possessed of these attributes that work in his favor that do battle for him. This is the prime connection, the Middle Pillar, which transfers, transforms below to above and above to below.

Lift up meaning raise your awareness to this level in order to partake in the divine essence.

Ask the question that brings about the answer symbolized by the three patriarchs, the result of questions that arise from contemplating the divine.

Everything that leads to and promotes the divine connection is the realm of Higher Shekinah. It represents the higher thoughts, or the host of the heavens comprising all that is Shekinah.

The reflection of the hosts of heaven the Higher Shekinah is that which is directed to become the essence below, the lower Shekinah by which that reflection is recognized called by name.

(Yishayahu 40:26) ...*from greatness of strength*... that of which it is said, (Bereishis 48:16) ...*let them grow into a multitude in the midst of the earth.– and this is the Righteous One.*

And it is ...*greatness of power*... *the Righteous One.*
His power is the power of the act of creation,
of which it is said:
(Numbers 14:17) *And now let the power of ADN"Y be great*;

לא נעדר מהשכינה לעולם. וזה וזה הכל עמס. שבעים פנים לתורה
Not absent from Shekinah forever.
And this and this are all truth. Seventy faces to the Torah.

86a) This vast perfusion of holy thoughts has an exponential effect on the revelation we experience. This is known as the righteous one because what we envision will surely take place.

Significant here is the power of the act of creation. This happens when we make the connection between the source and the outcome. It is only via that connection, that awareness, that the act of the power of creation takes place at all. The 70 faces of Torah are also the 70 places of the act of creation.

They are all there because they have all pondered the mysteries of creation. Therefore we too must ascend in similar fashion. All comes to be as a matter of vibration on the inner sphere. You connect with that which you resonate with.

Mighty in judgment is the quality to discern the higher worlds. It is in this way that Jacob achieves perfection. Judgment is the ability to be able to choose the perfect path in mind to rise up to the highest in unification.

The power flows from above to below and below to above. It is the same power regardless of where we choose to focus upon it in its journey. That power seen as a whole is SHEKINAH.

Tiqun 50

בראשית ברא עלקים פתח רבי שמעון ואמר, שאו מרום עיניכם וראו מי ברא אלה,
Bereishis *In the beginning ELKY"M created...*
Rabbi Shimon began to speak and said:
(Isaiah 40:26) *Lift up your eyes on high and see who created these...*

ראשי תיבות ש׳או מ׳רום ע׳יניכם ש׳חרית מיי׳נחה,ע׳רבית. שלש תפלות.
The initial letters of *Lift up your eyes on high* are: the morning service, the afternoon service the evening service' The three prayer services.

About them it is stated:
(Job 33:29) *Behold all these will E"L do, twice or three times with a man* because they are the chariot for the three patriarchs, and about them it is said, (Bereishis 2:4) *These are the generations of the heaven and of the earth when they were created.*

We start with "the way things work." It is a process that is continuous and ever resolving itself. The three patriarchs represent ascending levels of prayer. Therefore each prayer service builds one upon the other. In this way the generations of prayer come to be. This is the template of creation. It is there we find the promise that EL will do.

Yes creation was filled out of the initial play of the chaos and the void. However, everything that came after was made from HEI including the five types. In this way creation modeling after its own perfection brings forth that which is out of the perfection that always will be. It remains to this day a self-sustaining all abiding influence

Once again a template for creation is alluded to. The Hei is a place, a habitation, the same place discussed previously.

It is where Shekinah operates moving above and below to effect the transformations that result in life experiences. In order to make this clear it is stated that not for chaos, meaning not just to make the nothing into something was this place established. It is for what is good and evolving in good, i.e. Israel is Shekinah laboring or working Her timeless journey above and below.

The three prayers services are seen as the vehicle for the movement of Shekinah; these three are the excuses for composition meaning that during these services as the mind is occupied with prayer Shekinah moves of Her own accord.

The Higher Mother is the drawing force of that which is the sublime connection throughout the body inherent in its spiritual structure. This is the kundalini that rises and falls.

Our connection is with our thoughts above. Those thoughts that are called the host are the higher thoughts that are already awakened above. When Shekinah rises within the body the spirit is experiencing unity. This unity increases during the ascending of Shekinah including inside of all thoughts.

The idea of Shekinah is central to Her liberation and Her return from Exile. Therefore we are reminded by the various agencies that come into play. All of these agencies refer to our heavenly stature any one of which is enough to recall Shekinah to Her rightful place within.

She receives from her connection, which is VAV. Father and mother implies that one is giving to the other and in turn they establish a template for both giving and receiving. This is Shekinah.

When Shekinah descends food descends from Him above. This is the sustenance of the body and more important the enhancement of life's circumstances. The flow of being is dependent upon this food from above awakened by Shekinah that opens the inner doors to the awareness of the unified being.

וכאשר יורד בה שמתחברת ו' בה', לא צריך להוריד מזון לה על ידי שליח בעולם, אלא על ידו.

When Vav is joined with Hei, then He does not need to lower food to Her by means of any agent in the world, but by His hand.

And when He emerges through Her,
He ascends withdraws to the Infinite אין סוף which is א'.

מזון שלה לא בזכות תלוי הדבר. ולא בחיים שהם אבא ואימא. ולוא בבנים שהם נצח והוד. אלא במזל הלוי הדבר.

Then Her food is not dependent upon any particular merit,
and not upon life which is Father and Mother, and not upon children who are netzach and hod, but upon מזל *mazal* does the matter depend.

And when She descends from Her place, and Ha Kodesh Barachu descends to dwell with Her, it is said of Him and Her children:

בו ובבניה אין מזל לישראל. אלא הקדוש בורך הוא רוכב אל כרו'ב שהוא מטטרו'ן, והוא ברו'ך

there is no *mazal* for Israel,' but Ha Kodesh Barachu rides upon a cherub who is Metatro"n which is ברו"ך blessed.

86b) When there is divine connection everything is as if all is one. The flow is then continuous coming from the levels of Mazal above. This is the awakened reality of unity wherein the essence and the thought are together. Because of this there is no parsing, no separation. Male and female are fused together; one purpose one intention and one unlimited outcome.

Ha Kodesh Barachu is the servant of Shekinah delivering all that She requires sustained by His hand that is always giving. She contains all the blessings and is never separate from Ha Kodesh Barachu. It is like the earth is never separate from the sun. They both travel together as a singular unity.

Thoughts are the deeds of Israel. Our thoughts make up the sustenance for Shekinah for it is there that the agent for her being is derived.

She is raised to Her place by our thinking our aspiration for holiness, our work within Torah seeking connections and identifying over and over again the unity that is there. Ha Kodesh Barachu is raised to His place by the making of a vessel into which He may flow.

It is the consciousness of connection that returns Ha Kodesh Barachu to His place because it is there within that connection that we come to know to whom it is that we speak to or of. The prayers establish the pathways however, it is the intention that ignites and maintains the holy flow.

In essence place equals unity. The unity of the divine name YKV"K.

It is only when Ha Kodesh Barachu is united with Shekinah that place is established. It is the joining of giving and receiving, the male and female aspects unity as a whole without separation.

Tiqun 51

בראשית ברא אלקים את השמים ואת הארץ
(Bereishis 1:1) *In the beginning ELKY"M created the heavens and the earth*

What is את *et*?
But thus have the sages established:
All '*et*"s' are meant to indicate inclusiveness of something else'
and this *et* is the Torah, comprising all the letters from Aleph to Tav with which were created heaven and earth.

And furthermore:
the heavens (את השמים) – the heavens are Ha Kodesh Barachu,
this is what is written: (1 Kings 8:32) *And you shall listen, O heavens!...*
and את is His female partner. *and* ואת – this is the Righteous One and its female partner, *the earth* – made of all of them,
issued her seeds and fruits, and the mystery of the word: (Bereishis 2:5)
And every bush of the field before it was in the land..

Connection is the key to creation. Therefore tying together the heavens and the earth, the male and female God principal and the seeds and the fruit all bring us into the meanings of this connection one to the other just as the word ET suggests.

The field is consciousness. Throughout the field the aspects of creation support each other. Thought seeks a complementary partner.

Thought seeks direction and that direction is Adam. Adam is both the principal of reflection and the principle of combining complementary thoughts.

The 72 Names are each comprised of three levels of meaning referencing the three patriarchs, the three branches of Shin, and the three ways you think about something; contemplation, reaction, active reflection. These are the souls of the righteous.

Torah is what ties us into Shekinah. It is the bread of Torah meaning those insights that are always available for us to digest and learn from.

מהו ליבדת האדם. אין עבדה כאן אלא תפלה. שהיא עבודת השכינה, עבודת יקו'ק ודאי.

What is for the work of humanity? There is no work here except prayer, which is worship of Shekinah, the 'work' of YKV"K certainly, about it is said:
(Psalms 104:23) *A man will go out to his labour and to his work until evening, A man will go out to his labour* – this is the morning prayer, *and to his work until evening* – this is the afternoon prayer, of which it is said:
(Bereishis 24:63) *And Isaac went out to meditate in the field before the evening...*

87a) All day long we are thinking. When we are conscious of the effects of that thinking we arrange our thoughts in prayer so that we may be continuous in promoting a good outcome. Good thoughts...good results.

We worship Shekinah by arranging our thoughts our prayers to produce the continuous flow above and below that is Her pathway via which Ha Kodesh Barachu the all within becomes all that comes to be.

Tiqun 52

בראשית ברא אלקים. אלקים, חמש אותיות כחשבון ה'

(Bereishis 1:1) *In the beginning ELKY"M created...*
ELKY"M: composed of five letters like the value of Hei (5)
א'ד of אדנ'י also adds up to five, and the mystery of the word:

(Bereishis 2:6) *but there went up a mist from the earth, and watered the whole face of the ground.*

Come see. Arousal needs to be from below to above,
and after which: *...and it irrigated the whole face of the land.*

...and it irrigated... Vav is an irrigation from Above to below,
which is: (Judges 5:21) *...a river of ancients...*
which is drawn from the brain המוח

The question has to be asked. Something has to be done. The vessel is forever in a state preparing itself below. We prepare ourselves by aligning with unity above. Once we are in alignment the streams begin to flow. This is what it means when it says "it irrigated the whole face of the land." This is the awareness of the connection or consciousness of SHEKINAH.

The river of ancients refers to the wellspring of Shekinah that is released and flows as a result of the holy alignment.

It is the flow Shekinah that gives the body its awareness. It is a higher awareness of the unity of God.

If you envision the body as a system then the power that floats above to below and below to above is a sustaining power.

The point that is Yud becomes the sea that is Ya"M wherein the river of Vav empties into it or irrigates 'the whole face of the land.' All of this is from the streaming of Shekinah flowing through us from us above to below.

Shekinah is light that is another symbol for the flowing of the life force that connected with holiness.

Torah is by its study and our pondering of it an inspiration to give forth new meanings that are the basis for the flowing of higher thought. Our consciousness needs higher thought in order to evolve.

Therefore Keter has designed it so that the fountain of waters Chokmah, is the well that overflows. We reach this by our inquiries, and our intention to bring forth these higher waters.

See how the brain is the wellspring that arises to bring forth the waters that overflow. This is a direct reference to the kundalini power that is synonymous with Shekinah, the connection that provides all of the holy pathways.

Therefore Shekinah irrigates the body. It receives its life force from the realizations that we have as we go along. In youth these realization are basic and naturally arrived at. Later on we have to work at producing these same flowing forces because of all the blockages the world might place in their way. Therefore it is established that there are 'buckets' containers of wisdom, of connection that are tipped over in response to the awakening of higher thought.

Unless you strive to release the wellspring through Torah study nothing is released from above and you become as a dry tree.

The Torah in action is the ideal state. It is the sustenance that you produce from Torah that is the main thing and not merely pursuing its pages.

Tiqun 53

בראשית ברא אלקים שם ב"ת, שם א"ם, שהוא א"ם מאלקים. והם גן עליון בן תחתון

(Bereishis 1:1) ***In the beginning** ELKY"M created...*
ב'ת (daughter) is there; א'ם (mother) is there,
which is the א'ם from ELKY"M, and they mother and daughter are the Higher garden and the lower garden.

Rabbi Shimon **began** to speak and said:
(Shemos 2:8) *And YKV"K ELKY"M planted a garden in Eden from the east, and He placed there the man that He had formed;*

And YKV"K ELKY"M planted a garden , this is Shekinah.
in Eden – this is Higher Mother. *From the east* is Higher Father.
and He placed there the human that He had formed,
this is the Middle Pillar.

And about him the man it is stated:
(Bereishis 2:7) *And YKV"K ELKY"M formed the human out of dust from
the ground, and He breathed into his nostrils the breath of life...*

87b) Higher and lower garden refer to the mystical place within where the flows of Shekinah emanate from. Mother refers to above to below and daughter to below to above.

The human is place inside of Shekinah the garden, which comprises both Higher Mother and Higher Father. The human is the Middle Pillar the connection that arises within the garden.

The human is the central repository of life both receiving and giving forth imaging above and transferring below. The soul or the identification of the human comes from lower Shekinah, from the sense of knowing their connection to the body and to all that is.

The 'man of creation, the man that acts as though He-She is One. The moment man is brought into existence there is the flourishing, the sending forth the imaging of above into the below.

The Middle Pillar is the human who consumes of himself to produce all that is.

All that is man or the Middle Pillar are contained in the sense of the body and the covenant, which is that man should recognize God and there would be no distinction.

You behold the unity which is Shekinah, the divine connection and this is what you draw what is good to eat from.

We partake of the wisdom of Torah, of the insights of connection and this is what gives life to us in the sense that our consciousness is expanded many fold.

So the essence of holiness or the connection with unity and its realization are what flows into our consciousness from below to above since we keep getting this understanding every moment.

The possibility of choice comes from the Tree of Knowledge of Good and Evil. Therefore Metatro"n is the choosing of good and Samae"l the choice of evil. It represents another place another kind of thinking that does not embrace the unity as does the Tree of Life.

Therefore a principle is set into motion that keeps producing the righteous Tree so that from "his place" meaning exactly where we are in the moment, it may sprout.

Each realization that preserves the covenant meaning that recognizes the basic unity of man and God produces the son. These mysteries of Torah are the food for our thoughts to contemplate.

Likewise were we to be caught up in the choosing of good and evil without relationship to the covenant then there will always be a mixture since choice still remains in effect.

You guard yourself by not dwelling upon good and evil. Therefore you just consider the covenant the unity of man and God and this is what governs the circumstances of your life.

Yes choosing the Tree of the Knowledge of Good and Evil causes death since the choices then place you upon the wheel of life bereft of spiritual sustenance that might have granted you immortality. All this comes from the fruit of an errant thought that then produces its own antecedents making matters progressively worse.

Tiqun 54

בראשית ברא אלקים, את השמים עץ החיים. ואת הארץ כל עץ נחמד למראה. והארץ היתה תהו ובהו זה עץ הדעת טוב ורע.

(Bereishis 1:1) *In the beginning* ELKY"M created the heavens the tree of life; and the earth
(Bereishis 2:9) *...every tree pleasant to behold.*
(Bereishis 1:2) *And the earth was chaos and void.*
This is the tree of knowledge of good and evil.

And this is the mystery of the word:
chaos תהו – the depth of evil עמק רע
void בהו – 'the depth of good עמק טוב.
And this is *the tree of the knowledge of good and evil.*
(Bereishis 11:9) *...because the LORD did there confound the language of all the earth.*
And from here emerged all the mixture of good and evil,
which is the mystery of the righteous person for whom it is bad, the wicked person for whom it is good.'

The earth arises from the principle of unity. This is the Tree of Life. Chaos and void are the Tree of Knowledge of Good and Evil.

Therefore the mixture of good and evil are seen from the different aspects of wicked and righteous. With unity there is perfection which creates an unerring reflection. It is consciousness expanding. With good and evil there is this back and forth and going from one to the other that dilutes the image.

Tiqun 55

בראשית ברא, בי"ת רא"ש והם אבא ואימא.
Bereishis BaRA the letters of which also form: בית (house) רא'ש (head), *and they are Father and Mother.*
ברא (He created) is the translation of בן (son),
It is the Middle Pillar,
and about it is said: (Bereishis 2:10) *And a river emerges from Eden...*

יש עדן ויש עדן.
There is Eden and there is Eden,
this is what is written: (Psalms 36:9) ...*and of the river of your delight*
You shall water them;

And the river of your delight עדניך rehabilitate, certainly.
This is Higher Eden, Higher Keter. The Eden below is Yud,
and there is an Eden below this is Higher Mother.
The letter 'ר is Eden in relation to the river below it;
this is what is written:
And a river emerges from Eden to irrigate the garden.

88a) The middle pillar as we learned previous to this is man. The river that emerges is man co creating with God the two as One.

So first the essence of all that produces all-this is the Higher Eden.

Below this there is another mirror image of Eden. This is Yud and then below this is the Higher Mother-Binah. So the letter Reish is the relationship of higher Eden to lower Eden and so on down the line. This is the river that emerges from the connection that links one to another in various gradients of revelation or pouring forth.

The river of the water of Torah is where the revelations come from and descend flowing from the inspirations above, and the light above.

There is a river whose constant streams water the most high, shining from the overflowing of abundance that is the heart of the king.

It is called the river of the ancients, the source of their inspirations arising into seven rivers, revelations that reverberate in the mountains the high places, the subtle mysteries of Torah.

There is river of fire, the cleansing fire, the clearing of kelippos, the exaltation of holiness, and the transcendence of the body.

Vav is of course the connection Shekinah that flows. Depending upon your vantage point it is one river or another but always the same in carrying the higher wisdom below and the understanding that ensues above.

Emanating from the rivulets of fire are sixty warriors to clear away the discrepancies and reveal the holiness.

These rivers of fire, of wisdom, and of Shekinah are symbolic of the emanations of revelation and correction that come upon us.

Arising from the hidden source 'your delight' emerges in response to your revelation, which has been shown to you. All you can do is to experience this. It always goes beyond words encompassing bliss as the light that shines through an open door.

It is the relationships that thoughts have with one another that are being alluded to here. The four sides of Aleph represent what happens to a thought, however we remember that His Name is One meaning every thought that is related to One is also One.

It is reiterated that no matter what shape the relationship assumes there is still no separation and no partnership simply one.

The river that becomes separated is Vav. This is the Divine connection and its separation is the result of veiling the unity. Still the key to unlocking the unity is to remember that these four rivers all resolve themselves into Vav the divine connection.

Remember that Shekinah already resides within the body. What is drawn into the body is the understanding, the recognition of holiness, and the covenant of unity. Then similar to what we have learned above the process is repeated diverting into four streams flowing into the arms and legs.

Consider that in the Higher Garden there emanates the divine flow which is received by the lower garden i.e. the understanding, that is the practical basis for that flow. Then there is the return flow. Call it the loop of meaning that arises on high as a kind of feedback loop to keep the whole thing always in motion. Therefore sitting in garden is to be aware of this back and forth motion and the ability to participate fully conscious of the process as it is ongoing.

The four way split in Metatro"n mirrors the four way split that has been happening all along. The gold in the north represents the pathway that Shekinah takes in bringing insights into fruition.

These movements are the various relationships becoming conscious of one another. In this way the holy influences interact.

The river Pishon represents those angelic influences that help you by giving you just the right amount of encouragement to persist in your studies. The revelations that you receive are from the side of the holy Chayot the aspect of the lion. The strength of meaning is what is presented here.

Unless you take the time to contemplate Torah's mysteries you miss out on the life giving properties that are streaming from above and reflected below. This is the punishment for those who transgress Torah.

פישון שם שפיפון להאעניש למי שעובר על תורה שבעל פה
Pishon – viper שפיפון is there, in order to punish one who transgresses the Oral Torah.

88b) Entering into holiness we have to let go and think holy thoughts otherwise the flow is subverted. When we remain on the pathway we enter the mystical Eden.

Once entering Eden man is taught to remember the covenant, to remember his holy estate, and to identify with holiness which is the unity that is the fundamental status of his being.

What he is to guard against is his creative nature (female) which allows for all possibilities so that he doesn't stray away from the unity. The possibility of separation was always there in the garden and yet man remained true to the unity. However as things happened he tried something else and found he could not get back into the garden.

For it is within Torah that the image of man is revealed, the image that is true containing both male and female and not the separation which has dominated humankind since the fall.

The positive precepts 'to remember' the unity are there.
The negative precepts to stay away from the possibility of evil were also there.

Therefore the ascended man Jacob, and the ascended people Israel have always had the unity within them. This is something that is ever present.

The new moon represents another level of ascension.

Unity is the King that resides in Malchus.

Remember the unity of being

The sound of the shofar is the Middle Pillar Shekinah by which the flow of unity is resonated throughout the body.

In the beginning (בר׳א שי׳ת פי׳ שש) ELKY"M created...
this ELKY"M is Higher Mother, who rides and ascends in tru'ah
for She is Rosh HaShanah.
this is what is written,
(Psalms 47:6) *ELKY"M God is gone up amidst shouting, (tru'ah)*
of which it is said,
(Numbers 23:21) *None hath beheld iniquity in Jacob, neither hath one seen perverseness in Israel; the ELKY"M his God is with him, and the shouting for the King is among them.*

Through the sound of the shofar the reestablishment of the unity within occurs.

והיא חרות על הלחת.
for writing is there; and it is *engraved* הרות upon the tablets.

יד כותבת ויד חותמת.
A hand writes and a hand signs.

One is the great hand of which it is said,
(Shemos 14:31) *And Israel saw the great hand...* and the second is the strong hand this is what is written:
(Deuteronomy 4:34) *and with a strong hand...*

89a) This writing is the imprinting of intention that follows for the New Year arriving from both side right and left and entering the middle pillar to ascend. It is the determination of the pathways of Shekinah.

This writing is also the higher engraving the ascension of unity that arises with the influence of intention. It is a retooling and a return to operational status of Eden.

There is the writing that goes deeper than words called engraving. This produces 'cherut' or freedom that is the aspect of free will that only happens within Gan Eden. It is

Shekinah that inspires this 'freedom.' We work with our hands literally to become the vehicle for ELKY"M in order to complete the circuit that is the purpose of Shekinah all along.

Hand implies intention since it is the last act that completes the thought. So the great hand is the higher intention and the strong hand is the carrying out of that intention hearing the impress that is to follow through with the plans of the unity

It is the recognition of this 'power of the act of creation' that gives it strength. Without this recognition the power is diffused, ineffective. Consciousness is the key here. To embody ADN"Y means to become master of that power.

When you identify that power with the self, you recognize what is above you and what transpires coming through you, which is the making of this world of experience.

Without this recognition, this particular consciousness, there is no power.

It is through writing that the thoughts are focused and that power that comes through the recognition of the unity is realized. This is a self-produced power initiated by the act of writing.

The source of writing is the Higher Mother. Out of this source, this crown comes perfection, wealth and righteousness.

What you are taking hold of is the ability to express the divine, to give meaning to the awesome source. It is the expression of Shekinah and the recognition of Her pathways.

Two fingers signify the unification of the male and female. This is the act of producing that which you have received.

The female provides the inspiration from the higher mother in the male and Ha Kodesh Barachu acts upon this by writing it down.

There is the defining moment in writing which brings about the commitment of the pen to the paper of the idea in its realized form. This is my name. Uriel.

It is in this writing that the higher voice is heard. The thoughts that appear on paper are a result of the weavings that take place via the various pathways of Shekinah,

When we write our intention is focused. That focus is what is signed above. When we rewrite that focus it is the Vav that awaken our connection to Shekinah.

Each name which is the implied intention evokes the expounding, and the teaching of the writing. The servant of YKV"K is that intention that rides with it. These are names of power that are brought into focus by intention.

Tiqun 56

רשית ברא אלקים. אלקים הרי העמידוהו, שם יראה, מצד האות ה' (ה"י) שהיא
לשמאל. שאף על פי שאות י' היא רחמים, במקום ששולטת ה' עליה (עליונה),
נקבה נקראת.

In the beginning ELKY"M created... ELKY"M: they have established fear is there, from the side of the letter Hei {or. H"Y} which is to the left; for even though the letter Yud is mercy, in a place where Hei is above it, it is called female.

This is speaking about how the letters flow one into the other and their attributes are determined by their place. This is something that is revealed over and over again here.

All who receive are female, in the location from which they receive.
And the mystery of the word:
(Ecclesiastes 5:7) *...for the highest over the high waits...*

וכמו כן השליח למעלה מתתרו'ן

And like as well the emissary Above is Metatro"n.
And some are the appointed ones under his hand,
who are the emissaries of Shekinah.

And Shekinah is female. There is no permission to go to any place,
without the consent of Her husband.

89b) Everywhere there is a flow of the divine giving and receiving, opening and projecting, and ingesting and assimilating. Thoughts are a prime example of this principle as they begin lofty in nature and then as their essence is gradually evoked they are put into practice producing other thoughts of a similar nature and so on.

There is no connection, experience of Shekinah unless by definition we connect on high. The intention is always unity.

Whatever is received there must be consciousness of intent.

While the divine influence is always good because there is choice we must, however, be on guard to make the right choice to choose the good and not make something else lesser in nature.

One develops out of the other. The male develops out of the female and the reverse is also true. It is a matter of direction and again intention.

The drops are called vowel points, which clarify the nature of the design, the words, the thoughts, and the actions that are mirrored from above.

Anger destroys holiness and subtracts from its essence leaving only the shell or the idol left which is less than useless.

Therefore the connection that is enacted with Shekinah cannot be effected unless there is a unity a love that unites the two thought forms. Anything else is a diversion of purpose.

What joins together are our thoughts. If they are most high then the joining continues the principle reproducing it in kind. If those thoughts are less than holy they cause a downward spiral interrupting the cycle causing death.

Unification must take place in a holy state of mind never allowing the rampant expressions of chaos to dominate.

The holy experience of unity happens as it will and not because we wish it so. Two must be together in harmony otherwise the union is off kilter and the flow of holiness does not reveal the inner sanctification that must take place.

וסוד הערבה נרמז בשתי (עם) אותיות ע'ר ו'ה. ע'ר ר'ע בעיני יי'.
And the mystery of sexual immorality ערבה is alluded in these two letters combinations of E"R, V"H;
(Shemos 38:7) 'E"R was......evil (R'A) in the eyes of YKV"K...

And these branches are not spread out such that 'ervah (obscene nakedness) can be between them, which is not the case except outside the place of Ha Kodesh Barachu, which is ADN"Y, this is what is written: (Psalms 5:5) ...evil does not abide with You.

שבספירות תמצא אב ואם ובן כאחד, בבינ'ה ב'ן י'ק
For in the sephiros, you find Father and Mother and son as one in Bina"h: the letters of which form be"n (son) and Y"K and there is no 'ervah there.

90a) Holiness resides within its own domain unaffected by evil the ervah that results from an incomplete union.

Unity places all together as in Binah, Father, Mother and son in their right aspects to each other.

The idea is that there is no separation.

The entire understanding of the Sephiros in Kabbalah depends upon the unity of their expression. There is giving and receiving from one level to another, male and female one hundred percent linked together. If there is a contrived separation that acts as a wall so to speak between male and female than by definition the unity is no more. This separation of male and female is the essence of evil.

Therefore seek the unity that is male and female together, giving and receiving and all partaking of One. In your mind tear down those walls that block your awareness of the unity.

Recognize that the higher has to flow through a willing vessel, which at the moment of its flow becomes female to what is above and then subsequently this flow becomes male to the one it flows into. Tear down those artificial walls because in the end they are what hold you back from the essence of unity the marriage of male and female within you.

Shekinah is distributed throughout the body connecting all in concert with the divine directive above. In this way all partake of the divine influence depending upon the consciousness that has been achieved.

The opportunity for connection occurs during the time of letting go, and the sacrifice of the ego in order to unite the letters above in our understanding.

This unity is all encompassing and rests on the Righteous One called Yesod that is the cornerstone of unity. For the wise this will be easily understood.

This unity must unite all the parts and not just one segment as in brother and sister because then it is incomplete and cuts off that particular union from the whole.

Consciousness has to be present in order to reveal the holiness above and the intention below.

Therefore you proceed when you have the unity in mind and the blessing of heaven that ties you above while flowing towards the unification that is Shekinah and Ha Kodesh Barachu.

This act of unification is nullified without the blessing from above. The mind may conceive of a unity, however, it makes no headway unless that unity is truth. This is the truth of the marriage of Shekinah and Ha Kodesh Barachu.

The arousal of the flow of connection can be for no other purpose then to carry the intention forward in the fruition of unity. These judgments that are made come from the incomplete nature of arousal without holiness as its goal.

The attention to the unity must be supreme otherwise going off in an errant direction causes the exile.

Our thoughts conceal the secrets of unity. If we hold them close and do not indulge in aberrations then the unity is promoted. If we stray then it is as though we are unifying with a lesser 'god.' and this causes separation.

The way of holiness is a narrow path that requires attention, intention and the acceptance of Shekinah to flow freely through you.

When Shekinah is sent away it is as though there is no connection. Even the way back is obscured. However Her basic nature, or the basic nature of connection is never kept away. It is there to be discovered by the righteous one.

The sephiros embody the days of week accordingly.

From the ten sayings we derive the inner flowing of Shekinah sourcing from Keter, coming from Bereishis the start of it all.

The righteous one stands for unity above all things. There is separation when there is no Righteous One. There has to be a Middle Column to connect to and a foundation to anchor the holiness from above.

Bring together holiness from Sabbath to Sabbath uniting Shekinah and Ha Kodesh Barachu and promoting feeding the realms above.

וצדיק שקרב לאשתו בימות החול, אותו בן שעושה עליו נאמר צדיק ורע לו.
And of the righteous man who approaches his wife on weekdays of that child that he makes, it is stated, the righteous person for whom it is bad.

For he causes the sacred which is the seventh day to be made mundane; and that time is the mystery of the righteous person for whom it is bad, the wicked person for whom it is good.

90b) The time of holy connection occurs during the Sabbath during the time of the recognition of holiness. Holiness has to be present otherwise the circuit cannot be linked together and the intention becomes diffused.

Adam and Eve were created as twins and yet they were one person without any separation. All the sephiros were included in them equal above and below.

It is the unity that sustained Adam and Eve the two that are always one.

It is the mixture of good and evil and then the attempted unification that causes death to appear. Any who separate Adam and Eve are as if they too are participating in the sublime delusion and eating of the knowledge of the Tree of Good and Evil. Within the mind this separation is especially apparent when the intellect argues for its way and fails to consider the female the accepting of the male influence. It is this blocking that takes away the female prerogative causing separation.

When Adam strays from the unity he deviates from the image that was made of him from above. Just as a prism must catch the light just so in order to shine the rainbow colors so too Adam has to be in perfect aspect to his creator in order that all the Sephiros be included him that they also shine. Every color described depends upon vantage point from which you were looking. This vantage point is an exact representation of the relationship between Adam and his creator. When Adam perfects this relationship all the colors shine giving him dominion over the above and the below in relationship to his awareness of the rulership of God.

וכמו שנכללים כל גונים ממעלה למטה בצדיק,
כך נכללים כל גונים ממטה למעלה בעמוד האמצע
And just as are included all colors, from above to below, this is included in the Righteous One, This includes all colors, from below to above, in the Middle Pillar.

91a) Shekinah includes all the colors radiating in infinite connection.

Connection, the Vav is the measure on high.

There are infinite connections great and small.

The hand symbolizes the infinite connections culminating in the palm symbolic of that which you hold and that which has come to be.

The symbols of the bones in the arms show the pathways of connection by which all things are brought into being. When you follow these pathways and are aware of their influences you may trace the entire field of Creation in regards to the connections of Shekinah.

In the beginning male and female are one there is no separation. Then because choice has been introduced Adam chose to separate, to interfere with the connection of Ha Kodesh Barachu and Shekinah. Because of this separation this fateful choice, that connection is interrupted.

It would appear that Adam denied his feminine nature at least for a moment that was enough to cause the separation.

If we accept the creation myth that woman was initially part of man and then removed because Gen 2:18 "it is not good for the man to be alone," this presents a paradox. On the one hand the female partner is removed and yet this makes man alone.

It is like an alternative reality when Samae"l takes over. It represents the choice that is away from creation a kind of dissembling of reality. The tendon of the foot directs the pathways in which a man may travel symbolizes this choice.

By trampling with the heel the pure physical act of being without spirituality places the soul under the yoke of the seventy nations.

Shekinah the creative force, the feminine aspect is a must have component of connection. Without it the intention can make plans but they do not come to fruition.

This second female partner from the tree of knowledge of good and evil allows Adam to choose between what is right or not. Therefore if he chooses right then she is for him encouraging him to connect, whereas if he chooses wrong then she effectively blocks the unification.

It is the first archetypal woman that is the essence of Adam and has to be recovered by unification via Shekinah to connect with Ha Kodesh Barachu. It is a call to the original state of innocence.

When Adam is reunited with Shekinah, with the female aspect of his nature then his intentions are directly related to his accomplishments. Nothing good can be denied him.

Again another paradox here since if this first one was removed from him, then she was never involved in the sin of the eating of Tree of Knowledge of Good and Evil.

Then the separation it would appear is brought about from above. However this also speaks to the dual nature of consciousness that can wall off a part of itself and also conversely unify with itself depending on the aspect of intention to the higher force of creation.

Therefore Adam must be in a constant state either of return in merit or decline accepting that part of himself that is always there or denying it.

It is the synthesis of Ha Kodesh Barachu and Shekinah that makes up the unity. When there is separation this is called the 'nakedness of your daughter', or daughter in law or a woman and her daughter. All these are symbols of Shekinah without Ha Kodesh Barachu.

In this way there must always be a uniting of the influences causing connection resulting again in the unification of above and below.

Tiqun 57

בראשית תר׳׳י שב׳א. והן שתי נקודות, שתי יצירות.

Bereishis TRe"Y (two) ShV".
And they are two points of the two formations (יצירות).
of which it is said:
(Bereishis 2:19) *And YKV"K ELKY"M formed formed every beast of the field, and every fowl of the air; and brought them unto the man to see what he would call them;*

באראה כמה נשמות וכמה ציורים צייר הקדוש ברוך הוא בדיוקן המרכבות שלמעלה, שהן חיות הקדש.

Come see how many souls and how many depictions did Ha Kodesh Barachu depict in the image of the chariots High, which are the holy angelic beings.

שלמעלה בני אדם נשמות מהן.
והביא הקדוש ברוך הוא את האדם בגלגול על כולם.

Above the sons of Adam inherit souls; and Ha Kodesh Barachu brings humanity through reincarnation over all of them.

91b) Consciousness presents itself in order to make itself known. It is the self aware-moment. It is the relationship of all things to a central point of perception in this case the 'forming' is the forming of thoughts to bring about the visions that are presented from the ground to place them in aspect to each other.

It is the experience of life that exists eternally on high and its expression in the world of form brought about by the reincarnation of form thereby exerting control or intention upon them.

It is curious here that Adam who is male female does not find a helpmeet when there inside of him is her, his helpmeet. This is the naming that results from consulting the host above. The host above are the angels, etc., the vast sea of consciousness on high. And yet there is no helpmeet there since he would have to find this within himself.

The host on high, the sea of consciousness has designated missions to perform and these directives are translated into the naming of the denizens below.

This example of Metatro"n shows how an angelic influence may be transformed according once again to its specific mission. In consciousness this applies to a seed thought that changes according to the specific connection it makes with another adjacent or compatible thought.

The thoughts and miracles they perform all goes into the naming of the angel according to its mission.

All of this takes place within the world at a predetermined time and place under the configuration of the planets and zodiac all according to the performance of their (the angels) mission. The changes that take place here determine the performance and the mission.

The transformations of Metatro"n therefore takes place via Chasdei"l, Gavrie"l SeTURYE"L, ChOTMYE"L and KOTVYE"L according respectively in regards to kindness, mightiness, concealing, sealing and writing of sins and merits.

Therefore the angels each are described by a specific sephirah.

We are linked to every cause that we a part of which sends to us or receives from us including the Cause of Causes. YKV"K permeates all aspects of being meaning there is no where that YKV"K is not present.

From the book of Raziel: "There are three secrets corresponding to the Torah of the prophets. All secrets correspond to these three. The first commandment is the first wisdom, reverence of the Lord. It is written, reverence of the Lord is the first knowledge. The beginning wisdom is reverence of the Lord, corresponding to three wisdoms."

And because when you rise together with these four letters

they are called, through Him, YKV"K, in one unity:
(Zechariah 14:9) ... *YKV"K is one and His Name is one.*

And because this is where the faith of Israel is in four of these letters;
and all those Names are designations for this Name.

אין שם ע¯ אין סוף ועד אין תכלית, גדול ושולט מן זה, למעלה עד אין סוף ולמטה
עד אין תכלית
There is no name to infinity and to the uttermost greater or more
dominant than this, above up to infinity, and below to the uttermost.
And all hosts and camps of angels fear and tremble from it.

92a) The unity rules above all since everything refers to the
unity. It is central to the understanding Torah and to opening
of those secrets that the righteous may only know.

This unity, this YKV"K when understood in its entirety goes
beyond awesome into the realms of Mazal emanating the
cause of causes.

Tiqun 58

בראשית ברא אלקים *(היא)* את. בת יחידה היא בת מלך פנימה *(היא)* את האמה
שלה. ועליה מאמר ויפל יי' אלקים תרדמה על האדם ויישן וכו'.
(Bereishis 1:1) *In the beginning ELKY"M created*
(She) is *et.* The singular daughter,
(Psalms 45:14) ... *daughter of the King within the palace...*
(She) is *et* - includes Her maidservant, about whom it is said:
(Bereishis 2:21) *And YKV"K ELKY"M*
caused a deep sleep to fall upon the man, and he slept

The universe as we know it is but a shadow of the whole; an
imaged representation. This sleep is but a further shadowing
of the image of holiness allowing the dreamer to experience
the dream world of apparent separation while remaining
attached to the whole.

She is barred from within from returning whence She came.
This means that Adam has to seek Her, Shekinah within even
though there She is represented without. Another paradox

and yet via synthesis both within and without are made whole since they each stem from the same source.

In like manner the outer and inner temple are described. The outer and inner temple are comprised of the body of man and his own inner reflections upon the nature of things.

It is all there in Torah and yet without the artist to envision the form within the clay there is nothing. The artist experiences the vision and then the hands work the clay. In like manner our thoughts envision an outcome for our hands to shape accordingly. Within Torah its insights are the clay that is shaped into the unity that is the goal of all revelation. Hint: You are the artist, the clay, and the seeking, as well as the end result, the unified awareness that is the continuous creation of heaven and earth.

Holiness needs a holy container. This is what is built in the realm of thought as the connections occur and synthesize the 'buildings' described. Before there can be a temple in physical form the holiness of spiritual work must proceed, otherwise it does not stand.

These two temples do not, however, refer to those physical structures we know of but are rather the spiritual constructs that our thoughts are attached to.

This closing is the closing of improper entry, which means not unifying with the Yetzer Hara. There can be no mixture. Instead there is a purity as in a virgin.

The purity of holiness from Shekinah the holy connection cannot be entered into unless there is a state of mind that is aligned with that holiness; therefore the three days of purity.

Male is always to be united with female.

It is the speaking of the realization of holiness, the emotional breakthrough that rises above linking prayer with intention that brings about the certainty of fruition.

They are naked meaning nothing gets between them. There is a unity of purpose that is realized and brought to form.

He said to him:
'My son! In the place that is sexual immorality there is shame and this is: ירא בשת (same letters as Bereishis) and one who has no shame, then surely the feet of his ancestors did not stand at Mount Sinai.'

And shame is in three colors, white, red and green of the face, of which it is stated: (Yishayahu 29:22) ...*now Jacob shall not be ashamed...* with the colors red and green; ...*and now his face shall not pale* with the color white.

92b) There is clarity and there is a covering, veils, colors and illusions. The mind follows after one or the other and the results are according to which path is taken. The clear path is where the illusions are removed and the link up between Ha Kodesh Barachu and Shekinah are joined. All of these symbols are aspects of remembering to remove those husks and those shells of thought that block the awareness of the clear light.

The seventy-two names align themselves into the magical transformations of reality.

Wherever we look we see connections and each connection increases the light and shows its precursor.

Everything is presented by the following of one aspect after another. The world is created continuously in this fashion and for the wise the seventy-two names carry the keys to the awareness of each careful step taken.

Tiqun 59

בראשית, כבאש יי' נשפט, שהם כתנות עור שצריך בהן הבדלה. כאשר אומרים
ישראל בורא מאותי האש, ואומרים המבדיל בין אור לחשך.
Bereishis (Yishayahu 66:16) For by fire will YKV"K contend

which are the tunics of leather for a separation is required in them.
When the People of Israel say, *Who creates the lights of fire,*
and they say, Who separates between light and darkness....'

Light and darkness symbolize the choices between clarity and
illusion. More importantly they show that the creator of both
makes the separation so that we can realize the difference.

חשך שחור. כתנות עור שלו, שחורי שחרות כעורבם שנאמר בהם
Darkness is black, its leather tunics are black,
of which it is said: (Song of Songs 5:11) *...black as a raven.*

(Bereishis 3:1) *Now the serpent was more subtle...* of it,
because all the living creatures He created garments,
as well as for all the creatures that were created in the six days of
creation, and yet there remained the bodies of the destructive agents to
make, and He did not make them because it was Sabbath eve,
and this is: (Bereishis 2:3) *which ELKY"M created to do.*

93a) The serpent is time or perceived time. Eve is the
progenitor, the womb of Creation. The Garden is what is
impressed with our thoughts that take form. The Tree of the
Knowledge of Good and Evil represents the choices we make
if we are cut off from Creation or the awareness of the unity.
The serpent says see what is possible and yet he lies because
Creation is instantaneous. Every possibility exists. Choice
happens when we start weighing this and that whereas by
trusting in the process of Creation we are always brought to
the perfect outcome.

Tiqun 60

בראשית זו ברי'ת שנאמר בו עץ החיים, והרי העמידוהו. ובהיפך הבי'ר, שגרם
שבר לאדם הראשון. וזה עץ הדעת וב ורע.

Bereishis this is contains בר׳ת (covenant), of which it is stated:
(Bereishis 3:24) *the tree of life;*
and this has been established; and in reversing ובהיפך the letters of הבי׳ ר
(broken), for it caused a breaking for the first human,
and this is the tree of the knowledge of good and evil.

Good is the tree, that which it is written:
(Bereishis 3:6) *And when the woman saw that the tree was good for food,*
and that it was a delight to the eyes... but its fruit was evil,
according to her vision, (so did it) does it appear to her externally.
Like the mouth of the snake, beautiful words externally, and a heart filled
with filth inside.

The breaking that takes place in the human is the thought of
separation. This is shown by the rearrangement of the letters
of broken. It represents free will, which ultimately resolves
into freedom to choose God.

Interesting that the woman has a vision of something and it
appears. It is the substance of what is within that reveals
itself without regardless of the outer description. It is the
heart of the matter.

The poison of death is the choice of death or transformation.
Since She is of Adam what she gave him was the same
choice. Once shared with one the other is bound by the
results.

Free will takes us into chaos, void, darkness and the abyss
because they are possibilities. To experience free will these
possibilities need to be explored. This is why transformation
i.e. death arrives on the scene as a correction for taking the
wrong turn in life.

Now given free will we realize the propensity of evil and
recognize it as in the waters of Marah. It is a place that
experience has shown us we dare not go.

Likewise the sweet tree the choice of ultimate good is also
our possibility.

ומפני זה יש עץ שענפים שלו מתוקים, ועץ שענפים שלו מרים. ועש מים מתוקים
ומים מרים

And therefore: there is a tree whose branches are sweet, and a tree whose branches are bitter; and there are sweet waters and bitter waters.

For this that corresponds to this did Ha Kodesh Barachu make.

And there is a tree, half of which is sweet and half of which is bitter,
and this is the tree of the knowledge of good and evil,
like silver mixed with lead.

And there is a tree whose husks are on the outside bad
and on the inside is sweet fruit.

93b) The tree represents our choices of good and evil in regards to the thoughts we choose to eat, to ingest, to latch on to.

All of these symbolic representations are to enable you to discern the true nature of good and evil thereby letting you choose good and to recognize when the path diverts from good.

It is a subtle difference discerning the nature of evil since many times it is enclothed in good.

For deed is the proof of the thought. It anchors it in holiness.

Judge them indeed by their works.

The staff that is Metatro"n represents the capacity for connection each of us has. It is through this connection that we transform everything below.

Now this staff or this capacity may be used to uplift or pull down.

Always it is the weight of our thoughts that lay our fates in the balance. When we are mindful of this we access the staff or wand to transform our troubles into mercies, and blessings.

In essence we only need change our mind about what it is we are intending and then all else follows through. This is the secret of repentance and the active place of mercy in our lives.

At our core is Ha Kodesh Barachu unchanging and always good. This is the place to access continuously.

When we realize the nature of evil and that we can turn away from it then we can have a change of place moving from the attraction of evil to the ever present good that has always been there for us.

The enlightenment is to know good and evil and the choice we are asked each moment.

Therefore we live our lives according to our choices that we make in what to think about and what those thoughts bring forth in terms of deeds.

Tiqun 61

בראשית זו מהשבה. אלקים זו אימא עליונה, מעשה, ששניהם יראה ואהבה. את השמים זה קול. ואת הארץ זה דבור.

Bereishis this is thought;
ELKY"M this is Higher Mother,
The fact that both of them are fear and love.
The heavens this is voice, And the earth – this is speech.

And in everything did Adam and Eve sin.
They separated between Father and Mother, who are thought and deed;
and between voice and speech which are son and daughter.

Following along with the theme of thought we see the permutations of thought, action, voice and speech. Now that which comes to be, Bereishis is thought. And the subsequent result is ELKY"M action. Taking it further along the line there are 'the heavens which is voice, and the earth which is speech.

The original sin is separation so that thought, action, voice and speech are disconnected. The way of return is the unification of all four. In the beginning all were connected flowing effortlessly together.

They heard the voice of YKV"K ELKY"M whereas prior to this all was one. It was an integral part of them.

And because of this:
(Bereishis 3:8) *And they heard the voice (of YKV"K ELKY"M walking in the garden to the spirit (cool wind) of the day...*

א'ת קו'ל זה עמוד האמצע, והשכינה עמו יי' אלקים אבא ואמא.
The voice this is the Middle Pillar, and Shekinah with Him;
YKV"K ELKY"M – Father and Mother.
and these four letters YKV"K: Y' –Father, K' – Mother,
V' son, K' daughter, which are: thought, and action, voice, and speech

and the mystery of the word, thought combines with action,
and this is the mystery of YU"D which is Y',
and voice and speech which is heaven and earth and all their host.

94a) So it is that the permutations of ongoing Creation take place. All are linked together in the divine unity of expression.

Thought and action are a singular entity combined with voice and speech the expression of that singular entity.

Hearing the voice that was echoing in the garden was because he Adam no longer heard it within.

It is Shekinah the voice of connection the same connection that is meant to be eternal with the Tree of Life.

When expression does not follow the form of intention it is left dry and cannot be restored unless both, wellspring, the source of connection and the expression of connection are one.

The gathering of the waters, the meeting place of the wellspring, the recognition of holiness, the awareness of eternal unity are all symbols of the One.

Man cannot hide from the voice within. He may in error project it without however that voice is resident within him and cannot be hidden.

What they became aware of was their state of separation. In truth it was a false denial and yet the allegory is that it persists as long as we give truth to the lie.

Hiding causes another level of separation since realizing that there was separation the first step is to bring about the return to unity.

Moses by his recognition of the separation came to understand the unity to recognize it once again.

Unity is the recognition of the fruit tree, the reawakening of the covenant and the symbolic separation of falsehood that clothes the truth, the foreskin and removal of the membrane.

Without the recognition of unity Adam has no place in the garden, which represents a unified field of awareness.

Tiqun 62

בראשית, שם ב׳ת, שם א׳ש, (שם אשרי).

Bereishis - Ba"T (daughter) is there; Ei"Sh (fire) is there; (AShRe"Y happy) is there.

At that time, Ha Kodesh Barachu withdrew from His Shekinah,

and She remained the singular daughter, this is what is written:
(Lamentations 1:1) *How* איכה *she sits alone.*

And the mystery of the word:
(Bereishis 3:9) *And YKV"K ELKY"M called unto the man, and said unto
him: 'Where art thou?* איכה*'* composed *of:* איה *(where) is* כה *(thus).*

To Adam He said where is your recognition of our unity.
While we may say that Adam caused this separation the facts
in the story suggest that this separation was part of the
original plan since the serpent, Eve and Adam were creatures
that were made by God. All played a part in this Creation
drama.

Adam answering explains that he found himself in a state of
separation and was afraid never having experienced this kind
of thing. Think about it like this. Imagine taking a child to a
big city who has never seen traffic and this child ends up
standing in the middle of the road because someone told him
to stand there. Now you could punish the child for listening
to this someone. You could kick him out of the garden out of
the city but then why not explain to him about the traffic.
Another paradox.

You hide from evil by not partaking of it and focusing on
good.

אלא בא ראה, בזמן שיש רשות למשחית להשחית,
But come and see at the time when permission is given
to the destructive agency to destroy,

It is said, (Shemos 22:5) *If fire break out, and catch in thorns,*
and at that time,

(Bereishis 18:25) *...that so the righteous should be as the wicked;*
And because of this: a person should, at that time, hide and be concealed,
so that he should not be found among them, for at that time,

(Proverbs 13:23) *...but there is that is swept away by want of justice* and
because of that, *...and I was afraid for I was naked and I hid.*

94b) Once Adam realizes that there is evil in the world he is afraid of being caught up in it so he attempts to hide from the evil. Likewise by not partaking of evil or contemplating evil we in turn also hide from the evil.

Repentance is the turning away from evil even before it comes and when it appears on the horizon.

This concealment of the mind of our thoughts is the ability to not choose an evil thought to think about thereby causing the chain of associations that makes more evil possible. We cut it off at the root by dismissing it.

The simple way of connection is to always walk in the image of above.

So now there is a refinement to Shekinah. She is the ideal person. This means that Her connection is the same as unification

The human is the connection the middle pillar.

Emanation should be used instead of creation referring to Shekinah as the prime mover that brings all things into being.

It should have said H' created the human since one Heh is the reflection of the other Heh.

It is the moving force of connection Shekinah that is ELKY"M 'the way things work' the process of emanation the animus to the soul that is in a person.

We must guard this image this reason from above that makes us who we are and never be separated from it.

Shekinah withdraws when there's no connection. Therefore maintain your awareness of the unity at all times.

Tiqun 63

בראשית ברא אלקים. מהו אלקים, מי אלה. ועל זה מי.
In the beginning ELKY"M created.
What is ELKY"M? And that's who these (the letters of אלקים) are

And about this M"Y (who) it is stated:
(Bereishis 3:11) *Who מי told you that you are naked?*
Which אשר *I commanded you...* and that of which it is said:
Who אשר has sanctified us with His commandments, and that of which it is said, (Psalms 1:1) *Happy (ashrei) is the person who* אשר
has not gone in the counsel of the wicked... for it is the public domain, the whoring wife.

These questions and answers the who and which are the domain of the realization of holiness. You recognize the divine within. The wicked are in the public domain, where reaction is the normal way of viewing the world instead of the cause of all causes.

Egypt is the public domain. The way that these reactions of the public domain take place seemingly outside of the holy connection, are fueled by the kelippos.

There is a healing of the lower Shekinah the place where there arises the holy connection, the imaging that proves itself above.

Via repentance or the letting go of the "outside domain" you re-establish the holy connection above. In a sense you return the image to its source.

Without Shekinah it is as though you were a shadow every moment reacting to what is not there.

The 'life' is the awareness of connection and the idea that the imaged form and the source are one being.

We impress upon our souls the memory of that image and then we reflect upon the wonder that fills us because of this. There is no other way of connection but by the recognition of this connection.

The answer to 'what is truth,' is that recognition of the imaged form.

If you operate from an illusory image than your works are bound to fail.

The truth is what is learned from the connection that is Shekinah which is the fulfilment of Torah, its purpose and its inherent design.

(Isaiah 59:15) *And the truth shall be missing...*
and falsehood rules in the world

ובזמן שנתקנת אמת ועולה למקומה, נמחה שקר מהעולם, זה הוא שכתוב
and at that time when truth is corrected rises above to its place,
falsehood is wiped from the world; this is what is written:

(Proverbs 12:19) *A language of truth shall be established forever...*
it is not written You have established rather, truth shall be established;
but a lying tongue is for just a moment.

95a) Truth is the connection. It is when the image recognizes its own reflection from above. This recognition is the divine connection. It is Shekinah. The correction of truth is like removing the veil that reveals the image and its reflection.

By extension it is truth that calls into being the whole world since it is thought, word, speech, and action that shapes the unique fabric of the universe.

In essence the word is turned against itself causing its own destruction as in the return to the darkness upon the face of the abyss.

Truth is the builder and falsehood the destroyer.

When we become so enmeshed in the lower things of this world we forget that the underpinnings of that world are the words we speak. Therefore when we speak falsely Shekinah falls, and our connection collapses.

Yud is the beginning of the divine name, which brings all into being. When we start with something false the entire structure is compromised.

The foundation of everything is that the word is inviolate. It sanctifies everything.

There are core installations within consciousness that when uprooted cause chaos and void. This occurs due to indifference and a path that is opposed to good.

The transformation of the name is the ability to view it in its various aspects so that we can see the operation of the divine wherever it reveals itself to us. Therefore the Yud seen in YKV"K is that transformation looking at it from below.

We see Yud in the middle as well emphasizing the all presence of unity.

The essential point of everything and its foundation is the all presence of unity.

Tiqun 64

בראשית ברא אלקים. שמ איש שם אשה עם ח' של אלקים

Bereishis BaR"A ELKY"M there in the word בראשית is the word איש (man), there is the word אשה (woman) together with the Hei of אלקים

and about them it is stated:
(Song of Songs 2:5) *Support me with barrels,* with man and woman.

And who or what caused this?
It is because the light left Adam and Eve with leather—skin to wear.
and thus: *support me with barrels, with leather to wear* עור
which correspond to: (Bereishis 25:5) …and reddened skins…etc.

The being of man and woman brought forth from the beginning contained are the first two phrases. Since it is the word that creates and forms this shows us the true purpose of TKZ, which is that out of this simple word BeREiShY"T the entire universe of being is wrought.

These skins are the veils of consciousness that hides itself from the unity.

When Adam says 'the woman that you gave…" he is already wearing a veil since the woman was always a part of him. Instead of saying we he errs in separation.

The error is not in the act itself or the hiding but rather in the perception that separates one from the other. There is no sin without separation. Shekinah conversely represents unification. So what is being asked is, 'what have you been thinking, what have you separated?

A man should fear or be exceedingly aware of the connection that is between what is thought and what is coming to be.

When you are not mindful of that connection, specifically the connection between your thoughts and the world around you, you then suffer the consequences.

שאדם ואשתו נבראו בדיוק הקדוק ברוך הוא ושכינתו. ומפני זה חטא האדם היה
תלוי בעמור האמצע, וחתא חוה בשכינה. ומפני זה מה זאת עשית.

For Adam and his wife were created in the image of Ha Kodesh Barachu
and His Shekinah, and therefore, the sin of Adam
is dependent upon תלוי. it affected the Middle Pillar,
and the sin of Eve upon Shekinah; and therefore what is this (zot) you
have done? You have done it to זאת (this), certainly.

95b) The sin is breaking the connection. Since the Middle
Pillar is Shekinah both Adam and Eve are joined in their error
which is the misalignment of source. 'This' refers to the
misalignment. There is then a disconnect between the image
and it's source.

The state of being called Shekinah devolves when this
misalignment takes place. What changes or goes awry is our
relationship to that connection.

In "This" I trust. It is the connection. It is Shekinah. It is
that connection that has to be re-established. As this
connection is re-established then a place for HVY'H becomes
apparent.

For it is Shekinah that is the wisdom of the poor meaning that
all have access to Her, the holy connection.

This is a spiritual ascent and descent. When Solomon
descends it is for the purpose of rising again higher.

Shekinah takes on the aspects of learning (Torah) and their
expression (below) in the world of action. They are both the
same only different in aspect and perception.

This wisdom of awareness of the consciousness of Shekinah
rules over all other knowledge. It ascends and descends with
that knowledge and is the inner pnimiyut of its essence.

The wicked act without this knowledge of Shekinah. Those
that have fallen under the influence of the wicked need direct
intervention to enter a unified awareness.

There was a time in which thoughts were placed in a kind of equilibrium. That is no thought rose above the other and no thought descended below the other. They were all together as one thought complete. Now the serpent for whatever reason appeared to challenge the higher thought.

Because of this challenge it was faced with a break in the unity. Because of this apparent breaking of the unity the completeness of thought became fragmented. Call this the preponderance of thought one over the other that disregards the unity.

The unity of thought refers to the fat places, the places with the unified awareness produces plenty.

The earth has consciousness and there is earth and there is earth. We are talking about the perception that is seen through the awareness of being throughout creation.

Adam is connected from the beginning to all. He-She is a part of everything. These curses come about as a result of the separation but not in the way you might think. This separation is by design since Ha Kodesh Barachu-Elohim took the female from the male. This was the first separation in consciousness that took place. Now it was possible for all to reunite since this is the inherent design, however possibilities cannot be dismissed. The serpent represents that possibility of further separation. The repair work that is left to us to contemplate is also the design imprint since by definition creation is self-repairing and we are as much a part of that return to Eden as any higher decree.

These seven lands are seven states of consciousness.

And Adam sinned against Bat Sheva (lit. daughter of seven),
and it is said of him:

(Proverbs 24:16) *For seven* times *shall the Righteous One fall...*
he meditated upon repentance, and it is stated of him: *...and he shall rise*
and he rose.

וכאשר ירד שם היה עושה מעשים ותולדות בכל ארץ וארץ. מהם היו צומתים
ומהם לא היו צומחים

And when he came there, he things and the history in all the land and the
land. In some of them they grew and in some of them they did not grow.

96a) He rises through recognition of the various states of
being of consciousness.

When he descends it is for the purpose of correction on a
grand scale. The consequences are always in line with the
actions that are taken.

An allusion is made to descending beyond the light into
darkness reflecting the poverty or lack that is inherent in such
a situation. Again the various stages are demonstrated here.

All of these states of being darkness and light, wealth and
poverty, refer to the consciousness of a person who is either
the reflection of the light or has become opaque to the light.
It is the awakening of the light that we are born into when we
recognize the connections that we have with the light and
with the precursor of light; the all essence of primary being.

There are states that proceed directly from the primary being
and those that are secondary offshoots of darkness and
everything in between. Such is the tale of the various
dimensions of being that we encounter on our journey
towards unity.

Tiqun 65

בראשית ב׳רא׳ א׳לקום׳ (ראשי תיבות וסופי תיבות א׳ב וא׳ם שם שהם י׳ק)
Bereishis: BaR"A ELKY"M the first and last letters there
acronyms of , A"V (father) and Ei"M (mother),
which are Y"H

And the mystery of the word:
(Shemos 3:20) *And the man called the name of his wife Eve for she was the mother* אם *of all life,* for like this of Her it is said:
(Proverbs 2:3) *Yea, if* אם *thou call for understanding,*

The mother of all life is the prime progenitor wherein all things good take their iteration from. What is called here the 'woman that you gave' is the action without the definite purpose. It is the evil inclination that arises not from good but from the endless possibilities of reflection some of which are evil.

Again it is a matter of perception in terms of which wife we are referring to. Eve is the primary wife that is always a part of Adam. When the separation comes she is called a maidservant from the Tree of knowledge of good and evil.

Still the essence of good remains. Eve remains from the aspect of the tree of life. Therefore both Eve and maidservant are the same seen from different aspects.

The 'power of what,' the higher mother, the question that is answered, and the unity of both; all of these expressions raise the awareness towards its higher goal the opening of connection.

באראה, אדם הראשון בדיוקן של יקו'ק נברא. ובדיוקו של עשר ספירות שהם
יו'ד ק'א וא'ו ק'ק מצד יקו'ק.
Come see: the first man was created in the image of YKV"K,
and in the image of the ten sephiros, which are: YU"D H"E VA"V H"E.

From the side of YKV"K from the side of Yud,
he is called איש (man); and from the aspect of Higher Hei,
his wife is called אשה (woman) – the mother of all life;

and from the side of V"H, Eve, his wife;
and from the aspect of יו'ד ק'א וא'ו ק'א Eve is called Adam;

96b) The unity that was prior to the fall was taken for granted. Afterwards they realized that they were perceptually alone except perhaps for the aspect of woman that persisted to revive the connection. The distinction then between wife and maidservant is that on the one hand the wife always remains attached while the maidservant is that part of woman that is separated. All of this occurs in terms of man's thinking.

A body was formed over the spiritual entity of Adam and Eve.

It is from existence, from understanding, and from the aspect of mother that all of these tell us what the divine state is. It tells us what is the unity and what that separation is in terms of the sin that was misread and the substance of being that is to be restored.

When we look at the image of the Sephiros that embodies YU"D K"E VA"V K"E we can see how these reflections are all spiritual counterparts of the initial source emanating from above. What we are saying is that this divine principle lives in man who is the demonstration of this principle.

There is a unity of design that includes man and woman and Adam and Eve. They are reflections of one another and are affected in turn by the image that sees not clearly.

Tiqun 66

בראשית ברא שית (פי׳ ששה). זה אדם שכולל ששה. והם שתי שפחות מצד האילן
של טוב ורע, עצם ובר.איש ואשה,

Bereishis includes the words: ברא (He created) שית (six).
This is man, who includes six, and they are two maidservants from the side of the tree of good and evil, bone and flesh; man and woman,

of whom it is stated:
(Shemos 2:23) ...*for from a man she was taken* – thus four;
Adam: male and female; this is what is written:
(Shemos 5:2) *Male and female He created them...*thus six.

And therefore:
(Shemos 3:22) *And YKV"K ELY"M said:*
'*Behold the man has become like one of Us*

knowing good and evil...which the early ones קדמונים established to mean as *one of the angels*.

It is the unity of being that is expressed here. We also have the six aspects of the Divine reflection.

Man has taken on the qualities of the above becoming as angels.

The initial intention is for Adam-Eve-Man-Woman-two handmaidens to eat of the tree of life meaning to understand the purpose of life, the way things work and their application since the reflection was after all a true reflection from above.

Because of the single Hei or rather the contemplation of good and evil there arose the possibility to choose evil somehow equating them each other. Because of this the consequences that followed were meant as a correction.

Once separated from Eve Adam could have returned but did not because he was already contemplating the separation.

Adam is forced to work the ground meaning he has to come up with the entire chain of association that leads him back above starting with the basest element and making it holy increasing his connection.

Adam's thoughts were not of Torah and that was his transgression since he turned to the world as his witness and the focus of his attention.

The task remains for us to choose of the fruit of tree of life by the insights given by Torah to pick up the reflections of the source and return via these pathways of holiness.

Adam has the knowledge of good and evil and yet does not possess the discernment of good over evil. For Adam it has become a choice when it rather would have been a lesson that he learns.

שאם זכה לכול מעץ חיים שהיא עץ חיים היא למחזיקים בה, מה כתוב בה בהולקה
גם מעץ החיים וגו.

For if he had merited to eat of the tree of life,
which is: *a tree of life to those who take hold of it*,
what is written of that, and he will take also of the tree of life.

Rabbi Shimon said:
'Woe to them, to those who are assumed to be (but are not) studying
Torah, of which it is stated: ...and he will take also of the tree of life...
and in its commandments, which are the fruit of the tree,
of which it is stated: ...*and he will eat and live forever.*'

97a) It is not enough just to know that there is good and evil in the world. You have to be schooled in the good so you will choose it like grapes on a vine. It is the good that Torah revelation is meant to provide. Without Torah revelation there is only knowledge and not its correct application.

Therefore knowing good and evil without Torah study is to strive with the angels in cause and effect without a divine purpose in mind using this power of good and evil for selfish gains.

Understanding the nature of things without the essential ingredient of good dooms the person who works in this knowledge of good and evil. They choose evil because it suits them and their selfish interests. This was the result of the events leading up to the Tower of Babel.

Therefore having the image that does not correctly reflect the divine means that the image itself was flawed and must be removed.

The destruction of the temple came about because of the intentions of the priests that tried to use the temple ceremonies for their own selfish interests paralleling the generation of the dispersal.

The prophets warned the people of the results of that would surely bring about ruin.

These warnings were the common sense appraisals of using the divine power to choose evil causing the blocking of rain, and the blocking of fruit. The intention must be turned to repentance in order to reverse the course of evil that was rampant.

Therefore the temple was destroyed since any temple that chooses evil is no temple at all. The people were killed and the remnants scattered to prevent such abominations from ever occurring again.

The sin of Adam in summary then was to think that because he had the knowledge of good and evil he could somehow control his fate sans the connection with Ha Kodesh Barachu.

The hidden things always remain hidden. By definition anything that you bring forth in meditation is grist for the mill. This admonition, which occurs frequently is to discourage inquiry into those matters that you might be unprepared for and therefore draw the wrong conclusions from.

Therefore having the knowledge of good and evil and the way things work gives you a choice of what to work upon or rather what to think about. In those times they realized this but lacked the integrity of unity which is why their efforts were tinged with evil.

ומפני זה כוה הקדוש ברוך הוא לבן אדם במה שהורשת התבונן אין לך עסק בנסתרות

And because of this, Qudsha Brikh Hu commanded a person

you have no business looking at the hidden things.

He said to him: Certainly that is how it is.

97b) There is a paradox here. The admonition not to inquire into that which should not be inquired into and then the explanation of what it is that should not be shown. The reason given is because it is the holy companions that are together and therefore it is permitted to reveal these things.

What is forbidden is the mixture of good and evil caused by the tree of the knowledge of good and evil. The idol worship refers to seeing the holiness in something that is a shell of awareness and not the awesome being that is Ha Kodesh Barachu.

The lesson as it comes through is that there cannot be any mixture at all. The consideration of good must be pure because it is Shekinah that makes the connection and that which flows through must also be pure.

זכאי הוא מי שמעלה אמונת הקדוש ברוך הוא שהיא שכינתו כלולה מעשר
אמירות, מבחשבה אחת ברצון אחת בלי ערבוביה כלל.
Worthy is he who elevates the faith of Ha Kodesh Barachu, which is Shekinah, comprised of ten utterances, in one thought, with one will, without any mixture at all.

One thought, one will with no mixture at all is the pathway of Shekinah the faith of Ha Kodesh Barachu.

The focus of your attention has to be singular when contemplating the connection that is Shekinah and Ha Kodesh Barachu. You have to divest yourself of all extraneous thoughts and drill down to the unity that is the divine connection.

The mind becomes one with the thought of the Eternal. There is the unification that occurs twice each day and even beyond this becomes a way thinking about God as singular and contained within itself.

There must be continuity of focus and a singularity of thought. This is something that is the inheritance of consciousness; that consciousness that began with the revelation of I Am.

Now out of this revelation of I am, the awareness of being, of process and of form there arises self-reflection. However, this self-reflection becomes clouded by those extraneous thoughts as motes of dust will cloud a mirror giving an imperfect image. Just as we wipe those motes of dust away with a cloth to reveal the perfection of the image so too can we operate in thought to remove everything that clouds our image of the divine.

During our recital of the SHMA twice a day there is the opportunity to remember this singularity of thought and to apply it to the experiences of our lives. The SHMA represents the unification of Shekinah and Ha Kodesh Barachu. This unification ties together our aspirations on high with the complete application to all that is around us. We do not just unify in some ethereal plane but are rather unified throughout the entire experience of self identification.

(Proverbs 19:21) Many are the thoughts in the heart of a man… We have to recognize that the world around us provides us with so many directions and that those directions all lead to dead ends except for the one that unifies above and below. This unification is the awareness of connection and its source and then we see the unity that exists forever between the two who are always one.

Tiqun 67

בראית ברא עלקים זה מטטרו׳ן, שבר אותו חקדוק ברוך הוא קדמון וראשית לכל

419

צוא השמים שלמטה.
Bereishis BaR"A ELKY"M, this is Metatro"n,whom Ha Kodesh Barachu
created as the original and first of all the host of the heavens below

And this is the small man אדם קטן
For Ha Kodesh Barachu made him in the image and depiction of above,
without admixture, and about him it is stated:
(Bereishis 1:24) ...*Let the earth bring forth living soul to its type...*
And he is: (Bereishis 1:11) ...*the fruit tree making fruit to its type...*
Like that above.

98a) The image is explained as being the archetype Metatro"n
the initial soul of creation that is the primary reflection of the
above.   Because of this everything that comes after is
generated by this image, 'the living soul,' and the 'fruit tree.'
The principle then of reflection is what initiates here.

Mixing the image only produces error, a degradation of the
image and punishment for the wicked who revel in this kind
of combining.

The One of this image is Ha Kodesh Barachu

Much is learned here about the male Adam and the female
Adam in terms of their unity and how their expression
represents both. The essential point is that man must live in a
world of action in order to prove himself, prove the image of
above and mirror the above in all ways.

Anything else that occurs detracts from this image, which is
always perfect. Adam is rewarded or punished according to
his adherence to the image of perfection.

ועם כל זה הראה הקדוש ברוך הוא לו, כל מה שקורה לו, אם היה מתה כלפי חסד
שהוא כלפי זכות או אם היה מתה בה כלפי חובה.
שאם הקדוש ברוך הוא רצה במיתתו לא היה מראה לו שני דרכים שהלו,
שהם מות וחיים לשון.
And with all this, Ha Kodesh Barachu has shown him everything that
happens to him, if there is chesed, then it is for the right thing,
or there is guilt; and if Ha Kodesh Barachu wished his death, He would
not have shown him his two paths, which are:

(Proverbs 18:21) *Death and life are in the hand of the tongue...*

And He showed him that good is not mixed with evil, for Ha Kodesh
Barachu had separated them, as it says:
(Bereishis 1:4) *...and ELKY"M divided between the light and the
darkness, and the mystery of the word:*
(Bereishis 26:33) *...and the curtain shall divide for you...*

98b) We have to know the difference between good and evil
so that we can choose good. We have to recognize that we are
not limited in this knowledge of good and evil. We choose
good because we must separate the evil from the good in
order to experience the purity of good.

Consciousness is the arena in which all of this takes place.
Therefore our thoughts are the building blocks and our words
are the cement that locks them in place. Without this choice
there is no divine connection. The divine connection is the
ability to choose good over evil.

The inviolable nature of good is shown. The separation takes
place between the light and darkness mirrored in the Mishkan
in terms of the holiness of the meeting place between man
and God.

Adam has to guard against the thought of evil and yet he
accuses woman wrongfully of being to blame when it is the
thought of evil that is to blame and Adam's acceptance of this
thought as the reality of his life.

What is the solution to good and evil since it was ordained in
the world that preceded man?

There is the archetypal or original man Adam Kadmon. It is
the template for Adam to come.

Here is the man of the body and the man of the soul. It all depends where the identification takes place; where the focus is.

The path of evil (Samae"l) is a slippery slope. The two females are one level following another. In either case it is the distance that keeps us from connecting above. The defilement is the distance from both Father and Mother.

In order for connection to take place there must be purity. It is all or nothing.

There must be a joining above and a connection below. None of this takes place in an impure state.

In order to reside in the realm of holiness all who enter must be holy. This singularity of purpose of holiness resides in the thoughts that we think. The direction and content of those thoughts determines its single focus that is good.

The tent represents the false covering, the husk of public domain thoughts that veil the holiness making a man of wickedness since the tent shields the holy thoughts.

If you start with wickedness then there can only be wickedness all the way through unless there is repentance. Conversely starting with holiness assures a man of their holy place above.

The decree comes from the thoughts we hold and the beliefs we attach ourselves to including that of death itself

As before stated there can be no mixture. Holy and unholy cannot be mixed. Likewise there is no moral equivalence between the two. Holiness is the singular aspect of Ha Kodesh Barachu and his Shekinah.

The initial emanation called Metatro"n, is the divine name incarnate, the image of perfections.

The ideal vision has no death no sin. Evil cannot attach itself here.

Because of this the heavens were divided as well the light and the darkness.

The theme of mixture is continued in terms of purity and impurity. Purity must be set aside in order to experience its elevation.

Tiqun 68

ב־אשית ברא אלקים. מהו אלקים, להט עץ החיים מתה האלקים ודאי, וזה מטטרו'ן.

Bereishis BaR"A ELKY"M:
What or Who is ELKY"M?
(Bereishis 3:24) *...the flame of the switching sword to guard the way to the tree of life*;
(Shemos 4:20) *...the rod of ELKY" M,*
and this is Metatro"n,

והרי העמדנו אותו שמתהפך מדין לרחמים.

and thus we have established that it switches from judgment to mercy.

ובו משתנים (נמצקים) צל דיוקנים שלא דומים זה לזה

And through it are changed (are found) all the images that are not alike.

One to another: when it switches from right to left, it shows the face of ox, and when it switches from left to right, it shows the face of lion; and when it switches from both of them to the west, it turns its face away and is switched to an eagle (to a man) and when it switches from both of them to the east, which is in the middle, it is changed to a man (to an eagle) below the eagle.

99a)Metatro"n the first image, the idealized image is always there to return to on the other side of the switching sword. Therefore the definition of or the 'what or who' is ELKY"M.

It is that idealized state which we can to refer and become one with.

The images take their forms from the vantage points of perception depending upon how you are looking through the switching sword, the angle of vision etc. The idea here is that there is oneness amongst all of these images.

It is an eternity of images that is being presented here all through Metatro"n.

The image of Adam begins with Metatro"n and goes through various permutations of which all of these, heaven and earth, stars, moon, sun zodiacal signs and throne, etc. are brought about out of this one image of perfection.

It all depends upon the first image. The way to mirror that image is to do what is good.

Tiqun 69

בראשית ב' שתים חכמה ותבון (ובינה). שלישית יראת יי' ראשי'ת דעת
Bereishis Beit chokmah and tevunah and (binah).
The third is: (Proverbs 1:7) The fear of YKV"K
is the beginning of knowledge דעת
and with this knowledge it is stated:
(Bereishis 4:1) *And the man knew Eve his wife*
for there is no coupling except with knowledge (*da'at*),
which is the Middle Pillar the unity of Father and Mother.

So it is below, the Righteous One is the unity of the Middle Pillar and Shekinah below; and of body and covenant it is stated:
(1 Samuel 2:3) *...for YKV"K is* ל'א *of knowings* דעות.

Knowledge-Daat is the great connector between thinking of a thing and seeing a thing. There is conception and there is realization with consciousness in between.

The upper image, the Metatro"n and the lower image the body realized as a unity of being. There is a synthesis of being.

424

Body and covenant are this synthesis meaning the agreement that what is above is the template of the body.

The righteous one is that which recognizes-knows this principle of as above so below since it is the rock upon which the world is built. It is the sustaining principle.

There is the unity of Father and Mother, then Mother and Daughter, all depending one level upon the other. The unity of one 13 and the other 13 making YKV"K.

Therefore wherever you find one the image of the other there is unity, the mystery of Aleph of One. The divine name itself a symbol of this unity and the inherent connection that is that unifying principle.

Always there is the connection between them that is Shekinah where two become one.

What is forbidden is the mixture of good and evil which is to say that there are no forbidden sexual relations.

The stumbling block is the evil that is the skin that is in between. This is the perceptual veil that must be released in order for the purity of the relationship between above and below to be fully realized.

שהרי רע מן עור, הוא ערוה שהבדיל בין ו'ה שהם אח ואחות,
כאשר התלבש עץ החיים בעץ של תוב ורע, זה הוא שכתוב
...which is evil of to blind
It is 'ervah (forbidden sexual relations) which separates between V"H
Who are brother and sister.
When the tree of life is enclothed in the tree of good and evil,
this is what is written:

(Bereishis 2:9) ....and the tree of life in the midst of the garden;
and the tree of the knowledge of good and evil.

We have to be aware of the consequences of our actions. Therefore if we are blind to our actions then the fruit that it bears is evil.

Here is a deep mystery. The tree of life is contained within the garden in which the tree of knowledge of good and evil resides. It is one inside the other. The tree of life is the absolute. The tree of knowledge of good and evil represents the random occurrences or rather the chaotic occurrences that may happen.

The Tree of Life is inherent in the soul and yet the Tree of the Knowledge of Good and Evil enwraps it. The admonition here is to not let the preponderance of evil gain sway so that dissolution takes place. Within consciousness the analogy is to thoughts that are holy and unholy. Once again there must be no mixture between the two. If there is it destroys the presence of unity or the divine connection, Shekinah.

The rainbow is the symbol of connection arching across the horizon. In its perfection the contrast of evil is revealed. Evil cannot approach perfection.

Stretching the foreskin conceals the evil, and covers it so that is cannot turn towards good. The bow is the connection that must be established above and below. It is like taking one covering and putting it over another in order to block out the light or in this case the connection with the Tree of Life.

The choice in consciousness is between accepting the unity or veiling it. Accepting the unity is the rainbow and veiling it causes the sorrow, the hard spirit signifying a shell covering spirit.

Stretching the foreskin or the masturbation that it alludes to refers to the thought of separation. The covenant implies unity as its central purpose. Everything we do has to keep the unity uppermost in mind. Therefore we guard against separation and go towards unity, echad.

והאדם ידע כו' קם דזקן פתח ואמר, רבי רבי, ועד כאן לא היה יודע אדם את אשתו. אלא בזמן שהטא הסתלקה השכינה ממקומו וכך העמידוהו בעלי המשנה, שבזמן שאין שכינה במקומה אסור בתשמיש המטה.

(Bereishis 4:1) And the man knew, An Elder rose and began Rabbi! Rabbi. And until here, did Adam not know his wife? But when he sinned, Shekinah was removed from its place, and thus have the masters of the Mishnah established, that when Shekinah is not in Her place, conjugal relations are forbidden, because of Her it is said:
(Bereishis 47:31) ...and Israel bowed upon the head of the bed.

99b) When Shekinah is removed or rather not thought of in her place then the knowledge of connection is missing. It is as though our thoughts are cut loose and roam at random. It is the antithesis of creation.

North and south symbolize the correct alignment of consciousness without which chaos results. The birthing of a child, male, means the promotion of the unity in its active connection.

Following the sin once again Adam knew his wife meaning the connection was re-established, the alignment set right.

Both good and evil are now apparent in the world and without Torah written or oral they are naked of the truth of the way things work.

The sin takes place in consciousness and yet the return also takes place here. The text is explaining within the elements that have come previously that a return to Metatro²n must take place within consciousness. Here is "the power of what."

Qayin is the result of the thought of separation. Therefore he comes from the root of the snake. The snake is the idea of separation.

Qayin's pollution is rectified by the Kenite who recognizes that there is unity and then turns away from separation.

Rabbi Shimon said to him: 'Elder! Elder!
And why does Ha Kodesh Barachu trouble with them
to bring them through reincarnation?'

אמר לו, מפני כבוד הצדיקים להעביר החטא מביניהם שעד שקין שב בתשובה פגם
של אדם לא נשלם.

He said to him: 'For the sake of the honor of the righteous to remove sin from amongst them; for until Qayin had returned in repentance, the defect of Adam had not been made complete.

And therefore, for his honor, Ha Kodesh Barachu troubled with Qayin, and so it is with all the wicked who are the sons of the righteous.'

100a) Reincarnation offers the opportunity for correction along a timeline that spans the Eternal. It is for this purpose that the defect that resides within Qayin is corrected. This is a lesson within consciousness that no matter what the obstructions or previous veils we can always approach the Eternal by correcting and removing the veils to purity.

The error, or the leaven in the dough, and the putrid drop all refer to the idea of separation that permeates the good and invalidates it causing death.

It is through reincarnation that the idea of separation is corrected. Consider that each thought goes around and then returns. In its return it can be modified, ameliorated, dissipated or completely diffused into nothing. The generations are the generations of thought.

Eve adds sacrifices. She removes the veils to her awareness of unity and as a result gives birth to righteousness, Havel.

Again these generations represent thoughts that must be corrected or developed depending upon their adherence to Shekinah, the Eternal connection that thought aspires to.

Mazal is something that refers to the aspect of the heavens and the heavens are the symbol for consciousness and the thoughts that are contained therein. Therein in the moment each has the aspect either of a favorable or malefic attitude. This literally depends upon what you are thinking about in the moment, the direction of your thoughts and your alignment with Shekinah.

There is no sign for that which is Eternal.

Mazal takes its aspect from each thought in relation to the other. The most important indicator for Mazal is the Vav the connection that unifies the one in this instance Aleph.

For Mazal rises in thought and is the essence of the higher thought which transforms that which is below into that which is above.

Israel exists as an Eternal since it has ascended a verity of being, call it a constant amidst a sea of change. The arrangement of thoughts provides the masala of everything.

When your thoughts are in right aspect to the heavens meaning they mirror correctly the heavens than good results are in order.

Reincarnation is the beginning of another level of being. The wheel turns through a cycle and then turn again via the connection that is the Vav of one cycle to another. It is one life to another. All cycles are for the building of that middle pillar which are the pathways above from below.

Each cycle goes through its appointed rounds and then rests meaning there is a timeless moment, the breathless moment that assesses and then moves on to the next cycle.

For these sixty myriads represent the transformations of ten, the iterations of the sephiros, the establishing of the Middle Pillar, and the central point of which is Keter.

והכל נרמז בצדיק שבו גלגול, ועוד יסוד שם יו״ד, שמתגלגל בו ונח בו מכל גלגולים שמתגלגל. וימפני זה ויכל אלקים ביום השביעי מלאכתו אשר עשה

And it is implied for the righteous in reincarnation that secret of the Yud cycles through and in Noah are all reincarnations that cycle through.For this reason and on the seventh day God rested from the work that he did.

And the letter Vav indicates sixty myriads of incarnation for the righteous. The righteous are six. And the middle column indicates sixty. And Higher Keter this is Aleph indicates sixty myriads.

(Ecclesiastes 1:4) *A generation goes and a generation comes, and the earth stands forever.*

100b) There is an initiating force that continues throughout the process becoming itself and the thing unto which it is sent. It is Yud that transforms and remains the same after another fashion.

The soul and its female partner come in together working as they have always been correcting the errors and ascending in the connection of Vav, the pathway of Shekinah.

It depends upon the aspect of one thought to another. If you cognizant of the moment then the moment works in your favor.

Your thoughts are eternal and via reincarnation you bring in not only the focus of your continuous contemplation but also the help you have received along the way. Therefore your contemporary or true partner will reincarnate with you. This is an extension of the helpmeet meaning your mate will arrive with you. Your thoughts are the spiritual component of that helpmeet.

We learn also that sometimes the contemporary does not reincarnate together with the righteous.

Consciousness is illumined in the midst of thought. What this means is that the identification with holiness depends upon our right relationship to the world around us. We have to make not only the right choices but also as well we have to make the determination as to our primary aspect to Ha Kodesh Barachu.

Time and space make up the dimensions of the world and the offer to change one or the other or both comes because of a person's ability to be conscious of their own soul's purpose. This is an example of choice extended to the maximum conception.

For the sake of every righteous purpose the Shekinah must connect with the world. Without this connection the world passes away meaning the body.

The Sephiros represent the myriad worlds, wheels, and gilgulim-reincarnations, that flow together from generation to generation. They are the transformations of soul.

Throughout these transformations of soul Shekinah resides Eternal as the connection that brings about the transformations in the hour of sustenance.

The person, R. P-dat has to make a correction in their alignment with Ha Kodesh Barachu. This alignment includes Shekinah the link between above and below. Essential to this right aspect then is the letting go of the shells of awareness that block the free flowing of Shekinah.

In spite of good deeds there has to be an unbroken (without guilt) pathway to the above. Any lingering doubts (guilt) will clog up the works.

The Elder is speaking about our identification with Shekinah. Livelihood refers to how we think about Her; what is our aspect to Her? Clothing refers to the connection that we experience with Her, the inner garment that we wear. Conjugal satisfaction is how we let go of our ego to allow Her to become all that is to unite with Ha Kodesh Barachu

Sustenance from the right again is our aspect to Her, how we see and experience Her. Her clothing is disregarding the outer covering for the inner garment.

Moses concealed his face because of the blazing truth the ELKY"M represented which dismisses the ego and leaves only the essence of reality, the way things work.

Tephillin and Tzitzit represent the inner garments since they are spiritual markers to the unity of Ha Kodesh Barachu.

ועונס מצד עמוד האמצע שהא ישראל, שמע ישראל. לשם היחוד שלא
from the aspect of the Middle Pillar, which is Israel;
(Deuteronomy 6:4) *Hear O Israel* for Her unity is there;
this is what is written:
(Shemos 21:11) ...*and if these three he shall not do for her,*
then she exits freely without money;
for (Job 33:29) *Behold all these will E"L enact twice or thrice with a*
man.

אבא שהוא חכמה באלו שלש יורד בגלגול
'Father' – which is chokmah – descends through these three in reincarnation;

And behold it is written of Adam and Eve: that two went up to the bed, and seven came down.
He the Elder said:
'That is precisely how it is, for they the seven are: Adam and Eve, Qayin and his twin sister, Hevel and two female twins.

Connection is the essential element here. Each connection, Adam and Eve, Qayin and his twin sister, and Hevel with his two twin sister each link to Shekinah and the soul that symbolized by the unity of the Middle Pillar, Israel.

The connection exists above and below and when this is interrupted causing lower Shekinah to descend from Her alignment then the unity was compromised.

All takes place by the perception of a thing. Adam realized that the connection creates or sustains the wellspring that is withdrawn after it descends to its starting place. Everything is thereby lifted up. Even Ha Kodesh Barachu in this way is a work of art constantly becoming more sublime.

In this subsection we find a summary of the preceding ideas. When we cut past the imagery we see that Shekinah the connection is the way to the highest mysteries. Mazal depends upon connection and if you are not in synch then your good deeds cannot overcome this lack of awareness.

Now we will see how by effecting changes in our way of thinking we change the life experience.

Place is where you reside within. It brings about your aspect with relation to everything else. What thoughts are you thinking? Where is the flow of your being? What is your purpose? All of these questions arise when you contemplate the divine. Every change comes to be as a result of this place in consciousness. Change your mind and change your circumstances. The Divine does not change. It remains inviolable awesome in its contemplation.

The mystery is enclothed within the divine name no matter in what perspective you look at it. The many 'names' of God speak about particular aspects of their influences. Within consciousness what you identify with (your name) determines the path you are taking.

It is thought that may be a tail for lions or a head for foxes. It is the recognition of thought as the precursor to action. It is the active use of thought to predetermine actions.

בא ראה, גלגול האות ו' הוא שיוצא בשעתו, שעלין נאמר מזל שעה גורם, כמו
שהעמידוהו אין מזל יום גורם אלא מזל שעה גורם, באברהם מה כתוב בו כאשר
באה בגלגול,

Come see: Reincarnation is of the letter Vav,
for it emerges at the hour of which it is stated:
'the *mazal* of the hour causes,' as they have established:
the *mazal* of the day does not cause, but the *mazal* of the hour that causes.
What is written of Abraham, when he came through reincarnation?
(Bereishis 19:27) *And Abraham rose early in the morning,
to the place,* in order to greet Her

101a) Consciousness contains every possibility of thought so that even were we to consider for moment the lower thoughts we would still be able to rise up with the higher thoughts.

It is every moment, it is 'the Mazal of the hour' that determines where we are in thought. Call it the atmosphere of our thinking including not just surface thoughts but the general tone of our thinking. It is this that determines our divine connection.

Abraham rose early in the morning meaning he reincarnated to the place of holiness so that he could greet Her, Shekinah.

Isaac did the same. He approached Shekinah in the field for she was the 'guest lodging in the desert.'

He encountered the place within where Shekinah resides therefore he encountered Her.

When you encounter Shekinah the angels surround you, awaken you fill you and you are there in Her presence, the presence of holiness the link to Ha Kodesh Barachu.

He waited with Her, for Ha Kodesh Barachu whose appearance was sent by Moses, the dawn that arrived with His reincarnation. It is the realization of holiness that unites above and below. There we find the recognition of unity coupled with the pathways of unity that are Shekinah.

Shekinah threads Her way through body and soul via the Middle Pillar connecting the essence of life (the soul) with the body of life (all of our experiences.

The true nature of Shekinah is to be with Ha Kodesh Barachu. There is no connection with unity.

R. P-dat has the revelation of connection without the same revelation of unity there can be no authority, no realization of the perfection of holiness.

So if the person is reincarnated into that hour of connection-unity that hour is not relevant to his person. It is not his time so to speak.

Aaron shall not meet with connection, without unity. Unless Shekinah be married to Ha Kodesh Barachu he should not approach. This is the state of consciousness in which such a holy approach is allowed.

As is said, timing is everything. The coincidence of reincarnation at the exact hour as in the beginning offers perfect synchronicity for the soul to absorb the lessons of unity and connection. This in turn gives knowledge throughout of the divine purpose that is happening through them.

Half an age refers to the relative period of incarnation whether it is a lifetime or in between lifetimes it calls for reflection on the completion of the Middle Pillar.

Half the kingdom is like the paths through Tipheret from Malchus below.

The Middle Pillar is the meeting place of above and below, the left and the right, the entirety called together in unified awareness.

The plane of opposites defines the possibilities from the Tree of Knowledge of Good and Evil that are described here alluding once again to the unity that underlies all.

In Torah the examples of right and left are numerous and they are caused by our attention to Shekinah.

Aaron approaches unifying left and right and Shekinah and Ha Kodesh Barachu, the connection and the unity.

With the moon there is a filling and an emptying.

Mazal causes birth to be at the beginning of the moon or at its waning cycle.

Therefore for R. P-dat who is born in the waning cycle he is offered a choice to start again chancing that he will be born under a better aspect. The point here is not the birth but rather our reaction to it; what we may overcome in terms of Mazal.

שלזה בן אדם שנולד בי'ד שמאל, קשים מזונותיו כקריעת ים סוף
For a person born in the 'hand of the left.

Sustenance is as difficult as the splitting of the Red Sea;
for the sustenance of the soul is Torah,

the sustenance of the body is bread, and whether this one or that, his sustenance is difficult.

Because these are from the aspect of judgment,
for they were created through judgment, which is ADN"Y.
And whomever was created though mercy, which is YKV"K,
their sustenance is not difficult; the food of the soul is Torah,
the food of the body is bread of the five grains.

101b) There is a predetermination or a predisposition of the soul. This of course refers to Mazal the timing of things. With judgment the effects are more severe in that the consequences are more swiftly applied. With Mercy there are mitigating factors. A person deeds and thoughts determine his place in the world.

You can only rule over your awareness. It is that which creates the heavens the Earth and the sea.

Timelessness is introduced into the art of creation. The plan of creation is inclusive. Therefore our sense of being includes every reincarnation.

What is it we are pursued by? It is your thoughts. Specifically it is the evil inclination that pursues you. ELKY"M seeks the pursued because this is what we need to remember if we are to resist the evil inclination. In other words we are to remember 'the way things work.' When we are able to remember then we can put into place the correct thoughts that will move accordingly.

The sin is always separation. Hevel whose sacrifice was accepted did so without acknowledging the unity of all. Therefore he repeated his father's sin.

There are multiple levels of consciousness. These many levels have to be harmonized within each other. This is why it is possible to do the right thing in one level and not do the right thing in another.

Reincarnation results because of a level of consciousness that must be rectified or harmonized with the unity.

Hevel was replaced by Seth in terms of the levels that needed to be corrected. It is following the principle that nothing is ever lost. Hevel then rises up via Seth.

Therefore within Bereishis the letters forming shame also appear because the possibility of sin does occur and therefore one of these correcting influences is shame which teaches us to remember and repent.

Through Bereishis the correction is already built in so that the perfection that is envisioned may return to its place.

It is the Yud that is transformed each time in each of these words Israel, ADN"Y, and YKV"K. This represents the result of reincarnation, and the levels of fulfilment of these three states of being.

And so Moshe gains the letter Hei reincarnating from the ten generations from Abraham.

It is the transformation level by level that splits the sea of Consciousness releasing the captives (negative thoughts) from the bondage of the status quo.

זה הוא שכתוב הנה יד יי' הויה, ה' חמש אצבעות. ובה בקע הים, וזה הוא בוקע
מים מפניהם, ובה עתיד להיות בוקעים התורה מימין.
this is what is written:
(Shemos 9:3) *Behold the hand of YKV"K shall be...*
the letter Hei is 5 of AVRaHa"M representing the five fingers
with which he Moses split the sea, and this is: (Isaiah 63:12)...*splitting
waters before them...* And with it the right hand, he is destined to be the
splitter of the sea of Torah from the right.

At that time, that which was to the left in the heart,

which was Hevel, which is HaLe"V (הלב) Hevel is withdrawn to the
right, and from there it ascends to the brain intellect,
which is chokmah, for the heart is Higher Mother,
about Whom it is stated: the heart understands, after which it descends
upon the earth, to bring the Torah down to earth.

102a) The sea of Torah is split by rising above the surface
meanings penetrating to the deeper insights that awaken there.
It is also a surging above within the levels of awareness that
operate from the higher worlds.

There is a transformation that takes place in the body refining
the evil inclination into the essence of the Tree of Life in a
sense bring Torah down to earth meaning we are transformed
from within by our contemplation of Torah.

Because the sin is in thought so too is the correction in
thought. The same analogy applies for action as well.

אין ספירה שלא התגלגל אדם עליון, שהוא יו'ד ק'א וא'ו ק'א, כ'ח מ'ה,
חכמה ודאי, כדי לצרף וללבן עת אדם שברא בדיוקנו למטה,
והאציל בו אצילותו, וכל הטורח השלמעלה
לא היא באדם אלא מפני אצילות האדם שלמעלה.

There is no sephirah into which Higher Adam (אדם עליון) is not
reincarnated for He is YU"D H"E VA"V H"E.
ko"ach (power) of Ma"H (what [=45]), specifically chokmah [anagram of
ko"ach ma"h], in order to refine and purify the man that He created in His
image below, and emanated into Him His emanation, and all of the effort
Above was not effected in Adam, except for the sake of the emanation of
Higher Adam

102b)Through reincarnation the refining process continues
operating on Abraham, Isaac, and Jacob refining the thoughts,
the deeds and the person completing the work; in this instance
Jacob.

The divine template is shown flowing through the patriarchs.
In Jacob it is the synthesis of the essence of the tree of life.
Here we see the extension of the Sephiros and the awakening
of connection.   This awakening is the awareness of the

'hidden thought' the thought of unity the thought that is immersed in connection.

This joining occurs in consciousness.

The refinery is consciousness. It is the repository of thought. Abraham Isaac and Jacob represent the levels of the refining process each one more than the other.

The Higher Adam is the principle that remains throughout. Call it the organizing principle or the impetus for your highest good. This higher Adam is therefore reproduced below becoming the inspiration for all connection and attachment to holiness.

'Days of his youth' refers to the divine image of perfection that resides within flowing through us in successive reincarnations building itself into an image of perfection that stretches throughout our life experiences ever new and always growing.

The divine remains inviolable. In its roots carried the Eternal image of reflection.

In Israel the divine image was nurtured and grew through the three patriarchs their awareness of holiness deepening until Jacob who then became Israel. The bearer of the divine image is therefore Israel.

The divine image grew until it attained the image of his youth, the tree of life, 500 years long. It ascends through everything and indeed is the connection that enlivens everything.

This image again is the operating principle that all spirituality comes from. It is the essence of holiness the river that is Shekinah and the source of life for all flesh.

It is the original tree reborn as it were and yet as if it had never been lost. It defines the pathways of the sephiros where Shekinah flows through.

The divine emanation is described as it originally operated.

It is the thought of separation that interrupts the divine flow.

It is the thought of unity that restores the divine flows.

אבל בן אדם שטרח עליו הקדוש ברוך הוא בגלגול ולא הצליח ממקומו,
עוקר אותו ממקומו ושם אותו במקום אהר, ומשנה לו מקום.

But of a person over whom Ha Kodesh Barachu has bothered to bring through reincarnation, and was not successful in his location in time and place, He tears him from his location and places him in another location, and changes his place.

And the mystery of the word:
(Vayikra 14:42) ...and he shall take other dust and plaster the house.
And this is: change of place.

103a) Creation continuous and everlasting flows through each person. Our thoughts determine our aspect to creation and also the direction in which our lives flow. Therefore we strive to align ourselves with holiness for the sake of holiness producing a positive outcome for us.

A person has a destiny to fulfill and if they do not complete their mission they are uprooted to another place.

Each of us is a vehicle for the expression of Ha Kodesh Barachu. The prime directive is always brought forth into being. Since we are that expression our vehicle the body is taken up and transformed time and again until that expression is realized.

This expression is nothing less than the fullness of awareness of holiness, the sense of divine connection and the realization of unity.

Once enshrined in unity the process continues world after world building the continuous creation endlessly.

We become subsequently become immersed in holiness achieving lives of perfection.

The wicked were given the opportunity for connection yet refused it and were therefore not able to become another link in the chain of holiness.

This story of the man on crutches who travels instantaneously and then becomes transformed into a body that shines with radiance is an allegory about the transformative powers of holiness. It continues the themes presented previous to this passage in that the life that is Torah infused becomes one of transformation even to the point of emanating light.

בינתים החזירו ראשם אצלו וראו אותו שהיה רץ כשרביט של כוכב
Meanwhile back in his head running like a ramrod of a star

He performed for them a jump קפיצה and they found themselves,
in the blink of an eye, at the mouth of a cave

(he pronounced for them the Name of 42 letters,)
and they skipped 500 parasangs in one instant; they found)

He said to them: 'Rabbis! Enter'
They entered after him into a cave within a cave, until they entered an orchard, and there was the one with crutches now divested of that body.

103b) Initially the sages are led into a mystical realm where they see the transformed vision of the lame man wearing another body. There the elevated (on the throne) transformed lame one has students reciting, Vanity of vanities or breath of breathes.

The master on crutches takes a hold of the sages bringing them into seven chambers in which is written vanity of vanities. The master realizes that these sages are not as learned as he thought.

The realization that comes from the inner meaning of this verse, 'Vanity of Vanities makes possible this mystical realm; something he inherited going back through all the generations. He does not tell them the secret.

Instead he gives them a lot of money symbolizing their worldly view, which disqualifies them from the mystical realm they have just witnessed. In short their efforts would have been better spent contemplating this verse but now they take their worldly reward.

The explanation of Rabbi Shimon is that these vanities are corresponding to the seven verses of Ana Bokoach. Each letter covers a specific area and each verse a day of the week. He intimates that this has to do with the elevation of the soul in regards to its imaging (form of a seal of wax). There is, however, much more to this since when we refer to the breath of breaths taking that meaning we are talking about the original spirit of Adam and its ascension, fall, return and the transformation of the holy connection.

רבי, אמור לנו שם רמוז (פ'א שום רמז)
Rabbi tell us where this is alluded to

בזה הפסוק, שלא התכסתה חכמא זו מן החברים
But this verse is not covered in the wisdom of the friends.

אמר להם, חכמים, בודאי סוד עליון יש שם
Surely there is wisdom that is higher mystery there
But I shall say it to you by hint (ברמז).

There are seven *havalim* and worthy is the one who does not take his reward in this world.

And they are included in Bat Sheva (lit. daughter of seven)
and they are in this verse:
Vanity (HaVeL) is one; *of vanities* (HaVaLY"M) is two – so there are three; *vanity of vanities* (HaVeL HaVaLYM) is three – so there are six; *everything is vanity* (הכל הבל) – there are seven;
and corresponding to them are the seven Names of AVGYTa"Tz.

104a) The vanities, the breath build one upon the other leading us to the secret of AVGYTa"Tz (Ana Bekoach-1st verse).

It is within the letter as demonstrated by Sepher Yetzirah wherein the light represents the instantaneous appearances of Creation. The constant of deity seven times and the correspondence of the seven names of AVGYTa"Tz.

We begin the association of the elements with the spiritual counterparts of spiritual ascension.

The vanities, the seven breaths, represent the pathways from thought through intention to demonstration. Therefore to speak a thing is to know it via the breath and to whisper it into existence so that once spoken it becomes what the breath has prepared the way for in manifestation.

The seven doubles of Sepher Yetzirah are the pathways of light and the speech of the secret process of continuous creation.

We elevate prayer with intention and a heightened awareness. All that is made is made by this intention and awareness.

The four legs of the throne Dalet represents a spiritual center. It is a place of higher being from which to anchor our awareness. It is also the center of meditative thought. The six steps are the six words in each of the seven verses of Ana BoKoach.

The awareness of being, and the sense of continuous creation emanate from this throne. It is the source of Higher Shekinah the joining of Yud and Hei.

Metatro"n the divine image, is the emanation that is ongoing. This emanation produces reflections called the intellectual spirit, the intellectual animating soul. There are levels of awareness that this refers to including our own perceptions of deity and the inner core of that which is the center of our being.

You elevate the breaths thereby elevating the soul. This is a conscious union of mind body and soul, the joining of above and below. The dual meaning of havel, breath or vanity, both speak to these levels of soul perception. Either we see it in the material and that is all or we recognize the spiritual and take our cue from there.

Your breath cannot be separated from your thoughts. Therefore an evil thought is produced by an evil breath and conversely a holy thought by the holy breath.

The divine image of perfection is continuously emanated by the divine name in its spelling and vowing. There can be no mingling of that image with any other especially the images that are false produced by evil, by demons, etc. Therefore Israel taken together represent that image which is the Tree of Life to all who make it whole.

וכולם עולים מהלב לפה.
And they all ascend from the heart to the mouth,

Seven 'breaths' ascend, seven descend to water them,
and therefore: *seven, and seven tubes*

There are three that are hidden above, whose garments are
אמ'ש (last night) which are represent fire, water, wind these are ten that
rise from the 32 paths, and there are, corresponding to them, the ten
utterances and the 32 mentions of ELKY"M of creation thus 42.

104b) The sacred pathways are described, spiritual conduits
for holiness arising and falling with the breath, awakened by
awareness, by the connections that are consciousness.

The symbols of those hidden above in fire water and wind,
representing the flashing of light, the pooling of water and the
dispersal of air all akin to thoughtful representations of
holiness.   Now these ten from the 32 paths the sephiros
awakened once again by awareness and contemplation of
principalities they concentrate in. It resolves to ELKY"M of
creation becoming then the 42 letter name that is an acronym
for the awakened consciousness of continuous creation.

Everything begins in its spiritual phase and then becomes
material. So all follows the original pattern, the ELKY"M of
creation, the 'way things work.'

So we see that as an element becomes animated it performs
the tasks that are common to it, winds moving mountains,
fires of emanation, becoming the essence of the wind. The
synthesis of these, wind, air, water and fire are the voice that
breaks the cedars. It may be called the active voice.

The vowel points emphasize the desire and the intention of
the words spoken, acting as specialized points of higher
connection so that the awareness is always engaged.

The actions of spirit are detailed by Qame"Tz 'upon the
waters' and then chile"m 'hovering over the waters.'

Shv"a demonstrates the hidden action of fire becoming the strong wind. The spiritual counterpart is explained in a hint that suggests further study.

Permutations and transformations take place becoming this aspect of ko-ach. YKV"K becomes what it needs to be in the moment. The voice directs and infuses and the intention shapes and forms.

The wind of the Middle Pillar represents the pathway of Shekinah and the rising up of the awareness of YKV"K and the imminent connection that is taking place, thus representing the cleaving each man to his brother or each thought to each thought.

The continuity of creation as described in levirate marriage is related to thoughts, which are eternal and though seeming to be gone are taken up again by the complementary thought, or the brother of thought.

The exile represents a falling away from the awareness of this connection. It is therefore called hollow and faint.

Contained within the breath is the power that animates all. This power is contained within the AVGYTa"Tz prayer spoken specially with the emphasis on the wind, the fire, the air, the water. All of this shows us the intention in the thought.

Wind, Fire and Water are symbols of the sephiros and the levels that are ascended and descended corresponding to the divine name. We see how the letters form the various combinations that make Mother-woman, wisdom and the seas moving through the lower sephiros until Malkhut. This is the flow of being coming into manifestation.

These seven voices represent a hierarchy of thought. They speak to the inner awareness awakening the template of primordial thought. We are being shown the awareness of manifest being.

There is a synthesis of vowel notes and cantillation notes. We see how one resides in the other in each individual letter as well as the associations that exist between them.

We see how the metaphor is continued in reference to the elements and for each individual Sephirah. All of this points to the emphasis that is produced by the complementary associations between Sephiros and by extension thoughts. It is analogous to the dendrites that produce the synapses in the brain.

Vowel points emphasize the speech that is the substance behind the thought. They accentuate the meaning of thought in essence grounding the thought that is produced by the vanity of vanities.

Divine connection comes from the Yud expressing itself through Hei while grounding it and raising it level by level above and below via the pathways of the Sephiros.

אותיות מתלבשות באש בשמאל, ועליהן
Letters are enclothed in fire on the left hand side,

And about them it is stated: *the voice of YKV"K hews flames* להבות
which are breaths of fire.Cantillation notes are clothed in air, in the
middle. And cantillation notes are from the side of Keter,
and vowel points are from the side of chokmah,
and letters are from the side of binah for whose sake
and are clothed in water, fire and wind, which are chesed, gevurah,
tipheret; and thus are they clothed in netzach, hod, yesod.

105a) The water in which these vowel points are enclothed is the flowing of wisdom that carries the entire structure of Sephiros in its pathways.

These breaths are the energizing influences, and the points of inspiration. Via the breaths these inspirations connect everything together.

These cantillation notes add the component of melody that is harmonized (water, wind and fire) throughout the Sephiros.

The vessel repeats the impetus it is given and is the center of the expression of all taken together.

The pulse of spirit is a cycle of connections like the gears that intermesh turning making another connection in the same manner over and over again no matter where the linking takes place.

The breath, the beginning of the cycle, and the pulse repeats the unity of the flow of wisdom that was began from above.

This pulse transforms the coals into a great flame arising from the awareness of being.

This beating in equal measure is the image taking form in exactly the same manner as it was sent to it from above. It is the perfect form and the pulsing keeps it that way.

In the aspect of chesed that the long flowing river the sustained pulse is generated and generating.

With this pulse the fire jumps up and then subside growing in power.

There in the Middle Pillar the pulse is harmonized evened out and takes on through its mold of form the substance from the above that is being imaged.

Acting via the breath the lower Shekinah is aroused because She responds to that image above presented to Her silently.

In exile She cannot respond because the pulse does not beat evenly or with power. It is as though She is asleep.

She sleeps because we have turned our awareness away from the One, which is Ha Kodesh Barachu.

She cannot be awakened without our awareness of the above. The process of ELKY"M is not speaking or rather is not being listened to. Without the understanding of the 'way things work,' all of our actions and thoughts are disorganized without purpose or intention.

It is after all the Voice that carries the heavenly flow. It is this specialized pulse that we need be mindful of. The potential remains in the silence but the Voice must be activated.

With pulse the melodies are promoted and the harmonies are thereby produced. These are the thoughts that produce substance and the awakening of Shekinah.

David's songs encouraged the pulsing of the flow of wisdom from above. They promoted it according to the divine name, which is the signature of that pulse and its perfection.

The spirit flows through us animating our bodies and more importantly raising our level of soul perception. By understanding the breaths, the havalim, we are able to send spirit where it will go.

The spirit of the holy does not participate in decay. Where there is decay there is no pulsation.

Without awareness the potential exists for holiness (my heart is awake) but there is no connection to holiness.

In exile the voice is missing its power and therefore the flow of wisdom from above gets short-circuited.

The still small voice is what moves and pulses.

With Messiah the voice returns and knocks on Shekinah's door meaning our awareness opens up and the divine connection is restored.

וסוד הדבר, יי׳ בחכמה יסד ארץ כונן שמים בתבונה. באבא שהוא י׳ יסד בת שהיא ה׳ קטנה.

And the mystery of the word:
(Proverbs 3:19) *YKV"K by wisdom founded the earth, by understanding He established the heavens.*
with Father, who is Yud, He founded daughter, who is the smaller Hei,

about which it is stated:
(Shemos 37:11) ...*but his father kept the saying in mind,* with Mother who is Higher Hei, *He establishes the heavens* which is Vav and is son of Y"H ב׳׳ן יי׳׳ק

105b) Consciousness lets go of thoughts that spiral downwards and attaches itself to thoughts that rise above.

With wisdom meaning with the perception of what the results of every action must be and with discernment it is able to direct those actions in just such a way.

The imaging then produces the daughter that is a reflection of the initial impetus from above as well as the Mother that is the higher Hei. Consciousness builds itself from within. The initial thought (father kept the word) goes out and becomes the thing itself.

Thoughts each have their counterpart; one is a sustaining influence and another is a directing influence. This is the male and female together as one.

We see how the letters combine making the template of awareness. The letters have inherent within them the core properties of consciousness. These properties in combination produce the mystery of the word.

The burnt offerings symbolize thoughts that are stripped of their impurities. Imagine consciousness as a pool and then imagine that within this pool there are streams that break apart from the main flow to become rivers. It is in this way that she arises towards the father. This is the flow of the connection of Shekinah.

There is always the mirror and its reflection. This is the burnt offering, the rising of its influence and the answering reflection.

Linking this to the pulsing of life our thoughts are seen in an altogether new light as the electrical connections between each positive and negative flow attracting each other both rising and falling.

Holiness corresponds to the joining together of the divine principle YKV"K.

As reflections of holiness the angels appear as wind and fire, and water and earth.

The conscious awareness of holiness is given a place in the body and is composed of the ultra spiritual worlds of the angelic forms in their elemental forces.

The breath rises with the connection Vav to link together above and below. It is the way of Creation, the imprint of holiness and the 'way things work.'

The reflection of the voice which is the thought is the speech that the word made form.

There is the consciousness of the unification of letters and words to bring about the Middle Pillar that is the connection above. The mouth demonstrates intention by speaking the words and the spirit meditates upon these words making the connections that unify the thoughts.

Worlds are brought in and out of being and from such a realm the secret of the four letters and their unity appears. It is the making of these connection that initiates the unity of their coming together in the holiness of the Righteous One.

In consciousness thought ascends upon thought. These are the two levels of the voice above and the voice below.

Think of this as two cylinders one inside the other, the voice above is the outer cylinder the voice that descends below is the inner cylinder. This is how Hei the inner voice rises while Vav the outer voice descends making its combinations with Vav and Yud respectively.

The contemplation of the master is the highest undertaking. It is like building a structure in which all will benefit and therefore all come to your aid in building this structure. The structure is the holy temple within that is the center of the throne of your highest awareness.

Our conscious prayer contains the breaths and speech that is the natural way of communion above. Here we take the intention and raise it via the breath to combine with the holiness above producing the unity that is One.

You build worlds when you unify the concepts of Creation and Manifestation making new heavens and new earths. You build with words of unity coming from thoughts of unity coming from unity itself.

You have within you the Creation that is ongoing. It responds to your comprehension, to your intention and to your invention. What you stand upon is the throne of glory, that fundamental singularity which infuses everything with its pulsing, with its reflection and with its eternal life.

Out of the midst of consciousness (shade of my hand) your thoughts seed the heavens and bring forth all that is on earth. Since we are the thoughts that make up the vast infinite expressions of Ha Kodesh Barachu, these thoughts are those that have been placed in our mouths. Everything we do is an expression of the One.

And about them it is said,
Open for me – with the letter Beit:
(Psalms 118:19) *Open for me the gates of righteousness...*
(Psalms 24:7) *Lift up your heads, O ye gates, and be ye lifted up, ye everlasting doors; that the King of glory may come in.*
and because of this: *Open for me* – with the letter Beit; (Psalms 118:20)
This is the gate of YKV"K... and this is the letter ב in בראשית

(Song of Songs 5:2) ...
my sister אחתי – with the letter א of בראשית
my beloved רעיתי – *with the letter* ר *of* בראשית
my dove יונתי – *with the letter* י *of* בראשית;
my perfect one תמתי – *with the letter* ת *of* בראשית
for my head שראשי – *with the letter* ש *of* בראשית

106a) We are the expression of all that is. Each person together and as a each to express the divine will.

She is Shekinah separated from Ha Kodesh Barachu. Many philosophies are tried to heal Her but they are all unsuccessful for her illness is separation.

There is the woman who is sick because her husband is gone and may only be healed by the doctor who knows that it is Shekinah that is absent.

She recognized the doctor meaning she responded to the connection of holiness or rather the pulse of holiness. He reminded her of the connection above and She started pulsing in response to His knocking.

She can only be healed by unity, which is within the already existing image of perfection. This image of perfection is inherent in BaR"A SHY"T.

Therefore the gates are opened. It is the gate of YKV"K symbolized by the letter Beit. It is enough just to begin to query the mysteries for the opening to take place.

Likewise each letter of Bereishis may be contemplated for its entrance into the mysteries

The dew is the rising up of the divine connection. Here it is overflowing like the manna that appears. All of this comes from the recognition of the unity. Each discovery causes another drop to come into view.

It is within this fullness that there is the rising and the descending of connection. Therefore at the point where they are both rising and descending it is the point where they meet where one becomes the other. The sixth becomes the seventh and vice a versa.

The crown is the place of collection where the unification takes place.

Then the Yud emerges into the many streams that form the nexus of all the worlds to come.

What is being described here is the hidden action of Shekinah in its aspect of becoming this or that. It is the energized flow of consciousness that awakens every cell.

The Vav, the spirit arouses the connection bringing together YH and H. Then the six words of the unity, the days of creation all come together and the connection is restored above and below.

'Open for me,' meaning be open to the connection that is above and below. It arises from the left and descends to the right. It is the flow of spirit. Those who learn seek deeply into this mystery.

The dew or the essence of connection that appears is like manna because of the YU"D H"E VA"V that fills the thoughts and brings together that, which is disparate.

We begin with unity and end with unity like a song that start in the key of C major and ends in C major. It is the resolution of one that is continuous and everlasting.

Throughout the body the dew forms above and below. Again this is the collection of holiness that overflows. These are the drops of the night. They awaken Shekinah and She effortlessly flows above and below beginning below then rising above.

The Sabbath represents the overflowing too of holiness that results in the extra soul in the anticipation of the connection that is accentuated during these times. The concentration and attention is on holiness. It is Ha Kodesh Barachu that appears in remembrance of the deliverance from Egypt.

Every opportunity to study Torah and to reveal the mysteries is also an opportunity to awaken Shekinah.

(Song of Songs 2:13) *The fig* tree *has put forth its green figs…*

שהם תלמידי חכמים בל״ב נתיבות פליאות חכמה,
בל״ב שהוא ב׳ מן בראשית, ל; מן לעיני כל ישראל
For they are the scholars in the 32 (ל״ב) wondrous paths of wisdom
with through/in the 32 mentions of ELKY"M of the act of creation,
in the heart which is composed of: Beit of (Bereishis 1:1)
בראשית and Lamed of (Devarim 34:12) to the eyes לעיני of all Israel.

106b) The 32 mentions of ELKY"M points of connection to the unity of the beginning the fundamental place of return, the template of perfection.

She, Shekinah is healed in revival of connection above and below. It is this connection that we find in both written and oral Torah.

The commandments symbolize the opening of the flow into the heart or the center of the expression of holiness. Negative commandments allow us to restrain that flow and positive commandments let it overflow.

The Middle Pillar can be compared to the valve that controls the flow going and coming, above and below, and right and left. It is the abode because it is the place that is routing control throughout the entire system of holiness.

The 'voice is knocking' suggests the inner voice that responds when we receive an insight on the oral Torah. This is what is awakened. It is the voice of the oral Torah.

'Vav is distant' meaning the connection is far away, and the wisdom of Yud is what awakens that voice that is the oral Torah within.

The initial idea for the world contains everything that would be needed to build the world and all its inhabitants. This idea that founded the world is in effect even in this moment and continuously brings forth all that is. It is the daughter, and the reflection of above that is the template for all becoming.

The heavens may only be established by connection. This is the Vav or the awareness of above and below.

Connection is for the purpose of making you conscious of holiness. There are levels to this consciousness called Binah for it's overflowing.   There is Tevunah for its active awareness. Again with Tipheret there is the harmonization of the connection, the Hei with Vav.

We have to become active in our awareness of divine connection in order to wake up the essence of connection that is Shekinah to Her place above.

'There upon the waters' meaning there within consciousness is the catalyst which opens the door for connection via chokmah opening the flow of chesed.

Redemption means the complete consciousness of connection with everything in its perfect place. It is a transparent place where form and spirit are one inside the other with the awareness via the connection holding all together as one.

Without connection all is not right with the world regardless of wealth, wisdom or might.

There is only the connection that unites Ha Kodesh Barachu with Shekinah that is significant or worthy of praise.

It is also the unification of male and female the recognition that there is no separation.

The initial reflection is sent through Binah where it expresses itself in the manner in which it has come into being in the first place.

The unification of male and female spiritually restores the divine image as it was when it all began.

Consciousness relies upon unifications to maintain it holy status. This is the point of bringing together Yud to Hei and Vav to Hei. The end result is always holiness and the consciousness of Ha Kodesh Barachu.

The offering is the setting free of the small man for the ADAM that is the unified YU"D K"E VA"V K"E. It is the joining of the perception of man with the perception of God.

זמן דופק יורד ועולה מארבע דפקים לעשר. דופק בארבע אותיות, עולה באש ורוח, וירד במים ועפר.

At that same time, the pulse descends, and rises from four pulsations to ten. The pulse, in four letters of the Name, ascends in fire and wind,
and descends in water and earth,
and the mystery of the word,
(Bereishis 28:12) ...and behold angels of ELKY"M were ascending and descending upon it ascending two, and descending two.

And they are, water is the vowel point קמ"ץ
the vowel point שב"א is fire; the vowel point חל"ם is wind;
the vowel point שור"ק is earth, the vessel of all of them.

107a) Unification is the cause Above of all causes. The letters in their coming together create everything out of all of the possibilities inherent in their associations.

The pulse is the continuous Creation taking place throughout the four worlds of Yud He Vav Hei, in the unification of holiness.

The angels are together in pairs of two symbolizing two thoughts that come together. These are two complementary thoughts such as air and fire and water and earth.

Vowel points are the connecting links between letters symbolizing the connecting links between thoughts. Think of them again as a kind of gear interchangeable in some ways and it is the universal gear, the earth that is the vessel of them all.

We see how the divine name is connected in just such a fashion. Water quenches fire. It is fire raised a level through the agency of water. What we can see from this is that the initial Inspiration or fire is transformed into the water so that the flow is controlled.

We are talking about the power of speech but it's true when the breath comes into the manifestation it is the earth that appears. These transformations take place in the heart. It is our awareness of this influence that makes the transformations flow from the breath into the earth.

The way of prophecy is that you're aware of the thought and then the breath prior to it becoming part of the earth. This awareness is of the pathways of holiness flowing through the heart.

The progression of unification is described as, two ascend and descend and then rise to ten signifying the Sephiros in extension.

Aleph is one and the ten sephiros mirrors in the ten fingers and the ten toes the divine image of reflection.

Shekinah ascends through Vav meaning that She becomes that which is ascending.

She is those vowel points which are the gears of connection. As She flows through She makes the various connections. These in turn are the basis for the unified awareness seen in the symbols of YKV"K

Vav is the connection. Shekinah starts with our understanding below of the way things work in the world as Malchus. Then from these insights we enter above with Yud, that is the wisdom that connects with the spiritual essence Hei. Therefore we bring together below and above accordingly.

The bride is Shekinah and She doesn't awaken and flow unless there is unity above and below including the four sides or directions. It is like having a force that radiates outwards which does not come into full operation until it is flowing thought all of the chambers freely connecting one with the other.

As She flows via the breath She reaches on high Chokmah the breath that rises and Binah Mother the breath that sends out, the warm breath.

The path that consciousness takes makes itself up as it goes along. Consider that everything emanates from this central path. The left, right and center paths are described all emanating from the breath warm or cold, in and out and the harmonized central path.

The breath becomes dry transforming into the earth below uniting together the four letters being a part of the process of

Creation and 'the way things work.' The four that amount to ten take the subtle pathways from ideation into fulfilment.

Mikha-e"l, Gavri-e"l, Nuri-e"l, and R-pha-e"l are the intelligences that shape the winds as they are flowing into being.

We see how the primordial air that is composed of the essence of being works its way until it becomes that which stands dry or fulfilled in the Sephira of Malchus. All of these principalities act together in producing that which is coming to be.

The essence of a thing is its 'sweet smelling savor, the recognition of what is coming to be, and the consciousness of being.

The bread for the fires are those thoughts that are fed to the holiness that is flowing at this point through Netzach and Hod. This is therefore a refining process.

The three levels of holiness are each in turn transformed via the connections taking place all along the way.

מרכבה של כולם שכינה
The chariot of all of them is Shekhinah.

Because there are six תיקונים revisions,
from the side of the letter Vav =6,
which is the holy spirit הרוח הקדוש
(of Ha Kodesh Barachu) which beats and blows in all of them.

The chariot of malkhut comprises four winds,
and this is the mystery of 'two faces ד״ו פרצופים
which are the ten pulses, which are the Hei that comes from the heart,
which is 'breath' הבל made up of the letters ה ל׳ב (the heart);

107b) Shekhinah is the current that flows through all of Creation called the holy spirit, the ruach hakodesh.

Imagine that thoughts come together fueled by their momentum. This momentum is described as four winds and ten pulsations. It is the breath that arises and directs all to the destination Hei which is a mirror of above and below.

The six levels Zeir Anpin, the archetype of Emanation and the issuing of souls from this point of sublime awareness are unified and yet each has a separate divine purpose.

This throne is the directing influence of higher Shekinah and is a mirror of the lower Malchus.

The momentum of the ten wheels, or sephiros that emanate from the throne make the template of awareness by which all awareness flows in or out of being,

Man the image encompasses consciousness containing within the divine image all the wisdom that initiates these pulses.

Higher Hei unifies with mercy to cool the flow since its start up is abrupt and because of the distance that the connection has had to undergo. There is the realization and and then the flow pulses but in order that it be sustained and controlled it has to be controlled with a kind of resistor like conceptual construct.

The redemption is the restoration of connection where the awareness is One with YKV"K and by definition the rising sacrifice attracts the higher Hei which is the culmination of form and its reason for being.

Jacob switches his hands with Ephraim to signify that the direction of the pulsations is determined by holiness alone and not by status or birth or anything else. Inside of this meaning is the place where we change our minds from one thought to another. The levels of thought are determined from the throne of thought. This throne is built by the choice of our thoughts and the determination of the image there within.

Observe and recognize the awareness of holiness, Remember when the veils are in place, Remember the Name which is the key to the unification of the mitzvos.

The opportunities for connection abound throughout the year contemplating the various festivals. You learn to recognize the flow of pulsation in the year corresponding to your life experiences and then as well their relationship to the festivals.

The middle pillar is completed meaning that the connection with Ha Kodesh Barachu is established symbolized by the joining of ADN'Y with YKV"K making the two fold divine name alluding also to the Dalet that is two plus two and the four that become ten.

The inner dwelling, the tabernacle, the throne of glory, the place of becoming the Middle Pillar, all of these come together here within the place where our thoughts are set free and pulse with the holiness of above and the experience of the holiness below.

Your focus has to be holiness otherwise the momentum that is Shekinah, the current, the pulse recedes and will have to be promulgated again. This attention to holiness is the arousal of redemption.

This tempest wind is chaos and veils the holiness, blocks the flow causing the world to err. What does this mean? It is as though you have no clear picture of the direction you are taking in the world and therefore the results are always mixed with the reactions to things instead of flowing through them.

If you paddle in a river with force you can go against the current. If you let the current take you wherever then you are subject to indeterminate result. Or seen from another perspective if you are in the current of Shekinah there are no counter currents that can hinder your progress or block your holy connection.

Evil is chasing the wrong current. It gets you somewhere but never the place you started out wanting to be. All of this applies to thoughts, the ones you are inspired by or the ones that take over your life for evil.

Without your active intervention these evils, these negative thoughts build their own momentum and become agents of destruction.

A sick person dwells on negative thoughts, which causes their illness.

All of these effects the 'back breaking work, etc., are symptoms of us not paying attention. This is why Israel were slaves in Egypt. They were slaves to their negative thinking, to thinking like the Egyptians and ignoring their own holiness. As a result they suffered until Moses came along and said, "Listen and Remember."

When we Observe- listen and Remember we realize that we are the source of holiness and of connection. They are both contained in our thoughts. Holiness is the symbol of HYV"H and Remember is the symbol of ADN"Y. It is the marriage of Qudsha Brikh and Shekinah, the Dalet that is two letters, the connection, and the four that become the ten. All of these refer to our awakened awareness that then emulates the divine template of emanation.

(Deuteronomy 8:3) ...*for not on bread alone shall a man live,*

שהו הבל לב השכינה הקדושה, להב המזבח, ומיד שעולה בהבלי פיהם של ישראל
בתפלות הקדוש ברוך הוא שואל בגללה מי זות עלה מן המדבר. בזות עלה ודאי.
Which is the breath הבל of the heart of Holy Shekinah,
the flame להב of the alter, and as soon as She ascends through by means
of the breaths of the mouths of Israel in prayer,
Ha Kodesh Barachu enquires of Her:
(Song of Songs 3:6) *Who is this (zot) rising from the desert?*
– *Who is This rising*, certainly.

108a   The desert is the man who does not drink of Torah.
When there is intention to connection Shekinah arises and is
met by 'who is this?' This rising and the corresponding
answer make up the unity of being.

The breath releases the thoughts whether they be for good or
ill. Breath for good, the breath of prayers seeks connection.
Breath for ill seeks disunion.

The Redemption takes away the false vanities (breaths) that
lead people to sin.

The spirit of holiness is the pulsation of the beginning once
again and rules by overcoming every other impulse.

The ship the body is the direct result of the Breath the spirit
that moves through it. All things that occur are the result of
this breath and spirit. Is because of this breath and spirit that
all things come to be. It is also true that it is not just the body
of a person but the body of a person's experiences that results
in everything that goes on around him.

The Spirit, the wind, and the Breath all are the same. We can
see from what Ezekiel is saying that he is speaking about the
action of the breath, the wind, and the spirit in the body. It is
our connection with holiness that connects all of Creation
together.

The body is the vehicle for Shekinah. It's waves are constantly coming up on the shore of the body. In this way the body moves with the ebbs and flows of spirit.

Shekinah sets the boundaries and the pathways through which she must flow.

Now when you recognize the effects of the breath in the lungs and the spirit correspondingly in the chambers of the heart you begin to see how these pathways are built and how "the four become the ten."

The beat, the pulsation and the rhythm are defined by the vowel points.

The rhythm of the words and their timing exists in the vowel points. Above, below or in the middle refers to the location of the pulse that is being repeated.

Beating above denotes the hot and dry opening caused by fire or by the transformation of anything that is blocking imitating the action of the burnt offering.

Beating below reveals the collection point is moist, the heavens below, the wind upon the sea, and the spirit entering the flow of the ship.

Equal pulsations are a key to the summoning of holiness and also the action of the breath in the three-fold breathing of pranayama.

When the breath is held above and below the complete breath is shv"a,

There are reflections of the breath called fire and water. There is a meeting place in between its outflow and inflow that is the meeting place of fire and water.

The breath is aroused via fire, water and wind in the middle symbolized by shure"q. Visualize the spacing here, and then visualize the pulsing within.

Consider the timing in music half time, four/four three/four, etc. The pulse produces the vowel or you could say that producing the vowel makes the pulse.

A long pulse or a wide pulse is where the beat is lengthened as in holding one vowel for a four count or eight count. This refers to qame"tz.

The simultaneous pulsing with nine vowel points becomes the one all-inclusive pulse of Shekinah because all pulses are included in Her via the vowels merging and becoming one.

When the spiritual understanding is one the body is one with the spiritual understanding. Each aspect enlightens and as a whole all come together in unity above and below.

Vav is the measure of the connection meaning its strength or stature; how well connected. In unity this connection is endless.

וכאשר נקודות דופקות בו. הן דופקות כל הדפקים בנחת ברחמים.
And when the vowel points are beating in it,
they all beat with ease, with mercy.

And when there is no Vav there, they beat quickly,
and they are judgments דינים beating with oppression after oppression,
and they are: (Jeremiah 30:7) ...*it is a time of trouble for Jacob,
and from it he will be saved.*

108b) When the vowel points beat together in Vav all nine together in consonance then there is harmony and they beat with ease, with mercy. When they beat quickly without harmony there is dissonance caused by judgments that clash with each other.

The initial inspiration comes from the movement of letters and vowels, which is thought. Then the points themselves speech, then letters and finally action. We are speaking of the movement of thought into speech into action.

The unity is shown between left and right, speech and action and thought and form.

When there is complete connection to say and do are simultaneous, one.

The snake and the staff going from one to the other is the transforming influence. It is the connection of the Middle Pillar that brings all that is coming to be.

Either the pulse is even and calm which is the good inclination or agitated which is the evil inclination affecting the body accordingly.

The good inclination transforms the body from agitated to harmonious intending towards unity.

The snake prevails in agitation and is adverse to the body causing sickness.

If we listen to the pulse we determine the state of being. In this case the sick house of exile.

Chaos like the tempest destroys all it touches causing disunity.

This wicked pulse assumes its own hierarchy affecting those that are attracted to it. It doesn't make anything but rather takes from everything.

The depths covered them meaning the truth of holiness subsumes the evil or the uncleanness.

In all cases it is the unity that transforms the chaos by its strength and song.

The hierarchy of evil causes a cutting off from the harmony of unity.

Therefore is a perverse barrier formed between unity and chaos.

This perverse barrier protects holiness from contamination allowing Shekinah to flow as She will.

Because of this barrier from the husks below good is pristine forever.

These husks above are coverings to protect Israel from the evil hierarchy below so that Israel may rise without interference. Evil thoughts fade when we turn our attention from them. While they may still reside they are stripped of their power to attract us. Instead thoughts of holiness surround us by using our attention acting as husks to protect us from the influence of the evil. The images of horse and rider cast into the sea refer to what happens to these evil thoughts. We provide the imagery for their binding and covering.

בראשונה נתן אותם ביד השליח שהוא גבריא״ל,
ולא היה מזון לסמא״ל ולמחנות שלו אלא על ידי השליח
At first, He gave sustenance to them by the hand of an agent who is Gavriel, and there was no sustenance for Samae"l and his camps, except by the hands of a messenger.

470

Because of the sins of Israel, He becomes clothed in them the husks
and then, as it were, it the sustenance came to this one Samae"l
by the hand of Ha Kodesh Barachu.

And this is if the People of Israel walk the straight path
and fulfill the Torah and its precepts.

109a) Your thoughts rise and fall according to your attention
to them. When you withdraw that attention they fall. When
you focus that attention they rise. Thoughts have no power of
themselves. It is your attention that provides momentum to
the wheel of thought.

The operations of thought proceed regardless of their
direction. This means that if your thoughts are taking a
negative direction then all the power that is contained within
them will be derived from that direction. Conversely if
thoughts are taking a positive direction the same power issues
for good and leads to holiness.

Pharaoh speaks from the lower hierarchy of chaos.
Initially it was the nothing out of which something was
refined all of this in the hand Ha Kodesh Barachu. For Israel
is given the awareness of this making and therefore all the
world sees their connection above.

However, when Israel sins more chaos is made. It is as
though now Israel is responsible for cleaning up the mess of
chaos it has created by its sin.

The separation comes because of the downward flow that is
induced by sin leaving the consciousness under the influence
of the lower hierarchy veiling the relationship above.

When the holiness is revealed the inner essence is made to
shine overcoming everything with its light restoring the

connection. Shekinah and Ha Kodesh Barachu are united as they were always meant to be.

When you are conscious of the lower hierarchy you obviate their effects by attaching yourself to the holiness above.

You have to attach your attention above and detach your attention to the husks below.

During the weekday the time of doing work we are enclosed in the husks to protect us from the chaos all around us. Still while enclosing the husks we have the responsibility to keep clearing up the mess that was left behind by sin.

Within the realm of the universe of sephiros the divine name is enclothed by veils so that it cannot rise to the level of conscious thought protecting or veiling the holiness within.

This separation symbolized by the days of the week and the Sabbath tells us not to partake of one and mix it with the other. Holy thoughts rise and mundane thoughts remain in place. A mixture would pollute the nature of the holy thoughts.

So this idea of mixture whether in the field or with garments to wear shows us that our attitude in mind when seeking the divine has to be equal in kind; that is we need to rise with holy thoughts to enter into the realm of holiness.

The holy place is sacred by definition. Even when we go about in the world and are veiled in its flow we still have the inner dimension of holiness that is revealed every Sabbath. What this is saying is that when we stop to consider divinity as on Sabbath the divinity becomes unfettered by worldly thoughts.

This inner fruit is the holiness that resides within even in the midst of the mundane.

Even below in the Tree of the knowledge of good and evil there is the purity of holiness whose inner fruit is by way of emanation. Still there cannot be a mixture because holiness cannot be touched by impurity.

Consciousness is constantly in a state of transformation. The thoughts that are below are the ones that are being transformed. This is by definition a refining process. It seeks out the good and refines the evil.

Thoughts which do not pursue connection are soon brushed away. They are a tree without any roots.

הקדוש ברוך הוא להעביר כל אלו קליפות למעלה ואמצע ומטה,
ולא תהיה ערבוביה בפמליא שלמעלה
Ha Kodesh Barachu is destined to remove all these husks:
Above, and in the middle, and below; there will be no mixture in the
supernal household בפמליה שלמעלה.

At that time:
(Devarim 32:12) *YKV"K alone did lead Israel and there was no foreign god with him*. At that time
(Shemos 4:2) *And she further gave birth*
A spirit of holiness will be added upon Israel,
this is what is written:
(Ezekiel 36:26) *And I shall give you a new heart,
and a new spirit I shall place within you...*
And moreover, And she further gave birth, to his brother Havel.

109b) In the Redemption there is complete focus on holiness thereby removing any hint of mixture.

Prior to the redemption our thoughts arise or they fall according to our attractions. When the spirit of holiness is added to Israel there is only one way for our thoughts to travel, which is within holiness itself. This is the new heart, and this is the new spirit.

You encounter Shekinah through rising in holiness and seeking the higher wisdom.

The angels are the bearers of higher wisdom in that when you seek they are called to your side. It is as though your thoughts seeking holiness call holiness to itself attracting that which is like unto itself.

She gave birth to the spirit of holiness. This is what is added to Adam. The higher and lower Shekinah are the connecting points above and below.

Thought goes through three transformations above each time transcending the other and giving rise to three incarnations of being one inside of the other.

The three drops that are the three incarnations of a thought that are compared to the vowel point segol in the 'first dough' are the connecting points for the inspiration of thought. It is the same for the dough itself as it goes through its transformations assuming various forms.

Now out of each transformation there are secondary appearances analogous to three Yud's from the priestly blessings that bless, enlighten and lift. These follow the initial pattern of one thing becoming another all the while maintaining the original primary influences.

So therein is the mystery of reincarnation from Adam into Abraham.

Also we include in this analogy the Sephiros and their transformations.

Thought speech and action the transformations of being are described similar to the above version.

The idea of the connecting link of segol is expanded here describing each Yud and its transformation.

We are given then the template of manifest being in three incarnations, which are the pattern of Creation throughout all things.

They made preparation for the three pieces of matzoh on Passover:
one *matzah* above, with which to bless,
the One Who brings forth המוציא
he second is 'the double bread לחם משנה
the third is 'the bread of affliction לחם עוני without salt,
for it is stated:
(Vayikra 2:13) ...*upon all your offerings, you shall offer salt*,
and because it is 'the broken matzah פרוסה מצה like:
(Daniel 5:28) *Your kingdom has been broken up* פריסת פרס...
then until She Shekinah shall be complete, one should not offer salt מלח upon Her, which is the letters of chole"m. And what is chole"m?
The Middle of all three drops higher actions incomprehensible-hidden to know.

110a) The completion of Shekinah meaning Her total connection with Ha Kodesh Barachu occurs from the Middle above (Gevurah, Chesed and Binah) and the Middle below Netzach, Hod and Yesod) .

The hidden brain is where thoughts arise via the Ancient of Ancients which then connect via sego"l giving rise to the second incarnation, the imaging of the soul that takes place during reincarnation.

This imaging of the soul takes place from the Middle below netzach, hod, y-sod corresponding to Noah, Shem and Japheth continuing the image of Creation Bara Shy"T "He created six." These six are the Middle above and below as mentioned previously.

The Yud's are generated as connection points from their tips.

We see the progressions, reincarnations of Adam, three from the first another three from the second.

The progression of Creation is imaged into form. The image above becomes the form below, the higher Adam the second Adam. So when Moses asks 'what is His Name," the answer is the imaging of the One.

Now these three drops are transformed by baking in the brain or rather the consciousness. There within is a constant guide for this baking, the Minister of Bakers presiding over these subconscious images. The arrangement of thoughts comes and then the shaping of thoughts corresponding to the rear brain.

The three drops, the three Yuds in YU"D Ke"Y VA"V Ke"Y provide the template through which the awareness proves itself in form.

The six constructs made from three above that Middle and three below that Middle symbolize Seth to reveal within him the three reincarnations of Adam and Hevel. The Yud that flew away becomes the Foundation stone or the anchoring point from where the world is set into place.

Joseph sinned in the image.

It is in the consciousness of Joseph that the sin occurs misreading the image that is from above representing the sons of Jacob.

These drops are thoughts of holiness that must be kept pure since they are the images of holiness and cannot be mixed with the 'whore.'

These divine images of reincarnation are the template for the life force of the worlds meaning that all who enter into this place of being have these images as their own prima materia.

The answer to "what is His Name," is the image above and the image below.

The three drops or images including the Yud that flew away to establish the anchor point of the world.

(Psalms 114:3) *The sea saw and fled...*
And if not, Israel would not have emerged from the sea.

והוא קיבל עונשו באלו עשרה הרוגי מלקות, שהיו עתידים לכאת ממנו עשרה שבטים ומפני זה היו עשרה הרוגי מלכות כמו עשרה שבטים שהיו עתידים לצאת ממנו, והיו חושבים החברים שעשרה בני יעקב היו

And he received his sentence in those ten lashes martyrs, who were beating him ten tribes and because it had ten martyrs like the ten tribes that were to come out of it, and would think that the ten members were sons of Jacob.

He said to him:
'If so, who placed this mystery in Seth?'

He said to him:
'The souls of the righteous were created before the world was created,'

110b) The sea represents the status quo while the uplifted thoughts part the status quo creating another reality altogether.

The souls of the righteous in essence represent the divine soul, the original plan.

A thought contains both the inspiration and fulfilment of its purpose.

This purpose of this original thought goes through three reincarnations above and below.

Out of these incarnations the six sides are generated alluding to Moses and where he has come from and what he generates in turn.

Seth and Enoch being from the earliest generations provide the impetus for all further reincarnations including Moses. All are related by letter and number.

Therefore She'T becomes another starting point that was already built into the system, 'wisdom in its inward parts.'

Moses is drawn from wisdom the waters above.

The generation or production of Moses is from the Mem and Shin, the heart and Shekinah and their merging. This shows how thoughts come together to produce the whole that is greater than the sum of its parts.

Moses name is doubled twice to give sustenance above and below revealing above 'what is his name,' and below 'what is the name of his son.'

The idea of Moses is actualized by uniting above and below making Moses the connection that unifies by relating simultaneously to both above and below.

Moses contains within himself the three patriarchs in their mystical appearance as lion, ox and eagle giving rise to the man Moses completed above and below.

The chariot contains images that resolve to the human image Adam. It reveals through study the answer to what is his name and what will I say to them. It shows the relationship of the image to the Creator and visa versa and is another cornerstone in learning the mysteries of Creation.

Here we have a restatement of the spiritual law as above so below and as below so above.

Ezekiel's vision describes reincarnation with one stationary wheel. It is the soul and the revolutions of the soul that are the reincarnations that take place above and below.

These reincarnations are like the earth that is a constant to the appearance of one generation following another.

The animating soul assumes its place in the body rising or falling according to the thoughts one focuses on. The revolutions that take place are the revolutions of thought. They represent the levels of meaning that come about the closer we move to the center of being.

The various levels of the soul move in tandem with the vibrations of the animating soul which is locked firmly in place within the heart.

Shekinah may be thought of as the life force that transcends time ever present always as a will to good. It is the connection through which we must travel to ascend the levels of holiness that lead to unification.

He began a discourse and said:
(Ecclesiastes 1:5) *And the sun rises* זרח *and the sun sets...*
And the sun rises – this is the Middle Pillar,
which is Moses in Its image; *and rises* – this is what is written:
(Deuteronomy 33:2) *...YKV"K came from Sinai,*
and shone זרח *from* סעיר *to them...*

ובא השמש כאשר נאסף משה. ועם כל זה שנאסף, אל מקומו שואף זורח הוא שם,
וזה יהושע שהיה כמו הירח שהיא השכינה.
And the sun sets – when Moses was gathered up,
even though he was gathered up, to its place it yearns, it rises there
and this is Joshua, who was like the moon which is Shekinah.

111a) Shekinah stands alone as the sole current of connection. Her current is inviolable so it cannot be merged with on any level. This is an important concept since it brings together the ideas of the soul that stay constant while the Ruach moves level by level and is analogous to Shekinah which provides a constant anchor point for the soul.

The sun rises, Moses, and the Middle pillar refer to its image which is the image of perfection that is divinely sent forth. It points to the mystery and its source.

The sun rises and sets referring to reincarnation and the adherence of the soul in the righteous and the leaving of the soul in the not completely righteous person. In consciousness it is thoughts that rise and fall according to their attractions for one another. This occurs so that righteous or holy thoughts may be strengthened and negative thought may be cut off or fall from the awareness.

The sun rises or Ha Kodesh Barachu appears where there is any connection or Shekinah. Shekinah only dwells where thoughts of holiness are being generated. In consciousness these thoughts are those that build one upon the other in a unity of purpose.

It is therefore can be our constant purpose to awaken Shekinah throughout each moment. The connection is served by attention. The converse is that chaos will ensue through inattention.

If your thoughts, your words and actions are devoid of connection then it is a false making since only connection brings about unification.

There is the breath that is called vanity meaning it is without connection and there is the breath that seeks connection and is the beginning and ending of Torah and everything in between.

There are the five books plus the voice that rises in breath, call it Shekinah call it the connections that exist between the five books.   Five books separately and yet one Torah six books considered altogether.

Consciousness is constantly perfecting itself. It always seeks the highest unity. This is why a righteous person can have negative things happen to them. These negative events clear the consciousness of error so that the consciousness may be perfected.

In the beginning there is the image of perfection. If this image is in anyway compromised this is the sin of perfection. By definition if the body sins then the sin began in thought.

The merits of the wicked follow every reincarnation so that even though they are wicked they still receive the fruits of their merit in the next life.

בינתים הרי רבי פנחס ירד מישיבה עליונה, ונראה תחת צל רבי שמעון, ואמר לו,
מהו הבל אשר נעשה אל הארץ, וכי על הארץ נעשה הבל.

Meanwhile, Rabbi Pinchas descended from the Higher Academy and appeared beneath the shadow of Rabbi Shimon,
and asked him: 'What is the meaning of:
(Ecclesiastes 8:14) ...*hevel (vanity/breath), which is made upon the earth*? And is hevel really done upon the earth?

But, as it says:
(Bereishis 2:6) *And a mist rose up from the earth...*
for this is *hevel* (breath) that is made upon the earth: the breath of prayers and the breath of Torah, is made upon the earth of Ha Kodesh Barachu, which is Shekinah, of Whom it is said:
(Isaiah 66:1) ...*and the earth is My footstool...*

111b) The connection of hevel is that Shekinah which is the earth is awakened by the breath of the Torah of prayers that are as the mists that rise from the earth.

The breath that is made upon the earth is that which comes from the heart that is the animating soul which inspires speech.

The soul branches out into the tree that is the body and it expresses itself through speech.

The Tree of Life is the divine image of perfection that Adam chose not to see and therefore uprooted this tree by his inattention. This tree of life is connection, the yud above the Vav and the Hei of YKV"K.

In spite of missing the tree of life, the hei at its foundation remained intact.

The unification of the name takes place whenever we attach to the rooted Hei and hear the HV"Y that comes to us in the night or in our silent mysterious places i.e. the three watches of the night.

The question asked, "where are you?" refers to where is the tree and how does Hei remain alone.

The reincarnations of Adam into the three patriarchs are the correction for the uprooted tree, which via the patriarchs becomes rooted again.

The second Hei is restored in Abram, who is called the branches of the Tree. The fruit of the Tree, the Yud is Yitzchak, and the connection of the tree itself is in Jacob.

The tree of restored via Moses because he brought down the five books of Torah completing the tree, the divine name YKV"K.

Moses completed the name YKV"K since he learned to related everything to Torah. The unification of the name is just that; seeing that there is unity in every part of Torah and that everything relates to the divine name and everything relates to unification of that name.

The divine image is restored in terms of it's original intention. It is the divine plan of Revelation.

Moses then becomes the extension of She"t restoring the Yud of ShY"T of B-REiShYT.

Torah begins with a BRaKhaH in order to provide a constant correction from the sins of the earth. This is the predominance of spirit over matter.

The letter Reish in the same manner provides a correction against ignorance.

The Tree is complete in all of its pathways ten of the commandments and Sephiros relating to Adam and his redemption.

The letters provide the meanings within B-REiShYT including their fullness relating to the unity of their relationships with each other therefore completing them.

So it is that with ELKY"M the fundamentals of the way things work is presented and made a constant throughout all of Creation.

What has been revealed is 'the way things work' in regards to the unification of all of the above and below.

The fulfillment of unification is the restoring of the divine image complete in all of its parts.

אשרי העם שככ״ה לו בגימטריא מש״ה,
Happy is the people whose lot is thus is the same as as Moshe

Happy is the people whose God is YKVK as it is said...
(Ecclesiastes 1:4) *A generation goes and a generation comes*
– and there is no generation less than sixty myriads;
and about him it is said:
(Psalms 105:8) *A word He has commanded to a thousand generations*,
and his Moses' extension היתפשטותו is in each generation,
in every righteous and wise person who is occupied in Torah,
up to sixty myriads, in order to perfect them from all their defects.

112a) Happy is the nation that understands it can unify with God through Torah and its devices of unity.

Every generation has the ability to unify their consciousness because of the unity that Moses presented and enshrined within Torah.

Moses corrected in the moment all of those sins by the unification of Torah. This rectification that is within Torah exists for always and generation after generation for those whose partake of its mysteries.

The extension of ELKY"M blossomed within Jacob.

There is united within Jacob the image of perfection.

The Yud transforms through reincarnation operating through the patriarchs with Jacob correcting and Moses perfecting, the one ADN"Y, the other YKV"K.

Jacob completed the rectification of Adam in that the soul was not ready to accept the divine image, which wouldn't happen until Moses.

Moses is the transformation of that rectification into perfection in terms of the recognition of the divine image.

Qayin brings only that which is left over or that which was unused, not a fitting representation of what makes the connection above.

Qayin does not bring of the best to make that divine connection and it is refused.

Hevel brings the best of what he has to offer and it is accepted. The connection must be made like in kind in order to rise above accordingly.

Qayin's gift was from a lower place sensual in nature.

And what is it?
It is the mother of the evil mixture,
the fruit of the tree of good and evil,
of which it is stated:
(Shemos 3:6) *...and she took of its fruit...*
...and she gave also to her husband with her...

ומה היא, לילית, משם באים ערב רב שהם מעורבים בישראל,
שנאמר בהם הוי גוי חטא, שהם זרי מרעים בנים משחיתים וכו׳
And what is it? It is Lyly"t: from where comes the mixed multitude who are mixed with Israel, of whom it is said:,
(Isaiah 1:4) *Woe to a sinning nation!* those who are the *wicked seed, corrupting children etc.*

112b) Qayin tried to unify separateness with unity and failed.

His sexual obscenity was separateness.

The evil resides in attempting to make holy that which can never be holy. As discussed early there can be no mixture of good and evil. Good remains good. Evil remains evil.

Just as in the golden calf where the evil of idol worship was mixed with holiness; its outcome was chaos and destruction. This is why Qayin's offering was rejected. It wasn't of the right type.

Qayin knew better and therefore his intention in offering was bad since Ha Kodesh Barachu would forgive, ignore and spread mercy but not for an intentional act of separation.

Hevel's intention was motivated by unity to bring Shekinah to Ha Kodesh Barachu.

We see that it isn't so much the kind of offering as is the intention with which it is offered that is the deciding factor.

Qayin is mad but YKV"K tells him that he can be forgiven if he changes his intention; if not then sin will crouch at his door constantly.

The sin of Qayin is corrected when Moses kills the Egyptian. This alludes to the correction of Qayin's killing of Hevel and coming upon Hevel's twin sister.

וסוד הדבר ויפן כה וכה, ואמרו קדמונים מהו ויפן כה וכה, אלא ראה מה עשה בבית ומה עשה בשדה. ואין שדה אלא אשה, כמו שאתה אומר כי בשדה מצאה. זה הוא שכתוב ויהי בהיותם בשדה.

And the secret of it : (Shemos 2:12) *...and he turned this way and that*?
But he saw what he did and had done in the house,
and what he had done in the field, and there is no field but woman, as it says: (Deuteronomy 22:27) *For in the field he found her...*
This is what is written:
(Shemos 4:8) *...and it was while they were in the field...*

And he turned this way and that
– he looked to see if there was of the aspect of good in him,
for sometimes good becomes separated from bad,
and from there come converts,
and therefore he looked from every side up to sixty myriads,
but he did not see there any convert emerging from him,
and so: *he struck the Egyptian.*

113a) What the Egyptian did was to cause separation between above and below. Moses looked around to see if there was any good in the Egyptian. When he did not find any good or any reason to continue he struck him down. Moses was looking for anything with which he could unify within this Egyptian but he did not find it.

There must always be a place to connect with Shekinah, otherwise it is sin that crouches at the opening meaning the opening of your thoughts.

It is Torah that takes us out of exile and guards against the chaos that is the burden we cannot bear.

The burden of exile is the result of the misplaced intention begun with Qayin. This intention gets in the way that heavy burden increasing as we refuse to lift up our thoughts on high.

An evil intention may bring riches but there is a heavy price to pay where sin enters at the door of the gate of Gehinom and justice/revenge occurs.

These innovations, inspirations, new insights on Torah provide anchors for connection arranging for Shekinah to be united with Ha Kodesh Barachu. The Ancient of Days is the wellspring for these innovations.

The violence of that initial act represents the taking of life, the taking of something without raising on high the unification that is 'the way things work' in terms of Ha Kodesh Barachu and Shekinah.

(Shemos 4:3) *And it came to pass* at the end מקץ *of days*.
Rabbi Shimon opened, and said

מהו מקץ ימים. אלא מאותו מקום שעתיד לומר בו קץ
כל בשר בא לפני, קץ שם לחשך,

ותרגם יונתן בן עוזיאל קץ כל בשר השחתת כל בשר, מלאכי חבלה

What is the meaning of *at the end of days*?
But from that place of which it is destined to be stated:
(Bereishis 6:13) *...the end קץ of all flesh has come before Me...*
(Job 28:3) *An end קץ he has made to darkness...*
and Yonatan ben 'Uziel translated the end of all flesh as
the corruption השחתת of all flesh as "angels of destruction."

He God saw that there were destined to emerge from him Qayin:
those (Song of Songs 2:15) *...who ruin vineyards...*
who are Israel i.e. Israel are the vineyards of whom it is stated:
(Isaiah 5:7) *For the vineyard of YKV"K of Hosts is the house of Israel...*
Because of this: ...and to Qayin and to his present He did not heed.

113b) The end of all flesh is the end of the attractions of the flesh which cloud the higher spiritual imperatives.

It is foreseen the chaos that Qayin will bring because of the thoughts that are reincarnated through his descendants.

By contrast Hevel's aspect of righteous souls provide a counter to Qayin throughout the generations.

Initially Qayin takes the brunt of the harsh judgment of the snake because his birth had not been sweetened meaning infused with the good that is ever present. Therefore there was a mixture.

Therefore that good intention in Qayin became weakened.

However after Qayin Hevel had that sweetening, that good which was sweeter was then subdued by the forceful judgment.

When they were in the field of the consciousness of Ha Kodesh Barachu the harsher judgment prevailed.

It lasts until this harsh judgment is placed into the great abyss and is thereby transformed into the higher tears.

It is from these higher tears containing both harsh judgment and sweetening that souls descend into one body containing both the spirit or soul of Qayin and Hevel.

Therefore there is a choice that is continuously occurring siding with Qayin or Hevel. At this time the holy body is made up of all of the holy connections.

(Bereishis 4:9) *And ELKY"M said to Qayin: Where is Hevel your brother?* Rabbi Shimon said: And did Ha Kodesh Barachu really not know where Hevel was, when He asked him? For surely nothing is hidden from Him, as it says,
(Jeremiah 23:24) *If a man were to hide in the hidden places,*

אלא אוי להם לבני אדם הטפשים אטומי הלב סתומי העין, שעליהם נאמר עינים להם ולא יראו באור התורה

But woe to them, to those stupid people,
who are blocked of heart and closed of eye,
about whom it is said: (Psalms 115:5) *they have eyes but they do not see* with the light of the Torah.

They are comparable to cattle who do not look, and who know only the straw of the Torah which is its external shell and chaff, of which it is said chaff and straw are exempt from tithing.

114a) The bundling of the cluster, the joining of holiness the stars in the heavens, and the galaxies of light all refer to the thoughts that ascend on high.

Thoughts align themselves according to their attractions and the attraction of holiness operates upon the same principle. Where is Hevel meaning where is that thought which is ascending and is the principle means of connection on high. For Qayin separated himself from holiness.

Qayin lost sight of Shekinah and felt himself separate. In essence he lost the center of thought and could only operate on its periphery.

It is the higher image that descends to imprint man with the visions of holiness that are the aspects of perfection.

The aspect of Hevel will not be stopped but must continue. The sixty myriads arriving through the patriarchs and culminating in Moses are still continuing as a constant source of holiness.

Therefore in ever generation those sixty myriads find their place inside of the souls of the righteous.

אמר רבי אלעזר, אם כן נודע שכל צרה זו תהיה בגלות האחרונה. מדוע נאמר
קניתי איש את יי'.

Rabbi Elazar said:
'If so, then it is made known that all this trouble will be
in the last exile, so why is it stated:
(Bereishis 4:1) ...*I have gotten a man with YKV"K?*

אם תאמר מפני קני שיוצא ממנו זרע מעולה. אחר שיאסף הוא, יתעוררו בני קין
להחריב העולם, ומהם קול דמי אחיך צעקים.

If you say it is because of the Kenite Jethro, who emerged from him as
superior seed, yet after he was 'gathered up,' the sons of Qayin were
aroused to destroy the world, and from them comes the sentiment that:
the voice of the blood of your brother is crying out;

This is what is written: (Psalms 12:6) *'Because of the plunder of the poor, because of the cry of the need.*

114b) The evil that Qayin initiated keeps on producing evil, the evil of murder, the evil of killing each other.

There comes a point in which all the troubles come together in order to be wiped out once and for all. The man with HVY'H will transform the trouble into holiness.

Not only does the evil continue to destroy but the need to contain and conquer the evil becomes the blood of your brother that is crying out for revenge over all the misdeeds that have been carried out in the name of evil.

The good in Qayin reached its culmination in the Kenite, Jethro. After that the evil continued.

The evil throughout the generations was shown to Qayin; the results of his killing of Hevel.

Qayin also could see the recompense for that evil that is carried out to his descendants.

Reincarnations take place with Qayin's soul so that none know where he will pop up from time to time.

Now Qayin is given the chance to rectify three times and that is it. He reaches his level of completion but then in the fourth redemption; that is for the soul of Hevel.

Because Qayin lost sight of Hevel or the idea of Hevel he is doomed to wander until he rectifies and at that time he is complete.

And furthermore:
Where (אי) is Hevel your brother?
Come see regarding these two letters Aleph and Yud,
I have heard that they rise to to a High place שלמקום עליון
אי. Aleph stands for 'designer wondrous and concealed,
Yud stands for 'thought;' for it is in this place that Adam and Hevel
sinned; and it has been said that they are:
Aleph –Supernal Keter כתר עליון
Yud – thought מחשבה
Above and Above למעלה למעלה this was where the sin was.

115a) It is in thought, in the perception of what is all around that the sin takes place. Sin by definition is any thought without the recognition of the unity. It is separation that is sin. The sin caused damage to the conception of holiness; made it less that it was.

Thought ascends level by level until entering the initial hidden of all hidden ones.

Thoughts are concealed within thoughts so that on one level perhaps it is that there is no sin.

The clarification here is that if you sin in one level if affects all levels except for the hidden one of all hidden ones. This is why Moses could not see this level of thought.

Moses could not see the face that is the place of where the Cause of all causes is made known.

Moses could not see this cause of all causes because of the sin of Adam that introduced the separation. This blocked the clear sight of what is meant to be. This separation threatened this sublime thought so that it withdrew and so that nothing could compromise its essence.

What Adam sinned in was the perception of separation. He lost sight of the unity. He thought that he was alone, naked and afraid. This place of higher thought where there is no death withdrew from Adam's perception.

Since Adam never breached that level of higher thought, the cause of all causes. He only penetrated so far which is called the garment of thought.

אמר לו רבי שמעון. במחשבה שהוא מוח אף כך חתא שהזרע משם יוצא.
Rabbi Shimon said to him:
'My son, in thought, which is brain, he also sinned.

For seed emerges from there, for it is the wellspring of the tree of life;
for it is the primordial light אור קדמון and the pure light אור צח,
and the most clear light אור מצוחצח.
These three drops that are alluded to in Higher Yud,
a tip above and a tip below and body in the middle.

And he Adam mixed darkness there, which interrupted
between the Cause of All Causes עלת העלות and Hidden Mind and
therefore: (Shemos 33:20) ...*for man cannot see me and live*

until that darkness is removed from there.

115b) This hidden thought comes from the template of thought that is the designing force behind the hidden thought or rather impetus that we or Adam was initially able to perceive. It is the shock of separation that has Adam trembling.

Adam made a veil that caused separation between the primordial light, the pure light and the most clear light. These are the three drops or degrees of opacity that are alluded to with the Higher Yud.

Adam introduced the darkness of separation between the Cause of All Causes and Hidden Mind. In essence he lost the ability to track his thoughts and to be at one with the effects of his thinking.

It is this separation of thought from itself that is the illusion. It is the illusion that one thought could hide from another

This darkness is introduced because the sin goes through a progression that sustains this darkness, this separation of thoughts. We find out about this because of this particular discussion revealing the extent of the sin and also the projected higher realms that now cannot be seen.

Hidden thought is beyond the cause of all causes. This is because by definition once a thought is revealed it becomes part of the cause of all causes.

This image making capacity comes from the Hidden of all hidden. It is the generator of these images divine. Just as the soul animates the body and yet remains hidden so too the primordial light animates the Cause of all Causes, which cannot produce for itself an image.

The joining of Mind and Mother is the consciousness of connection and it is this that awakens the link above to reconnect with holiness.

These garments of leather, of skin are so that Adam who felt cut off from above would not be afraid of the void that had interposed itself between him and holiness.

Repentance begins the process of connection. It creates what is akin to a ladder that is between Adam and Higher Mind.

Because Higher Mind is in effect covered with tephilin Shekinah remains with Adam to continue the connection above.

The process of letting go of sins is because of the Higher Mother, Shekinah rising within Adam to connect above then grounding or rooting lower Adam as the current flows from above to below.

The flow of Shekinah takes place during reincarnation to carry the soul on its journey attracting those influences that will benefit it on its way.

Because Israel broke the connection of Shekinah She is sent away, withdrawn being single above and single below.

For the masters of repentance Shekinah is reunited above and below. This is through Torah study that brings down those insights which provide the pathways of connection.

ומפני זה, בני. א״י הבל אחיך. אם יכולים אנו לומר א׳ י׳ מן אקי״ק אימא עליונה.
And therefore, my son,
א״י (where) is Hevel your brother?
we could say, is Aleph Yud in the midst of the Name EKY"K
Higher Mother.

And Hei Hei remains, about which it is said,

494

(Ruth 1:19) *And they went, the two of them* here is where Hevel sinned (where his sin reached to).

116a) When you keep letting go of separation and reach for connection She stays with you.

Hevel repeated the separation of Adam separating one Hei from another or the above from the below.

Without connection or without unity Adam experiences fear, the nothing, chaos.

It is thought itself that is denigrated by this separation losing its ability for connection leaving the V"Y or half Aleph.

The way to connection is on high connecting to that higher Yud that has been separated.

The Thought that is brought down is the higher Thought that allows for connection and to re-establish the holiness above in terms of our perception of that thought.

The higher Yud is initially one with YKV"K until it is no longer connected. Without this unity it acts alone or without any other letter.

There is none to separate the Creator Above. It always acts from unity.

Therefore the Creator above maintains this partnership with the letters of Creation revealing and producing the Sephiros.

It is through the connections of the Sephiros that the continuity of Above is maintained as in a how a garment protects the inner core or body.

Again the Creator Above, the Highest Above all High Ones generates that unity without any other.

What is revealed is that unity is never compromised. It is only the seeming garments of unity in which the appearance of separation may appear.

Aleph represents the anchor of connections and appears large, smaller, and intermediate with the letters

These Alephs of connection are the links that align with the above via the Adam of creation, formation and action.

These garments veil the inner mysteries of emanation, the Supernal light and the ten sephiros of emanation.

It is through the extension of these sephiros of emanation that the image is made both internally and externally.

The sin of Adam caused a breaking apart of that unity of connection that the sephiros has accomplished within him, and without him. Therefore nothing remained of connection following the sin.

Adam did not preserve the glory above, the unification of the Sephiros and their connections on high.

אבל עלת העלות כאשר ברא אותו כמו שאתה אומר
ויבר אלקים את האדם בצלמו, הוא נטל הצל ממנו, ונתן בו בלי שותפות של אחר.
But the Cause of Causes,
when He created him like it says:
(Shemos 1:27) And ELKY"M created the human in His image...
He took all from Himself and gave it to him without the partnership of
any other, for Father and Mother made him in their form,
in two forms ציורים, this is what is written:
(Shemos 2:7) And YKV"K ELKY"M formed
formed with two forms, the form of Father, which is YKV"K;
and the form of ELKY"M, which his Mother;
and this is: And YKV"K ELKY"M formed...

ואחר כך עשה אותו כלי
And then did the same making for him a vessel כלי

This is what is written:
(Bereishis 2:7) ...*dust from the ground*...
It is not only written *from the ground*, but dust from the ground...
and this is lower Shekinah, of whom it is said,
(Job 34:15) ...*and man shall return upon dust* which is his reincarnation.

116b) This image of Father and Mother is a poured image from the Cause of Causes. This is to set up the parameters of one thing coming from another by reflection. Father and Mother intertwine to produce the image that is one.

The vessel or the dust from the ground is what holds the essence of what is Adam and is the dwelling place of lower Shekinah.

Adam is of the same essence as the cause of all causes.

Adam is seen through the garments of expression culminating with the body.

The domain of emanation is not created within Adam. Adam is imaged from creation throughout formation and action. Creation in terms of the sephiros are the external garments of what the effects are.

The human is the Middle Pillar partaking of these constructs of emanation and acting as a pathway for their expression. The human is the connecting link between lower Shekinah and Higher Shekinah.

In each world emanation, creation, formation, and action the human sits in the middle with the Vav between the two Yuds of the letter Aleph. It is wisdom that builds the house, and the capacity of self awareness.

Adam is born without separation, without the foreskin.

Adam it says tries to influence his world directly.

Adam takes on the image of above becoming enclothed in all images and husks. In this sense Adam is the result of the realm of possibilities and therefore has to make a place of his own.

The image of Adam is contained within all of the sephiros and therefore has the ability to rise above his station and transcend the husks and the images that have been cast upon him.

Each sephirah is connected to Adam in that his being is the central waypoint for all movements and cycles.

Adam inherits the Kingdom that he is possessed of including both Higher and lower Shekinah. He moves as he will and transcends all.

Adam is the resolution of higher Man and lower Shekinah or the Adam of action. Again Adam is the nexus of creation in all four worlds.

ושכינה תחתונה דמות אדם שהוא עמוד האמצע.
ועוד עמור האמצע בדיוקו הכתר וזה אדם של ברואה.
And the lower Shekinah that is the image of man is the Middle Pillar.
And furthermore: the Middle Pillar is in the image of keter
and this is the man of creation ברואה.

And the man of formation the righteous one – is in the image of chokmah, and because of this:
(1 Kings 5:26) *And YKV"K gave wisdom to Solomon...*
who is the Righteous One, the covenant of peace,
שלמה (Solomon) is composed of שלם (complete) and the letter Hei.

And lower Shekinah, the man of action, is the form of Higher Shekinah. And all is truth and Shekinah is surely included in all..

117a) The 'man of formation contains the image of chokmah.

The synthesis of all that is the lower Shekinah contains the 'man of action' and all is included in all.

Shekinah rules through all since She flows through all becoming a part of its essence.

Shekinah guides where she flows discerning between brain and fruit and the husks of the other side. She knows where she moves and through what she is moving; towards the light and away from the darkness.

The awareness of manifest being comes when we make conscious choices, i.e. intercourse for the sake of birthing.

This 'knowing' then is that conscious choice that brings about unification. Any other reactions are of a world in which Shekinah is missing and therefore the connections are not made. The parallel is with the weekdays in which Shekinah does not unite with Ha Kodesh Barachu.

Just as Mordecai knew what would happen with Esther, so too did Adam when he knew Eve, become conscious of the outcomes.

The direction that Shekinah takes provides the pathways that we build up within consciousness. If we build up ill-conceived pathways Shekinah does not enter here. However, if we build up pathways that flow with good Shekinah enters and strengthens them even to flowing through the incarnations that take place as a result.

Adam knew the result of sin that would appear through Qayin bringing about the Angel of Death.

LYLY'T is the attempted mixture that comes from good and evil and not being conscious of the pathways that we build up within our thoughts. Since Eve tasted of another pathway she communicated that taste to Adam, which set the chain of events into motion.

The way of return is indicated by Qayin's repentance via the sign of the covenant, and the acceptance of unity as the end goal.

Hevel appears to ameliorate the evil that is destined from Qayin and to provide a clear path for good to travel throughout the generations in order to cleanse the pathways. He stopped knowing Her meaning he stopped the evil pathways from entering into his life, his thoughts.

Hevel's pathways are destined to purify the pollution as it did with the times of Moses allowing him to take Israel away from the tainted culture of thought they were living in.

These pathways of good are ever present. We turn to them to unify above. The mixture we must avoid whether good from evil or evil from good. The lesson is to only partake of and follow the good.

(Ecclesiastes 2:15 and Shemos 6:3) ...*in that also* בשגם =345),
this is hevel (vanity), *and they have established,*
that בשגם (also) refers to Moses:

Moses is Seth, and he is Shem, and he is Hevel: (Job 33:29)
And behold all these will א"ל *enact, twice or thrice with a man.*

And the mystery of the word:
(Isaiah 63:11) *where* א"ה *is he in whom He placed* השם *within him...*
(Shemos 3:13) ...*מה is His Name...*
And this is Adam in his fourth reincarnation, and because of him it is said: (Amos 2:6) ...*and upon four I shall not return him*
I *shall not return him* in another reincarnation.
Since his father, who is Adam, had descended into him,
at that time is made known,

(Proverbs 30:4) *what is His Name, and what is the name of His son if you know?*

117b) Moses is the fourth incarnation of Adam. When Moses asks he is speaking from the standpoint of Adam saying 'what is the name of that to which I have returned.

So there within Moses is the complete chariot. It is the awareness that recognizes its own movement throughout consciousness and then rides with intention.

For evil there is the correction of good, Hevel. In thought the same takes place on all levels. Within the consciousness of good the pathways are corrected and the way made clear.

Hevel is the awakened awareness, the heart of good of wisdom.

The evil inclination takes away, destroys, is unclean and does not add whereas Hevel is the addition. It is this pathway that we need to attend to.

The container is Qayin and Hevel is what is inside. It is what we are looking for seeking truth, insights and wisdom, or the kernel of the thing, and its hidden essence.

Since Qayin is also built in the same way with the inner good always present he also has access to this aspect of himself.

The realm of opposites persists until the good is fully realized.

The continuity of Moshe is evidenced throughout the Torah. It is the flowing of unification symbolized by Moshe and his connection above that infuses the words with meanings, the phrases with connection and the stories with inspiration.

It is the flow of letters that show the intentional arrangements of Torah meanings that arise from beginning to end.

The seven breaths of Ana Bekoach, six arising through the windpipe one through the mouth prepare the way for the expression of the intentional meaning of thought.

The seven voices, energy centers, chakras, transformations and breaths that issue from the emanated image enlivening the spirit make the pathways that fulfill the life force.

Again there are seven voices of transformation from the left that descend to express itself.

There are breaths that connect. These are the breaths of life. There are breaths that take away from or pull down. These are the voices of death.

Through speech we express the good that is centered in the Vav of the six levels of the throne that then evolves into the ten utterances.   The Vav or connection of these breaths becomes light, the five mentions of light in Shemos 1, and the Higher Hei via the Yud of speech of utterance.

Voice symbolizes the connection above and below and is the Voice that carries meaning above and expresses that meaning below.

The angels travel via the pathways of Vav in conjunction with Y, and Y"V that are the breaths rising and descending from heaven to earth and from earth to heaven.

The movement of breath is directed by the unification of YU"D K"E VA"V K"E, and the awareness of the unity that is contained therein.

The other breaths are of separation from bad thoughts that are also combined with deed.

The place of manifest being or Malchus is revealed.

שכל מי שנוטל מלצות בלי תשע ספירית הוא מקצץ בנטיעות.
For anyone who 'takes' בנטיעות malkhut without the other nine sephiros, he cuts the shoots.

And anyone who takes nine sephiros without malkhut,
is a heretic כופר בעיקר.
And about the breaths of 'the other side' it is stated:
(Jeremiah 10:15) *They are vanity, deeds of illusion...*
For there are the breaths that rise in base speech and in falsehood,
and all ascend towards the brain.

There is a sun and moon and stars and zodiacal signs in the firmaments
which are shells קליפות about which it is stated:
(Isaiah 5:18) *Woe to the drawers of iniquity with ropes of falsehood*
and about them it is said:
(Isaiah 51:6) *...for the heavens like smoke will vanish*
(Isaiah 24:23) *Then the moon shall be confounded
and the sun will be ashamed*

118a) It is unity that makes the connection all inclusive of the sephiros otherwise there is the illusion of separateness that speaks only for itself and is a veil a blocking for unity.

When your thoughts are not based on unity they go astray and your connection to life vanishes, the whole basis of 'the way things work' becomes polluted.

Thoughts that bring about destruction and misdeeds have their own angels that make note of these constructions bringing what was uttered into evil manifestations.

Qayin chooses evil even though he has access to both good and evil.

The aspect of Qayin chooses the snake not considering the good.

503

However, Qayin does choose repentance afterwards, and the sign of the covenant in order to regain, or reconnect on high. The allegory is that we may always connect when we choose good and seek unity.

The same thoughts that make up the pollution of Qayin may be made clear as in the case of Jethro who becomes one with the thoughts of Moses.

Vanity of vanities meaning there is good and evil and the choices are always there in front of us to choose hevel or good.

The ways of connection are six levels, four angelic beings representing the Middle Pillar that connects on high and below to unify the awareness of being.

Prayers rise above ascend in breath and unify with holiness.

The distinction is made between lower thoughts and higher thoughts (breaths).   This is something we must learn to become aware of.

We learn here about those other debased thoughts that must be separated from the holy thoughts.   The separation or Havdalah is symbolic of the conscious awareness of the difference and the right choice of thoughts to attend to.

We build our own temple within by the thoughts that we intend.   Our world is made up the same way the entire Creation has come to be. One thought at a time linking with other complementary thoughts all arising in holiness to become the unity that is One.

אבל אחרים שמוציאים מפיהם הבלי שבועה, אליהם

But about others, who produce from their mouths the breaths of false oath,

It is said: (Proverbs 7:26) *For she hath cast down many wounded;* – and they are called *casualties* הפילה, for they profane the Name of YKV"K; and breaths emerge from their mouths,and the voice and speech of falsehood, and false oath; and they mention His Name in vain and falsely.

With that Name that emerges for nothing and falsely, they build themselves constructs that void them from the world; This is what is written: (Jeremiah 2:30) *In vain I did strike your children.*

118b) When thoughts are destructive they produce casualties and they produce death.

When thoughts are promoted for other than unity they are in vain.

Thought is the precursor of action and a good thought is what Hevel had and Qayin had a bad thought. Standing both before Ha Kodesh Barachu they were judged according to their thoughts.

Hevel thought well in line with unity. His thoughts were of making connections.

Qayin's thoughts were destructive in nature and yet even so these thoughts could be forgiven once Qayin recognized his error, however if he persisted in this kind of making or unmaking he would be cursed.

It is the intention which rules over sin or lets sin rule over the person.

The wicked take no note of consequences and therefore keep on sinning.

The consequence of sin was the killing of Hevel. This breaks the connection to unity and promotes separation. Therefore

Shekinah which is connection must have recompense. She must have connection.

Qayin by carrying through on the thought of Adam now makes a cycle of death since the proof is now in the world that this may be done.

Think of thoughts as coming one from the other. Therefore if you take what is there and it is false or evil and add to that then you are following in the footsteps of your father's using these thoughts to make your world. Conversely if you intend unity then unity is the result.

Qayin disregarded unity and went ahead to build upon the errant thoughts of his father acting like they were a center of focus.

It says woman here but the sense is that of separation and of letting the reaction determine the focus of expression.

Hevel is killed by Qayin for something that he thinks will benefit him in the short run. He loses sight of the bigger picture.

Qayin is cursed by the effects of his evil act. He dismisses holiness and therefore condemns himself to live in a world of chaos where he will directly experience these results from the very land that he committed them on.

Until Qayin repents fully he will be alone, a nomad a wanderer since by definition he has rejected the unity that brings all things together.

Qayin's fate is bound up in the pollution or separation that was cast upon Eve. It is similar to the prohibition against having relations with a menstuant.   This is similar to the mixture of good and evil that is likewise forbidden.

נד , מפני שאתה מצד ננחש. נע בעולם הזה,
נד בעולם הבא. שהם שכינה עליונה ושכינה תחתונה. שנוטלים שניהם נקמה ממך.

N"A (a wanderer), because you are of the side of Samae"l,
Na"D (a nomad) because you are of the side of the snake.
You are a wanderer in this world, and a nomad in the world to come,
which are Higher Shekinah the world to come and lower Shekinah this
world. For both of them take revenge upon you.

And because of this, when he Qayin heard
that Hevel was derived from such a high place,
then immediately: (Bereishis 4:13) And Qayin said to YKV"K:
'My sin is too great to bear'
thus he returned in repentance and showed regret.
Therefore: (Bereishis 4:15) and YKV"K placed a sign upon Qayin..

119a) When you leave the realm of unity you are subject to chaos. It is as though you do not leave a pathway of return to connection. In this case there will be nothing for you either on high or below, or the Lower Shekinah and the Higher Shekinah.

Qayin repents once he understands Hevel's high place and how he came to be there. In that moment he understands that he must repent.

Now we see that Jethro by his circumcision and correction to the law of Moses fulfills Qayin's correction in that righteousness has been built up in order to allow connection to once again take place on high.

The extent of the Creator's mercy, forgiveness are endless which is why we may turn around our lives in a moments repentance recognizing the connection that we seek is already there.

Qayin accepts his fate. This means that we have to accept that our thoughts produce the actions that we must deal with first before we may repent.

In order to save Qayin the mark of Vav or connection is placed upon him so that others may recognize the one who separated himself from Ha Kodesh Barachu and His Shekinah and is on the path of return to that divine Vav, the connection.

When we return in repentance we connect again on High entering into the state of grace called Eden. It is connection that brings us to Eden and keeps us there.

These descendants carry with them the aspects from Qayin for good or evil.

In one stream of the descendants of Qayin the evil inclination destroys unto death.

When the evil inclination rules over a person they carry a shadow that makes them aware of their sins so that even though they sin they realize in the core of their being that they are doing wrong. It is this shadow that calls them to repent their sins.

The consequences of sin are clear. There is a poverty of life. The heavens meaning their connection on high dissipates like smoke. The earth and its material treasures will wither. Without a higher connection there is no holiness, and no thriving with abundance.

Even though a person has a fortune gained through their sins perhaps they would still be in poverty in their souls.

The cure for this poverty of spirit, this death of meaning is to return in repentance to the awareness of unity.

The person who spends their time in frivolities not seeking unity brings destruction upon themselves, their houses.

When your music is for the sake of holiness and to promote unity it is another story altogether. At this time it is as though YKV"K plays through you.

The counter to the evil inclination is to study Torah and become immersed in its mysteries in order to reach up for unity and the sense of all that is One.

The sins of Qayin and the corresponding effects of these sins will be avenged, they will be corrected and in the end, 'death shall be swallowed forever.'

Adam knew his wife again setting in motion the seeds for the correction that will take place with wisdom.

מה חכמה זו. שחסר ממנו י'. שבה היה שית. שהוא ברא ששה, והוא ראשית.
What is this chokmah? It is that letter Yud representing chokmah,
that is missing from it i.e. from the name Shet, with which he would have
been six.

Which is ברה ששה (He created six); and it chokmah is
ראשית beginning. And it would be said of him,
(Isaiah 46:10) *He tells the end from the beginning...*

119b) Chokmah is the link between inspiration and knowing. It sees the end in the beginning.

Shet represents the possibility of completion the end and beginning, the wisdom that all is one.

Shet also represents the eight days of circumcision the new beginning arising from the cutting off of the old false start.

Prayer then is the way to connection since via prayer thoughts have to be intentionally directed above.

Through prayer the correction keeps becoming established. By making things right above this is the vengeance of shepherd upon shepherd.

In clear speech via prayer the correction becomes the way of connection.

The mixed multitudes have to be wiped out. This means that our thoughts can only contain holiness, so they will call in the Name of YKV"K.

Tiqun 70

בראשית ברא שית (פי' ששה),(וזה מטטרון, אות בצבא שלו, ובגללו נאמר
Bereishis BaRA ShYT (He created six) and this is M-TaTRO"N
a sign within His Host; and for his sake it is stated:
(Bereishis 4:15) ...*and YKV"K placed a sign on Qayin*...
to protect him, and that which he Qayin was going wandering
and as a nomad in reincarnation, was made into NOD.

Immediately, (Bereishis 4:16) ...and he dwelt in the land of Nod, east of
Eden. And this was the sign of the covenant of circumcision,
since he had envy of his brother who was born circumcised.

The template of the beginning contains M-TaTRO"N and is contained in the sign that is impressed upon Qayin so that he would be able to reach up when in trouble.

Hevel's thoughts were circumcised in that he only thought of holiness. So Qayin in a land of holiness is to partake of the same thoughts as Hevel.

Therefore in the Kenite Jethro Qayin's repentance is completed by the essence of the thoughts of Hevel. The land of Nod, being next to Eden are those that are reincarnated until the body of Jethro gave proof to the reawakening of holy thoughts.

Meanwhile Qayin still in Nod also had thoughts of evil, which is the evil inclination that he brings forth in his children.

Chanokh transformed the evil inclination and walked with the ELKY"M and became one with them meaning his consciousness transformed into the principle of ELKY"M merging with it into a fiery torch. So there are three incarnations, Adam, Shet, and Enoch.

Enoch began the return to YKV"K, the return to unity from which all reincarnations of the righteous are extended.

There is Metatro"n from the template of the beginning flowing into and becoming Chanokh.

We see that Ezekiel's vision contains this template of the beginning called Nuriel rushing and Metatro"n returning two aspects of the same being.

The rushing and returning of Metatro"n/Enoch describes the action of reincarnation that occurs because of the revelation of the beginning providing all the angels of reincarnation that preside over each soul.

Moses is called to see and make the pattern shown to him by YKV"K which is the template of Creation. It is the Menorah and the constant reminder between the eyes of this template that calls you to holiness every moment.

Call in the name of YKV"K means to seek the unity in consciousness everywhere and every when.

The six chambers of Creation are the levels of the unfolding of the way things work. Higher Mother may be compared to let it be meaning let things proceed now as they have begun.

Shet is the redrawn level of Hevel, the level that reaches on high for connection.

In the same way Moses too embodies the level Hevel, reaching on high coming from the waters of consciousness.

This chokmah is that reaching on high. It is the awareness that connects above that signals the awakening of the light.

The beginning of the first reincarnation is the awakening of the levels of light that transcend and culminate in Moses. It is the call on high. It is the call for the awakening of light. This is the call of the connection on high.

This extension of the Yud above from Shet through Tipheret the level of Jacob is the foundation stone of the world. This tells us that reaching on high for the connection to holiness is the primary principle upon which the world is founded. This is what Moses teaches in Torah to reach on high and to remain connected all the while.

וזה משה שמזכירים אותו אחר יעקב ומפני זה אז הוהל לקרוא בשם יי׳. משם
ואילך אז תקרא ויי׳ יענה

This is Moses, who is mentioned after Jacob;
and because of this, *then it was begun to call in the Name of YKV"K,*
from there then onwards:
(Isaiah 58:9) *then* אז *you shall call, and YKV"K will answer.*

And therefore:
You have placed שתה *after* שת, *is the letter Hei.*
And they are Y"H: Yud from שית Hei from Hevel; and they are Father and Mother;
שית is Vav -6– the son in the middle.

120a) With Moses 'you shall call, meaning with the awareness of the awakened self now reunited above. Because of this awakening YKV"K answers.

Yud and Hei and the Vav in the middle complete the awakened awareness that are the Father, Mother and son. This makes the holy connection viable once more.

Moses takes the meaning of this awakened awareness and puts it to work for Israel thereby completing the final Hei in the name Moses since the other three levels or letters already resided within him.

Therefore the three patriarchs each had a piece of the puzzle but not the connecting links which became one with Moses. The 'what is his name,' is saying what is the result of all of these connections that we are learning.

Moses completed within consciousness its connection between 'the way things work' and the active awareness of holiness. This is why YKV"K is completed in Moses and allows for the answer to 'what.' Because of this revelation YKV"K is once again in place within consciousness so that all may call in the name of YKV"K.

The original connection is restored above and below.

The 'what' first is a quest and then is the same answer. The question is what is this that we are learning. The answer is the connection between the above and below in all of its ramifications.

Therefore mah (what) above and mah also below.

In this way the Cause of all Causes returns to the awareness that descends upon everything.

Moses can then explain this awareness in shorthand via the SHMA.

The 'way things work' and the awareness of consequences is brought to another level of insight. Initially Adam is part of 'the way things work' but has no idea of consequences until he sins. Then after being reincarnated through Moses he now is fully aware of the consequences of his thinking and of his actions. He began as innocence, was corrupted and then returns to a higher level of self awareness that reawakens his consciousness of the consequences.

The six levels of awakening bring forth the seventh level of the Higher Mother.

Aleph is Keter, Beit the two millennia, and Gimel is the Higher Mother reaching down to Chesed bestowing kindness.

Yud is chokmah the wisdom of Solomon, Tav is Tipheret and Tzadi is the righteous one Yesod.

Aleph is the wondrous designer creator of the image of Adam within Adam. Aleph is the first of all the first ones.

The first Adam, supernal Keter, hidden of all hidden ones, cause of causes, and the primordial of all originals above are the Adam that runs through all the sephiros.

This supernal Adam is the nursling of Creation, that which was built within Creation to continue Creation in the manner in which it is born.

This supernal Adam is given the power of Creation and the faith of Creation. He is given the awareness of Creation that it takes place within.

This higher Adam is Higher Chokmah that is in the image of Keter and is indeed the instrument of Keter, itself the instrument of the cause of all causes.

Now this image cycles through Creation as the Middle Pillar like the divine image that is Chokmah and the divine form which is the Higher Mother.

Therefore this image of Emanation flows through Creation, Formation and Action. It is the same Supernal Keter Chokmah and Binah that are all one in contemplation.

The Cause of causes speaks to YU"D H"E VA"V H"E inside of the Sephiros which represent Ale"Ph H"E YU"D H"E or that which is coming to be and always was. This is an eternal statement a kind of master control to the operating system of Creation.

'Let us make a human' means let us make an instrument that will carry on this work with the complete understanding of what this work is all about.

(Isaiah 44:6) *I am first and I am last, and besides Me there is no ELKY"M* meaning that the 'way things work' continues as the basic principle of Creation. This principle knows no other as the three Yuds of YU"D K"E VA"V K"E in their absolute unity testify.

The first chamber the ten things created are the sephiros that represent the pattern perfected.

The heaven above the heavens, the light far above and the sealed darkness are the components of everything that the cause of causes brings into and is by their interactions the basis for the actual workings of consciousness.

Chaos and the void above are there within the spirit of holiness, the transformation of consciousness and all of its interactions.

(Bereishis 1:2) ...was *hovering on the face of the waters* of Torah.

מדת יום ומדת לילה, מדת יום שכינה עליונא,

מהו יום עמוד האמצע, שמממנור ימים ארוכים זה הוא שכתוב ארך ימים בימינה.

The attribute of day and the attribute of night: the attribute of day is Higher Shekinah. What is day? It is the Middle Pillar, from which days are long, this is what is written:

(Proverbs 3:16) *length of days in its right hand*;

This is what is written:

(Psalms 42:9) *By day YKV"K shall command His kindness...*

Short days are from the side of the small countenance זעיר אנפין,

the Righteous One. The attribute of night is lower Mother.

To here is the explanation of A'leph of AV"G (from Ana Bekoach).

120b) We can link together Higher Shekinah and lower Mother or Lower Shekinah via the Middle Pillar which is analogous to connecting day and night. All of this completes or summarizes the action of the Aleph of AV"G. It is a description of the initial phase of consciousness both of light and darkness one taking from the other and transforming all in between.

Two faces represent the Beit of Higher Adam one turned above another anchored below. The Gimel in the three worlds of Creation, Formation and Action are the physical dimensions of Adam.

We are made as the connection between above and below and between consciousness and its actualization. The face is the image and the tail is that earthly connection.

It is the fountain that overflows that produces the wellsprings of life and of the existence of manifest being. It is wisdom that provides all the connecting links and the strength for the completion of the vision. It is the starting point that is everlasting above everything. It is the knowledge that is inherent and revealed. It is the three Yuds of YU"D K"E

VA"V K"E, the head of the world. All of these metaphors roll themselves into One.

From this wellspring then come the blessings arising from their source which is the head and source of all blessings.

Therefore what arises out of this wellspring that is the source are the blessings that are the motion, and the flow, of Shekinah which is derived from the ongoing Creation. The valley that is raised up is Shekinah. Her flow permeates throughout all.

The symbolism of connection showing wisdom-Reish, Connection-Vav and Higher Keter-Khaph all are contained in the word Baruch. It is as if to say that blessing issued from the source flows forth with wisdom via the connections of Vav, or of the flowing of Shekinah.

Therefore be mindful of the blessings and the bending and the standing to activate consciousness to remember these symbols to build within the temple of meaning that has been the purpose all along of this discourse.

It is consciousness that is to be exalted and filled with higher meaning throughout via the prayers and the blessings.

It is the Yud that continues from the source. It is the image of perfection. In this way the beginning is seeded with the end.

It is the High of All High Ones that permeates all of existence

The perfection of the beginning is the Torah which relates all things to One.

It is your thoughts that arise and speak to the flowing of One. They rise with insights (hills of hills) that show you the truth about this experience with you at its center.

You are the center; the joining of all thoughts, building of all chambers and the consensus of all the images of Creation that the righteous (those that perceive the deeper meanings behind it all) inherit.

ובו מנקדות כל נקודות התרה,
שהן נקודות בהיכל שהיא שכינה תחתונה ומאירים כולם על ציורים

And in it are the vowel points, all the vowel points of the Torah,
which are pointed in the chamber, which is lower Shekinah,
and shine upon all the depictions,

like precious stones which shine upon the top of a crown,
and similar to the stars shining in the firmament;
and because all the points of the chamber are in it,
it is said (Bereishis 1:17) And ELKY"M placed them
in the firmament of the heavens to illuminate upon the earth
this is lower Shekinah (these are the souls of the righteous),
who strive in the Torah to bring to light her hiddenness,
this what is written:
(Daniel 12:3) *And the wise will shine like the radiance of the firmament...*
etc..

121a) The vowel points are the indicators of holiness compared with the lights in the firmament, and the souls of the righteous and the wise. This is to show the pathways of illumination from Higher Shekinah to lower Shekinah. The radiance of Shekinah within this chamber or consideration of light is also shown. Similarly Torah in its treasures provides these shining pathways.

The stones of marble in the second chamber are the heavens of rakia this second heaven.

Within this second chamber is the split that separates the waters and also uproots Satan from Torah. This means that there is no doubt in Torah; its unification is complete.

The invocation to revelation is presented.

These generations of Adam are arranged in the twelve zodiacal signs of Adam above corresponding to the twelve tribes of Israel. Then within this set are the four faces of ox, eagle, lion and people through which all faces are known. This is the imaging process being described from above to below.

The image of Adam is YU"D K"E VA"V K"E. Adam dwells with YU"D K"E VA"V K"E.

It is Shekinah that takes on the form of Adam both higher and lower so that in our thoughts we may image the holiness within and reveal the wonders without.

The study of this work must not be construed as to allow us to imagine any attributes of the Creator in terms of physicality.

(Rabbi Shimon) opened and said:
(Shemos 18:21) *And you will see appoint from all the people, men of valor, those who fear ELKY"M, men of truth, those who hate* ill-gotten *gain...*

men of valor, from the side of chesed for the letter Yud is there and for its sake it is stated,

הרוצה להחכים ידרים
One who wants to become wise should head south.

121b) The physical body represents in ways incomprehensible the super hidden and concealed things.

We study the Creator via the sephiros.

Any physical dimensions apply only to the attributes of the Creator and to the sparks that are the letters and combination of the alphabets of Sepher Yetzirah with which things were created.

These revelations are self explanatory to those who seek in the right way.

You will appoint men who seek holiness.

The letter Yud via chesed the pathway of the wise.

The letter Hei via gevurah the pathway of the wealthy

The Middle Pillar is Vav the path of truth.

The letter Hei via Malchus the proof of truth.

The source of imagination is ADN"Y the four visions.

All those leaders come from the aspect of ADN"Y their numbers verified within Torah.

עשר תקונים אלו, כל תקון ותקון יש לו (בו) ארבעה שיעורים שעולים לעשר, כמו רשות היחיד שרחבו ארבעה וגבהו עשרה. ארבעה יקו"ק, עשרה יו"ד ק"א וא"ו ק"א

Ten constructs תקונים are these, each construct has (within it) four measures which amount to ten, like a private domain, whose width is four and whose height is ten, Four' is YKV"K, ten YU"D K"E VA"V K"E.

122a) The keys to understanding this section is 'there are the four and there are the ten," YKV"K and YU"D H"E VA"V H"E. These constructs are what make up the comparisons to Torah and to the physical aspects that are described. In addition the Chariot and its wheels within wheels are also a direct comparison here to the four and ten via the sephiros. It is as though there is a nexus being formed in mind by the associations that are centered around the four and the ten and their extensions.

In this way there is a continuation of the divine image in greater and greater detail merging with the concept of unity that has been presented previously. In addition to the faces and physical aspects there are also the senses that are considered in terms of their relationships to the unified awareness.

באלו ארבע תקונים אמר למשה. ואתה תחזה מכל העם וגומר. וצריך לחזור עליהם: אתה תחזה, בשער. עליו נאמר ראשו כתם פז זה כתר עליון. ומבפנים מוח, שמנו יוצאים מעינות לכל צד להשקות לכל שערה ושערה שהיא עולם סתום.

Those four constructs did tell Moses, *And you shall see appoint of all the people,* and now we need to repeat them.

And you shall see appoint by the hair about it is said,
(Song of Songs 5:11) *His head is of fine gold...* this is Higher keter,
and inside it is the hidden brain from which to water in every direction,
to water each and every strand is a hidden world, and every wellspring is
made a spark, and every hair strand is made a sceptre.

'Hidden brain המוח הסתום is called the Infinite אין סוף,
which is divided into three intellects מוחות (lit. brains),
which are Yud, Yud, Yud, which are alluded to in this Name:
(א"יק ו"אי ק"יד יו"י =45) ק"יי ו"אי ק"יי יו"ד =63

122b) The wellsprings issue from the higher Keter via the strands making sparks and the symbols of the sceptre. All are connecters of light.

The three intellects or levels of becoming issue from the Infinite, the hidden brain, and the three Yuds of the spelled out Name.

The Name also seen as YU"D K"Y VA"V K"Y is called the three atmospheres because there are three Alephs. The three scepters of this name are the three Vav's and the hair leading to comprehension of the dimensions of the stature of Ha Kodesh Barachu. These descriptions open up the heavens in terms of the imagery presented here.

Out of this imagery each strand is a soul and some are angels, some are sparks such as Ophan and others and galgal or wheels are imagined. This is the imagery of holiness.

So too we envision these strands of judgment and mercy of Tipheret, and so on in order to arrange the mind in the order of holiness in the image of the above.

The measure of holiness is envisioned to give us a sense of the infinite nature of what we have in mind in thought within consciousness and throughout the entire atmosphere of holiness.

Each part of the body is included in this measuring of holiness each according to its aspect one to the other.

KVY"Y is throughout each and every limb.

The unification of the body like the soul is complete with YKV"K.

Moving from the body of man to the body of the earth or King of the earth also we find YKV"K throughout.

The two limbs work together as in YKV"K ELKY"M the connecting links between heaven and earth.   ELKY"M is King, the principle of 'the way things work.'

There is an interchange between HVH"Y and ELKY"M that brings about the Higher Image of which there is no other.

It is through the body that a person comprehends how the world comes into being according to the awareness of holiness that KVH"Y and ELKY"M are at all times present.

The aspects of holiness throughout the body are enumerated.

First YKV"K over voice, the voice that speaks words of power and brings things into being. Next there is EKYe"K

and the heart giving meaning to all existence. Continuing is
the High One of All High Ones this Voice that is hidden and
concealed ruling over everything.

EYE"H proves the word the voice that comes into being and
illustrates principle that is called the Cause of Causes.

אקי״ק מראה על עלת העלות שהוא היה הוה ויהיה, והוא הבל שעולה עד אין סוף.
The Name אקי״ק demonstrates about the Cause of Causes,
that He 'was' היה... ...'is' הוה, and 'will be' יהיה;
and It the Name אקי״ק is the breath that ascends to the Infinite,
and in it rides the Cause Above all causes.

The Name על demonstrates the עלקות (like the Shekinah)
of the Cause Above all causes, and about It did Job say:
(Job 5:8) *I shall seek* towards אל א״ל, אל אלקי האלקים

123a) The breath that ascends, EHY"H the upper connection,
is the Shekinah carried by the Cause of Causes.

The supernal attribute, E"L is what you find when you seek
connection in the initial revelation of holiness.

These angels that are called by this E"l are the inherent
connection, the constant source which resides within the
recognition of the unity of the Infinite.

These voices respond with holiness since they are called in
the Name of holiness.

The unity of the Cause of Causes permeates throughout all
changeless and ever present.

The perception via the limbs of the senses is all the same to
the Cause of Causes giving meaning where there is none and
bringing prayers and insights into Torah.

That which speaks with the divine connection is called ADN"Y synthesizing thought and speech.

The connections of the body are summarized in the Sephiros here to show the ever presence of holiness throughout the body.

E"l appears throughout the conceptual revelations of the patriarchs contemplating holiness in all aspects of the sephiros.

The arrangement of threes YKV"K YKV"K YKV"K beginning with the fire that does not burn via the three patriarchs. This arrangement is to add yet another connection to the pathways of unity that are being arranged here. This is the purified awareness.

It is the fire that gives momentum to Shekinah arising above and below via EKY"H EKY"K EKY"K.

It is the all encompassing fire, the merging of heaven and earth the soul and Ha Kodesh Barachu, and Shekinah with both via ADN"Y ADN"Y ADN"Y.

The voice that is connected that is one that is 'the way things work' is the crown and the Aleph above all Names.

Through Yud He and through wisdom channelling through Binah the essence of all letters is generated beginning with Aleph which is the Higher Mother or Binah.

Here is another combination, a construct of holiness EKY"K on high Keter, The middle pillar YKV"K, and below Shekinah ADN'Y.

It all depends upon the vantage point we are looking from. From EKYe"K Keter, "I shall be" there is Chesed E"L Gevurah ELKY"M, and the Middle Pillar YKV"K. Then completing with TzVA-OT Netzach and Hod, ShD"Y Yesod and malkhut ADN"Y.

In prayer or meditation the Righteous One Yesod and ShD"Y the life force.

At 'You' (atah) the lesser Hei wherein blessings are sent into via the middle pillar YKV"K.

The combinations then of Higher Mother, Father and all the sephiros of the Middle Pillar together complete a unified whole.

ומפני זה צריך לכלול בו תהתונים בכריעה ואחר כך עליונים בזקיפה

Because of this, one needs to include the lower ones in the bending of the knee, and afterwards, the Higher ones in straightening up.

Supernal E"L, *presenter of good kindnesses, superior to all and Who remembers the kindnesses of the patriarchs* this is keter, superior to all of them.
And *bringing redemption to the children of their children of the patriarchs*, these are netzach and hod,
for the sake of His Name in love this is lower Shekinah.

And the Middle Pillar includes the first three blessings, which are:
the blessing they are the patriarchs, the blessing regarding acts of might;
and the blessing regarding the sanctification of the Name,
and it includes the three last ones in the service and it includes the middle ones, to fulfill through it:
(Yishayahu 44:6) ...*I am first, and I am last, and besides Me there is no ELKY"M.*

123b) Thereby incorporate in the actions of prayer the various meditations on the holy names.
Keter supernal above all flowing through the patriarchs via Netzach and Hod encompassing love shows the pathway of the lower Shekinah.

The ritual of the service is now aligned with the constructs of holiness providing unification in every portion

It happens when you learn the various levels of holiness that when you pray you are activating these levels via your conscious awareness of them.   Then via that conscious awareness you may ask rightly and receive in kind.

So we see that at every level the sephiros require mastery and consciousness of their activity.

You raise unity in hidden thought, machashavah stima.   All your thoughts bind themselves together on every level including the hidden levels.

All that comes is out of this hidden thought via the constructs you are learning about or rather, which are being inscribed within you.   It is at this point that the awareness becomes self-knowing.

The pathways already existent become illuminated like the hair that shines forth including those thirty-two paths that flow from the effortless above.

These likenesses, these images need to be affixed. This is so that you may forever return to them as an established point of reference.   It may seem as though there are disparate constructs. However, when considered in terms of the light of the hidden constructs that are in essence bringing about all of this, these disparate or separate ideas are brought together within the reality of unity.

Everything that is being brought forth via the initial creation has a special luminous color.

Now the Garden of Eden below also brings forth images that are he husks of the fruit of the higher Eden. They take the form of the vessels of the Tabernacle. In this case the Tabernacle is a construct below that is wrought by the imagination, which is a mirror of the above.

We are speaking of the images that are to be considered, long hair mercy, the Long Countenance, Arikh Anpin, the letter Aleph, and then the two Vavs that found in the word Vav. This is the Elder of Elders. It speaks to the most ancient of constructs.

Judgment is what occurs in the consideration of all that is transformed.

There is a comparison between the long and the short Countenance from the aspect of Vav and Yud respectively.

It is the connection of short and long constructs like the notes of the shofar they link together making points of attachment.

We envision hair in a circle as a metaphor for the firmament that surrounds everything. It is physical and yet it is also metaphysical.

All of these descriptions of hair, long, short, stubby, shriveled, in between and hair in a circle are the way in which thoughts connect despite their differences.

David connected via the thoughts he shared including the Tehilim which were seven kinds of golden words. They are golden between of their transcendent value.

זהב שבא וזה הוא זהב מזקק שבעתים. וכך הם שבעה מיני לובן ושבעה מיני אודם.
כל ספירות נקראו שביעיות מצד הצדיק

… the gold of the vowel point shva, and this is gold refined seven-fold. And so there are seven types of white hairs, and seven types of red; sephiros are called sevenths.from the aspect of the Righteous One.

The Middle Pillar comprises all colors.
White hair is of the right side, red is of the left side,
green is of the side of the Middle Pillar, and all of them are seven, seven.

124a) The sevenths from the aspect of Yesod up to Binah making the composite Middle Pillar composed of all colors.

These are seven sacred pathways that ascend right, left and center simultaneous in their expression of the unity that is the answering call to Binah that expresses all in the initial phase of becoming.

The darkness conceals the light and yet they are one in the same. Shekinah flowing along the pathways concealed and yet revealed to the wise.

From here on the allegorical takes over. The red hair being indicative of a lower pathway that attracts the evil inclination.

The Levites want to achieve a purity of purpose therefore they eliminated all blocks to their holy awareness.

The woman like Shekinah hidden and concealed in the light; her pathways are revealed only to the holy and the wise.

The hairs by the ear, the listening hairs are removed to open the way to receive the higher wisdom.

The hairs on the top of the head express the flowing of Shekinah, which is the flow of Creation.

The hair of the Middle pillar harmonizes all that it attaches itself to.

Black is the symbol of purity if he is good, from the aspect of Shekinah depending upon the intent.

Hairs are the pipes, the conduits, the channels through which Shekinah flows. Colors represent the frequency or the ease or difficulty that these channels present for the ongoing flow.

Lower frequencies starting with red are the evil inclination. The higher frequencies or the range blue purple violet indigo are the pathways of holiness.

How do we know this? It is because on Sinai there was a sapphire stone on which Moses stood receiving the Decalogue.

If he is wicked the black is uncleanliness. These are the nights of fear, the chastisements, and the blockage from holiness.

The judgments are in the order of the intentions that are held on to and cause judgments upon the world.

The sounds of the shofar are symbolic of breaking up the lower patterns so that they can rise above joining the holy flow.

Do not curse the wealthy because the curse is a part of you and you are as much bound by it as the person towards who you are aiming it. Curses put you in league with Samael.

She is the evil inclination and her movement is of darkness.

It is the lower thoughts that go upon the belly and walk upon four legs in uncleanness.

The moment you give attention to the evil inclination it acts to make it easier for you to do unless you are mindful and stop.

The sin is your responsibility and can only be mitigated by your own repentance.

Sins subvert the flow of holiness.

If your sin is great or prolonged the soul of emanation departs.

וסוד הדבר, ויאמר אלקים יקוו המים מתחת השמים אל מקום אחד ותראה היבשה
וגו'. מסתלקת נשמתו ממנו ונשאר גוף יבש.

And the mystery of the word:
(Bereishis 1:9) *And ELKY"M said: Let the waters be gathered from
beneath the heavens to one place and the dry land will be seen*
His soul goes away from him, and his body remains dry.

What is the body here? It is the soul of the throne of glory
(of Ha Kodesh Barachu YKV"K) which remains dry,
because the soul of the way of emanation has been withdrawn from it;
for his soul is the body for that Higher soul.

124b) The dry land is the body that is without the soul's driving presence that is related to the unity of above all working together for the divine purpose.

The soul of the throne of glory is the soul of your connection to the 'way things work' or ELKY"M. If this connection is compromised it the body, becomes the dry land.

The dry land becomes the throne of glory when the mist enters upon the land. This mist is the repentance that is given to the land when the sin is removed via that repentance or the return to the land in connection.

Apparently the knowledge of divination is not forbidden especially if this knowledge helps a person in repentance and only if they are returning to the principles of Jacob the perfect man.

The example of Bil'am is given as one who wished to manipulate with spells and snakes the fate of Israel but could not find a handle to work on them with.

The mystery of Laban and his divination has to do with reincarnation in that whatever he was there is also the possibility of what he Laban will be.

There is nothing that is forbidden to know even though it is something that we do not practice. It is the nature of things to provide answers even when their source is not permitted since knowledge is of a free nature.

The movements of ravens, their ascending like the cantillation natore r-vi'a isolates the sin above, or through t'vir and shvarim the sin that descends in this world and then must be t'viru broken up below.

Therefore the knowledge of the ways must be learned so that we may avoid their dire consequences.

Those with a depressed disposition drive away Shekinah so instead Shekinah becomes gathered in Jacob, the consciousness of unity and remains even in exile.

When there is resistance to unity this aspect is set apart in prison in exile along with those low of head that do not reach for the unity above.

This change of name of place of deeds refers to the consciousness that while not engaging in the contemplation of evil recognizes it and must then actively move away from those thoughts, patterns and actions that are indicative of it. The principle is the same as studying divination and yet not using it since the main goal is the recognition of it in order to move the mind to a higher place of intention.

When the consciousness is pure from the right all goes along with this aspect of everlasting love and kindness. This represents a unity of thought and action.

However without kindness and love none of these other 'white aspects' are true and are rather eating away at the consciousness like leprosy.

The recognition of this white leprous spot means that the consciousness is separate, disparate and diseased.

וכל זה במה ניכר, שאין בן אדם שלא נכללו בו אלו ארבעה גונים
And by all of this there is not a person who does not have included in him these four colors.

But by that color which rules over all the others, by that he is called, and in it he is known what to be called white, or black, or red, or green.

And these four 'bad' colors are the four husks Kelippos of the nut: (Shemos 1:2) *void and chaos, and darkness* and *abyss.*
And they are: (Deuteronomy 8:15) *...snake, serpent, scorpion, and thirst...*

125a) Anger then in these four colors speaks to the vibrations of thought that transform the consciousness away from connection and towards separation.

These four colors that separate white, black, red or green represent the state of mind a person is in and this state of mind rules over all the other colors or states of mind.

These bad colors, the kelippos, void and chaos and darkness and abyss represent the state of consciousness prior to its awakening with the light that was good. In a sense it represents devolution.

All these colors are without kindness and love as described in the earlier definition. They represent the breaking down of thoughts into their baser elements.

The same power that builds can also destroy when it is turned to these four colors of separation even to the fire of Gehinom.

Therefore looking closely at consciousness you see these colors in the eyes, face and the hair.

These are the colors made by intending bad thoughts and dwelling on them as in depression mentioned earlier to the point of becoming a poison becoming death.

Therefore the extent of Mars, red, is the killing and destruction.

By contrast these same colors imbued with love and kindness describe Shekinah the consciousness of unity as apparent in the white of chesed, the red of gevurah, the green of the Middle Pillar and the black of the Higher Mother. These are the transforming colors of purity that are the product of a unified consciousness.

All of these colors flow with the unity of purpose which is the free flowing of Shekinah throughout consciousness This raises the forms of the sephiros and activates the purity on high that dwells below.

Higher Keter indescribable is above while the Middle Pillar radiates with all colors.

The symbols of color are linked to the mystery of hair, and the vibrations of purity through which the flow of Shekinah moves through truth, valor, fear of ELKY"M, and those who hate ill gotten gain.

The divine name too is linked with the four colors.

These colors woven by the Name show up in the lines of the forehead.

Specifically their dimensions are high and low and east and west.

The small lines-wrinkles of the eyes are described in terms of Yud.

We read the dimension of stature of a person from the aspect of HV"H

Long lines indicate men of valor. Short and wide denote men who fear ELKY"M. High lines show truth and small circular lines those who hate ill gotten gain from the aspect of Yud.

These descriptions of the lines of the face and throughout the body are compared to the lines in Torah, and the prayers referring to the pathways of YKV"K.

אוי להם לאלו שמכחישים דיוקנם למעלה, כאילו מכחישים סדרי בראשית, וכאלו ממעסים את הדמות, שאלו ששרטוטיהם ארוכים, וקומה שלהם ואברים שלהם

Woe to those who deny their own likeness דיוקנם Above;
it is as though they deny the arrangements of creation,
and it is as though they reduce the image which is the (ששרטוטיהם)
blueprint Above,for those whose lines are long,
and their stature and limbs are long, they need to be masters of kindness,
long patient of anger, masters of love
that of which it is stated: (Yishayahu 41:8) ...*the seed of Abraham, my beloved.*–

125b) The key to these lines in the face and also the hairs on the head is the image above. It is to this image that all is compared. This is an Eternal image. Therefore the secret of the image is contained in the seed of Abraham. Because of this they become masters of love and kindness their connections or lines are long matching their limbs, which are a measure of their stature above.

In terms of Isaac, ELKY"M, this stature also is reflected in the face.

Given a certain stature and yet not conforming to it is to deny the image above.

For Jacob, masters of truth a tall proportionate body, the seed of truth.

There we have within the letters and the images of the face. This is the divine image that is reflected in ADN"Y.

The small lines represent those who hate ill got gain, and the Yud. All is for the sake of remembering, recreating and bringing out once again that image above.

The circular eyes, the small mouth, the body, the nose and the beauty throughout are more of the divine image that is revealed.

In sound, vibration, and the notes too reflect the divine image.

The divine image is via Yud below to above and all the sephiros throughout ten thousand myriads.

Now Vav the connection, the dimension of each and every sephirah, and all possible worlds are included along with Hei and Hei from above to below and below to above. Once again it is the divine image represented by the divine name that is being built here within our consciousness knowing just what connections go here or there or above or below or in between.

Connections are truth. They are straight. They are holy like the cantillation note below and above the word. So too it is with the holiness that is the connection between the lines of the divine image. Crooked lines veer off and do not make the connection.

There is the balance of the Middle Pillar one opposite the other making sure no unclean images intercede.

Therefore the divine image has only lines of straightforward connection. It would have to be so since holiness can never be compromised. It is either is or it isn't as we learned previously studying about the mixtures.

The complete lines link with holiness and the divine image above.

Separation is the cause of the blemish, the damage, the error, the sin, the defect in the line. For if a person carries these signs he is damaged below and must correct himself.

The correction is the wiping out of the blemish and then starting over and becoming clear and staying that way.

It is the divine image that is the sole comparison and the place where all thoughts have to turn to for their sustenance. There is no compromise here since the divine image is eternal and its verities are the only ones that are to be likened to.

מי שרושם.ומצייר אלו שרטוטים, הוא אמון מופלא ומכוסה.
Who makes these lines?
It is the wondrous and concealed designer;

To whoever looks below the Tabernacle (mishkan),
these impressions and paintings are made known, of which it is said,
(Psalms 139:15) ...*I was wrought* רקמתי *in the lowest part of the earth*
the depiction of these four lines, the painting of these four drawings are a
lion bull an eagle four persons in all of them.

536

126a) These lines are the pathways of connection linking our thoughts with holiness. They are set up by the wondrous and concealed designer and present themselves via the four lines and the four faces.

The lion to the right is Mykhae"l being the impression of the image of chesed revealed.

To the left the ox, Gavrye"l that is the image of gevurah revealed.

The Middle Pillar, is the eagle Nurye"l revealed

The divine image is the face of the human, R-phae"l prince of Shekinah.

The divine image requires our recognition because in repentance we reacquire the image.

The lines show the state of reincarnation.

The last reincarnation shows no lines.

These lines show the etchings upon the image that reflect the divine name.

So what can be inferred from these lines in terms of incarnations is also represented in the vowel points.

It is within the image that we see the firmament in terms of the holy chayah.

The spark that ascends and transforms and then supports the fallen is that which the image brings about in its shining reflection.

There is a meeting place between spark and reincarnation. It is a rising above and a transformation below.

Once in the world he descends and is under the laws of the world as a wheel repeats the lessons not learned.

It is the sense of meaning that we carry with us through each reincarnation. Without this sense there is no context and there is no shining light to reach for.

The chayot discern formation and creation in terms of the reincarnations in that they are always connected above and below.

The third incarnation completes the face. Through it four worlds unite into one. The key is given by the vowel points that have their own higher connection.

The star that passes through the two Ophanim symbolic of shv"a made up of drag"a and shure'q is the thought that touches above and below linked in unity.

It is one point. It is the unification of the vowels and their markings and the reincarnations that are unified one with the other.

The three incarnations each have their own vowel distinctions and letters of the divine name.

The unification of the three Yuds, the three vowels are linked to the 'wondrous designer, (amon) hidden designer, the concealed designer' and the wondrous designer flowing as one through all.

There has to be a place where thoughts are collected first in memory then in movement as in thoughts that flow and the third way is in the depiction or the image making capacity of thought. It is the container of thought that is described in three ways here just as the container of tephilin surrounds the prayers within.

שרטוטים כמו זה יֵהָוָ״ה יְיָ׳ בהם מלך. הרי כאן שרטוטי המצח
Lines which are like this:
יֵהָוָ״ה יְיָ׳ the King is within them, until here are the teachings of the lines of the forehead.

Eyes: through them: *And you shall see appoint of all the people men of valor* through the color white;
those who fear ELKY"M through the color red;
men of truth through the color green; *those who hate ill-gotten gain* through the daughter of the eye the pupil, which is black.

126b) These lines of the forehead refer to the divine image above and how it reflects below. The appearance of these lines and their variations are learned to restore the image above.

The eye is explored in terms of restoring the divine image. The three colors of the eye are introduced and their associations with the three verities, valor, truth, and those who hate ill gotten gain.

There are three branches, three colors, and the daughter of ShaBa"T, and the daughter of the eye. The restoration of the divine image is through the perception of the eye in its acute awareness likened to Shabbat.

One Sabbath is above the Higher Mother, and one Sabbath is below the lower Mother. Connecting all the six sephiros of Zeir Anpin, these six levels all are comprised of one another.

The eyes of love, the perfect vision, and the contemplation of connection is the pass through Shekinah happening effortlessly.

Perception makes direction in that seeing falsely all we encounter is of a false nature coloring all we see with that false perception.

Looking or seeing from the viewpoint of the divine image everything that it beholds is holy. Therefore every part of the eye is like a wheel suggesting a becoming that is meant to be holy like Israel, the world, the land and the sea.

Blue is like the firmament the sea, and the Throne of Glory. Making the image above in terms of this color produces the divine reflection and gives substance to that image.

The three colors of the eye refers to the fire that does not burn, does not consume and the fire that burns and consumes. We are making connections linking together these concepts into a whole whose purpose is the restoration of the divine of the consciousness of the divine.

The bush that doesn't burn, the daughter of the eye, and the Higher candle denotes the states of consciousness that are awakened in spiritual proximity to the Creator.

The daughter of the eye, which is Shekinah, is the flowing of holiness throughout.

Consciousness achieves levels of meaning and then lights itself up by relating that meaning to its life experiences. Going south means following the descent of the Sephiros to the lower Mother. In this way what has taken place above may be verified with what the outcome is below. These fires are the inspirations the soul has at various points in its journey.

Envision the divine image right and left and the Yud and the burnt offering, giving rise to the Higher Hei. Through the contemplation of the higher Hei there is wealth.

The relationships of the divine name are explained via the burnt offerings and the prayer service. If you are intending to correct the divine image above in terms of your perception of it then everything that can be connected with it or be a reminder of it works in favor of this correction.

In the firmament meaning in the consciousness you are becoming aware of, there is a spark, an inspiration acting like a chole"m in the point of the letter Vav.

What is desired is the divine image reawakened through Torah study, through the mystery of the name of forty two and all of its connections.

ויש מי שהוא מפרש אלו שלשה גונים ברקיע, שהם לבן ושחור ותכלת.
And he who interprets these three colors in the sky, which are white, and black, and blue.

One is white, above the candle, and one is blue, below,
black the middle, separates both of them, and they are not perceived
through its darkness בקדרות שלה.

And this mystery was established in the Mishnah like this,
From when do we recite the SHMA in the morning?
When blue and white can be distinguished.

127a) The precursor for the SHMA of the morning is the color of the light. Blue to the left while the right is white and via the Middle Pillar there is the unification of both meaning the awareness of Shekinah. The black is the pathway through which the light radiates just as the stars radiate in the blackness of space. The SHMA is the symbol of unity that unites the light and the darkness and the firmament is the Middle Pillar in between. In the morning this recognition is especially important to jump-start the consciousness for the day.

In the evening the unification with the Middle Pillar takes place when the light is out of the day and into the night.

We receive insight into the flow of Shekinah in terms of the candle and its flame. The colors symbolize the intensity of that flow mirroring the sun and moon and the soul of a person that is like the flame shining in a candle.

Instruction in terms of visualization is given. The color white, also E"L, the throne of mercy and kindness are symbols to meditate upon.

The color blue shows the throne of judgment EKY"H ADN"Y and the King who unites YKV"K YKV"K. Using the powers of discernment or wisdom the Middle Pillar is activated.

The throne of opposites comes into play when death is introduced with life as its counterpart. The two paths above and below are the choice of the Middle Pillar.

Visualizing the color blue the sages would punish the wicked.

White, chesed, and MykhaE"L are the surrounding fence of symbols and when broken chaos or the snake comes through.

Red, gevurah, and GavryE"L and its opposite the serpent.

UryE"L NuryE"L green, and peace, its opposite the scorpion.

Black R-phaE"L, and Shekinah its opposite a thirst, a dry pathway where Shekinah does not flow.

Sages revived with the color white.

In higher Keter there is the perfection of person the idealized YKV"K.

For when you go beyond thought there is Mazal, unexplainable yet all the same ever present or not.

Close and deep yet always there for those who call still alluding to Mazal.

Mazal is the sea above apprehended through the connection of chokmah and binah the light and its expression, and the realization of the way in which everything works.

When the Divine is withdrawn there is only Mazal in the final exile to intercede. This is where my help will come.

The nothing is composed of Mazal, chokmah and binah. It is the awareness of this that makes up the supreme unity. There is none above.

By making the awareness focus on YKV"K building mountains each day in these three prayer services we setup the throne of glory and 'my help comes from the Throne of Mercy and the Throne of Judgment is withdrawn. It is the awareness that is focused by these three prayer services.

YKV"K flows through each Sephirah awakening and acting beyond comprehension and yet intimately a part of our consciousness and our awareness of being.

The totality of YKV"K is in every place, in every sephirah, in all things, in every thought and even the conception that is above thought.

א׳ אור שמאיר באלו ארבע גונים א׳ אורפניא״ל והא מטטרו׳ין, אור פניאל

Aleph light that shines through these four colors;
Aleph stands for *AURPNYE"L* (lit: 'light of the face of E"L),
and he is MeTaTRO"N, the light of PNYE"L,

And therefore he is called the Prince of the Interior.
And he is RaZYE"L, and he is URYE"L,
which adds up to the numeric value of RaZYE"L (248),
and which adds up to the numeric value of the 248 commandments of the
Torah, like the numeric value of AVRaHaM (248)
and this Razie"l is an angel of chesed, from where the Torah is given.
This is what is written:
(Deuteronomy 33:2) ...*from His right hand, a fiery law for them.*

127b) The four angels represent the perceptions of the eye
like a kaleidoscope that is focused just so to produce the
mystery of the light.

RaZYE"L through which the light of Torah is given is the
Prince of the Interior, the repository of special meaning, and
the flowing of chesed.

This is a light that is turned on, it is RaZYE"L. It is where
the mystery expresses itself and when this place of light is
revealed no mystery can escape you.

The aspect of gevurah from the left is where the negative
commandments are given from.

The Middle Pillar symbolizes both left and right the synthesis
of the two that become one, with Moses the human and Moses
the image of the divine.

The light that comes through the eye is woven of points and is
not focused leading to an unfocused expression or deceit, or
becomes the blood spiller red, green in anger, and black as a
robber. It is this unfocused nature, which in turn causes
fragmentation.

The depth of eyes are good or bad depending upon their intent.

With a bad eye deep set there is no end to the wickedness here.

High protruding eyes mean life and mercy and a heightened perception that sees all.

High eyes see through the higher perception of holiness.

The higher wisdom gives a fuller vision that is a burden to see what must transpire below.

The Ophanim are the eyes of heaven providing the vision on high throughout the earth.

The three chayot, have four sides to each of them, and have vision in every spiritual direction revealing the various aspects of YKV"K.

The connections are threaded between each of these aspects expanding the view to the level of seventy-two eyes.

הרי כאן חמש וארבעים עינים כחשבון אדם, והם יק״ו, קו״י, וק״י.
Here there are forty five eyes, as the numeric value of Adam
and they are: YK"V KV"Y VK"Y.

And furthermore: *and their backs* – this is Shekinah,
Who is upon the backs of the chayot and all of the camps;
this is what is written:
(Psalms 103:19) *...and His kingdom rules over all.*

And they have height – this is the Middle Pillar, Shekinah is over the
Ophanim, and the Middle Pillar, which includes six sephiros,
is over the *chayot* which comprise Metatro"n; and this is:
(Ecclesiastes 5:7) *...for high above the high waits, and there are higher
above them*
These are Father and Mother, the crown upon their heads,
who are over the Seraphim suspended from the throne.

128a) Through the human the divine is watching.

Shekinah is the background, the 'backs' through which man operates. Her flow gives him connection above and below.

The Ophanim are rising and falling with Shekinah as their ruler-director in the midst of the Middle Pillar Zeir Anpin. High above the high are Father and Mother, the crown over the Seraphim suspended from the throne. The higher thoughts, the energy of thought, the organization of thought and the unification of thought are all represented here.

The Higher Mother, Binah is the expression of thought. The height of thought is chokmah until the all knowing thought, Keter sees through many eyes bringing about the conceptual state of, 'clear light, polished light and primordial light. These lights in turn illuminate reflect or transmit the lesser light that are within the throne room like the soul illuminates the body.

These backs, coverings, are the eyelids, like the cherubs of eye they filter the light and darkness.

The eye is a microcosm of the universe of spiritual conceptual reality; all things are contained within the one thing.

The four colors, YKV"K, and the four wings of ADN"Y all relate to the Higher Father and Mother. This is a setup for the imagining of the Sephiros.

The shape of the eyes of right and left show the place of a person in regards to their spiritual development, humble, meek, haughty or brazen faced.

Like the ark covering so too is the eye covering. Here again it is one inside the other.

In terms of the eye EKY"H, YKV"K and YKV"K are those aspects that relate to the symbolism of the eye. This is so that everywhere we look we find the Divine in all things.

Cherubs are compared to the eye and the body showing that the temple is within and the eyes are those cherubim that sit upon the Mishkan guarding and guiding.

Cherubs of the eye are compared to the priests and their garment. Again the relationship of the inner temple to the outer temple is indicated.

There is one measure and one equal constant to work from and discover. Therefore the eye is the constant that sees without and within and has the attributes of the Mishkan pointing to the temple within that builds the temple without.

Going further now the lungs are part of the entire process of 'seeing' in that the breath itself is transformed by the lungs from what is envisioned and what is meant to be. The breath thereby carries the visions within and is the fundamental art of building the temple.

Further still, the eye and the heart are one showing the pathways from eye to lung to heart, carrying the messengers of holiness, transforming and enlightening along the way.

In each measure of every limb the corresponding holiness is wrought. In this way the unified being is resurrected in the image of the divine endlessly.

When out of balance or out of measure there is dissension and a lack of truth.

When out of balance the wrong doer appears.

שכל מי שאין הוא בעל מדות, מכחיש שעור קומה שלמעלה, ולא ויטל משם

For anyone who is not a master of attributes בעל מדות
is a denier of the dimension of stature' Above,
and this demonstrates that he i.e. his soul is not taken from there;
for all of the ten sephiros Above go in measure from the side of the Yud
and in 'weight' from the side of the letter Vav;
the two balances of the scale are Hei Hei, one measure.

128b) One who doesn't recognize or embody the unity of the sephiros cannot connect via Yud or Vav or the balance of Hei Hei since without awareness the connection is no more.

Yuds is the point of comparison to the divine that is in all.

The Shekel which is a measure of balance indicates Hei Hei in balance just so in its aspect of connection.

Everything must be according to the divine in measure. Everything must be in balance above and below as the divine name YKV"K demonstrates.

Therefore speak only what is in your heart so that heart and thought and speech are in balance.

As long as the balance is maintained throughout even with variations then there is no denial of the act of creation, the image of the divine.

What is said in the heart must be repeated in the mouth otherwise there is not a balance and this indicates that the thoughts are coming from the tree of good and evil.

Conversely inside and outside are equal partaking of the tree of life.

The evil mixture is falsehood. This takes place when there is a recognition of the divine however its expression is perverted or twisted out of place.

Abraham purified the initial pollution of Eve the thought that strayed by entering the fire, which cleanses. The clear thought of the tree of life then emerged.

The sin of Adam or the mixture that his thoughts became were refined in Yitzchak moving the pollution to the outside or Esau. Jacob without this mixture then is able to produce offspring out of the tree of life.

Round eyes signifying connection or Vav via the wings of the eyes containing those four letters permeating throughout the body containing YKV"K.

There is a common thread between voice-speech-breaths-uttering and reciting. This is a unification between all of these elements which at every point must contain YKV"K throughout.

Colors contain YKV"K throughout and flow like the sephiros with their accompanying cherub demonstrating purity in balance. When this does not happen it is the other side taking on an imbalance of these same aspects. These are more hints as to the architecture of the temple within.

Seven planets, and seven doubles show the degrees of judgment and mercy that are running and returning. They always keep their positions just like when the planets revolve in their orbits.

When right aspects do not exist Gehinom is the outcome. Everything must be in order for holiness to flow from one to the other in balance and higher meaning.

Balance occurs when the divine name YKV"K resonates throughout heaven and earth.

פנים הם בארבעה גונים. יש בן אדם שפנין לבנים מצד אנשי חיל. ויש בן אדם שפנין אדומים מצד יראי אלקים.

Faces are of four colors: there is a person whose face is white from the side of *men of valor*, and there is a person whose face is red from the side of *those who fear ELKY"M*;

And there is a person whose face is green from the aspect of *men of truth*; and there is a person whose face is black from the aspect of *those who hate ill-gotten gain.*

129a) The four faces and the four sides of the chayot show the aspects of holiness that shine forth from the tree of life.

These other four dark, evil, lead, thick, coarse and unbalanced are in contrast to the right side of holiness which is white like silver. It is the refinement of thought that Abraham accomplishes turning all that is coarse into purity.

When holiness is withdrawn so too is the moisture replacing that with fear, darkness, and the pollution of the snake.

When we are unable to connect above we experience doubt, and cannot see the end for the beginning causing all kinds of confusion all from the aspect of the snake

Another kind of unholiness is shown with the green of the bile that seduces with appearances.

For one the heart shows itself clear. For the other the aspects of Gehinom take place within a person in variations of form. They are the result of a blockage or a denial of the heart that causes falsehood, which over time creates the green bile.

The other is the destroyer meaning that thoughts that are not linked together make their own unholy alliance pulling down the holy thoughts. This is the meaning of the snake and the serpent.

When consciousness is average containing both mundane and holy thoughts it is not coarse and dry while when the predominate thoughts are of destruction, red, and blood, these are thoughts to be avoided.

The various aspects of the other are described in terms of red, black green, happy, sad miser, and spendthrift, all determined by the state of disconnection that occurs when the heart does not speak truly.

In contrast for those for whom the connection to holiness is clear, the symbols are these: I n the brain-chokmah-men of valor, those who fear ELKY"M-the heart, men of truth-the mouth, those who hate ill gotten gain-the body. Also from the aspect of ELYKY"M we have men of valor and men of truth where ADN"Y demonstrates YKV"K inside and out.

Likewise with the Yud in the brain men of valor and chokmah, while in the heart there is fear of ELKY"M, love and fear with Y"K right and left pointing to that which is hidden in the brain and heart.

The same is true for the Vav in the mouth, for men of truth, there is Hei-in the body, and those who hate ill gotten gain, V and H are both Torah and precept.. From this insight are given the revealed things.

The vowels, round faces and malkhut indicate of them all.

The sephiros each have their own vowel pointings except in Malkhut that is without vowel pointing.

קמ"ץ נקרא בנקודה זו, מצד הכתר העליון שהוא סתום כקמ"ץ
Qame"tz is called – with this point actual

from the aspect of Higher keter which is closed up,
like a qame"tz,.

Which is 'closed up' in thought, and no person knows what is inside it;
and that which is within is closed up in thought,
the Cause of causes He is called.

129b) It is in the expression of YKV"K that vowel points reside in the sephiros with Malkhut containing all the aspects of the sephiros.

Higher Keter is described as 'hidden in thought,' 'closed in thought,' the 'Cause of Causes,' and Qame"tz in its outward vowel points.

Pata"ch is the aspect of chokmah opened and revealed one mirroring the other like the two halves of Aleph top and bottom. The divine image is opening to be expressed.

Tzerei shows two points and one below, this world and the world to come, the fashioning of Binah, the Higher Mother.

Shekinah is the dwelling on the left, Shv"a.

The Middle Pillar Tiferet chole"m is the anchor upon which the dream is dreamed.

Also Netzach, chore"q and the right thigh through the analysis of the Awesome One the Middle Pillar.

Shure"q is Hod, like the connection of the chariot also holding up the tabernacle.

Out of Yesod, the Righteous One, takes hold of Shekinah and passes Her through below to malkhut and then above to Tipheret, the seed of truth, the helpmate opposite him.

These vowel points are show YKV"K throughout the round faces, the points within points, and the omnipresence of the divine in the smallest of things and the largest of concepts.

These faces large and small, of love and fury represent states of consciousness that our awareness can focus on in terms of the recognition of holiness. For Moses that recognition is 'YKV"K YKV"K E"L merciful and gracious...' also alluding to the thirteen attributes of mercy.

This Va"V is the connection through which the wicked are shown forbearance meaning that YKV"K is in everything even amongst the wicked giving mercy and blessings, May YKV"K shine His face towards you and be gracious to you; May YKV"K lift up His face towards you...

Deeper are the meanings within the mouth showing the intricate nature of deity even here in detailed purpose.

Therefore change the thinking, change the speaking change the name, place, and deed to enact teshuvah a return to holiness.

The vowel point is like luminous treasure corresponding to the body parts and veins. The mobility of the limbs each have an aspect to consider, and each an opportunity to strengthen their connection to holiness.

On the mystical levels the angels too represent these vowel points.

And they are called by these names,
ונקראים באלו שמות.

ק״דומיאל, (קדמיאל), (קמואל)
מ״לכיאל, צ״וריאל, הרי קמץ בותיותיו.
Q"-DUMYEL or Q"admyel or Q"muel,
M"aLKhYEL, Tz"URYEL – comprising qametz in letters;

פ״דאל, ת״ומיאל, ח״סדאל, הרי פתח.
P"DaEL, T"UMYEL, Ch"aSDYEL – this is patach;

צ״וריאל, ר״זיאל, י״ופיאל, הרי צרי.
Tz"URYEL, R"ZYEL, Y"OPhYEL – this is tzerei;

ס״מטוריה, גזריאל (גבריאל), ו״ענאל, ל״מואל, הרי סגול.
S"MaTURYaH…G"ZRYEL alt. GAVRYEL,
V"'ANEL, L"MUEL – this is segol;

ש״מעיאל, ב״רכיאל, א״הניאל, הרי שבא.
Sh"M'IYEL, B"RKhYEL, A"HNYEL – this is shva;

ח״ניאל, ל״הריאל (ל״הדיאל), מ״חניאל, הרי חלם.
Ch"NYEL, L"HRYEL or. L"HDYEL M"ChNYEL – this is cholem;

ח״זקיאל, ר״הטיאל, ק״רשיאל (ק״דושיאל), הרי חרק.
Ch"ZKYEL, R"HTYEL, Q"RSHYEL alt. Q"DUShYEL – this is chireq;

ש״מועאל, ר״עמיאל, ק״ניאל, הרי שרק.
ShMU'AEL, R"'AMYEL, Q"NYEL – this is shureq;

ש״משיאל, ר״פאל, ק״דשיאלל, הרי שרק
Sh"MShYEL, R"PhaEL, Q"DShYEL – this is shureq;

Here are twenty eight names, of which it is stated:
(Psalms 111:6) *The power of His deeds has He told His people...*

130a) These angelic forces composed of these twenty eight names spread themselves out via their pointing's in Torah. They encompass the whole adding direction and pathways for the wise who seek those inner mysteries.

Through both hands fourteen on the right and fourteen on the left. The divine name reveals itself in every segment via the pathways of the angelic hosts. These hosts however are only there to show the way and are not to be seen as the way. Call them the technology of holiness then.

In terms of order of appearance we see that when the snake or the twisted pathway is involved there is sin whereas the clear pathway is holiness.

Therefore the continuity of prayer must be preserved going past the sin compensating for it in order to unify the consciousness with holiness.

However when the consciousness is in danger of being subsumed or overwhelmed by sin (the scorpion) we must pull away in order not to be drawn in deeper and lose ourselves.

The nose in terms of the breath of anger and jealousy indicates that breath like our thoughts carries the life within and without it. We are affected by those thought we take in and let go of. When holiness is the goal those thoughts must be holy with no mixture. The clarity of thought may be compared to the clarity of breath be it warm, cool, angry, or jealous. All of this applies to consciousness.

Now the ears are discussed including the listening within, the high one who waits, and that which is above the high one suggesting a layered listening that takes place.

If the ears are blocked below meaning our thoughts are on lower things than those gates above are blocked. We have to direct or intend our thoughts to reach above and concentrate upon holiness. Unification takes place by our design so that we immerse ourselves in the divine flow. This divine flow is what we are listening for when we intend 'Hear Oh Israel.'

In general when we are learning about the various sense perceptions we are training the mind to be aware of its own appearance and pathways to discovery. This begins with seeing the throne of the east. It is a throne because once we intend to listen there it rules over our perception to bring forth the light not just the physical light but also the light of inspiration that which lights up consciousness.

This may be compared with Judah in the east, the lion cub that seeks to master its domain by becoming thoroughly familiar with it and claiming it as its own.

Next is the mouth combining all the levels therein. Ephrayim in the west between north and south with the bed to the west. In this sense the mouth is part of the Middle Pillar arrangement since it is centrally located and through it speech synthesizes the thoughts in words.

Hearing corresponds to the north where there is fear and awe. This shows us that in that moment of connection when we make the initial contact there is this fear or awe that fills us immerses us in the flow of Shekinah.

This happens is the north demonstrating Binah via Aleph, which resembles the ear. By listening we learn to combine and then to bring forth the new which is exactly the role of binah amongst the sephiros.

The nostrils are mercy and judgment both Yud, Yud with Vav and the nose in the middle represents the two channels of awareness that combine into one sensory experience. All of this happens in the south in terms of the directions of Kabbalah. Reuben means to see a son, which is the joining of both nostrils to produce the straight path that is Jacob.

The fifty gates of binah come in via the twice reciting of the SHMA. There are twenty five letters each time making a total of fifty saying the SHMA twice daily. Israel the son of Ya"H, Keter and Chokmah produce Binah. Now all flow through YH"V, represented by father mother and son.

YKV"K the ten sephiros, seen as YU"D H"E VA"V H"E permeate the senses equally and are always the same in every place.

שינוים הם בכלי הגוף. אבל בו אין שינוי כלל.

There are changes in the vessels of the body,
but in Him there is no change at all;

This is what is written:
(Malachi 3:6) *I YKV"K, I have not changed...*

ובכל אבר ואבר (שהוא נר של כל מצוה), צריך בן אדם להמליך את הקדוש ברוך הוא,
ולהכין לו מקום טהור נקי להשרות אותו שם ומפני זה צריך בן אדם לבער ממנו מכל אבר
ואבר, כל מחשבות וכל הרהורים רעים של טנופים שהם קליפות, וצריך לשרוף אותם בכל
מצות כשרות, ששורות על כל אבר ואבר שהם נרות

And with each and every limb (which is the candle of every precept)
a person should crown himself with Ha Kodesh Barachu as King,
and to prepare a place for Him, a place that is pure and clean that He may
become imbued there.

And because of this, a person needs to rid himself from each and every
limb all bad thoughts and reflections that are filthy,
which are husks; and one needs to burn them with all the proper
commandments, which reside upon each and every limb. The lines of
which are the candles.

130b) From the aspect Binah it flows into Chesed to the right,
hovers via the Middle Pillar south (downwards) as in over the
'face of the waters,' and then west alternating the flow of
Shekinah revealing its mysteries to them.

The body is the receptacle of these flows and yet these flows
are always one thing despite the compartmentalization of the
body with its organs, veins, arteries segments etc.

The entire body is the temple of Ha Kodesh Barachu the King
that is unity and our preparation is necessary in order to
provide a fitting dwelling.

Therefore eliminate all negative thinking, all meditations that
do not unify and instead unite your thoughts with the light of
Torah of the all the commandments that reside within every
limb.

The precepts awaken the channels wherein Shekinah flows.

We are lit from within by holiness. Our soul is the vehicle for searching all the inner chambers of consciousness burning the chaff and keeping the wheat, which are those thoughts of holiness uniting us above. No mixture here, only the clean fine flour of holiness. In this way whatever we make of this holiness will be by definition holy.

The order of the act of Creation is in every limb so that denying this order disengages the flow. This flow is of all the angels and their camps and all those thoughts of unity that revolve around each other via the chayot as well. This in turn provides a protective energy level of awareness that wards off disease and unholiness.

In every part of consciousness there is a ruler and this ruler is specific to that area that is unified. Again there is no mixture or exchange with any other.

We open ourselves to Ha Kodesh Barachu who rules every place and is analogous to the soul that rules the body and every limb. If Ha Kodesh Barachu is recognized everywhere then truly wherever we call he answers.

With a blemish the unity cannot occur meaning if things are put together in consciousness that are unholy or have a flaw then we cannot work on these since they are of the other side and cannot be approached like the scorpion that would take away life if we approach.

If Ha Kodesh Barachu is King over each part then he rules the entire world. Ruling over the small world he rules the greater world.

The purpose then is not to declare sovereignty of the King over every limb for a reward but for the purpose of unity, which encompasses so much more.

For the wise the answer is in the doing realizing the holy awareness.

The throne or the inner temple built with tallit and tephillin is the overflowing of blessings that reveal chesed making the flow self aware then residing there in peace to awaken the SHMA or the listening that goes beyond words.

By arranging this throne we continue its sovereignty over all. By intending this throne we place ourselves within its seating and all honor is declared to those who honor Ha Kodesh Barachu by honoring the throne and intending the revelation of the throne.

The reward of prayer and its precept are the ascension that envelops you. Since having intended the throne you are in the right place to rise above with songs and praise and the thanks that you have given, however, these now serve as the winds that lift you ever higher unifying with holiness.

Remove the foreskin, the husks of the other preparing the place for Shekinah taking away all thoughts of other Gods and preparing just as the throne has prepared the body for the soul to ascend in its higher calling.

כך הקדוש ברוך הוא כאשר נשמתו עולה למעלה, זה הו שכתוב
So Ha Kodesh Barachu when his ascends Above this is what is written:

מ״י ט׳עלה׳ ל׳נו׳ השמימה׳.
(Deuteronomy 30:12) ...*who will ascend for us to the heavens?*...

הקדוק ברוך הוא מעביר ממנו כל מלאכי חבלה ומקטרגים שלא יקרבו אצלו, מפני
שהשם ע׳ל יי׳ שורה עליו, שתמצא ותות באלו תיבות מ׳י יעל׳ה ל׳נ׳י׳ו׳ השמ׳ים׳ה,
ראשי תיבות מילה וסופי תיבות יקו׳׳ק בשמו עולה למעלה נשמתו. ובאותו זמן
יכקיים בו וראו כל עמי הארץ כי סם יי׳נקרא עליך ויראו ממך

Ha Kodesh Barachu removes all angels of destruction, and denouncers from him, so that they do not approach him, because the Name of YKV"K resides upon him, for you will find in these words of: Who (M"Y) will ascend יעל'ה for us ל'ני'ו to the heavens 'השמימ'ה?

The initial letters of the words are מילה and the final letters of the words are YKV"K, in His Name does his soul ascend. And at that time will be fulfilled of him:
(Deuteronomy 28:10) *And all the peoples of the earth shall see that the Name of YKV"K is called upon you, and they shall fear you.*

131a) When you are surrounded by thoughts of holiness this acts as a fence against evil against negativity. It is like a repelling field constantly spinning inwards with holiness so that nothing that is not a part of holiness may enter. This inner spinning rises to heaven carrying the soul with it. There is then a constant identification with holiness that then shines out from you.

We accept the positive precepts by bringing them into our conscious field of intention. In this way we continually surround ourselves with holiness so that it naturally radiates from us.

By filling ourselves with the insights from Torah our souls become illuminated like the pillar of fire at night or the pillar of cloud during the day. Our thoughts become infused with YKV"K radiating from us.

Every level of being is illuminated, ruach neshamah and nephesh in the merit of Torah, in the insights that are observed.

Observing the Sabbath, honoring and delighting in it to fill ourselves with Ha Kodesh Barachu makes a place Above within the consciousness that is conceived through our intention. In this way we rise above the mundane and enter the holy absolving all reincarnation and deeds.

It is the image divine that resonates through the body of the 'young man' Above. This is where we partake of the divine influences throughout the body and the spiritual capacity for rising above appears.

The alignment of thoughts comes about via the intention that is focused upon holiness. Upon making the unifications above and below using the perceptual organs of eyes, head and ears we bring into play the angelic principalities that awaken and guide that intention into the pathways of holiness.

The face is symbolic of the divine image of YKV"K and has angels that guide these influences. In a sense the angels come into being when the intuition is focused upon holiness bringing about the connections between thoughts, which are then aided by the catalysts of the angels.

So there is the breath that is the taking in of holiness, There is the agency of the nose and the mouth and the speaking of holiness grounding it in this world with angels overseeing the speaking and the voices of Torah speaking through you.

Our image is constantly being perfected by the King since when we connect it is as though the King were our hands since the divine resides everywhere. The concepts of holiness therefore build one upon the other.

The body of holiness that we inhabit is because we take on the divine image. The conception of that image takes place by our attention to the higher voice. In the world to come the movements and actions are without a body since it is a conceptual although none the less real reality. Here in this world the body of the divine is considered to be Torah from which all precepts are derived and which is the shape of the image of the divine that we can ponder and learn the mysteries from.

The covenant is the acknowledgement of heaven that the earthly partner has agreed to participate consciously with Creation. Every sign is in the verification of this pact upon which the entire host of heaven depend and are appointed accordingly to administer.

The legs do their part with corresponding angels similar to the chayot running and returning.

So too the divine is infused in the hair; indeed the entire system is unified in this infusion.

We must be mindful of the precepts. They represent the divine image and that image is our own embodiment. If we ignore this the connection breaks and sin or error follows.

We do the work of heaven by accepting upon ourselves the image of heaven. In this case the eyes and ears become those of heaven and all the hosts and camp Above assist in our journey.

Our thoughts tie together the holiness that we attach ourselves to. Because of this attachment or constant turning to holiness, the angels rise and descend according to the intention that is building this temple within.

By attaching ourselves to the image of holiness, which is the divine we become that image and likeness. We restore the holy connection to the unity above and below and then it is declared, 'give glory to the image of the King!'

מצוה של כל מצוה, בה שורה יקו״ק.
A precept (*mitzvah*) of any commandment: in it resides YKV"K.

It the Name is found in each and every limb;
It is found in the four colors of the hair and in the four colors of the eye,
and in the four chambers of the ear, and in the four colors of the face;
and in voice, and in speech and in recitation and in utterance,
and in the action of the hands.

And in each and every limb of the body is the Name YKV"K appointed
over very precept; for in it is *mitzvah* in a"t b"ash: M"Tz is Y"H,
P"Tz is V"H; thus 'precept' is YKV"K = MTzP"Tz;
and YKV"K in A"T B"Sh = MTzP"Tz.

131b) YKV"K permeates all

YKV"K is linked with MTzP"Tz showing the unity of both.

It is solely through YKV"K that the angels are called and the
action of holiness takes place.

Using EKY"H as our vantage point the mystery of the ten
letters above to below appears and is the crown at the head of
all Names. Above this YU"D K"E VA"V or VY"V K"E
AL"Ph DL"T NU"N YU"D, for a total of forty two letters
describing the higher heavens from which come the lands of
life that are created from what is called the heaven of
heavens.

The Artisan of all, the Cause of Causes is inviolable above all
and blesses all with the blessings of the above.

These footsteps of ADN"Y the legs and their four sides depict
righteousness determining each footstep.

Throughout the 100 blessings, sockets, five books of Torah,
ninety amens of prayer, and four sanctifications, KVY"Y is
there permeating every action.

Tzedakah, Higher Mother, tzedek Lower Mother are the
aspects of YKV"K expressing itself above and below. All of

these are examples of the unification's that take place throughout Tikkunei Zohar.

All goings are permeated with KVY"Y.

The integration of mitzvos, tephillin of the arm and shoulder, head and left arm all are permeated with the divine name.

The mouth reveals through its sacred permeation of YKV"K through which prayers learning and teaching takes place. In addition the mouth reveals the blowing of the shofar, and the voice that is within and without. The same unification then takes place with that which is dependent upon the nose.

All judgments too depending upon the mouth and eyes are permeated with YKV"K.

The SHMA, all precepts that are heard, shofar etc., all these are infused with the essence of YKV"K.

All commandments dependent upon the limbs, sukkah and lulav upon the hands all suffused with holiness.

All constructs, all unifications of thought are recognized with YKV"K. That holiness is throughout revealing the angels of holiness in every corner.

Be mindful of the angels, and the signs of holiness that we recognize. It is because of these angles that we act for good from the aspect of the Righteous One.

of whom it is said...
(Jeremiah 10:2) ...and from the signs of the heavens do not fear...

ומלאכים שתלויים ברגלים,
And there are angels that are dependent upon the legs,

of which it is said:
(Ezekiel 1:14) And the chayot were running and returning...

ונענוע של כולם יקו״ק, וצריך לדעת נקודה שלו, בכל אבר ואבר נקודה שמתחייבת
למלאך שהוא (אור) מים.

And the shaking of all of them is YKV"K;
and needs to know its point in each and every limb,
a vowel point that belongs to the angel that is (light) water.

And an angel that is fire. And angel that is wind.
For all vowel points are fire, wind and water. Malchus is earth,
The vessel of all of those Above that are derived from the sephiros.

132a) This running and returning refers to thoughts that come
and go. They are like the chayot and are dependent upon the
legs and their association with YKV"K.

The common thread and the power that runs through all is
YKV"K in every limb in each vowel point and in all the
elements creating the pathways Above.

The body is the vessel of meaning. It is derived from the
throne and its angels and Ophan for the essence of a person.
The soul-spirit-animating spirit are all residing there flowing
with YKV"K throughout.

Mikhae"l is compared to the flowing of Shekinah, the
principality of water, and the awareness of Ha Kodesh
Barachu unlike any other. We see the organization of the
archangels, Gavrye"l, Urie"l and R-phae"l and all that issues
from their gatherings. In order for there to be anything below
there must be the hierarchy of thought that is the background
of the way everything works.

Thoughts unite via the pathways that carry them i.e. the body.
Each time we make this unification of thought it is as if we
unite Ha Kodesh Barachu and Shekinah. All the while we are
preparing Shekinah to unite above meaning we seek the
higher meanings uniting principle and precept with action.

The temple is made by a constant adhering to holy thoughts and arranging them as they were meant to be. When we have the intention to reveal the holy messengers, those angels that carry the higher wisdom above and below then we build the throne, awaken the heavens, and cause a sanctuary to come into being. Due to this awakening and coming into being the Sukkah is built for us below to protect us from negative influences and make it possible to move between this world and the world to come.

When we bless we are blessed in return. It is similar to the blessings of the wedding ceremony.

We unify with the SHMA twice daily comprising seven sanctifications, which produce their counterparts below. It is our intention that sets all of this in motion.

It is this unity with the SHMA that brings together our intention with its demonstration, which is a comparison to Ha Kodesh Barachu and Shekinah coming together as one.

The comparisons go further even to bringing together a person and their bashert. This is how creation matches our intention word for word and measure for measure.

When we strive to do the will of the creator it means we do what is right because we understand that there is always a connection above mirroring our actions below.

We set up the temple within with blessings and prayers and unifications and then there is a corresponding temple and an eternal building that is in the world to come in the world of Ha Kodesh Barachu.

Meditate upon the image of Ha Kodesh Barachu in all of your body; not a single part can be missed. There can be no mixture here either since a part that is not infused with our thoughts of Ha Kodesh Barachu is not complete and must be reborn in order to complete the image of Ha Kodesh Barachu.

In consciousness the blemish must be reborn and corrected.

We strive to make sure our mouth speaks what our heart says. This is because oral and written Torah unite V"K and Y"K, otherwise YKV"K is absent.

The aspects of the lips are discussed, wide, average and small.

Speech must be of holiness for the angels carry that speech above and it must be worthy to approach the Creator.

These five constructs of the letters frame the speech that rises above.

(Deuteronomy 27:6) ...*you shall build...* – to Ha Kodesh Barachu, with many prayers and acts of worship;

ועליהם אמר יעקב וישכב מבקום ההוא.
and about them did Jacob say,
(Bereishis 28:11) ...and he lay down וישכב in that place
וישכב (and he lay down) is composed of יי"ש (and there are) כ"ב (22) letters in that place.

יי"ש (there are):
(Proverbs 8:21) *To cause those who love me to inherit, there is* יי"ש...
כ"ב (22)
(Bereishis 48:20) By you בך, shall Israel bless...
(Psalms 22:5) *In You* בך *did our fathers trust...*
(Psalms 18:30) *For in you* בך *I have run through a troop...*
(Deuteronomy 14:2) ...*and in you* בך *did YKV"K choose...*
(Shemos 32:13) ...*to whom they swear to you* בך...
(Song of Songs 1:4) ...*we shall be happy rejoice in you* בך
of them:
(Ezekiel 3:12) ...*Blessed is the glory* כ'בוד acronym: בך
of YKV"K from His place.

132b) You build the temple within. You prepare the way forward in this life and the next. Always this is done with prayers and blessings. Prayers are the question and blessings the answer. It is consciousness that experiences both. Therefore be active in your building meaning be aware that every word and every thought is or is not fit for the building you are constructing within.

The various types of beard are discussed according to types of persons.

The soul resides everywhere.

Shekinah rises or drifts away according to the unifications that we are actively pursuing, like the soul emerges and descends and goes outside its place.

The soul returns when it sins no more and acts for unity. The Queen, Shekinah emerges from the heart no longer called Queen for she is away from Her place.

The holiness of a soul is gradually built up according to our merits until She arises back to her place in the heart.

It is possible to become entangled in the web of bindings that dissolve the unity and embrace the chaos. Even a small part of this web is enough to trap a person in thoughts of negativity.

Worthy is he who is on guard against this web of delusion because becoming aware of the delusion is the only way to dismiss it.

The delusions are many filled with evil seeming to be good.

Evil occurs in the place that is not your own since you departed the unity of Ha Kodesh Barachu and are then subject to the evils of that other who seems to attract souls that have strayed.

אוי להם לאלו הטיפות שאותם נצוצות ושרביטים הזדמנו ביניהם

Woe to these drops, for those sparks and scepters chanced amongst them.

Those fools who do not guard themselves in their coupling, in them are they the wicked souls grafted,
and the tree of the knowledge of good and evil is made.

He has a female (*nuqba*) who is called:
(Shemos 3:24) ...*the flaming, switching sword*...
for all reincarnations of souls are switching in it;
sometimes the staff transforms into the snake, sometimes the snake transforms into a staff, and thus is male switched into female, female to male.

133a) Consciousness works in a prescribed manner and when that process is diverted or perverted it brings about imbalances as determined here by the sexual unions taking place. In like manner there are unions between thoughts that have their own set of attractions and linkages. When there is a mixture as has been spoken of before the basic structures go awry bringing about the perversions spoken of. These movements that take place in the body are reflective of the soul trying to correct itself from the stress of imbalance.

The various ways the evil incarnation comes into being are discussed in terms of their animal traits. Similarly the tribes of Israel each demonstrate the various animal traits but without the evil inclination.

The evil inclination appears as the various animal types alluding to the way thoughts join together creating mixtures that are unholy.

The key is to ruling over the evil inclination because in this way a balance is always maintained.

When the evil inclination is not stopped or ruled over then all kinds of chaos results since there is no longer the balance of what you think in your heart becoming the words you speak. The evil inclination then gets in the way and perverts all.

There is the man of Creation that rules over the lion and makes the pathways of Torah. This is the way of making the channels of holiness. His thoughts direct the flow into the pathways above.

The Man of Action rides upon an eagle, and he takes wind in his mouth, and he turns with his face towards the east, and makes colors in the eyes, in the face.

מי אדם שהל בריאה ויציר ועשיה כאן.
He said to him:
Who is the 'Man of Creation, Formation, Action here

He said to him: 'My son, this is he of whom it is said
(Bereishis 2:5) ...and man was not
(Ecclesiastes 3:19) ...so that man hath no pre-eminence above a beast

And he is the Man of Creation, for with this keter
did the Cause of Causes create all creatures.

אדם של יצירה חכמה, עליו נאמר והחכמה מאין תמצא, שהוא י' מאין שבו צייר
כל ציורי העולם.
The Man of Formation is chokmah, about him it is said,
(Job 28:12) And wisdom (chokmah), from where will it be found?... for it
is the Yud of אין, with which he painted all the painting of the world,

With it he painted eyes, and nose, the nostrils, the holes of the ears, and the mouth, all the points and paintings that are a ring for the letter Yud, and it is in them like a stone at the top of a ring.

The Man of Action this is the Nun of אין binah;
She is: (Bereishis 3:20) ...the mother of all life, the act of creation
in Her are made all the workings of the act of creation, and colors.

133b) The man of formation emulates the Creator above imaging within these pathways directing further still the flow of intention into what comes next into activation.

The man of Action speaks the word with his face in the east completing the process of becoming.

Before there was man, there was combined with Keter what the cause of all causes created in all creatures. It is the directing force, the prime innovation, and the supreme plan that includes itself in its making. This is the man of Creation.

Understand that this man of creation exists complete in its original intention inside of every pathway within including veins, arteries, organs, nerve endings, bone sockets, and everywhere in short that the life flow penetrates. There you may identify with in unity with the One that is all.

See that this concept is beyond conception in that it resides sum and total of every part of you so near that there cannot be a single step, even the slightest movement in which this man of creation does not perform with you.

Then or always out of this flow or complete infusion comes the imaging that is a natural result of this flowing that continues forever. When these images arise it brings into focus the Man of Formation like the perfect instrument for the perfect job.

The Man of Formation is wisdom, or chokmah. It is the yud of Ayi"N (nothing) in which the flow of direction from Creation finds itself imaging the forms of eyes, ears, and nose. Then it creates in all these points and images a ring for the letter Yud and this Yud sits like a stone set in the top of a ring. The Man of Formation brings about the perfect instrument then for the expression of the divine will.

What is this like? A King conceived the perfect song and yet without an instrument to express this song he could only imagine how wonderful it was. So it happened that this King created instruments to express this song all the while retaining the complete composition of the King. This is the Man of Formation.

Next there comes the work itself, the shining example of what was above and is now to be expressed below. This is the Man of Action.

The Man of Action. This is Binah the mother of all life, and the expression of the above. This proves the act of creation, and sets into motion all the workings of the act of creation. The expressed composition fills Creation with the purpose it reveals. The plan is then complete and the ongoing work continues forever.

Now the King has expressed His great work and set into motion not only the image making capacity but also the proof of the vision. All this takes place in one smooth flowing that shifts from creation to formation to action via the channels set forth initially from above and now working together via their own momentum.

Therefore coming to chesed the sketch is made and then filled in with the depictions that are gevurah until Tipheret is reached coloring the depictions making sense and beauty out of the image. What comes next are the three patriarchs netzach, hod and y-sod for it is through these three that the image is reflected, and contemplated.

Culminating in Malchus is the form of man. Here in Lower Shekinah the imaginer of holiness gives rise to the holiness above via the reality of the imaged form below.

It is only through the realization of unity that occurs in Malchus that we may contemplate the divine. A point of reference has to be in place otherwise the resulting visions are too much to conceive of and the point of reference is no longer in sight.

Malchus is the looking glass. It is the completed image that allows contemplation of the above since it is both vantage point and the perfected image below.

Our actions are what determine our state of being because it is the result of our thoughts, speech and finally action that proves the work. This happens in exactly the same way as Keter is proved in Malchus. When our actions are good they are from the Tree of Life.

It is through Malchus that we contemplate the above in the closed thought (like Aleph and Qametz) with the Yud of the eye being the Vav and the lower and Higher Hei each becoming a pathway to the countenances and colors of the face of a person meaning their state of being.

(Ezekiel 1:1) ...*the heavens were opened and I saw visions of ELKY"M* which are the five mentions of light in the act of creation, which are included in Higher Hei.

חמשה אור שמאיריים בחמשה גונים
Five lights that shine in five colors.

134a) The five lights, the five realizations that occur in consciousness representing the Higher Hei, the awakening by degree, the flow of intention expressed via the sephiros are all visions of holiness.

The absence of color, the lack of expression, and the flow that has atrophied and turned into dust from thoughts that stands alone without connection is the absence of holiness.

בא ראה, לא לחנם אמרו קדמונים אין הרוכב טפל לסוס, אלא הסוס טפל לררכב,
שסוס הוא נקבה, לרוכב שהוא אדם
Come see: Not in vain did the ancestors say:'the rider is not secondary to the horse, but the horse is secondary to the rider'

for the horse is female in relation to the rider who is 'man'
if he merits, then it is said of him:
(Shemos 2:18) *...I shall make a helpmate for him*
and if not then, she will be *opposing him* the evil inclination...

The rider must control the vehicle. Thoughts are the vehicle and the soul is the rider. In order to control the evil inclination the rider has to direct thought away from this state of decay.

There are two types of woman meaning two types of receptacles for thought. One is the evil inclination that twists and turns thought stripping it of its connections; the other is the helpmate or Shekinah, which encourages connection for good.

Man can either be a slave or master to his thoughts.

It is what you do with your intention that counts. If you strive for good then good is what you will receive. Intention directs the thoughts for good or ill.

Your state of mind may be troubled. Your thoughts may be confused or negative but if you take hold of thought, take hold of mind, take hold of the body or your state of mind with a good intention then you can heal and make good out of all that you survey.

The perfect marriage is between a good intention that is operating upon good thoughts. The woman is the receptacle of thought.

The righteous person that has negative thoughts and yet who strives to do good is fighting to get above this situation. Then there is the intention that is good and yet because of a predominance of bad thoughts the image is bad. Then the person that thinks bad and does evil things he is bad and evil.

The three incarnations begin with a person who has a predominance of good. His image is good and yet his deeds are bad and the woman where the image is righteous; and things turn out good.

It is reincarnation that mixes the levels of good and bad and the punishment that corrects the bad into good.

It is only by uprooting the 'woman' or the image of the body of thoughts that has corrupted the soul that there is correction. In this case change of place-reincarnation, change of name-self image-intention, or change of deed that is choosing to do good is the way to correct this situation of a righteous person who has a bad image-woman.

Shekinah is here meaning the inspiration that teaches and flows and gathers in the higher thoughts that are about to be explained.

The dimension of stature in terms of Shekinah will be explained.

The pathways of Shekinah are compared to a palm tree, Her breasts like clusters, the blossoming of a palm even to its role as lulav describing an unbroken flow.

Shekinah is compared to the lulav the body Vav in extension with five branches growing from it.

וחמשה ענפים הם, שנים מזה הצד, ושלשה מזה הצד.
And the five branches are: two from this side and three from this side,

and about them it is said:
(Vayikra 23:40) *...and the branch of a braided tree myrtle and willows of the brook...* ...the branch to the left, braided to the right, tree in the middle; willows of the brook – two, braided – three;

134b) Shekinah is centered in Tipheret flowing to and from here.

The branches are braided together like the pathways that flow and intertwine amongst the Sephiros.

The allusion to the body two thighs, two arms and the covenant, the citron, and the heart, Tipheres make up the fruit of the tree, which flows the same throughout.
In this flowing there is the Higher Mother, binah, the brain of chokmah and above the fountain of the tree, Keter whose main source is the Infinite.

The leaves of the trees are the outward extensions of consciousness. The head is the perception above. All are green meaning they are constantly renewed with this endless flow. The hair too is green always renewed like the seven types of gold in terms of their renewal of the gradations of holiness. So too the etrog is green and Esther too represents the renewal of holiness.

The straps of tephilin receive their renewal from the heart the same as the daughter of the King measures the pathways of holiness one to the other.

The equal proportions show us the uniformity of the flow from above to below and through all the channels that it must flow determining the communication that travels instantaneously from one level to another.

Just a reservoir flows through pipes that are measured so too does the divine flow awaken each level equally and at the same time passes along the higher information and processes the lower information.

The fountain of Keter is visualized as a final Mem, a point in a circle quadrupled in a square. The flow moves itself along these passageways and then through the four worlds of being.

The same principle is found in the mikveh. All equal parts of immersion and all purifications taking place simultaneously. The nine from Keter to Yesod becomes the ten with Malkhut on each of the four sides bringing about purity in all directions alluding to the correction of the forty years of exile.

The fountain flows via the living waters forming a vortex from above to below equal in their elements of holiness.

It is the uniform flow where one thing not only becomes the other but also is the other in the transmuted sense of a dimension outside of time.

All have a part in the expression of the Divine Will including each and every limb, the higher, lower and middle. Just as the vowel points express the sound of the word so too do the limbs and messengers express the holiness and Divine Will throughout.

Above the timeless sovereign nature of YKV"K is illustrated by the different vowels.

Likewise below with Shekinah the image is expressed in similar fashion as above.

Throughout time without restraints, YKV"K shall be, will be, and his name is Higher Keter. One is thereby expressed via chokmah and binah.

In every sense YKV"K extends His influence via the unbroken flow of Shekinah. This happens through the breath, through every part of the body and all of the thoughts that connect with the essence of One.

The seventy two names from Ex 14:19-21 all contain the essence of יקו״ק branching through the root of the tree Malkhut or the world of action reflecting the holy intention above.

ע״ב עליונים כנגד שבעים ושתים תיבות, שהן מן והיה אם שמע עד ושמתם. וושבעים ושתים
אחרות הן של של פרשת ציצית

Seventy two higher in contrast to seventy boxes,
if you shall listen...until And you shall place...;
and the seventy two others are of the section of the tzitzit.

The top of the tree: its servants who are (Deuteronomy 16:18) *Judges and enforcers...* - are the forty two words from:
And you shall love until *And it shall be*;
The body. (swaying bough) of the tree: its appointees and messengers are the fifty words which are from, *And you shall place* until *And He said*.

135a) In all of these seventy-two names and others in the verses and in the section of the tzitzit you find YKV"K permeating every part so you will know the intricate holiness that is one.

There in the unity of the tree those forty two words and those fifty words are unifications within unifications that all point to one.

The seven Names of the head, and the Ana Bokoach prayer that adds to forty-two also point to the unity above.

The first firmament. Think of this as a chamber within bounded by AVGYTa"Tz, generating the YKV"K (YHaVehHei) according to with shva, qametz, segol, tzerei that emerges in eight chambers, eight sparks, and eight inspirations. It is out of this beginning that all things come to be from this single channel of awakening.

The second firmament is one inside the other as in a dimension of space, where Q"R"'E SeTa"N is the surrounding force of this chamber producing YKV"K as (YeiHehVHa). It is in the making of this firmament that there is a point of reference against which all things may be measured.

The third firmament is NaG-DeYiKha"Sh generating YKV"K as (YaHeVeeHa). The waters that are gathered are the waters of consciousness as to their attractions and linking's that make up the substrata of the universe. It is the swirling spiral clockwise bringing up from below and setting up the patterns of the developing awareness.

The fourth firmament with BaT-"Re Tz-t-"G produces HVY"Y (YaHehVH). Here is the realization of holiness and the looking back at the lights in the sky. The pathways are illuminated once and forever.

Enter the fifth firmament bounded by ChaQ-Ve Tin"'a with YKV"K as (YahHehVeeHa). The waters swarm with the variations of life produced here within consciousness as its connections are enlivened with meanings.

The sixth firmament is ground zero, with YaG-"Le PhoZa"Q setting up YKV"K as (YaHehVohHa). Out of this awareness bringing forth all the reproductions that are endless in nature demonstrating the divine will above.

Then the seven point, the heaven that is included in the sixth day, bounded by ShaQ-"Ve TziYa"T produces YKV"K with (YaHehVeeHa). The realization that is awareness or consciousness sees itself and its gift that is everlasting.

Out of all the divine names generated by Torah it is ELKY"M that is the first and the last. This is because without the process of becoming or being put into place there would be no way to relate back to the principle of divinity, the principle of the way things work.

The divine names are generated from the letters of Torah from two up until ten representing the sephiros.

The name of twelve letters is derived from Higher Keter.

Twelve channels emerge from the divine source Vav from Arikh Anpin and H'E H'E.

Ah-Tzitzah- ron: Refers to the glowing pre-luminescent light of expectation preceding the initiation of thought

Aklithah-ron: The 360 Degree pathways that opens for the expression of Intention

Shemaqtharon: The fires of inspiration once kindled shine eternally

Demushah-ron: An idea takes hold and desire is formed.

Ve-Tzaphtzaphithron: The thoughts begin to find their counterparts by matching the frequency and inner feeling nature of their expressions.

Hurmyron: New meanings come forth expanding and raising the level of ideation past the point of projection.

Brach Yah-ron: The blessing from within, the Lord manifest as supernal imagery

Eresh Gadra-aon: The canvas upon which all projections are cast.

Basavah Monahon: Acceptance and the initial presentation of form

Chazhavayah: All areas now coalesce into the idealized form

Havahayryhah: The form is revealed as well as a series of instantaneous transformations

Ve-Harayth-hon: The place of peace is revealed as vibrations match in both feelings and thoughts.

The long countenance is VA'V at the head of the Aleph.

Torah shows you its insights when you listen for them. The pathways of Zeir Anpin are the expressions of holiness that are shown in Torah.

These crowns are points of higher confluence relating to the inspiration that are called each, Torah, priesthood or kingship.

There is the crown of keter from the aspect of Aleph in the image of YU'D and also the Aleph of EKY"K and the Aleph of ADN"Y. All of these are the higher influences above that are the rulers and inspirations for these 'crowns.'

These crowns link us to Torah via the divine names in terms of our acceptance and meditation upon its mysteries.

Think of crown as a point of inspiration from which flows the meanings from Keter and the head throughout every sephirah. It is also the blessing of every precept and the resulting flows/ occurrences that ascend upon contemplation of the blessings and precepts.

Because of this there are ten out of ten adding to a hundred via Aleph to ten thousands rising to the Cause of all Causes.

It comes out of the meanings of these letters that are crowned in Torah, which go on to derive the blessings and wellsprings that fill and illuminate all the sephiros.

והם י"א י"א מן י'קוק ע'לקינו י'קוק א'חד, בא' נקרא א"ל עליון. בי' יקו'ק. וכן
בא' נקרא עלקינו אקיי"ק אלקים אדנ"י והרי העמידוהו. ועוד כתר עליון אף על פי
שהוא אור קדמון אור צח ואור מצוחצח הוא שחור לפני עלת העלות

And they are the letters י"א י"א of:
(Deuteronomy 6:4) *YKV"K ELHYN"U YKV"K EChaD* with Aleph, it is
called E"L 'ELYON, with Yud, YKV"K; and so, with Aleph, It is called,
ELHYN"U EHY"H ELKY"M ADN"Y
and thus have they established it.

And furthermore: Higher keter, even though it is primordial light,
clear light and polished light, it is black before the Cause of causes.
And, of all the forces that are derived from it, it is said:
(Song of Songs 5:11) *His fringes are curls, black like the raven*
no light exists before Its light, for all lights are darkened before It.

135b) Therefore Yud and Aleph are a part of every sephirah.
In this way the divine names are generated through Yud
(YKV"K) and Aleph (E"L 'ELYON, ELHYN"U EHY"H
ELKY"M ADN"Y) and Higher Keter is the all-encompassing
light.

These channels that radiate throughout the sephiros contain
the concealed supernal ones. They move about in relationship
to the high one of all high ones so that by comparison any
lights perceived below are darkened.

It is the same of the Cause above all causes in whose light
none exist and all is darkness. This suggests the ultimate
unity of expression that knows only itself and as itself is all.

These lights, these crowns are what the essence of the
sephiros exist upon. The holy names are examples of these
lights through Ale"Ph H"E YU"D H"E and YU"D H"E VA"V
H"E =45, YU"D H"Y VA"V H"Y =63 which are the ten
within the ten.   The dimension of imaging the divine
reflection describes the perfect light.

The rider upon all is the Cause of Causes, high above all the
high ones.

These Names are channels, fed by fountains or wellsprings that are the flowing of Being into being and then back again through all in equal proportions with all containing the essence of the One.

The Infinite Above is measureless and yet still exacts measure in its flowing via the five arrangements. The corrections of Higher Hei include Vav, Hei, and Yud, being that which expresses the Infinite in exact measure throughout every part of being.

Words are defined by the specific vowel points. This leads to a comparison with our thoughts that are often colored with nuanced expressions higher, lower and middle.

It is how we think about something that makes its impression upon our thoughts. The eight Yuds are a specific way of looking at something relating to the firmament, which is established prior to anything coming into being. What we are developing via the signet or the signified expression of thought takes place via a process of rational becoming.

All are openings, ways to connect and express the higher thoughts, those great lights that share the channels of the sephiros and engrave the sense of being that is experienced and therefore is the seal of all of them.

The covenant is the surety that our actions are one with the Cause of causes representing itself through nine points, eight sparks and a firmament. Therefore having a point of reference (the firmament) the realization of manifest being not only is made possible it is also sealed as the primary part of the fulfilment of being.

From Malkhut to Chokmah there are nine from below to above. Binah is the seal and the jumping off point for the correspondence of expression that is the flowing of being from the Higher Mother. Then receiving the influence from Keter all shine with the effulgence of the high of all the high ones each receiving its measured portion.

Through the vowel points the letters speak or have speech and this is the speech of all beings, and the expression of life at every level of experience.

There comes a point when the Cause of all Causes in its reaches Binah where its expression is spoken. It is the word taking form and just at that moment there is a reflection which is without words. It is the reflection of the essence of above and the signal proof of the way things work, the ELKY"M without vowels.

כשהיינו קוראים בספר זה, כך היו יורדים צואות של מלאכים לסבב אותנו כבני אדם שמתקבצים לחופה בשמחת חסן וכלה. והקדוש ברוך הוא היה יורד בכל מחנות שלו לשמוע דברים מאותו ספר.

As we were reading this book, hosts of angels were descending to surround us, like people gathering towards a wedding canopy at the celebrations of a bride and groom, and Qudsha Brikh Hu was descending with all His encampments to hear words from that book.

136a) In this book is described the birth of creation along with the vision of Ezekiel and the four animals describing the various type of operations that take place. There are four faces and four colors alluding to when Moshe spoke to YKV"K face to face.

The Higher Shekinah comes into play bringing about the higher thoughts that move back and forth between the holy animals and also begin to rotate at our consciousness of their purpose. It is moving and beyond the field of our awakening and yet still we are put inside of that holy place to become that which always was, is and will be.

פתה ואמר בראשית ברא עלקים. זו הנשמה כאשר יוצא ממעי אמו נאמר בה
והארץ היסה תהו ובהו וחשך על פני תהום, שיוצא עיניו סתומות.

He began and said:
(Bereishis 1:1) *In the beginning ELKY"M created...*
this is the soul; when it emerges from its mother's womb it is said
(Bereishis 1:2) *And the earth was chaos and void and darkness was upon
the face of the deep...*
– for it a baby emerges with its eyes closed.

It opens its eyes and immediately: (Bereishis 1:3)
And ELKY"M said: 'Let there be light' and there was light.
After it the soul is gathered from this world, what is said of it?
(Bereishis 1:9) *And ELKY"M said: 'Let the waters be gathered
from beneath the heavens to one place and the dry land shall be seen...*
since the soul has departed from it, the body remains dry.

136b) The birth of the soul is compared to awakening of the
world into being.   Likewise the departure of the soul is
compared to 'let the waters be gathered and the dry land shall
be seen. For consciousness too there is an awakening of light
and also a letting go as in letting false ideas go by the
wayside.

The generations of Adam also alludes to the birth of the soul
coming forth on the day ELKY"M created Adam the fourth
Chayah, the fourth face in the progression of four.

When we meditate upon the four faces and the four colors of
the chayot we receive insights about how the world comes
into being.   The conclusion that is reached is a direct
perception of holiness, of the Creator and of the conversation
that goes on between man and the Creator.

There are faces that are seen and those that remain a mystery.
The divine image brings about its own reflection, which can
only perceive this from its own perspective and not from the
perspective of the divine.

The perceptions of the reflected image are called men of valor, men of truth, those who hate ill gotten gain, and those that have shame because they fear or are in awe of the divine.

When the reflected image does not take on any of these divine qualities then it must return to the void and chaos since it is like a canvas that rejects the paint that is placed upon it.

We learn now the place of these righteous ones. Lower Shekinah show the men of valor-Abraham. From Isaac there is the Higher Shekinah and those who fear ELKY"M. Men of truth symbolizes Jacob, Vav and Tipheret. Those who hate ill-gotten gain are David Yud and the fourth leg.

More comparisons and linkings are shown. HVY"Y is the Higher Shekinah and the Lower Shekinah is the Middle Pillar between them and YHV"H is MOSES and Metatron. Seeing them together their meanings are unified.

The newborn sees with the eyes of this world after seeing the inner world from his mother's womb. These inner lights that he has envisioned act as way showers via Torah to help him to understand where his soul has been and where it is going. All of this teaches him that sharing that vision awakens many others in kind.

The child has many ways to get back on track with the visions of Torah that he experiences. It is therefore his Torah study that reminds him of the unity of all things shown to him in the womb of his mother.

The child in the womb also experiences Gehinom as a guard against committing sins just the same as he has been shown the rewards for his Torah study.

When he wakes his eyes are shut to the visions of the inner world. He will have to awaken them through his life experiences.

We have to change our thoughts to align them with Gan Eden. These thoughts are the colors of consciousness that shine in the light for good.

Therefore we partake of the divine influence contemplating holiness and good making appear within the image of reflection that intimately resides there shining forth through us like the sun, like the moon.

Our thoughts are colored white, red, green and black like the strands of hair and are the stars with angels appointed over them. All of this goes together to make the unity that is each thought awakening to its own sense of connection.

The expression of the holiness of the divine finds itself at the final gate in the mouth. It is direct and interfaces with the above. Here the contemplation and the generation of being is one and the same.

The sukkah that covers and awakens holiness defines and expresses YKV"K and ADN"Y via our prayers and the intention to remember this opening within that results.

Y"K and V"K are linked via chokmah and binah. The cherubs are the intelligences that connect each thought together knitting the framework for holiness and are also the filter for the awareness to rise up into.

Man is the divine image made form. His awareness is contained in YU"D K"E VA"V K"E: From this awareness he contemplates and knows his maker.

וכך הוא מי שלא עוסק בתורה, עיניו סותם מהעול הבא. אחר שעוסק בתורה, מיד ויאמר

And so it is, that one who does not strive in Torah, his eyes are closed from seeing the next world. After he strives in Torah, then immediately it is said:

(Bereishis 1:3) *And ELKY"M said: 'Let there be light' and there was light* for they illuminate him with the light of that world.

And as soon as he goes to that world, then immediately:
(Bereishis 1:9) *...Let the waters be gathered from beneath the heavens to one place...* the soul is gathered to one place,
this is what is written:
(Ecclesiastes 12:7) *And the spirit shall return to the ELKY"M Who gave it... and the body remains dry; this is what is written:*
(Bereishis 1:9) *...and the dry land will be seen..*

137a) The sight that is lost is the inspirational sight therefore leaving just chaos and void.

By striving in Torah the openings appear allowing entrance into the next world. These openings are the connections that Torah has built into its substance like a code that is constant in revealing itself.

It is then the light of Torah that is our discovery lighting the pathways that lay before us describing the world in which we live and the world into which we are entering into via our imagination and our thoughts.

He goes to that world in unity. His soul is gathered meaning his thoughts and his consciousness is collected to that one place whereas the body becomes the dry land devoid of the soul.

The soul is returned to its type carried by the same thoughts that surrounded him in this life traveling via the pathways of Shekinah. Here they are rising and descending containing within itself the consciousness of unity that has been built through Torah study.

The unification of male and female takes place and is the perfect answer to every question. There is subject and object, give and take, and openings and closings. Consciousness inherits this on its departure from the body.

The soul in conjunction with Shekinah produces the worlds without end. There the Garden of Eden resumes its true perception of the divine both above and below. Perfection is realized because it never departed.

Enoch came to this realization and was not meaning he didn't need the body in order to discover the higher worlds and the truth above Ha Kodesh Barachu and His Shekinah.

Adam departed Eden in the body but returns in his soul via Enoch restoring what was lost, his youth, his divine perception and his unified partnership above and below.

Joseph spoke against his brothers that they weren't acting in the name of the divine image, which in some cases they rejected.

Joseph's brothers had the knowledge of wisdom of the way things worked and yet still transgressed by acting in evil ways by not following the ways of heaven or being jealous of heaven and by extension Joseph.

It is the synthesis of intention-the tongue and expression the voice that emerges and is colored by the mouth and throat. It is the joining of Tipheret and malkhut which is the center column and the demonstration of holiness.

When the chamber opens (the heart) it expresses holiness and every pathway through which it passes is holy. This also leads back to speaking one way from heart to mouth as spoken of earlier. (Not having one thing in the heart and another in the mouth)

The soul of man burns with the candle of YKV"K and within the cherubs, the wings of the lung, the coverings for the soul channel the breath into holiness or through holiness. The face of one to the other is like the kidneys are in the body.

In the heart's two chambers there is the elixir of life or the fire, the poison of death depending upon the aspect with which one views holiness. If we are attentive to holiness we choose life. If not it is death that we choose.

One cannot approach holiness without a holy intention for the unification of Shekinah and Ha Kodesh Barachu is from the right side the side of blessings, mercy. In such a state of unity the thoughts must coincide with holiness otherwise they become polluted and death emerges from the left side.

The foods of consciousness are akin to Levites, Priests and Israelites, which form themselves out of the daily prayers filling our consciousness with holiness, acting as the sacrifices were meant to. It does so in a manner of giving the intention only holy food to operate from. We see good and want good, expect good and receive good.

If you pray for a sense of connection then the answering call is life. If you pray distancing yourself from connection the answer is poverty from the left side, the spleen and death.

It is always the intention that determines the attitude of prayer. If the intention is of spirit or the animating soul then there is life but if otherwise there is no connection resulting in death or dissolution.

There is no way to change the outcome if the initial intent is crooked since what follows always is a reflection of what is entered into.

אמר לו, והרי עז״א ועזא״ל היו אלו. אמר לו והרי אחרים היו נאספים עמו. אמר לו
רבי אלעזר, והרי הקדוש ברוך הוא עד שהתיעץ בצבאות שלו לא היה עושה את
האדם, שאמר נעשה אדם. אמר לו ללמד דרך ארץ לבני אדם שנוטל גדול עצה
מהקטן ממנו

He said to him: 'And yet 'Az"a and 'Aza-e"l were these!'

He said to him: 'And yet others were gathered with him.'

Rabbi Elazar said to him: 'And yet, Ha Kodesh Barachu,
before He took counsel with His hosts, had not made Adam,
for He said: (Bereishis 1:26) ...*Let Us make a human...*
He said to him: "This was in order to teach respect to humanity, that the
Greater took counsel from the lesser."

137b) In the making of man the angels questioned why specifically Az"a and Aza-e"l. These represent the consciousness that doesn't seek the image of reflection and only exists for itself, and is at the limit of its revelation, and cannot go any further.

So the greater inquiries of Ha Kodesh Barachu are to teach respect.

Furthermore out of that which he made that did his bidding he asks the question because he knew they were bound to answer truthfully and only then did he commence to make a human.

In making the human the angels are called to watch over him since this is a branch of His planting and the work of his hands to be glorified.

It is the divine image that is made beyond the capacity of the angels to conceive. It is that rulership that is given to him who now has the discernment to rule over even the evil inclination.

He is given a soul in "our image" the image of above.

The angels shall be a part of him in spirit and in the animating soul directly imaging above and below even to ruling over the angels who see that it is His Name that resides upon him. This reinforced by 'and My seal in his hand,' the seal of the covenant. Higher thoughts are the domain of consciousness that is eternal. These higher thoughts are those angels who are tasked with helping him.

So it is that Metatron-Joseph shall do and listen blessing YKV"K performing and running to do the word of Ha Kodesh Barachu in all matters relating to him as the image of reflection.

These other angels that hated man sought to subvert his influence and gave the bad report of Joseph's brothers to Jacob.

The composite human male-female is that which contains the evil inclination brought about by these rebellious angels and therefore is exempt from becoming via the festival gatherings.

These mixed souls cannot see Shekinah since they are immediately reincarnated in order to correct the fault in them.

Those over whom the evil inclination rules for example the hermaphrodite is exempt from seeing that it is the image above since their mixture must be corrected.

There is a correction via reincarnation of the animating soul, the spirit and soul until they are in their right places. The spirit speaks on behalf of the soul and the animating soul arguing that since they were not in their right place they cannot be resolved together until that right place is assumed once more.

One comes into reincarnation for the first time while their sins are completely gone.

The person is shown to be in whatever reincarnation, first, second or third by the voice that is like shvarim, t-ru'ah or t-qi'ah depending upon the level of correction that has taken place. Consciousness self corrects until unity is realized in total.

Unity takes place regarding the transformations of a soul. All of this takes place within a persons thoughts and the way they perceive the world. If white then this perception is good because it is closest to the divine image.

We also see the correction in the second or third reincarnation.

בא ראה, ואתה תחזה מכל העם, כאן העמדנו לדעת תקונים אלו

Come see: *And you shall see of all the People* here from this verse we have established in order, or the necessity to know these corrections.

(Shemos 18:21) *men of valor* – eyes;
those who fear ELKY"M ears, this is what is written,
(Chabakuk 3:2) *YKV"K, I have heard Your report, I have feared...*
men of truth – the nose; *those who hate ill-gotten gain,* the mouth.

138a) We can tell the balance of truth about those who reflect the image and are witnesses above by the lips, legs, long or short,with men of valor-the eyes, those who fear ELKY"M the ears, men of truth-the nose, and those who hate ill gotten gain-the mouth. We are looking here at the image of reflection and its relationship above and below.

So reincarnation reveals the animating soul, soul-neshama, and spirit all regarding the proportions and balances that we can see in a person's body. In essence the outward appearance mirrors the inner development.

The mouth which is the most general indicator of righteousness; if this is false, or not in balance then this person is in their fourth and last incarnation.

The mixed multitude come into being and are not corrected and therefore return in contrast to the righteous who are corrected each time until four up to sixty generations. The corrected soul in the example of Moses comprises sixty myriads and is the vehicle for Shekinah. These sixty myriads extend the image bringing all in right aspect above and below.

When the righteous are challenged by separation then the healing is to the naval, the center of life force that having been corrected returns the sick to a healthy state of being. In contrast without correction further sickness blackens the soul.

Sickness is always separation; whether it be Shekinah from Ha Kodesh Barachu, or the divine image and the human image, the Middle Pillar and the body, the seventh sephiros, and the exile of Shekinah.

The people of Israel are separated by this sickness, in that they no longer recognize the deeper meanings of the SHMA and do not adhere to the unity of Ha Kodesh Barachu.

The life force of the worlds is the realization that we build our thoughts into unity and this unity brings about the awakening and awareness of Shekinah making the house in which man is in his glory to dwell.

Moses recognized the awesome truth of this higher image and was able to see it or the lack thereof in others. The truth of this higher image is that it resides within us when we intend to recognize it. It then becomes the chariot for us that our experiences depend upon. By constant awakening and inscribing via thoughts and intention this image produces the throne of holiness that becomes engraved within us.

Adam produces the image that represents the three Chayot and the soul of man. He recognizes that he is the image of above and like this image above he produces an image below. The pattern that is followed is divine.

Adam lived his time in a higher world reflecting the image above. When it came time to descend into the lower world he had the foresight to give his remaining time to David realizing that his Adam's correction would take place there.

The pattern of reflection continues via Lemekh to Noah.

138b) With Noah the reincarnation cycle was paused and the corrections that were in place settled and then were able to move on throughout humanity forever.

Initially coming from arikh anpin the lifetime view was for correction to take place over long years and days and then with Abraham via Zeir Anpin or the workings of the reincarnation cycle the corrections would take place via Change of place, and change of name, and change of deed.

Second Tiqun 22

בראשית ברא אלקים. בראשית, בר״א תי״ש זה אילו של יצחק.

In the beginning ELKY"M created; the word Bereishis is composed of:
BaR"A (He created) TaYiSh (a male goat)
This is the ram of Isaac.

Second Tiqun 23

בראשית סם א״ש לעולה של יצחק. וסוד הדר

Bereishis, the word E"Sh (fire) is there,
for the burnt offering of Isaac; and the mystery of the word:

And about these three reincarnations it is said:

(Song of Songs 7:2) *How beautiful are your steps in sandals, O noble daughter;*
(Ruth 4:7) *And this was in former times,* this is Higher Mother, the world to come.

139a) Even before the sacrifice of Isaac the ram was created via Bereishis so that when the time came it would be there to fulfill the mitzvah of saving him.

Also the burnt offering of Isaac is also created prior to its need in the fire that is contained in Bereishis.

Reincarnation takes into account the past as well as the future as we see from the ram being created within Bereishyt prior to its appearance in the binding of Isaac. The beauty of this system is that all is prepared for. This is the Higher Mother that precedes everything and yet is there in all that comes after, i.e. the world to come.

The shoe is removed because it is a holy act of letting go just as takes place on the Day of Atonement where we let go our sins to rise above to holiness.

Likewise the lamb is already part of creation from the beginning.

The example of Isaac who seemed bound to die but instead lived a holy life creates the setup for similar actions that take place above with all of our actions that need correction. What becomes important is the act of return and the subsequent correction. This has been built into the system of Creation from the beginning.

Now here in the exile we can look to this paradigm of holiness that saves even when it appears that death is immanent. The mystery of the word is that we are saved by His holy arm that allows the right mercy to overcome the left judgment.

The principle is the overcoming of judgment with mercy. In terms of son or daughter it isn't clear how daughter must be judgment since both are a blessing.

Therefore before birth mercy is the ruler over judgment and because of this Israel emerges in redemption. Mercy is therefore the active ongoing force.

In YAKDVNK"Y – it is mercy that prevails and in AYDKNVY"K it is judgment that rules but because of the foresight of the binding of Isaac Messiah will not die and Israel will be saved. The plan of Creation therefore includes the redemption and the proof of this redemption is in the binding of Isaac. Once something has taken place it can be used as the template for all that comes after.

It is because of the merit of the patriarchs, i.e. their actions that Israel is protected since this is what Israel may always return to in spite of errors they may commit. The basic plan is the overcoming of sin and the redemption that all three patriarchs lived through.

Adam - Israel did not transgress up to those three precepts since Adam reincarnated in Abraham and proved via his trial by fire that he did not worship idols. Consciousness contains the seeds of its own redemption forever proving itself to be ready for redemption.

The fire from the Hei of YKV"K represents the five colors showing the aspects holiness.

So Shekinah or those inner pathways which is the faith of Ha Kodesh Barachu emerge from our attention tying into the Vav. This Vav contains the colors of that fire which is the burnt offering.   Connections are then made between the various aspects of holiness.

In this burnt offering the symbolism of YKV"K ascends (V'H) and descends (Y'H) to illuminate the divine Name and become unified through this offering.

ומתק רבות אותיות ומתיחדות ומתקשרות זו בזו וזוה הוא סוד הקרבן וסוד הדבר,
and the letters approach and are united, and they become bound one in the other; and this is the mystery of sacrifice;
and the mystery of the word:

(Bereishis 28:12) ...and behold angels of ELKY"M,
ascending and descending upon it two ascend in fire, and two descend.

And Abraham was saved through the Name of YKV"K,
for even though there are four angels that are appointed of the Holy Name, Ha Kodesh Barachu did not occupy himself for Abraham to save him, but actually He His Name Itself, would save him,
because he Abraham had been jealous for His Name,
and through him had the first Adam אדם הראשון, who is Israel, become cleansed since he Adam had not transgressed upon
(Bereishis 2:16) And He commanded – which is idol worship.

139b) It is through the vehicle of the divine name that the angels of ELKY"M ascend and descend. The sacrifice sets up the pathways for their movement. In consciousness there are holy thoughts that do the same and specifically thoughts that are tied to the divine name.

The holy name itself which represents the image above saves Abraham because he was zealous for in his meditation on the divine so that the soul of Adam was cleansed through him.

Because of this cleansing via Abraham Adam is further purified through Isaac who refined his soul even further.

Since the process of refining continues in Jacob he doesn't have to fear going down into Egypt since the divine name has already been established in him and will ascend with him. Jacob is already a part of the divine plan.   Our thoughts of holiness stay with us even through our most severe trials and it is those thoughts that ascend with us helping us to overcome difficulties by leading us in the ways of righteousness.

Second Tiqun 24

Third Tiqun

בראשית שם אר״י של הכרבן. שהיה יורד בקרבן בדיוקן אריה אוכל קרבנות, וזה הוא ראשון לחיות שהיו אוכלות קרבנות.

Bereishis the word אר״י (lion) is there, of the offering; for it would descend to the offering in the image of a lion, consuming offerings and it is the first of the angelic beings that would consume offerings.

The lion is the first of the angelic being to consume the offering. Our offering occurs when we let go of negative thoughts replacing them with holy thoughts. The lion represents the ability to overpower all negative thinking.

The animating soul, the nephesh, and the indwelling essence of life is guarded over by four angelic beings representing various aspects of the souls interaction with the body. This is a composite of holiness.

Sin is the separation of the body from its angelic influence.

The angelic beings exist together as a composite whole and produce the animating soul. Without this joining together there is sin or separation.

When the name ascends the evil inclination enters since where there is separation YKV"K is not there.

The offering is our letting go of our sins according to each type. This offering is the fire upon the altar that erases the sin sending away the evil inclination Satan. It is an operation of consciousness that reinvents itself.

Consciousness is enclothed in skin and yet it still remains part of its maker. Each of us are a specialized part of the unity and we are made aware of that connection via the offerings, which bring us, closer to YKV"K ELKY"M. It is this union that is the mystery of the offerings and the mystery by extension of Creation.

Consciousness clothes itself in precepts that are positive that bring about our life experiences including in the world to come revealing the light that is hidden for the righteous.

Evil thoughts must be corrected, (those that transgress the negative precepts), so that before we can move on there must be that correction alluded to in the offerings.

Man offers his skin meaning those thoughts that surround him for good providing the template for all that is to come.

We must let go of the evil inclination. This is the purpose of the offering, which is to transform the evil inclination in order for the soul to be cleansed and made holy. This is so that when Esau brings the evil inclination it is transformed (by Jacobs disguise) into good allowing the father to eat of the hunt of the son.

The living flesh is that which can be transformed by Chayah, by life, and by the holiness that is the intention behind the gift that is offered.

עצם, יש עצם טמאה ויש עצם טהורה, ובשר של טהרה ועצם של טהרה, עליהם
נאמר עצם מעצמי ובשר מבשרי, ועצם הוא אריח

Bone ,עצם there is impure bone, and there is pure bone;
and of flesh of purity and of bone of purity it is said,
(Bereishis 2:23) ...*a bone of my bones and flesh of my flesh*
and bone is of 'lion.

Sinew גידים is of eagle, eagle נשר there is the eagle of purity and the eagle of impurity.

Bone and flesh and sinew, upon them reside blessing, and holiness, and unity, which are Priest, Levite and Israelite.
Of the bone, when blessing resides in it then immediately:
(Ezekiel 37:7) ...*and the bones came close, one bone to another*;
hey approach and become bound,

One in another, in the offering, and then immediately, skin descends upon them, and blessing resides upon them.

140a) The impure flesh is that which is imbued with the evil inclinations. These are thoughts that defy connection and tear away at the fabric of unity.

Regarding impure bone and pure bone the distinction is in the building of thoughts that are holy and those that are not. All of this goes back to the divine image that is either adhered to or distanced from.

The bones are the framework for the flesh. These are the Torah precepts upon which all insights are based. When these precepts are linked together via Torah study and via the offerings of prayer these precepts and their insights act to cover them with holiness.

Holiness is what appears upon these bones upon the flesh and are the blessings that descend in response to the intention of prayers and the offerings of the people.

Everything therefore resolves via the SHMA which is the prime example of the unity that all thought is destined for when the levels of holiness commence to bring all together as One.

Therefore the image of our reflection, which is malkhut, is sustained by blessings, holiness and unity. These are bound up in the three patriarchs who have provided the way for the bonding together of holy thought, holy action and the blessings that surround us in the response to both. In this way our prayers are carried upwards and we receive the corresponding answer in the blessings that descend.

In such a case the flesh is sanctified by the thoughts that envelop it. Pure blood upon the flesh making the sinews and the unity upon the bones causing the waters of purity and to descend. All this is in the mystery of the offerings.

In a further explanation of the offerings we learn the heart is the altar of consciousness upon which the blood of the offerings (the letting go the evil inclination since it comes from the left side of the heart) is transformed allowing the lion of transformation to devour the offerings. Otherwise these offerings are not accepted and are eaten by the dog or the lower nature.

So the dog symbolic of the lower nature resides in the bile, the liver and takes from the higher nature saying 'give, give.'

The bile-Gehinom is the concentrated negativity, death, bitter, sharp like a two edge sword. What this means is that this level of consciousness is adverse to unity and seeks separation at every step.

The bile is the cause of death. Marah, represents those thoughts that destroy, tear down, and resist unity building up to overwhelm the soul.

Because of this bile the heart cannot operate from the right side and can stray and act from the left-the evil inclination.

Now this bile cannot overcome Israel except when they sin meaning they allow the build up of wrongdoing. If they return in repentance the right side of the heart is opened up healing the left side and the waters or thoughts become sweetened with the realm of holiness by our prayers and their good report.

The spleen that produces the bile is Lyly't, which is a symbol for that which separates from good never to return. This in turn produces the mixed multitude that is to be avoided at all costs unless it is for their transformation. Consciousness contains all types together and it is up to us to discriminate between our thoughts promoting good and letting go of the bad.

By definition the mixed multitude contain good and evil. However, the good is swallowed with the evil since the attraction of negativity overcomes the good part unless there is a totality of good, then the completely righteous cannot be overcome.

The curse of YKV"K is applied to those that adhere to evil because the evil overcomes them and enters into their lives like a plague (diphtheria).

ומדוע נקראו תינוקות, מפני שאין בהם דעת להנצל ממנה
And why are they called children תינוקות.
Because they have not the knowledge (*da'at*) to be saved from her.

The understanding heart is saved for the Righteous One is there,
and the mystery of the word:
(Ecclesiastes 7:26) ...The one who is *good before the ELKY"M,*
will flee from her, and the sinner will be ensnared by it.

140b) The sinner is attracted to the evil inclination and is drawn into its web of deceit whereas the righteous is attracted to holiness and can resist the evil inclination fleeing from it.

The kidneys are symbols of making the right choice, lighting the candle of prophecy and good is the place where evil is stopped.

The holy spirit, the concentration of Shekinah, and all the divine attributes of the sephiros reside there in concentrated essence. The cherubs evoke the divine image and the holy beings operate as they were meant to in concert with each other. There is a purpose to the breath that uplifts and carries holiness on high. It is for this purpose that the image is perfected moment by moment.

Within each soul you will find the holy of holies, the heart, and the place of the intimate interface with Shekinah providing the holy pathways above and below. These are the spiritual pathways with angelic beings as gatekeepers.

All parts of the inner sanctum, the animating soul, Neshamah and Ruach must be in alignment in order to communicate with the higher essence otherwise the light burns too hotly destroying the connection. It is for the purpose of illuminating the holiness from above that we even contemplate such things.

Shekinah dwells hidden in the stomach the ready to rise above according to the demands of holiness. During sleep either it moves above as in a dream for good, or lays dormant in the dream for bad trying to reconcile the chaos that surrounds it.

The six levels of prophecy, the rings of the windpipe, and Zeir Anpin, represent the flow of being via Shekinah to the higher centers of awareness from the body to the mind to the indwelling Divine.

The sleep for bad is when chaos has to be reconciled and fails ending up in the four exiles. There cannot be any reconciliation of chaos since like the evil mixture, the mixed multitude or any mixture of good and evil, there will always remain the taint that corrupts.

The dream comes from the stomach and is either of the tree of good and evil or the tree of life. In all cases the stomach is Shekinah, which is the connecting place of Ha Kodesh Barachu. The aspect in movement is determined by the thoughts that center in good or in evil. The stomach is the transformational nexus of being.

The stomach therefore transforms (grinds) for good or bad. If for good manna. If for bad shame. Give yourself holy thoughts then to contemplate for good.

Here in the stomach the result of everything that we take in is sorted and transformed or left in decay. What we gather in each day accumulates for good or for bad in terms of our thoughts and our food.

The Torah is self-evident but because of the mixed multitude many stand in the way of her precepts and insights. They prolong the meanings with expressions of logic and veils that obscure the truth of Torah. For the wise however, they see through all of this and with a hint get to the heart of meaning forthwith.

A gleaning process that removes the mixed multitude is forecast so that people won't be influenced by the mixed multitude and will be able to learn directly from Torah without the ignorance promoted by the mixed multitude.

There must be certainty when saying words of Torah. Meanings are built into the expressions of Torah so that when the words are spoken the appropriate meanings ride alongside the words. The mixed multitude on the other hand speak the words not understanding their meanings so their thoughts are choked and not linked together with the words of Torah.

Like Esau who was hungry for meat but not Torah he produced anger and not righteousness, which are destined for the deeper meanings of Torah.

וישחלב טמא שהוא נחש, שהוא אסור לאכול העם הקדוש, מפני שעליו נאמר

And there is 'impure fat,'which is the snake,which the holy nation is forbidden to eat,because about that it is said,

Bereishis 3:14) *...cursed are you of all animal*

Second Tiqun 25

Fourth Tiqun

בראשית, שם י״ש להנחיל אהבי יש ואצרתיהם אמלא
Bereishis the word yesh there,
(Proverbs 8:21) *To give inheritance to those who love Me there is* י״ש,
and their store house I shall fill

And because the treasure house is there which is (Isaiah 33:6) *the fear of YKV"K* – it is filled for the righteous from there, and those who fear Ha Kodesh Barachu inherit this י״ש.

141a) The impure fat is that which accumulates because of the evil inclination.

Yesh (there is) is the promise of things to come. It is the filling of existence, the substance of meaning that issues from the divine source. It is the treasure house fulfilled.

The evil mixture knows not of yesh seeking material gain only. The question is put to them 'is YKV"K in them' since they do not attribute anything to YKV"K except being afraid to lose what they have.

The evil mixture has no spiritual concerns so that all is well in wealth if not then in poverty they are forsaken because they do not recognize where their sustenance comes from.

Those who test Ha Kodesh Barachu by performing precepts for rewards don't recognize the divine when they do not receive their reward. They know nothing of time or of the world to come and are only centred on the immediate gratification of their desires.

Therefore the bottom line is to love YKV"K ELHY"Kha with everything you have since attaching yourself to the divine is of primary importance.

Performing the precepts are not for the rewards you get but rather for the alignment with deity that takes place. Without this recognition there is no true unity.

Those who value money over Torah do not make the divine connection. They disregard the world to come even to what happens next in this lifes experience.

Connection with Ha Kodesh Barachu is the foremost goal of life. To understand and become unified in this connection is above all things.

Likewise with one who loves his soul best. It is with that he praises and recognizes Ha Kodesh Barachu in his life with all his soul.

Fire, judgment, ELKY"M the way things work the fundamental principle of everything that is in the universe. All of this is contained in the beginning discerning every event every experience and all that is coming to be.

Second Tiqun 26

Fifth Tiqun

בראשית, כי באש יי׳ נשפט.
Bereishis (In the beginning):
(Isaiah 66:16) *For in fire does YKV"K take judgment*;

אלקים בעל הדין

ELKY"M refers to the Master of Judgment,

And about Him it is said:
(Shemos 22:27) *Do not curse the judges.* Surely, just as it is stated above,
(Psalms 75:8) *For ELKY"M is judge,*
this one He shall bring low, and this one He shall raise high,
So should he be, a judge below, this one He lowers in judgment and this one He raises, according to his deeds, for this one He turns towards kindness, for this one towards severity; truth in the middle; and because of this, He is called the Judge of truth.

141b) Truth is the action of above to below, the mirror of our thoughts, and the repository of our intentions giving us what we perceive to be the purpose that is revealed according to our holy connection.

The unification of ELKY"M takes place showing chokmah and binah together with Y'H of ELKY"M the aspect of the left.

It is your sins that stand before you. It is the way things work and ELKY"M that are judged by YKV"K Who is the judge. In consciousness it is our thoughts that are judged according to whether they are of the tree of the knowledge of good and evil or the tree of life.

Satan represents the negative flow of our thinking. It is this flow which prosecutes our life experiences. It is our repentance or the rejecting of that negative flow of thoughts that is adjudicated by YKV"K.

We hand over those negative thoughts releasing our attachment to them and then submit them for mercy. This is another word for transformation of those thoughts seeking to ameliorate the consequences and therefore receive the judgment that is tendered with mercy by YKV"K.

When our thoughts cry out against us it is YKV"K that stands above the Middle Pillar and determines the results of these thoughts regarding severity or mercy.

Therefore regarding Torah that is given in judgment we are called upon to follow its precepts and not transgress them.

Judgments come about because another word for these judgments are consequences. The relationship of the Middle Pillar is then reversed with judgment so that this becomes the primary action that takes place. There is forever a cause and effect and transformations.

An analogy is made about the corpse on the tree. The tree of the field is man.

Therefore he who has eaten of the tree of life shall live forever and his sin does not hang upon this tree.

The tree is also likened to the scholar in Torah, which is the tree of life. Again this person life is tied into the tree of life.

Do not let sins committed in the day not be followed up with repentance which is what is the prescribed course. Repentance ameliorates the sin. This is like mixing salt and water with a preponderance of salt (sin) and then later adding significantly more water so that the salt is diluted enough as to not affect the taste. The same is true with sin. Add repentance so that the sin is ameliorated.

Again do not leave his corpse. the sagely scholar upon the tree meaning the ignorance that goes to those that do not understand this concept and allow the sin to weigh them down or to effect them in such a way that it buries them.

This woman represents the sin that is a burden like a snake wound around his neck, and in effect is the cursing of ELKY"M because when sin is set in motion it curses the sinner unless there is repentance.

The Sabbath represents holiness and our thoughts must be holy for the Sabbath and we cannot carry our sins forward. It is the opportunity to let go and do repentance to bury our sins and Remember and Observe the Sabbath. In this way the extra soul that the Sabbath brings is not defiled.

A student that is not shown these principles is called a base student. All must endeavor to not leave this student without the knowledge of repentance and by extension an understanding of the way things work.

The same is true of Israel that she should understand the way things work and be taught that repentance follows sin in order to bring about mercy from above.

שכאשר עשו עת העגל השב משה שישראל עשו אותו ואמר למה יי' יחרה אפך בעמך.
For when they made the calf, Moses thought that Israel had made it, and he said:

(Shemos 32:11) *Why YKV"K is Your anger flared against Your People.*
For Ha Kodesh Barachu had said to him:
(Shemos 32:7) *...Go, descend, for your People have* become *corrupted...*
He Moses immediately descended and saw the calf, the image of the ox and the donkey.

He asked, Who made you. Said the donkey: 'The mixed multitude,
(Ezekiel 23:20) *...whose flesh is the flesh of donkeys...*
The ox also said thus, The ring on which is the *mazal* of ox.

142a) Israel has the option and the blessing of the transformation of sin by clinging Ha Kodesh Barachu so that the sins can be repented.

At the time of the golden calf the people did not understand holiness until Moshe was able to give them the Torah.

Because it was only Israel that clung to Ha Kodesh Barachu they were exempted from the punishment that is of the mixed multitude. They did not understand holiness and therefore when they received Torah they knew what their sin was and repented. In other words do not let the sin of the mixed multitude hang on Israel.

For Israel are the people of Ha Kodesh Barachu meaning that via Torah they understood the Divine was always with them and if they sinned because of the mixed multitude then they also knew that they must repent.

Evil speech causes a premature death since it surrounds a person and infects their thought atmosphere pulling everything down with it.

Likewise the evil inclination causes a similar corruption of the thought atmosphere operating upon the body adversely causing it to cut off (strangle) the access to the tree of life.

The mundane soul does not get mixed with the extra soul of Sabbath since holiness can only know itself.

The return of the secured item by the end of the day represents a statement of trust that cannot be broken otherwise the punishment is a cutting off of that trust, (beheading).

The same is true of the garment that is taken as security, the soul and the tephillin of hand and head representing the relationship of the soul to YKV"K ELKY"M. It must be returned before sunset meaning before the time of communion with holiness.

Tephilin symbolic of the garment for his skin is the prayer and righteousness that transforms the sin into holiness.

The analogy here is that we borrow the soul from Ha Kodesh Barachu and return it the same at the end of the day. What this means is that our lives must be dedicated to the service of and awareness in the unity of that Eternal Being. If we ignore the consequences of our thoughts, and our actions then we will take on those consequences as a result.

We return our souls to the Righteous One, to Shekinah, which is to say that our thoughts return to the consciousness of unity. Therefore make sure your thoughts while awake are holy so that it is holiness you are returning to.

שודאי השמש שהוא הקדוש ברוך הוא לא מאיר לה בגלות שהיא לילה, ונשארת בחושך

For surely, the sun, which is Ha Kodesh Barachu, does not shine upon Her in exile, which is night; and She remains in darkness.

And therefore, Israel needs to illuminate Her in the exile with *light* and *candle*, which is Torah and precept.

אור הנשמה נ"ר נפש רוח שהם סימן נ"ר

Light is the soul candle is the animating soul and spirit which are signified by נ"ר candle.

The houses of the tephilin are that in which Shekinah lies down to sleep in exile; and the covering of the tzitzit are that in which She is to become enwrapped in Her lying down.

142b) Shekinah is brought into our awareness by studying Torah and following precept. The light of Torah provides the pathways for Her to flow into.

Shekinah is concealed in exile by tephillin and tzitzit so that she will be readily available when the light of Torah provides those pathways for Her to flow into and through. The soul is illuminated by Shekinah in all its levels, including nephesh, neshamah and ruach.

With tephillin and tzitzit Shekinah lies in wait.

In the consciousness of the precepts, and of the light of Torah people inherit or get as a result the following: soul, spirit and animating soul. These come about as a result of the natural course of Shekinah traveling through these pathways to unite with Ha Kodesh Barachu.

Israel can be healed by a consciousness of the state in which Shekinah resides and then calling upon Israel to recognize Shekinah to raise Her. When Israel recognizes-raises Shekinah Ha Kodesh Barachu descends to unite with Her and all of Israel are one.

It is the SHMA that encapsulates the expression of the holiness that is symbolized by the pathways that Shekinah opened up for Israel. Israel always has access to the holy pathways. These pathways are Eternal kindness and mercy.

Shekinah resides upon a person so that when the time comes for unity with above there will be the pathways that have already been put in place.

When you speak your words you indicate your thoughts. Your thoughts direct your words into being the same way that everything comes into being. Therefore if you don't want something to come to be that would be harmful to you then you do not speak harmful words. This is just spiritual common sense.

It is because of your sins that your soul is taken from you as a security since it is your soul that has the ability whether through action in this life or with three reincarnations to resolve the issues or to do the necessary correction. The payment that is it extracted because of sin is also the same as the correction that is necessary to ameliorate the sin.

Merit provides a bank account against which the payment of sin may be extracted. Always it is in equal measure.

An accounting is kept each day and in this way a kind of ledger concerning the causes and the consequences of every thought and every action is produced.

You protect your soul each day by not committing sins that will be judged during the night. You also protect it by filling it with merit that will weigh in your favor.

When the sins become too great for the merit to account for the person loses the body perhaps because the body hasn't done him any good in terms of working to correct his sins.

We are judged according to our deeds and by those deeds a throne of kindness or chesed is established. Each moment we are being tested this throne of kindness works in our favor as both a fence to protect us and an outward manifestation of the good we receive.

Shekinah testifies regards secret sins since She is always present and by the pathways She inhabits those actions are written in a book.

The soul has to join in the sin for it to be truly evil. If the soul rejects the sins or otherwise does not allow the sin to overcome it then it is exempted, or if it does join in the sin it must pay.

Our actions, our thoughts testify against us.

There are sins that are conditional upon the age of the sinner up until twenty years and then the payment must be extracted rather then being paid back in place.

ויש חטאים שמעניישים למעלה ותובעים אותם למעלא בית דין הגדול

And there are sins which are punished Above,
and are prosecuted Above at the Great Court of Judgment,

And because of them these sins, the soul is taken as pledge Above,
and is not allowed to descend below; but of sins which are punished
below, it is not punished Above, and it is not detained there.

And there are sins of the soul which are collected in every place,
such as: (Shemos 21:17) *And one who curses his father and his mother,*

Of whom it is stated: *he shall surely die*; from the Court of Judgment

עלמעלה ומבית דין שלמטה, שנדונה בשני דינים. ומפני חתא זה, בכל מקום
שמוצאים אותה למעלה גובים ממנא ובכל מקום שמוצאים אותה למטה גובים
ממנה

Above and from the Court of Judgment below, for he is judged with both
judgments, and for the sake of this sin, wherever it is found Above, it is
collected from, and wherever it is found below, it is collected from.

143a) Up until the age of twenty the person is not charged in
the higher worlds but must give an accounting below in the
mundane world.

It is those sins that are prosecuted above that because of this
the soul is taken as a pledge whereas there are sins that are
not punished above but are punished below and therefore the
soul is not detained above.

There are sins where the punishment is collected both above
and below like 'one who curses his father and mother.' In
consciousness this is a denial of cause and effect and
therefore allows chaos to rule the soul, which then pays the
price below and above.

Every precept has the power to protect the soul. There are
also sins against the Queen, against Shekinah, regarding the
blocking of the pathways against which there is no protection.

The intention matters when performing the precepts called maid servants, which are done to receive a reward. In this case there is a shallow connection, which does not protect against the denouncers.

There are sins that are judged according to money meaning according to taking material things and those that are judged when taking things of the soul like another's person's life etc.

The sin is weighted against merits and if a preponderance of merits then this is the qualifying factor and if the merits are not enough then the punishment is through the animating soul and spirit.

The judgment above is based upon sins and merit and the one, which tips the balance, is the one, which is ruled in its favor. This is why we should always be eager to do good works for they stand as our angels on high in our favor.

In judgment there must be equality above and below otherwise it would be in denial of the act of creation. Creation produces one thing and then another from that one thing and there is no swaying this way or that. All is in equal proportion. If not then there is an imbalance, which must always be corrected.

It is truth that speaks to the judge with Shekinah the pathway through which truth travels.

Those who would malign the truth or subvert it create chaos and void.

When truth is supreme it is as though Shekinah were extracted from exile along with Israel.

It is for the sake of Shekinah that the Master is entreated to annul the oath of the student. This speaks to the thoughts that bind and the thoughts that are let go of. In consciousness the master is the all encompassing one. Father and Mother represent the initiating cause and the resulting effect being brought into motion. The all-encompassing Master can annul that resulting effect.

The letter Vav, the son, the Middle Pillar, all may have sworn not to redeem Her but the three patriarchs, Keter Chokmah and Binah can annul this vow. What this is saying is even if the tendency is to block the awareness through whatever veils we have self imposed upon ourselves that the higher worlds, the patriarchs, can break through this cloud and open us to the truth of the light of above.

Even if you do not regret the oath the Higher and lower Academy will request that you act for the sake of the above, the Faithful Shepherd who is one with Shekinah since you have already resolved many issues in just this fashion previously.

ומסר עצמו למיתה בשבילה ובשביל בניה
and he has submitted himself unto death,
for Her sake and for the sake of Her children;

This is what is said:
(Shemos 32:32) ...and if not, then wipe me please from the book which You have written.

And if the vow not to redeem until the proper time is from the aspect of Father and Mother, and they do not wish to release, then I shall ascend towards Him of Whom it is said:
(Deuteronomy 17:8) If a matter is beyond you...
Of which it is said: into that which is beyond you, do not enquire...

שנאמר בו במופלא ממך אל תדרוש, שיפטור נדר. ואף על פי שהשכינה היא בגלות לגבי בעלה כנדה
He should absolve the vow, and even though Shekinah in exile is, in relation to Her husband, as a menstuant,

143b) The Faithful Shepherd, Moses has pleaded on our behalf even unto death so that our sins would be forgiven.

Shekinah will be purified for the sake of YU"D H"E VA"V H"E no matter the decree or how circumstances seem to be arrayed against us, against Her. It is the All Encompassing One that acts alone to resolve the issues regarding Shekinah and Her exile.

Tiqun 27 also additional Tiqun 6

בראשית שם שתי אש, ואלו הם שתש אשים שהן בורא מאורי האש. ועליהן נאמר סמכוני באשישות, בשתי אשות.

Bereishis the words שתי אש (two of fire) are there,
and these are the two fires, expressed in the blessing,
Who creates the luminaries מאורי of fire אש and about them it is said,
(Song of Songs 2:5) *Support me among the barrels* באשישות
with the two fires.

The luminaries of fire, sun and moon, the solar plexus and the heart center that awaken Shekinah produce Her flowing and result in unification with Ha Kodesh Barachu.

The two fires are the soul and the additional soul, which supports Her during Sabbath. Shekinah represents the soul that is supported on Sabbath raising Her up to be with Ha Kodesh Barachu. After Sabbath this support withdraws and Shekinah must rely upon Torah study and insight for Her support.

It is Shekinah that needs the support; from the two Torahs, the two fires, the two lips, and the two apples. All of this involves the insights that bring about new revelations relating to Torah and our own interface with the world. This is what sustains Shekinah in exile.

Shekinah is sick without Ha Kodesh Barachu therefore we support her with apples that are symbolic of the understanding we receive via Torah study and the contemplation of the divine. This is what makes it possible for Shekinah to flow and overflow until She reunites above.

The spices of Havdalah too are symbolic of those Torah revelations that unite above and below. Because of this spices are good to bless for their essence is of Torah, of Shekinah and of the connection we have above.

We produce the blessing and in return it is Shekinah that awakens the animating soul making the pathways for connecting with Ha Kodesh Barachu. The essence of revelation is the Faithful Shepherd above.

בליל שבת נאמר קמתי אני לפתוח לדודי בשבת. וכאשר יוצאת שבת נאמר ודודי חמק עבר

Of the Sabbath eve it is stated:
(Song of Songs 5:5) *I arose to open for my beloved...* on the Sabbath,
and when the Sabbath goes out is terminated, it is said:,
(Song of Songs 5:6) *...and my beloved has slipped away, passed by...*

And at that time: I sought him and did not find him,
I called him and he did not answer me...
Until I swore, that when He shall come another time, that I shall take hold of his hand, and I shall not let him go, and it is said,
(Song of Songs 3:4) *...I took hold of him and would not let him go, until I had brought him to the house of my mother...*
This is the Temple Above, *and to the room of she who conceived me,*
This is the Temple below.

144a) It is Shekinah that flows on the Sabbath returning in the form of the extra soul that arises in connection with Ha Kodesh Barachu. She departs following the Sabbath, however there is the idea of opening and closing that brings with it the consciousness of a thing and then its obscurity. When we are open to Ha Kodesh Barachu it is as though Shekinah was always flowing and when we are closed to the idea of unity it is as though Shekinah were locked away in exile.

We seek out Shekinah to provide the pathways to holiness to Ha Kodesh Barachu. Sometimes this is a fleeting search filled with hits and misses. We strive for that connection that is ongoing permanent and even everlasting.

It is in this final redemption that the connection by definition becomes everlasting.

The soul clings to Shekinah because this is the unification of above and below. Each time we lose this connection it is as though we lost something precious and then our lives become filled with searching again in order to find Shekinah whom the soul loves.

Whether it is the passing cares of the world or whatever distractions that capture our attention, there is nothing that compares to the unification with Shekinah whom the soul loves.

By way of practice we bind Shekinah with the hand and head tephilin to emulate the day of redemption when Shekinah is bound to us forever.

Shekinah is the harvest of Israel wherein the vine and its pomegranates have blossomed. When we are filled with precepts, insights about Torah, holy intentions and a yearning for unification we blossom in consciousness the same way as described in this passage.

The mixed multitude were intertwined with Israel during the exile so that it is important to see if they have taken over the vineyard.

The blossoming of the pomegranates means that the mixed multitude are gone and have not overcome Israel and the fruits of Torah are coming forth in abundance.

Therefore the call is for the return to the state of being wherein the first and second temples stood above and the glory of heaven is once more revealed.

The return of heaven is the awareness of the unity brought about with the eyes of ADN"Y and YKV"K.

Israel returns via Shekinah through repentance, and the four cups of redemption that are analogous to the four cups of the Passover meal.

Also there is a return in the four unifications-elements, the four Chayot, in the heavens and the earth, with the awareness of unity complete and revealed.

There is the state of being called Zion alluding to the Sinai experience of unity. At this time the heavens and earth sing together. The patriarchs and their sublime journey is revealed and the people sing along with the birds (heaven) and YKV"K returns to the consciousness of all.

Like the head tephilin Shekinah is bound to all at this time and praised for Her devotion.

זה הוא שכתוב ראשך עליך ככרמל זה תפלין של ראש. ורצועות תלויות מכאן
ומכאן כזמורות שהן ככרמל שתלויות מגפן

This is written to put on the Carmel on your head, this is the tephilin of the head,and the straps dangle from here and from here, like vine branches, which are like the Carmel, which dangle from the vine.

And the braid of your head is like purple this is the tephilin of the hand,
She that was impoverished in the exile, the poor one
this is what is written, (Psalms 102:1) *A prayer for the poor man when he enwraps...* will be dressed like purple, which is the mystery of:
U"riel, R"-phael, G'avriel, M"ikhael, N"Uriel.

144b) The tephilin of the head is symbolic of the branches of that vine on which grows Shekinah or the awareness of Her that fills the consciousness with unity.

The hand tephilin is like the poor one in exile so that when he enwraps he becomes surrounded by the holiness of U"riel, R"-phael, G'avriel, M"ikhael, N"Uriel who are called into being in this way.

The four chambers of the brain, four housings of tephilin, ADN"Y bound with YKV"K as YAKDVNK"Y reveal the name within the name and the sealing of the name 'Amen.'

Shekinah is the truth of the windings of Bereishis here presented in these seventy Tiqun. This truth of becoming is the head of all thoughts. It is the background against which all creation takes place.

The King is Abraham because he first discovered the way of return. Isaac took this one step further and then again another with Jacob. The tephilin wound around the left arm like the tresses of braided hair revealing the unfolding of thoughts into expression via the four chambers of the brain called ADN"Y.

Here we have the adorning of the bride, which is the revelation of unity and the home or the meeting place of all those pathways that Shekinah flows through while becoming One with Ha Kodesh Barachu.

Elijah is called to descend to adorn the bride and to offer Her the revelations that crown her with the unifications taking place above and below.

Shekinah is adorned with revelation. It is the same revelation contained in the compartments of tephilin. These are a crown that is a mountain of insight like Carmel, deep and mysterious like the raven, and fresh like the green leaves that are in the vines. These vines are symbolic of the new revelations that grow around the Tree of Life adorning it like Shekinah and we see that there is a sublime connection between both.

Even though Shekinah is in exile She is lifted up by revelation especially by the revelation of the poor man who becomes rich in Her knowledge, and the awareness and consciousness of her.

The brain and its four chambers are like the four housings of tephilin of head and hand equating to EHYe"H with the numerical value of 21 the same as the mentions of YKV"K in tephilin. More unifications take place here to show that there is nowhere that Ha Kodesh Barachu is not.

EKYe"K is the king bound in tresses (tephilin) showing that the head of meaning is called YKV"K that is bound up in every mention of the Name. It is bound because there are pathways to travel and exist within and without this direction the meanings would be random. With this direction the pathways of unity are illuminated.

The head is infinite in composition unifying all aspects of holiness, aggad-ta, halakhah, alamos, Mishnah, like the strands of the hairs of the bride they each have their own direction and yet are inextricably linked to the whole.

The bride Shekinah rises above all the inspiration itself, and makes the connection that is supreme in unification.

Mazalot plus the moon and the thirteen arrangements or pathways are forever written into the heavens like strands of hair connected to the whole and then going beyond to the multi universe where Mazalot without number shine forth in emulation of the unity.

The poor become the holy like the moon that becomes as the sun the head of them all. The dual Name YAKDVNK"Y bound up in the unification of two and the angels unified in ARGaMaN revealing thought that empowers, enlists, adjusts and remembers.

Here is the sun and its reflection the moon. Shekinah is within the reflection of the revelation above like the Mazalot reveal each other night after night rejoicing in the patterns of awareness that are forever designed to unify the heart, soul, and mind.

When you look above to the sky see the Mazalot and remember the pattern. There is rejoicing since one thing always describes and encourages the other. She, Shekinah is the pattern in our own awareness shown above in a grandeur and inspiration for our own revelation and connection on high.

מה ו כגבור . מה גבורה ושה נזה. אלא שנים עשר חלונות יש ברקיע וכל הצואות מקטרגים אצלם שומרי שערים

What is *like a mighty man*?
What is *gevurah* doing here? But there are twelve windows into heaven in the firmament, and all the hosts prosecute the image of the watchmen of the gateways.

The sun is crowned with the letters of the tephilin, which is the Name YKV"K, and is enclothed in gevurah;
this is what is written: (Yishayahu 42:13) *YKV"K like a mighty one shall go forth;* and this is: (Psalms 19:6) *...it shall rejoice as a mighty man running a course.*

And it 'breaks through all the windows of the firmament,'and it makes twelve pathways, just as Moses made upon the sea;and this is, to run a course.

145a) The mighty man is he who understands that his power is on high and that those Mazalot are the openings for the sublime connection that protects (guardians) against the adversarial forces.

In the world above and in the world below the ruler is YKV"K seen this time clothed in g-vurah so that we see the power that issues from the ruler overcoming all obstacles to awareness.

Therefore the awareness is opened via these twelve pathways just as Moses made the same upon the sea in order to flow through that sea into freedom, into the awakening of holiness.

The sun symbolic of this unstoppable flow initially shows as red from anger sweetened by chesed in white to quiet the anger of its initial going forth.

Now the Middle Pillar shows green and then is enclothed in the white of chesed, which is the light that radiates to the moon. The two pillars of truth, the Righteous One and Shekinah show the green that is the transformed mercy. In such a way consciousness transforms itself by the operation of its eternal constructs, and its modes of operation.

The sun and moon are together at that time to flow through Higher Shekinah to malkhut's wedding canopy. All is a singular light.

Shekinah takes from the three colors of the eye, white red and green partaking of gevurah and chesed and the Middle Pillar.

It is an intense light and an intense heat that Shekinah generates and can be overpowering so therefore turn away your eyes from me.

The Torah is written on both sides. The revelations are written with the hand of ELKY"M from the flowing of Shekinah that connects above with below. Because of this Torah contains Shekinah everywhere. Her pathways are the insights that are studied in Torah and Her openings are the openings of Torah.

In comparison to the twenty-four books of Torah are the wings and faces of the Chayot and their colors lion-white, ox-red, eagle-green matching the colors of Shekinah above, the Middle Pillar and Malkhut.

The Chayot call to one another like the two sides of the Torah each expressing Shekinah and through that expression Her pathways are eternal one matching one in their expression.

These tablets of stone are the principles of Creation based upon the foundation stone of Shekinah, the daughter of the eye, and the seven eyes that transform and project the expression of holiness throughout Creation.

This cornerstone, Shekinah has been despised in the exile by the Masters of Mishnah. They make their laws but ignore the essential ingredient for all of Creation. Shekinah is the law unto Moses from Sinai the qabalah that is what Shekinah connects us with in her flowing into unity.

It is Shekinah daughter of the eye black in purity evincing the pure light that shines through Her from Ha Kodesh Barachu. It is the clear light that resolves all differences, all illusions showing the truth.

A person should be occupied with Torah constantly in order for the light of Torah to shine through them to give the truth of their lives its proper vision. What we see then is the holiness that is Ha Kodesh Barachu via Shekinah who acts as a conduit for holiness.

YKV"K ELKY"Kha is ever present. This is the message we are shown here. Throughout time and space in the deepest parts of being there it dwells purposefully and eternally.

There within the SHMA the eternal nature of being is realized and acts as a reminder each moment of that omnipresence.

וספר תורה הוא עין. שתי כנפי עינים שהי לוחות ועליהם נאמר תמיד עיני יי'
אלקיך בה מר(א)שית השנה

And the book of the Torah is the eye the two 'wings of the eye' eyelids
are the two tablets, and about them it is said:
Always, the eyes of YKV"K ELKY"Kha are upon it,
from the beginning of the year…

And what is the meaning of *upon it*?
Upon 'the daughter of the eye' who is Shekinah;
and of 'the wings of the eye' it is stated:
(Psalms 118:19) *Open for me the gates of righteousness…*

The three colors of the eye are: 'general principle' כלל,
particular detail פרט, general principle
and they are: (Shemos 3:14) …*I shall be that which I shall be…*
which are a general principle throughout the whole Torah:
I shall be אהי"ה is 'general principle, *that which* אשר is 'particular detail;'
I shall be אהי"ה is general principle.

145b) It is the perception of Shekinah that is offered by Torah and this perception that opens the gates of righteousness revealing the holiness that is the expression of holiness that YKV"K ELKY"Kha looks through.

In Creation the three colors are the three principles of seeing, being and becoming all related to 'I shall be that which I shall be.'

The eyebrows and the forehead the colors and depictions of the Temple above are showing in their lines large and small the expression of 'I shall be that which I shall be'

The aspects are what they appear to be as Vav of YKV"K and Yud of ADN"Y and cannot be altered. The divine plan is exceedingly precise.

Forty-nine pure faces left and right red and white, humility and fear all depending upon the perception that recognizes the action of Shekinah within consciousness.

It is the inspiration that Shekinah evokes that is the source of those transformations that make everything new (green) and reveal the unity between groom and bride, between Ha Kodesh Barachu and the Higher Mother.

The three colors of the face, the 72 faces-chesed, 216 letters-g-vurah shows how things come into being going through the process of awakening YKV"K in every step (YKV"K passed by).

This vision of holiness shows the four faces seeking the Bride and seeking the reflection of that image which is continually being broadcast and received.

We extend the unification of via the middle pillar VA"V to the comparison of a year; those thirteen months. This is the becoming that is shown here. It is the process itself being alluded to.

Things comes to be via the drop that is chokmah or the bran or the intention that continues to realize its potential. There within the womb of that pregnant substance that is growing that intention is intact and continuously expressing its particular specific will. The transmission of this becoming entity is the VA"V that is by definition the source of the connection that runs up and down the tree verifying the truth that is Ha Kodesh Barachu and matching the image of reflection with its realized counterpart.

VA"V, the Middle Pillar, and the nose centered in the face takes upon itself the image of YKV"K ELKY"M reproducing that which is sent along its pathways in truth.   If these pathways are veered from then the image (signet ring of the King) is not faithfully reproduced.

Therefore Shekinah in Her arrangements is suited perfectly with Her nose aligned in truth to faithfully transmit the image of above to below and back again.

Via Torah the truth of that image is timelessly demonstrated speaking the truth of that image perfectly and issuing forth with the beauty of that truth.

Then from the mouth issues the name of YKV"K with the breath of Hei. It is the distinct shaping of Yud, with both the voice and speech of V"K. All of this keeps the image faithful to the intention of its maker Ha Kodesh Barachu.

The adornments of truth in the neck show the grand architecture of holiness via Levites, Priests and Israelites all in the service of truth.

In the expression of holiness the three patriarchs expressed increasing levels of awareness that progressively allowed Shekinah to be adorned with the two prophets of truth. Jerusalem symbolizes the image that has come forth in perfection.

The neck is Torah with its 613 precepts that guard the Torah; the neck links the body and brain, symbolizing intention and its corresponding form.

It is the image that is being reflected that ascends offering the scents of truth of the fully realized image via the Righteous One. The Middle Pillar takes each aspect and fills it with holiness. This is the glory of Shekinah unrestricted in Her ascent bringing the delights of being realized above and now proven below. The unification is both sublime and complete.

Oral Torah is compared to the neck in that it is the Oral Torah which goes deeper into the mysteries of Torah to reveal its truth the same way the neck reveals the truth of the body to the brain

ומיד שהיא מתקשטת בכל מיני תכשיטם ירושלם שהיא צואר עולם, הקדוש ברוך
הוא מקיף אותה, זה הוא שכתוב ואני אהיה לה נאם יי' חומת אש סביב. והוא מחבק
אותה בשתי זרועות, זה הוא שכתוב שמאלו תחת לראשי וימינו תהבקני

And immediately She Shekinah is adorned with all kinds of jewels, then Jerusalem, which is the neck of the world, Ha Kodesh Barachu surrounds Her. This is what is written:
(Zechariah 2:9) *And I shall be for her, says YKV"K, a wall of fire round about...* and He embraces Her with two arms;
this is what is written:
(Song of Songs 2:6) *His left arm is beneath my head, and his right arm embraces me.*

146a) Jerusalem is the neck of the world meaning she is the both way station the station of transformation of the world. This is because Ha Kodesh Barachu surrounds her and indeed emanates from her as a primary source of being.

The divine image is described in Yud in the palm, Hei in the fingers, Vav in Her arms and Hei in Her shoulder. This is Shekinah residing within taking up her rightful place literally becoming that Tree of Life within.

The Torah is given from the left and the right the two tablets, the two breasts given to be imaged there in the body to see and hear in subtle fashion like two young roes, twins of a doe.

Vav is the written Torah. The two arms are the six parts. Zeir Anpin is the flow from Binah through Hod. Through the two tablets, two Yuds, and the two breasts, the formation of all is coming to be like the Zayin just as the tip of a pen communicates the writer's expression.

The oral Torah is the maiden whose secrets are guarded by the two hymens that are passed through when inspirations about Torah reach the conscious level of awareness. Once understood these thoughts cannot be sent away into exile for the oral Torah is what stays with us as our own connection to Her.

Her stature is the awareness that is growing within preparing us for the world to come, which is Vav, the Middle Pillar the connecting link to holiness. The Righteous One is the Middle Pillar. This represents the active connections to holiness accessible via study and meditation that grow like a flourishing palm.

Imagine that within there are twelve springs through which holiness flows in the form of the connection that Shekinah makes in Her unification above and below. Now these unifications resemble the structures of a building with pillars of marble and arms of six parts. These twelve springs of water are the impressed image that then expresses itself in the flow of Shekinah connecting one another until unity is experienced, is known.

The righteous come to know this flowing of Shekinah in their hands and in their legs bringing about the symmetrical expressions of holiness that flourish via the indicated unity that is simultaneously taking place.

The two Righteous Ones flourish like a palm because of the flowing of the waters there within that sustain the palm. These are the upward and the downward flow of holiness.

There is a movement then of Shekinah which strides within with such an unsurpassable grace that She is the essence of holiness. All of Her movements are within and as our awareness of Her grows we 'take off our shoes,' meaning we let her move freely without hindrance; we remove our earthly bounds, our shoes.

Therefore the holy and the mundane must always be separated in order to cause the attention to one or the other to be complete.

Shekinah emerges inside of our awareness gaining recognition from the entire body keying on Her movements. Now we are sensitive to each step She makes. As this is occurring the Groom, Qudsha Brikh unifies body, mind, and spirit all within the marriage steps of Shekinah who joins Ha Kodesh Barachu in the ultimate union.

As a result of this joining the Middle Pillar is fully realized uniting both lower and Higher Shekinah joining and filling all with the bliss of enlightened unification.

In this light the Bride that is the awareness of holiness, the light of unity, which is YKV"K Tipheret and the son of the King are one image reflected and joined together.

Seventh Tiqun or Tiqun 27

זה הוא באשית ברא עלקים. בראשית אבא ואימא.

This is: *In the beginning ELKY"M created;*
Bereishis is Father and Mother.

YKV"K ELKYN"U; YKV"K *bara* is the son חבן of Father and Mother.
ELKY"M is the daughter חבת and about them it is said:

(Vayikra 19:3) *A man should fear his mother and his father*;
(Shemos 20:12) *Honor your father and your mother*;
your father – this is Ha Kodesh Barachu; *your mother* – this is Shekinah.

146b) There is the initial intention and its expression; this is the father and the mother creating the son and the daughter. Images of both are created meaning that intention and expression are what are being imaged as a part of the nexus of creation. The word Bereishis contains within itself Father and Mother. The extended meaning comes back to verify that Father is Ha Kodesh Barachu, and Mother is Shekinah. It is the Intention and its Expression. The fear is the awareness of the process to understand that everything that we put forth has consequences, which are going to be expressed.

A simple relationship is established between doing what is right (the positive precepts) and refraining from doing what is wrong (the negative precepts) It then simply becomes a matter of spiritual sense to promote good thoughts and actions since these lead to their counterparts good works. The converse is also true that bad actions and thoughts lead to bad works.

When you abide by these concepts to do good and not evil then you are honoring Ha Kodesh Barachu by reinforcing the expression of good, which raises Shekinah from Her exile.

It is Shekinah that must be reawakened within each of us. When we are able to do this with meditation, Torah study and doing good and not doing evil then what we experience is unity that is the joining of Ha Kodesh Barachu with Shekinah, Intention with its Expression and fulfilment.

Shekinah is expelled because of our sins. These sins obviate the unity. When we do anything that promotes the unity we bring honor to Ha Kodesh Barachu meaning we bring

Shekinah closer since this is the main goal to unite both once again.

So it is true that when we sin we leave Torah and the freedom, which results from the awareness of Shekinah and the unity with Ha Kodesh Barachu. We leave unconscious of what we do like a servant fleeing her master.

In the final redemption we return to Ha Kodesh Barachu via the awareness of Shekinah with our expression of the meanings of what is to be or not. It is our thoughts that come back to us in unity leaving behind those that were enslaved by separation. Our thoughts come back letting us know Torah in its true form of freedom since the flowing of Shekinah is the freedom of insight that comes through Torah study.

It is via the central theme of Torah that the freedom of death, nations and evil diseases and the mixed multitude will be readily available. This because Torah is the unification of above and below, of Ha Kodesh Barachu and Shekinah of the Intention and its truthful Expression. Thought itself will be transformed via these unifications.

Israel is promised a complete redemption regardless of how she became enslaved or in exile since Israel put away idol worship for the recognition of unity. That recognition of unity once settled in the awareness is forever a part of Israel. It is the redeeming spark that awakens Israel to Her redemption which is the recognition of unity as an ongoing state of mind similar to the state of being experienced at Sinai.

It is the soul that is free from all these aspects of being including the body so that the soul striving in Torah is free from death meaning the body may perish but the soul is everlasting. This portends the eternity of soul in regards to its relationship with Ha Kodesh Barachu and Shekinah. The soul goes out untouched by the lower thoughts of the body rising above to join above the heavenly hosts all without the experience of death.

In a further clarification the soul bypasses the difficulty of death and is conscious of its state of being emerging from the body free from the angel of death.

Eighth Tiqun Tiqun 28

בראשית, זו באר (בא״ר שיי״ת)(פי׳ ששה)
Bereishis this is 'a well' באר or (well of six);

והן שתים, אחת באר חפרוח שרים כרוה נדיבי העם.
and they are two wells: one is:
(Numbers 21:18) *A well (b-er) have the princes dug,
the nobles of the People have mined it...*

One is the well of which it is stated:
(Shemos 26:21) *...and they disputed about that also...*
and the second:
(Shemos 26:22) *...another well, and they did not dispute it...*

באר שרבו עליה זו תורה שבעל פה
The well over which they quarreled above is the Oral Torah,

Of which it is said:
(Shemos 26:20) *And the shepherds of Grar argued with the shepherds of
Isaac saying: 'the water is ours!...'*

147a) The arguments of the Mishnah revolve around the Oral Torah those that are fit and those that are not. These arguments take us away from the center of this discussion of Shekinah.

Ninth Tiqun Tiqun 29

בראשית ברא ששה צדדים של אסור והתר כמו שאנו אומרים.
Bereishis – He created six sides of the prohibited and the permitted;

As we have said: - (Tiqun 28)

(Numbers 14:17) *And now let become great the power* כ״ח *of ADN"Y...* and it is the 28 כ״ח letters of the act of creation.

With this (which is) power כ״ח of scholars:
(based upon Bereishis 26:22) *...and they dug another well and they did not argue over it* which is 'the law unto Moses from Sinai, the received law קבלה to Moses from Sinai.'

It is via Creation that power of ADN"Y is realized. This is ongoing.

The scholars dug another well meaning the received law the qabalah of Moses from Sinai.

There is an attempt show that the Mishnah is a garment for Torah and that it is the result of the bat kol, however again the relationship to Shekinah is not presented which illustrates the futility of arguments that do not start with Her as a unifying force.

Now all of these arguments, these snakes subjugate Israel and even those rely on the 'a fortiori' argument. The tortuous serpent is the Mishnah since it clouds the mind with arguments instead of unity.

Therefore in the Mishnah there is no peace, no unity of purpose as there is in Torah. To struggle in these arguments going to this side and the next and then the other is the epitome of separation.

Now in order to resolve disputes they dug another well called the rendered decision that appears to resolve those disputes however the clarity becomes opinion and the true arbiter of all disputes is Torah and the unity of Shekinah.

When Elijah comes the disputes will be resolved because it is Elijah that has been teaching about Shekinah all along during this discourse.   Shekinah resolves because the ultimate resolution is unity, which means these disputes become moot.

Tenth Tiqun – Tiqun 30

בראשית ברא אלקם, זה בבא ואלו שלשה בבות שנרמזו בשלש פנים (אלפין) בראשית
ברא אלקים.

Bereishis (In the beginning) B"ara (He created) E"LKYM
this is the initial letters form the word:
בב'א (gate) and these are 'the three gates' suggested by:
the three alephs in *B-rEishis barA E"LKYM*;

and about that it is said:
(Shemos 22:8) *Upon every matter of liability* פשע:
about ox, about donkey...
This is the Talmudic tractate: The First Gate' בבא קמא
upon a lamb, upon a garment
This is (the Talmudic tractate: 'The Middle Gate' בבא מציעא
upon all that is lost, about which he shall say 'this is it'
This is the Talmudic tractate: 'The Last Gate' בבא בתרא
regarding an ox
The Masters of the Mishnah dispute in this topic;
one with the other.

147b) Three gates, three oxen and the donkey all alluded to by Bereishis Bara E"LKYM; these arguments also miss the point of the divine connection.

Thoughts cannot remain in the same place unless they are of similar disposition; therefore do not think on a thing with two kinds of approach, the donkey and the ox.

In order to keep our focus it must be one pointed and amenable like the lamb to suggestion.

These twenty-four legal consequences that are derived from four main principles show by analogy the consequences of our thoughts and actions.

Taking control over our thoughts produces the wondrous, the wise and the great one.

Those that do not take control over their thoughts will be fraught with questions. If they knew that the answer is always unity then their control would manifest itself and the consequences would be avoided by intelligence and wisdom.

The two messiahs demonstrate their control over their thoughts by riding the donkeys and oxen of Mishnah understanding their relationships and the unifications needed to resolve all questions. By our awareness of unity we overcome ruin.

The child who has been leading this part of the discussion is free to ascend above to resolve the sixty tractates of laws that lay there suspended until he can elevate them to their place.

The child is compared to the lad who guides ships, and scholars to those who travel in the sea of Torah. From the four directions the spirit of Torah provides the pathways for the holy journey.

In contrast those four other winds are of Satan bringing ruin to all who are buffeted by them. These are the winds of the arguments of Mishnah that lay unresolved and that cannot be unified unless we rise above them. They are seeds of doubt because of their obscurity and their resistance to unity.

The child expresses the opening words for the exposition of the Torah insights that were given at Sinai and now are inspired in the same way by the unity of above. These insights once again live inside the voices and breaths of the mouth.

When Shekinah ascends through the mouth She has completed Her journey, which is unification. Out of this completion She speaks the words of Torah. These words are in the image of their master that is now impressed upon R.

Shimon.   His words capture the attention of both holy academies, Higher and Lower throughout all sixty myriads of both.

Tiqun 11 - Second Tiqun 30

מיד פתח ואמר בראשית, ברא שית פי׳ ששה, והם ששה ימים. ברא אלקים, מהו אלקים, הים השביעי

Immediately, he began and said: B-reishis composed of *bara* (He created) *shyt* (six), and they are the six days.
ELKY"M created- Who is ELKY"M? The seventh day.

And the mystery of the word:
(Ecclesiastes 1:7) *All the rivers go to the sea, but the sea is not full.*

Listen to the high ones.
Of the fish that swarm in the sea of the Torah it is said:
(Psalms 104:25) *...there are creeping things without number;*
beasts, small and large;
and all of them roar over food and of Shekinah it is said:
(Proverbs 31:15) *And she gives food to her household,*
and a portion to her young girls.

These rivers are the pathways via which the six days are brought into being becoming one with the source which is the sea that never fills.

Shekinah gives food, and meanings to her household and a portion to her young girls. The pathways that reside within bring about the insights we have about Torah and about the way things work.

Now these six rivers, six days become seven rivers, the seven maidens of Esther, and the pathways that fulfil every measure of holiness.

(Esther 2:9) *...fitting to give her* – to holy Mother, who is *bat sheva* daughter of seven.

ים קוקתיס כלול משבעה ימים. ומדוע נקרא אוקינוס. מפני שכל מיני מים ודגים ורמשים שאין הם שלו ויבואו להכנס בו, הוא מקיא אותם.

The sea of אוקינוס includes the seven seas; and why is it called *Oqyanos*? Because there are all types of water, and fish and crawling things, which are not hers and yet arrive to enter her; she vomits them out,

And from there they: (Ecclesiastes 1:7) ...*return to go*; like Noah's ark, which did not accept any other species, except of those which Ha Kodesh Barachu commanded.

148a) It is only fitting that Shekinah be revealed as the holy Mother, the daughter of seven and the seven shepherds (Abraham, Isaac, Jacob, Joseph, Moses Aaron and David) that reawakened the awareness of Her each in their own age and way.

The all encompassing sea of holiness only accepts holiness and bars entry to all else for there can be no mixture only that which is by unification one with Ha Kodesh Barachu.

The seven shepherds represent the pathways via which we may enter the abode of holiness connecting with Ha Kodesh Barachu via Shekinah. There are no other entry points since there cannot be any mixture other than amongst the holy things.

Hei is the sea and our connection with holiness. Vav is the pathway whereby we make our connection and is the river that our soul travels upon. The meeting of river and sea represents Y"H or the awareness of holiness and its inherent unity. Without this recognition no entry is possible.

It is the soul that is unified above and below via Shekinah which is our connection.

There is the return to go which signifies a return to the beginning just as all journeys take from one point of departure to another. Here too in this concluding section of Tikkunei Zohar we are arrive at the end and are then reminded of the beginning. This is the essential 'way things work that has been a thread through these writings. It has been there all along in between the lines but nonetheless is a primary factor of the operation of creation. When we can see every part as an integral aspect of the whole then we are well on the way to unification which is the entire purpose of SHMA, and of these Tikkunim, corrections which allow us to see the hidden lights that emanation from the pages of Torah.

Afterword:

Throughout this discussion there has been on central focus and that has been meaning. The language of Tikkunei Zohar elegant, poetic and at times obscure and difficult to understand has to have been for a purpose and that purpose is to allow us to understand 'the way things work.' We have been making connections here within Torah and the practical world of experience showing that unification is what the endgame must always be about. This is what R. Shimon bar Yochai is attempting to teach us here both in the text and in those spaces between the lines where we stop and think about the insights that are presented to us.

There is a further extension too of this discourse in meaning that carries itself far into the reaches of your life experiences. There are real lessons we can implement to obtain both immediate and long lasting results. In a sense it is the mind that is being trained to look back upon itself and take a long view of consciousness unifying above and below with that which makes us what we are.

This journey is ongoing. Each time you read through you will be opening up another area of thought that expands and illuminates all that is around it. The results therefore are cumulative building a network of unification within that works together with Torah to offer an advanced perception of 'the way things work.'

When we ponder the Infinite our questions seek answers showing us the innate nature of Creation. Yes there is cause and effect and it has real applications in every day lives. The study of how all of this takes place is something that in one way or another the world has been pursuing ad infinitum.

Our ultimate goal is Moshiach, the unification of consciousness, and a world that is free from chaos. Your next moment is infused with unification the memory of which brings everything together as it should be. Look for the questions and the answers and do what is right. All of this is the take away from reading this work.

May your vision be filled with holiness, your heart infused with love and your soul enraptured ascending every level even to the throne of glory.

Printed in Great Britain
by Amazon